A·N·N·U·A·L E·D·I·T·I·O·N·S

Western Civilization
Volume I

12th Edition

The Earliest Civilizations Through the Reformation

EDITOR

Robert L. Lembright

James Madison University

Robert L. Lembright teaches World Civilization, Ancient Near East, Byzantine, Islamic, and Greek/Roman history at James Madison University. He received his B.A. from Miami University and his M.A. and Ph.D from The Ohio State University. Dr. Lembright has been a participant in many National Endowment for the Humanities Summer Seminars and Institutes on Egyptology, the Ancient Near East, Byzantine History, and the Ottoman Empire. He has written several articles in the four editions of *The Global Experience*, as well as articles in the *James Madison Journal* and *Western Views of China and the Far East*. His research has concentrated on the French Renaissance of the sixteenth century, and he has published reports in the *Bulletins et memoires, Societé archaeologique et historique de la Charente*. In addition, Dr. Lembright has written many book reviews on the ancient world and Byzantine and Islamic history for *History: Reviews of New Books*.

McGraw-Hill/Dushkin

530 Old Whitfield Street, Guilford, Connecticut 06437

Visit us on the Internet
http://www.dushkin.com

Credits

1. **The Earliest Civilizations**
   Unit photo—The Metropolitan Museum of Art.
2. **Greece and Rome: The Classical Tradition**
   Unit photo—© 2002 by PhotoDisc, Inc.
3. **The Judeo-Christian Heritage**
   Unit photo—National Gallery of Art, Washington, DC.
4. **Muslims and Byzantines**
   Unit photo—Aramco photo.
5. **The Medieval Period**
   Unit photo—WHO photo.
6. **Renaissance and Reformation**
   Unit photo—Library of Congress photo.

Copyright

Cataloging in Publication Data
Main entry under title: Annual Editions: Western Civilization, Vol. I: The Earliest Civilizations Through the Reformation. 12/E.
　　1. Civilization—Periodicals. 2. World history—Periodicals. I. Lembright, Robert L. *comp*. II. Title: Western Civilization Vol. I.
ISBN 0–07–254825–8　　　901.9'05　　　82–645823　　　ISSN 0735-0392

Twelfth Edition

Cover image © 2003 by PhotoDisc, Inc.
Printed in the United States of America   234567890BAHBAH543   Printed on Recycled Paper

Editors/Advisory Board

Members of the Advisory Board are instrumental in the final selection of articles for each edition of ANNUAL EDITIONS. Their review of articles for content, level, currentness, and appropriateness provides critical direction to the editor and staff. We think that you will find their careful consideration well reflected in this volume.

To the Reader

In publishing ANNUAL EDITIONS we recognize the enormous role played by the magazines, newspapers, and journals of the public press in providing current, first-rate educational information in a broad spectrum of interest areas. Many of these articles are appropriate for students, researchers, and professionals seeking accurate, current material to help bridge the gap between principles and theories and the real world. These articles, however, become more useful for study when those of lasting value are carefully collected, organized, indexed, and reproduced in a low-cost format, which provides easy and permanent access when the material is needed. That is the role played by ANNUAL EDITIONS.

What does it mean to say that we are attempting to study the history of Western civilizations?

A traditional course in Western civilization was often a chronological survey in the development of European institutions and ideas, with a slight reference to the Near East and the Americas and other places where Westernization has occurred. Typically it began with the Greeks, then the Romans, and on to the medieval period, and finally to the modern era, depicting the distinctive characteristics of each stage, as well as each period's relation to the preceding and succeeding events. Of course, in a survey so broad, from Adam to the atomic age in two semesters, a certain superficiality was inevitable. Main characters and events galloped by; often there was little opportunity to absorb and digest complex ideas that have shaped Western culture.

It is tempting to excuse these shortcomings as unavoidable. However, to present a course in Western civilization which leaves students with only a scrambled series of events, names, dates, and places, is to miss a great opportunity. For the promise of such a broad course of study is that it enables students to explore great turning points or shifts in the development of Western culture. Close analysis of these moments enables students to understand the dynamics of continuity and change over time. At best, the course can give a coherent view of the Western tradition and its interplay with non-Western cultures. It can offer opportunities for students to compare various historical forms of authority, religion, and economic organization, to assess the great struggles over the meaning of truth and reality that have sometimes divided Western culture, and even to reflect on the price of progress.

Yet, to focus exclusively on Western civilization can lead us to ignore non-Western peoples and cultures or else to perceive them in ways that some label as "Eurocentric." But contemporary courses in Western history are rarely, if ever, mere exercises in European tribalism. Indeed, they offer an opportunity to subject the Western tradition to critical scrutiny, to asses its accomplishments and its shortfalls. Few of us who teach these courses would argue that Western history is the only history which contemporary students should know. Yet it should be an essential part of what they learn, for it is impossible to understand the modern world without some specific knowledge in the basic tenets of the Western tradition.

When students learn the distinctive traits of the West, they can develop a sense of the dynamism of history. They can begin to understand how ideas relate to social structures and social forces. They will come to appreciate the nature and significance of innovation and recognize how values often influence events. More specifically, they can trace the evolution of Western ideas about such essential matters as nature, humans, authority, the gods, even history itself; that is, they learn how the West developed its distinctive character. And, as historian Reed Dasenbrock has observed, in an age that seeks multicultural understanding there is much to be learned from "the fundamental multiculturalism of Western culture, the fact that it has been constructed out of a fusion of disparate and often conflicting cultural traditions." Of course, the articles collected in his volume cannot deal with all these matters, but by providing an alternative to the summaries of most textbooks, they can help students better understand the diverse traditions and processes that we call Western civilization. As with the last publication of *Annual Editions: Western Civilization, Volumes I and II*, there are World Wide Web sites that can be used to further explore topics that are addressed in the essays. These sites can be hot-linked through the *Annual Editions* home page: http://www.dushkin.com/annualeditions.

This book is like our history—unfinished, always in process. It will be revised biennially. Comments and criticisms are welcome from all who use this book. For that a postpaid article rating form is included at the back of the book. Please feel free to recommend articles that might improve the next edition. With your assistance, this anthology will continue to improve.

Robert L. Lembright

Robert L. Lembright
Editor

Contents

UNIT 1
The Earliest Civilizations

Six articles discuss some of the dynamics of early civilizations. The topics include stone circles and their possible origin, the comparative freedom of Egyptian women, and an early civilization's military revolution.

The concepts in bold italics are developed in the article. For further expansion, please refer to the Topic Guide and the Index.

UNIT 2
Greece and Rome: The Classical Tradition

Seven articles focus on Greek and Roman societies. Sports, military conquests, women in Hellenic society, and the impact of philosophy and exploration on the development of Greek society are discussed.

The concepts in bold italics are developed in the article. For further expansion, please refer to the Topic Guide and the Index.

UNIT 3
The Judeo-Christian Heritage

Four articles examine the impact that Jesus, paganism, and concepts of evil had on the Judeo-Christian heritage.

UNIT 4
Muslims and Byzantines

Three selections discuss the effects of Hellenic and Christian cultures on the development of the Muslim and Byzantine worlds.

The concepts in bold italics are developed in the article. For further expansion, please refer to the Topic Guide and the Index.

UNIT 5
The Medieval Period

Twelve selections examine the medieval world. Topics include religion, health issues, military conquests, and culture.

The concepts in bold italics are developed in the article. For further expansion, please refer to the Topic Guide and the Index.

UNIT 6
Renaissance and Reformation

Nine articles discuss the importance of trade and commerce on the development of
the modern state, the role of art in the Renaissance, culture, and the emergence of
religion.

Unit Overview   **176**

The concepts in bold italics are developed in the article. For further expansion, please refer to the Topic Guide and the Index.

The concepts in bold italics are developed in the article. For further expansion, please refer to the Topic Guide and the Index.

Topic Guide

This topic guide suggests how the selections in this book relate to the subjects covered in your course. You may want to use the topics listed on these pages to search the Web more easily.

On the following pages a number of Web sites have been gathered specifically for this book. They are arranged to reflect the units of this *Annual Edition.* You can link to these sites by going to the DUSHKIN ONLINE support site at *http://www.dushkin.com/online/.*

ALL THE ARTICLES THAT RELATE TO EACH TOPIC ARE LISTED BELOW THE BOLD-FACED TERM.

World Wide Web Sites

The following World Wide Web sites have been carefully researched and selected to support the articles found in this reader. The easiest way to access these selected sites is to go to our DUSHKIN ONLINE support site at *http://www.dushkin.com/online/*.

AE: Western Civilization, Volume 1

The following sites were available at the time of publication. Visit our Web site—we update DUSHKIN ONLINE regularly to reflect any changes.

General Sources

Archaeological Institute of America (AIA)
http://www.archaeological.org

Review this site of the AIA for information about various eras in human history. It presents news about the activities and research of the AIA, AIA/IAA-Canada, and other archaeological research institutions and organizations around the world.

The History of Costumes
http://www.siue.edu/COSTUMES/history.html

This distinctive site illustrates garments worn by people in various historical eras. Clothing of common people is presented along with that worn by nobility. Provided by C. Otis Sweezey, the site is based on a history of costumes through the ages that was originally printed between 1861 and 1880.

Julia Hayden/Ancient World Web Meta Index
http://www.julen.net/ancient/

Julia Hayden's site will lead you to an astounding array of articles, museum displays, bibliographies, and Web links pertaining to the ancient world (and other eras), on topics such as religion, sexuality, and superstitions. The site offers hours of interesting information.

Library of Congress
http://www.loc.gov

Examine this Web site to learn about the extensive resource tools, library services/resources, exhibitions, and databases available through the Library of Congress in many different subfields of historical studies.

Michigan Electronic Library
http://mel.lib.mi.us/humanities/history/

Browse through this enormous history site for an array of resources on the study of Western civilization, which are broken down by time period, geographic areas, and more. Links to many valuable general history resources are also provided.

Smithsonian Institution
http://www.si.edu/

Access to the enormous resources of the Smithsonian, which holds some 140 million artifacts and specimens in its trust for "the increase and diffusion of knowledge," is provided at this site.

UNIT 1: The Earliest Civilizations

Foundations of Ancient Economies
http://www.csun.edu/~ms44278/ancient.htm

An overview and history of ancient economies. It includes aspects of demographics, class structures, trade, slavery, tribute, capital and debt, land, and welfare.

Hypertext and Ethnography
http://www.umanitoba.ca/anthropology/tutor/aaa_presentation.html

This site will be of great value to people who are interested in culture and communication. Brian Schwimmer addresses such topics as multivocality and complex symbolization.

NOVA Online/Pyramids—The Inside Story
http://www.pbs.org/wgbh/nova/pyramid/

Take a virtual tour of the pyramids at Giza through this interesting site. It provides information on the pharaohs for whom the tombs were built.

The Oriental Institute/University of Chicago
http://www.oi.uchicago.edu/OI/default.html

Open this site to find information on ancient Persia, Mesopotamia, Egypt, and other topics in ancient history.

WWW: Egypt and Near East
http://www.archaeology.org/wwwarky/egypt_and_near_east.html

Here is a guide to online resources for the archaeological study of the ancient Near (or Middle) East. An Egyptian fieldwork directory is included.

UNIT 2: Greece and Rome: The Classical Tradition

Diotima/Women and Gender in the Ancient World
http://www.stoa.org/diotima/

This site features a wide range of resources on women and gender in the ancient and classical world.

Exploring Ancient World Cultures
http://eawc.evansville.edu

This electronic, college-level textbook has been designed by a worldwide team of scholars. Especially useful are the links to related Web sites. Learn about Greece and Rome, the pyramids of Egypt, and many more eras and topics.

WWW: Classical Archaeology
http://www.archaeology.org/wwwarky/classical.html

Useful information and links regarding ancient Greek and Roman archaeology are provided at this site.

UNIT 3: The Judeo-Christian Heritage

Facets of Religion/Casper Voogt
http://www.bcca.org/~cvoogt/Religion/mainpage.html

Casper Voogt offers this virtual library of links to information on major world religions, including Islam, Judaism, Zoroastrianism, Baha'ism, and Christianity.

Institute for Christian Leadership/ICLnet
http://www.iclnet.org

This site of the Institute for Christian Leadership, a Christian organization, presents documents and other resources of use in the study of early Christianity. Internet links are provided.

Introduction to Judaism
http://philo.ucdavis.edu/zope/home/bruce/RST23/rst23homepage.html

Use this site as a launching pad to Web resources on the history of Jews and Judaism, including a link to the comprehensive

www.dushkin.com/online/

Shamash site. The page is provided by Religious Studies 23, a course at the University of California at Davis.

Selected Women's Studies Resources/Columbia University
http://www.columbia.edu/cu/libraries/subjects/womenstudies/

Click on extensive links to information about women in religion and philosophy and a wealth of other topics.

UNIT 4: Muslims and Byzantines

ByzNet: Byzantine Studies on the Net
http://www.thoughtline.com/byznet/

This Web site offers a brief historical overview of the Byzantine Empire, a collection of maps, and a comprehensive list of emperors.

Islam: A Global Civilization
http://www.templemount.org/islamiad.html

This site presents information on Islamic history. It chronicles the basic tenets of the religion and charts its spread, including the period of the Umayyad Dynasty in Spain.

Middle East Network Information Center
http://menic.utexas.edu/menic/religion.html

This site provides links to a cornucopia of Web sites on Islam and the Islamic world. Information on Judaism and Christianity is also available.

UNIT 5: The Medieval Period

EuroDocs: Primary Historical Documents From Western Europe
http://www.lib.byu.edu/~rdh/eurodocs/

This collection is a high-quality set of historical documents. Facsimiles, translations, and transcriptions are included as well as links to information on Medieval & Renaissance Europe, Europe as a Supernational Region, and individual countries.

Feudalism
http://www.fidnet.com/~weid/feudalism.htm

Feudalism is covered in great detail at this site, which offers subjects such as feudal law, agriculture,development in Europe during the feudal period, and feudal terms of England, as well as primary source material.

The Labyrinth: Resources for Medieval Studies
http://www.georgetown.edu/labyrinth/

Labyrinth provides easy-to-search files in medieval studies. As a major site for topics in medieval history and lore, make it a primary stop for research.

The World of the Vikings
http://www.pastforward.co.uk/vikings/

For information on Viking ships and travel—and other aspects of Viking life—visit this site from Past Forward Ltd.

UNIT 6: Renaissance and Reformation

Burckhardt: Civilization of the Renaissance in Italy
http://www.idbsu.edu/courses/hy309/docs/burckhardt/burckhardt.html

Jacob Burckhardt's famous book on the Renaissance is available chapter by chapter on the Net at this site.

Centre for Reformation and Renaissance Studies
http://citd.scar.utoronto.ca/crrs/databases/www/bookmarks.html

This list of bookmarks contains extensive links that are useful to a study of the Renaissance and the Reformation.

Elizabethan England
http://www.springfield.k12.il.us/schools/springfield/eliz/elizabethanengland.html

Prepared by senior literature and composition students in Springfield High School (Illinois), this unusual site covers Elizabethan England resources in some detail: Historical Figures and Events, Everyday Life, Arts and Architecture, Shakespeare and His Theatre, and Links to Other Sources.

1492: An Ongoing Voyage/Library of Congress
http://lcweb.loc.gov/exhibits/1492/

This site provides displays examining the causes and effects of Columbus's voyages to the Americas and explores the mixture of societies coexisting in five areas of the Western Hemisphere before the arrival of the Europeans. It then surveys the Mediterranean world at a turning point in its development.

History Net
http://www.thehistorynet.com/THNarchives/AmericanHistory/

The National Historical Society site provides articles on a wide range of topics, with emphasis on American history, book reviews, and special interviews.

The Mayflower Web Pages
http://members.aol.com/calebj/mayflower.html

These Web pages represent thousands of hours of research, organization, and typing. The site is a merger of two fields: genealogy and history.

Reformation Guide
http://www.educ.msu.edu/homepages/laurence/reformation/index.htm

This Reformation Guide is intended to provide easy access to the wealth of information on the Internet for this period. Topics include Martin Luther, John Calvin, the Reformation in England, Scotland, Ireland, and the United States, as well as the Counterreformation.

Sir Francis Drake
http://www.mcn.org/2/oseeler/drake.htm

Sir Francis Drake and, in particular, his "famous voyage"—the circumnavigation of the world during the reign of Queen Elizabeth I—are the focus of this site. It is provided by Oliver Seeler's site, The History Ring.

Society for Economic Anthropology Homepage
http://nautarch.tamu.edu/anth/sea/

This is the home page of the Society for Economic Anthropology, an association that strives to understand diversity and change in the economic systems of the world. The site presents data on the organization of society and culture, a topic of interest to students of the Renaissance and Reformation.

Women and Philosophy Web Site
http://www.nd.edu/~colldev/subjects/wss.html

This Web site provides online collections of resources, ethics updates, bibliographies, information on organizations, and access to newsletters and journals.

UNIT 1
The Earliest Civilizations

Unit Selections

1. **Stonehenge: How Did the Stones Get There?** Aubrey Burl
2. **Hatshepsut: The Female Pharaoh**, John Ray
3. **The Cradle of Cash**, Heather Pringle
4. **The Coming of the Sea Peoples**, Neil Asher Silberman
5. **Grisly Assyrian Record of Torture and Death**, Erika Bleibtreu
6. **Scythian Gold**, Doug Stewart

Key Points to Consider

- How does the author believe that Stonehenge was built? How does this differ from some of the other theories?

- How was Hatshepsut such an unusual pharaoh in Egypt? Why did Hatshepsut not have many military adventures?

- Why was the introduction of money important for the Mesopotamian civilizations? What did the Mesopotamians use for money?

- Who were the "sea peoples," and how did their weapons and tactics launch a military revolution in the ancient world?

- How did the Assyrian kings maintain control over their subject peoples?

- Why were the Scythians regarded as some of the fiercest warriors of the ancient world?

 **Links: www.dushkin.com/online/**
These sites are annotated in the World Wide Web pages.

Foundations of Ancient Economies
http://www.csun.edu/~ms44278/ancient.htm

Hypertext and Ethnography
http://www.umanitoba.ca/anthropology/tutor/aaa_presentation.html

NOVA Online/Pyramids—The Inside Story
http://www.pbs.org/wgbh/nova/pyramid/

The Oriental Institute/University of Chicago
http://www.oi.uchicago.edu/OI/default.html

WWW: Egypt and Near East
http://www.archaeology.org/wwwarky/egypt_and_near_east.html

Civilization is a relatively recent phenomena in human experience. But what exactly is civilization? How do civilized people differ from those who are not civilized? How is civilization transmitted?

Civilization, in its contemporary meaning, describes a condition of human society marked by an advanced stage of artistic and technological development and by corresponding social and political complexity. Thus, civilized societies have developed formal institutions for commerce, government, education, and religion—activities that are carried out informally by precivilized societies. In addition, civilized people make much more extensive use of symbols. The greater complexity of civilized life requires a much wider range of specialized activities.

Symbolizations, specialization, and organization enable civilized societies to extend greater control over their environments. Because they are less dependent than precivilized societies upon a simple adaptation to a particular habitat, civilized societies are more dynamic. Indeed, civilization institutionalizes change. In sum, civilization provides us with a wider range of concepts, techniques, and options to shape (for good or ill) our collective destinies.

In the West, the necessary preconditions for civilization first emerged in the great river valleys of Mesopotamia and Egypt. There we find the development of irrigation techniques, new staple crops, the introduction of the plow, the invention of the wheel, more widespread use of beasts of burden, improved sailing vessels, and metallurgy. These developments revolutionized society. Population increased and became more concentrated and more complex. The emergence of cities ("the urban revolution") marked the beginning of civilization.

Civilization combines complex social, economic, and political structures with a corresponding network of ideas and values. The Sumerians organized themselves in city-states headed by kings who acted in the name of the local patron deity. The Egyptians developed a more centralized and authoritarian system based on loyalty to national divine pharaohs. The Assyrians used force and intimidation to shape an international empire.

These early civilizations allowed for little individualism or freedom of expression. As historian Nels M. Bailkey notes in *Readings in Ancient History: Thought and Experience from Gilgamesh to St. Augustine* (1992), "Their thought remained closely tied to religion and found expression predominantly in religious forms." Elaborate myths recounted the deeds of heroes, defined relations between humans and the gods, and generally justified the prevailing order of things. Thus, myths reveal something of the relationship between values and the social order in ancient civilizations. The link between beliefs and authority, particularly in Egypt, is treated in the article "Hapshepsut: the Female Pharaoh."

We are inclined today to make much of the limitations of ancient systems of thought and authority. Yet the record of the Mesopotamians and Egyptians demonstrates, from the very beginning, civilization's potential for innovation and collective accomplishment. They developed mathematics, monumental architecture, law, astronomy, art, and monetary systems, as explored in "The Cradle of Cash," and literatures rich with diversity and imagination. The record of ancient civilizations is full of cruelty and destruction, but it also includes an awakening concern for justice and moral righteousness. These early civilizations are notable, too, for their heroic efforts to bring nature under human control.

For a time the great river valleys remained islands of civilization in a sea of barbarism. The spread of civilization to rain-watered lands required that outlying areas find the means to produce a food surplus and to develop the social mechanisms for transferring the surplus from farmers to specialists. The first condition was met by the diffusion of plow agriculture, the second by cultural contacts that came about through conquest, trade, and migration.

Several satellite civilizations evolved into great empires. Such enterprises grew out of conquest; their initial success and subsequent survival typically depended upon their relative capacity to wage war. "The coming of the Sea Peoples" describes how an ancient military revolution affected the balance of power in the ancient Near East and furthered cultural exchange between diverse and dispersed societies. The problem of governing scattered and often hostile subjects required that conquerors create new patterns of authority. The growth of the Assyrian and Persian empire were not mere acts of conquest; they were innovations in government and administration. The earliest efforts to impose and maintain imperial hegemony could be both crude and cruel, as the report "Grisly Assyrian Record of Torture and Death" attests.

Stonehenge

How Did The Stones Get There?

Aubrey Burl explains how the myth of the stones transported from south Wales to Salisbury Plain arose, and why it is wrong.

HISTORY IS FULL OF ENJOYABLE MYTHS but Stonehenge has too many. They mutate. Hardly had modern scholars got rid of the pre-Roman druids than those soothsayers reappeared in the guise of 3rd-millennium BCE astronomer-priests who are said to have designed the great circle as a celestial computer for the prediction of eclipses.

There are other common fallacies. The Greek explorer, Pytheas of Marseilles, who provided the first written account of Britain when he visited the islands c.300 BCE, is sometimes said to have visited Stonehenge. In fact, he landed near the splendid circle of Callanish in the Outer Hebrides 500 miles to the north. Just as mistakenly, Stonehenge is described as a British stone circle though it is not this at all, but rather an imitation in stone of a lintelled timber ring, with architectural influences from Brittany.

Perhaps the most persistent of these myths is that men ferried scores of enchanted Welsh stones hundreds of miles. Returning across the Irish Sea from the Wicklow mountains to their home in southern Britain some time after 3000 BCE, a group of gold- and copper-prospectors are said to have steered towards the landmark of the Preseli mountain range in south-west Wales.

Regarding the Preselis as magical and their bluestones life-enhancing, the crews felt compelled to plunder them one by one for an intended megalithic sanctuary on Salisbury Plain. The romance has been repeated so many times in so many books that it has almost become fact.

But there is no substance to the story. The early third millennium BCE, when the great monument of Stonehenge was begun, was a premetal age which had little contact between Wales and Ireland. That came only with the discovery of Irish copper ores around 2500 BCE. Even then, there is no evidence for prospectors from mainland Britain visiting Ireland. What Irish gold or copper did reach Bronze-Age Wessex probably arrived in the form of ready-made axes and lunulae manufactured in Ireland and carried overseas by Irish traders.

> The stones of Stonehenge: the massive sarsens were dragged from the Marlborough Downs; but what about the smaller bluestones?

The story of the transportation of the stones from Preseli is less than eighty years old. There is an alternative possible explanation, namely that glaciation was responsible for the appearance of the stones on Salisbury Plain. This is often discounted as many geologists argue that there is no proof of Pleistocene glaciation (from the era of the last Ice Age, which ended around 8000 BCE) on Salisbury Plain, and therefore there was no glaciation there at all. However, Geoffrey Kella-

way, who in 1971 was one of the first to support the idea of glaciation, suggested in 1991 that the ice ages of the much earlier Pliocene Epoch (5.4 million to 1.6 million years ago) provided a more likely candidate for the event that transported the stones to the region.

Stonehenge consists of two kinds of stone: sarsen (Tertiary sandstone) and bluestone (various grades of dolerite, an igneous rock and other varieties of stone). The massive vertical pillars that one thinks of as archetypically Stonehenge are sarsens that originate from the Marlborough Downs eighteen miles to the north. There has been little controversy about them. As long ago as the seventeenth century the architect Inigo Jones (1573–1652) wrote, in a book published in 1655,

> the same kind of Stone whereof this Antiquity consists, may be found, especially about Aibury in North-Wiltshire, not many miles distant from it, where are not onley Quarries of the like stone, but also stones of far greater dimensions then any at Stoneheng, may be had.

He said nothing about the properties or source of the smaller bluestones. Perceptively, though, he did mock at a myth. 'For, as for that ridiculous Fable, of Merlins transporting the stones out of Ireland by Magick, it is an idle conceit'.

The legendary history of Stonehenge is described in the caption below this drawing signed 1575 and first published in Camden's *Britannia*.

The 'ridiculous Fable' points to a geological fact, though an archaeological mistake. Unlike the sarsens, the source of the bluestones remained unknown for centuries until in 1923 the geologist H.H. Thomas deduced that the source was Carn Meini, 'the mound of stones', in the Preseli Mountains of Pembrokeshire. This immediately raised the question of how they made their journey from there to Salisbury Plain. The following year E.H. Stone remembered that Geoffrey of Monmouth's chronicle, more hysteria than history, had claimed in the twelfth century that Merlin had brought the stones of Stonehenge from Ireland. This, Stone speculated, was perhaps a half-remembered saga of Britain's first metal-workers returning from their search for ores in the Wicklows, using the Preselis as a landmark and carrying off boatloads of potent bluestones. But it was a conclusion based on a misunderstanding of Geoffrey of Monmouth. It was wrong about the type of stone and wrong about the prospectors.

In his *History of the Kings of Britain*, Geoffrey recorded that the Saxon leader Hengist of the fifth century AD treacherously slaughtered hundreds of British nobles at Salisbury. Their affronted warleader, Aurelius Ambrosius, ordered a memorial to be erected on the site of the massacre. He sent for Merlin who advised,

If you want to grace the burial-place of these men with some lasting monument send for the Giant's Ring which is on Mount Killaurus in Ireland…. The stones are enormous, and there is no one alive strong enough to move them.

A British contingent went to Ireland but were unable to shift the pillars. Merlin laughed and 'dismantled the stones more easily than you could ever believe' and erected them in a circle around the burial-place on Salisbury Plain.

It is a fable unique to Geoffrey. Earlier the same century, Henry of Huntingdon had remarked of Stonehenge, 'no one has been able to discover by what mechanism such vast masses of stone were elevated, nor for what purpose they were designed'. He did not mention Merlin, nor Wales. Three hundred years earlier the Welsh monk Nennius had written of the massacre but not of Merlin, Wales or Stonehenge.

3

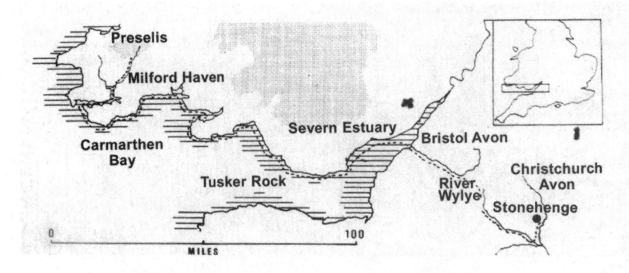

STONEHENGE: HOW DID THE STONES GET THERE? The 'traditional' route for the bluestones from south Wales to Salisbury Plain involved a long sea journey in treacherous waters, then along the river Avon; overland to the Wylye, and up to the Stonehenge site (above). The unfeasibility of this was starkly revealed in AD 2000 when an attempt to transport a relatively small bluestone along smooth paths and modern canals proved harder than expected and ended with the stone sinking into the sea.

Geoffrey, although probably a Welshman himself, said nothing about bluestones, nor the Preselis, nor even Wales. He did, though, emphasise that the stones were gigantic and beyond mortal strength, which surely suggests, even to the most sceptical reader, that he was referring to the sarsens—which are up to 30 feet long and weigh twenty tons or more—rather than the much smaller and five-times lighter bluestones. He may even have been unaware of them. Nor are they shown in a mid-fourteenth-century manuscript showing Merlin at work at Stonehenge.

Geoffrey's garbled report can be explained. Writing in the late seventeenth century the antiquarian John Aubrey remembered that,

Mr Gethin of the Middle Temple London, told me, that at Killianhill (or a name like it) in Ireland, is a monument of Stones like those at Stone-heng; and from whence the old Tradition is that Merlin brought them to Stone-heng by Conjuration.

He added in Latin that the pillars were 'located on the plain, not far from Naas' in Co. Kildare. Some such menhirs do still exist, enormous grey, granite columns like Craddockstown West, 14.5ft high, Punchestown 17.5ft, and the 21ft high Longstone Rath. They were not in fact sarsens, but to the clerics travelling from England to St Brigid's Abbey in Kildare they did resemble them and seemed to be the remnants of a gigantic Irish ring that had been a quarry for the massive circle of Stonehenge. Merlin had carried the pillars away on his back, not stopping at the Preselis on his way.

In 1185, fifty years after Geoffrey's *History*, the Welsh cleric Giraldus Cambrensis saw the monstrous Irish menhirs on his way to visit the Kildare abbey and its magnificent illustrated manuscript, 'that wonderful book… so delicate and subtle'. He was astonished by the size of the stones and wondered how they 'were ever brought together'; it is obvious that it was their similarity to the Stonehenge sarsens, not the bluestones, that he and Geoffrey had in mind.

There was a dilemma. Geoffrey had the two ends of the story but lacked ways of bridging the 250 miles of land, sea and mountain between Kildare and Salisbury Plain. Aware that humans were incapable of freighting such huge pillars, the medieval chronicler turned to the equally acceptable superhuman. He invoked Merlin—the sixth-century seer Myrddin, already popular in Welsh legend and poetry—and it was that wizard who dismantled the stones and had them brought to Britain.

Once it is realised that Geoffrey was writing about sarsens being transported from Ireland, the farrago about talismanic bluestones from the Preselis is discredited. There are no sarsens on the Preselis. The Irish links with Stonehenge had nothing to do with the dolerite of the Preselis but everything to do with the mineralogical ignorance of medieval English visitors. The megalithic 'epic' is merely wishful thinking.

Although the bluestones may have originated in the Preselis, the notion that humans moved them to Stonehenge is confronted by many archaeological difficulties. Transporting the bluestones from Wales to Wessex would have been a form of seafaring suicide. Metal prospectors, even in the third millennium, could quite feasibly have made such a journey with a manageable cargo of ores, travelling in easily-beached canoes, but in contrast the endeavours of crews attempting to manoeuvre a heavily-laden, clumsy raft along the seas of the Welsh coast would have been perilous in the extreme.

On a floating platform without sails, with propulsion dependent on paddles and poles, with little control over steer-

COURTESY OF THE AUTHOR.

The bluestones are smaller than the sarsens, being typically four or five tons in weight. Today they stand inside the sarsen ring; originally they formed a horseshoe or unfinished circle before the sarsens were erected.

ing, and affected by every capricious current of the Bristol Channel, the crews would have faced the vicissitudes of weather and a recurring series of threats: strong tides, undertows, lethal sand-banks. Added to these difficulties is the fact that natives of land-locked Salisbury Plain are unlikely to have been experienced seafarers. To cope with the treacheries of the southern Welsh coastline and the swirling waves of the Irish Sea they would have needed the assistance of local fishermen knowledgeable about the currents and the signs of suitable weather.

Even at the end of the sea voyage further challenges remained. When the Bristol Avon had been reached the seagoing raft would have had to be abandoned and the stone transferred to a vessel more suited to narrow and winding rivers. Further on it would have had to be unloaded for an overland portage of several miles up exhausting slopes until the cargo could be lashed to a third craft for an up-river crawl along the twisting River Wylye—the 'tricky or treacherous' stream' (according to the authors of *The Place-Names of Wiltshire*, 1970)—then northwards up the Christchurch Avon towards Salisbury Plain and Stonehenge. This unparalleled undertak-

ing would have had to be repeated almost eighty times, over a period of many decades.

The demands of such an enterprise were underlined by the attempt by a group led by Phil Bowen and given lottery money last year to reproduce the journey. As a scientific experiment it was sadly flawed. From the beginning the project was compromised by a series of economies, precautions and shortcuts. A bluestone one ton lighter than any at Stonehenge was chosen. It was dragged on a sledge from the Preselis, though not over rough ground but along mesh-covered roads. A lorry was used to take the load over difficult slopes. At the coast the stone was lashed on a cradle between two lightweight curraghs or coracles instead of being laden onto a sensible, well-constructed raft. At the end of the intended voyage the team planned to avoid the challenge of rivers and an arduous cross-country haul by floating the cargo on a barge along the Kennet & Avon canal—not an option that would have been open to the people who built Stonehenge. Yet even with these spurious adaptations the mission ended abruptly just four miles out to sea when the stone slipped from its lashings, fell into the water and sank 60 feet to the

muddy bottom of Freshwater Bay, Pembrokeshire, with its sharp currents.

The 'reconstruction' was an ill-researched, ill-prepared fiasco. But its failure does emphasise how difficult and dangerous a genuine adventure would have been.

Whatever the method by which the stones arrived on Salisbury Plain, they were apparently set up in about 2800–2700 BCE inside a much older earthwork, in either an unfinished concentric circle or an incomplete horseshoe open to the south-west. A century or so later (c.2500 BCE) the great sarsen circle was constructed, and the bluestones were dragged from their holes (called the Q and R Holes, after John Aubrey's *Quaere*) only to be returned some centuries later to form an irregular circle and an elegant horseshoe inside the towering sarsens. Some remain today in these positions.

In 1983 a systematic archaeological search of the Preselis was undertaken to look for signs that the Stonehenge bluestones might have been quarried or removed. It concluded: 'The field survey has not yet produced any direct evidence that the Stonehenge bluestones were quarried or collected from the Preseli Mountains in the third or second millennium BC'. Yet the indisputable fact remains that stones originating in outcrops found in south-west Wales were used in an early phase of the building of Stonehenge.

If the people building the monument indeed brought them there, it was probably from close by, a few miles from Stonehenge where there was a convenient glacial deposit of the only stones among the chalk and flint of Salisbury Plain. Of the more than 1,300 stone circles in Britain, Ireland and Brittany, not one has stones brought from more than six miles away. There is no reason for Stonehenge to be an exception now that Preselis' 'magic mountain' has been shown to be irrelevant. To answer 'Stonehenge is unique' is a convenient evasion.

Those who argue for the human-transportation thesis rarely explain why men would have chosen to transport crude blocks all that distance without first removing unwanted, heavy protrusions from the stones. Professor W. Judd asked this question in 1903, twenty years before H.H. Thomas:

The old tradition concerning Stonehenge [is] that it consisted of a circle of 'bluestones' which had acquired a certain sanctity in a distant locality, and had been transported from the original home of the tribe. If so, the stones, brought from so far away, would have been reduced to something like half their bulk…. Is it conceivable that these skilful builders would have transported such blocks of stone in their rough state over mountains, hills and rivers (and possible over seas) in order to shape them at the point of erection?

Yet whatever 'dressing' the stones received, occurred when they reached Stonehenge. The mass of bluestone chippings found there, 'the Stonehenge floor', testifies to that. In contrast, Judd continues, those who hauled the sarsens 'would appear to have left only the final dressing to be done after their transport', in spite of moving them a much shorter distance. Thomas attempted to answer this by suggesting that the chippings

found on the site were the result of an original unshaped bluestone getting being smoothed later for a reconstructed ring, a conjecture that leaves Judd's criticism intact. Logic, though, insists that it would have made sense to lighten a stone at source, and this would also have made it easier to secure the half-shaped block for its long, perhaps stormy, journey.

As the 'magic mountains' in which the stones were found, the Preselis are doubly discounted: firstly by the Merlin story, and secondly because there was plenty of suitable stone much closer to Stonehenge. It was available to the north on the Marlborough Downs, to the south in Dorset and to the west in the Mendips, all less than a sixth of the distance to south-west Wales.

Meanwhile, about twelve miles west of Stonehenge in the vicinity of the Boles earthen long barrow near Warminster, there was a litter of glacially shifted stones from the Preselis. This has been known since 1801, when William Cunnington excavated the barrow and found a large bluestone buried deeply within it. So firmly accepted is the legend of human transportation that Cunnington's discovery is ignored or dismissed for a variety of reasons: it was the wrong stone; it was not a bluestone; it was deliberately concealed in the mound 4,000 years later by murderous Saxons. None is credible.

By the time that Stonehenge was built, men possessed a centuries-old expertise in recognising the best stone for their axes, and exploited sources as far apart as Land's End, the Lake District and north-eastern Ireland, while rejecting unsuitable stone such as sarsen or slate. It is inconceivable that for their first stone circle at Stonehenge, a prestigious monument that was to endure for lifetimes, the builders would casually accept not fine-grained durable stone but third-rate material such as tuffs, rhyolites and calcareous and volcanic ash, when excellent dolerite blocks were plentiful on the slopes of Carn Meini. Some of the Stonehenge bluestones were so imperfect that they weathered into stumps in a few years. Rather than envisaging the transportation of such rubbish these distances, it is probable that there was a muddle of good, bad and ugly stone

within a few miles of Stonehenge, brought there naturally some millions of years earlier.

Believers in human work-gangs assert that the stones were taken from the Preselis because these stones were believed to have special powers. Yet those superstitious men searching for health-giving slabs were so incompetent that they also apparently chose the Altar Stone that now lies at the heart of Stonehenge. This also originated in south Wales, though not in the Preselis themselves but from about twenty miles away. It was not bluestone but sandstone of which an abundance was already available in the sarsens of the Marlborough Downs. It had no special shape, bore no arcane carvings. Yet this nondescript seven-ton slab was apparently selected and transported on the hazardous journey. More feasibly, surely, this stone simply lay among a clutter of others on Salisbury Plain.

The theory for the transportation of the stones by glaciation is not without supporting evidence. There are unsubstantiated reports of bluestones having been found on Salisbury Plain not far from Stonehenge, at Seend and at Edington, and there is proof of at least one substantial dolerite deep in the mound of Boles long barrow, a Neolithic burial-place blocked up and abandoned centuries before the ring was contemplated. William Cunnington, the antiquarian and fair geologist who found it in 1801, also wrote something pertinent, implying that he had recognised not only the bluestone but other types of Preseli stone in the barrow:

a great variety of the stones found in an oblong barrow near this place that are of the same kind with several of those at Stonehenge.

Other than the medley of 'bluestones', there is no variety at Stonehenge, just homogeneous sarsen. One wonders if Cunnington had also recognised rhyolites and tuffs in the barrow, neither of which are local to Salisbury Plain.

Nor were the true bluestones, plain and spotted dolerite, ever thought to have special powers. There are stone circles around the Preselis, but they are built, like all circles, of stones in the immediate locality, dolerite being just one of a mixture of tuffs, rhyolites, sandstones and volcanic ashes. Only Gorsfawr, in the immediate vicinity of Carn Meini, was composed solely of dolerite and its moorland is strewn with the slabs.

To this long list of objections to the notion that human transportation accounts for the presence of the bluestones must be added the identity of the so-called 'prospectors'.

Until recently they were believed to be the people known as Beaker Folk. The earliest peoples given this name were immigrants from the European mainland in the later third millennium who settled warily on Salisbury Plain, well away from Stonehenge and its natives. But their successors, users of the attractive sealing-wax red Wessex/Middle Rhine beakers, whence they take their name, were wealthy leaders with copper daggers and gold cruciform discs and button-caps. These people might conceivably have gone to the Preselis. The authority on British beakers, David Clarke, thought so in 1970 when he wrote:

It is at least possible that these powerful chieftains directing the trade and exploitation of Southern Ireland, by way of the Bristol Channel and South Welsh coast, may have had the Prescelly [sic] stones brought along the copper/gold route to Wiltshire and Stonehenge, remembering that Prescelly Top, at 1760 feet [537m], is every sailor's landmark on the shortest

crossing from the gold bearing hills of Wexford—a veritable Welsh Olympus.

When Clarke was writing in 1970, Stonehenge was still thought to have been an Early Bronze Age artefact, built about 2000 BCE. The makers of the elegant Wessex/Middle Rhine beakers were seen as having arrived in Britain around 2200–2100 BCE, a century or two before the impressive circle was erected. Recent studies are in agreement with Clarke's chronology for the Beaker Folk if not for Stonehenge itself, accepting a date of 2300–2100 BCE for the beakers. Recent radiocarbon dates from Stonehenge, though, show that the sequence of its three megalithic phases was: (1) on or before 2700 BCE, the first bluestone setting was erected; (2) the bluestones were removed from the Q and R Holes and the imposing sarsen lintelled circle and trilithons were constructed around 2500 BCE; (3) finally, about 2250 BCE, the bluestones were restored as a circle and horseshoe inside the sarsens.

The fact that some of the stoneholes of the sarsens of 2500 BCE cut through the Q and R pits, demonstrates that the latter must be earlier than this date. This kills the notion of the Beaker Folk having brought the bluestones to the site. The 'prospectors' were as many as seven centuries years too late.

Pre-Beaker prospectors did not go to Ireland; they had no need. Theirs was not the time of gold or copper and there was already good stone for axes in Britain. Archeologically, there is no evidence of anyone who could have fetched the bluestones.

It has never been explained why the Q and R Holes project was left incomplete. The simplest explanation is that people found, to their dismay, that there were insufficient half-buried glacial dolerites, rhyolites, sandstones and tuffs for their ambitious Stonehenge project. In frustration they abandoned the scheme and turned to a more imposing source, the sarsens of the Marlborough Downs. Those massive stones *were* hauled laboriously over dry land by natives of Salisbury Plain who really did exist.

FOR FURTHER READING.

Richard Atkinson, *Stonehenge* (Pelican, 2nd ed. 1979); John Aubrey, c.1665–93, *Monumenta Britannica*, I (Dorset Publishing Co, 1980); Aubrey Burl, *The Stonehenge People* (J.M. Dent, 1987); *The Stone Circles of Britain, Ireland and Brittany* (Yale University Press, 2000); David Clarke, *The Beaker Pottery of Great Britain and Ireland, I, II,* (Cambridge University Press, 1970); Rosamund Cleal, Karen Walker & Rebecca Montague (eds)., *Stonehenge in its Landscape* (English Heritage, 1995); Geoffrey of Monmouth, c.1136, *The History of the Kings of Britain*, trans. L. Thorpe (Penguin, 1966); Giraldus Cambrensis, c.1185, *The History or Topography of Ireland*, trans. J. O'Meara (Penguin, 1989); Leslie Grinsell, *Legendary History and Folklore of Stonehenge* (Toucan Press, 1975).

Aubrey Burl was Principal Lecturer in Archaeology at Hull College of Higher Education, and is an authority on stone circles.

Hatshepsut

The Female Pharaoh

Continuing our look at women in ancient Egypt, John Ray considers the triumphs and monuments of Queen Hatshepsut, the only female Pharaoh.

John Ray

The Pharaoh of ancient Egypt is normally described as the typical example of a divine ruler. The reality was more complex than this, since the Pharaoh seems to have been a combination of a human element and a divine counterpart. This duality is expressed not only in the ruler's titles, which often have a double aspect to them, but also in the king's names. Every Pharaoh had a human name, given to him at birth and used in intimate contexts throughout his life. These names are the ones by which we know them. Since such names tended to repeat themselves in families, we now need to distinguish kings with the same name by numbers. In addition, there was a throne-name, conferred at the accession and containing the immortal form of the ruler's divinity. The king was an embodiment of the sungod, an eternal prototype, and the human frailties of the individual ruler did not affect this embodiment: a convenient system, surely, for having the best of both worlds when it comes to government. The Pharaoh was essentially an icon, much as the imperial Tsar was an icon, and even the president of the United States sometimes appears to be.

How far can icons be stretched? Pharaoh was the manifestation of the sun in time and place: he could be old, young, athletic, gay, incompetent, boring, alcoholic or insane, but he would still be Pharaoh. Examples of all these types are known, or hinted at in the sources. But could he be female? The theoretical answer to this question may have been 'yes', since there are several ancient Egyptian texts describing creator-gods with both male and female attributes, but it was one thing to concede an abstract possibility and another to welcome its embodiment. Female rulers are attested in the long history of dynastic Egypt, and later tradition puts the names of queens at or near the end of both the Old Kingdom (*c.* 2200 BC) and the Middle Kingdom, some five centuries later. (The Old Kingdom one, Nitocris, later

attracted considerable legends, and appears prominently in Herodotus). However, the important point was that tradition placed these queens at the end of their particular dynasties: female Pharaohs were unnatural, and meant decline and retribution. Egyptian society gave remarkable freedoms and legal rights to women—far more than in the rest of the Near East or in the classical world—but limits were limits, even by the Nile.

Egypt was, and is, a Mediterranean country, where the most powerful man can frequently be reduced to confusion and paralysis by a remark from his mother, but women were limited to their sphere: if they had no other title, they could always be honoured as 'lady of the house'. If they stayed within this domain, they could expect to retain status and protection. Agriculture beside the Nile was intensive, and this meant that women's contributions were essential, as opposed to the more nomadic societies of the Near East, where females were often seen as an encumbrance. Many Egyptian women may not have thought their position a bad bargain; pregnancy and childbirth were expected but dangerous, and support outside the family was unknown and perhaps impossible. Security, and the real possibility of influence over the holders of power, may not have seemed so poor a prospect, especially if a woman produced a son or two, while divorce and inheritance rules for females were relatively favourable. Why break the mould?

The early part of the Eighteenth Dynasty is often known as the Tuthmosid period, after the name of its principal rulers. Tuthmosis I (*c.* 1525–512 BC, although another reckoning would lower these dates by twenty-five years) was a warrior ruler, who took on the scattered principalities of Lebanon and Syria and carried his arms far beyond the Euphrates, setting up a victory stela on the banks of what the Egyptians described as the 'topsy-turvy' river, since it flowed the opposite way to the Nile. In ret-

A granite head of Tuthmosis III, the sidelined young Pharaoh who took revenge on his over-assertive aunt by erasing her inscriptions after her death.

rospect, this is the beginning of something resembling an Egyptian empire in Asia, a subject which was to preoccupy foreign policy throughout the next two dynasties. However, retrospect is a one-way street, and contemporaries may have thought that one show of force was enough. It may equally be that the modern concept of empire is an anachronism for the period: 'sphere of influence' might be a closer guide to Egyptian thinking. Tuthmosis I was followed by another Tuthmosis, a Pharaoh of whom little is known and arguably little worth knowing. However, he was married to Hatshepsut.

Hatshepsut was Tuthmosis II's half-sister (marriage to close relatives was not a problem in the Tuthmosid royal family, and this may explain the prominence given to queens in the early years of the dynasty; all were equally descended from the dynasty's heroic founder). However, it is likely that the king was worried about his wife's ambitions; her name, after all, meant 'Foremost of the noble ladies'. On his premature death (*c.* 1504 BC) he and Hatshepsut had produced only a daughter, Nefrure, and the official successor was Tuthmosis III, a young son by one of the king's minor wives. Clearly the boy was in need of a regent. His aunt thought herself qualified for the job; more importantly, she had convinced enough others of the same truth that she was able to stage a coup. She and Tuthmosis III were declared joint Pharaohs. There were precedents for this in earlier dynasties, and this may have gone some way towards blurring the innovatory fact that one of the co-regents was not male. In a few early scenes she is shown dutifully following her partner, but this soon changes. This was to be a co-regency that was far from equal. For the next twenty-two years it would be 'goodnight from her, and goodnight from her'. The reign of Hatshepsut had begun, and her throne-name was Maatkare, 'Truth (a female principle which also embodies the ideas of justice and harmony) is the genius of the sungod'.

There is a sense in which all history is about the meanings of words, and it is certainly true that to change history involves colliding with the language in which it is expressed. Hatshepsut does this. Traditional Pharaohs were the embodiment of the god Horus; Hatshepsut is also Horus, but the epithets she adds in hieroglyphs are grammatically in the feminine forms. Furthermore, she describes herself as 'The she-Horus of fine gold', fine gold (electrum) being an amalgam of this metal with the rarer and more valuable silver. It is as if she were to style herself the platinum goddess. Like other Pharaohs, she regularly refers to herself as 'His Majesty' (a closer rendering might be 'His Person'). However, the word for majesty is turned into a new feminine equivalent. One is reminded of Elizabeth I of England, with her doctrine of the dual body of the monarch, one of which happens to be female. Rewriting language in the light of gender is not a twentieth-century discovery. It did not work in ancient Egypt (and it might not work now), but the attempt was none the less made. The changes either originated with the queen, or were approved by her, and they must correspond with her thinking. In conventional temple scenes, where the icon of a traditional Pharaoh is necessary, she appears as a male ruler. In sculpture, on the other hand, she is shown as female but imperial, with the typical Tuthmosid face and arched profile. Her portraits are unmistakable.

Hatshepsut's standard bearer is followed by men carrying herbs and spices from the Punt expedition, underlining the possibility that its motive was economic.

(Below) Loading up the Egyptian ships at Punt (from Howard Carter's drawings at the turn-of-the-century of the Deir el-Bahri reliefs): among the `booty' were the frankincense trees that stood in front of Hatshepsut's temple.

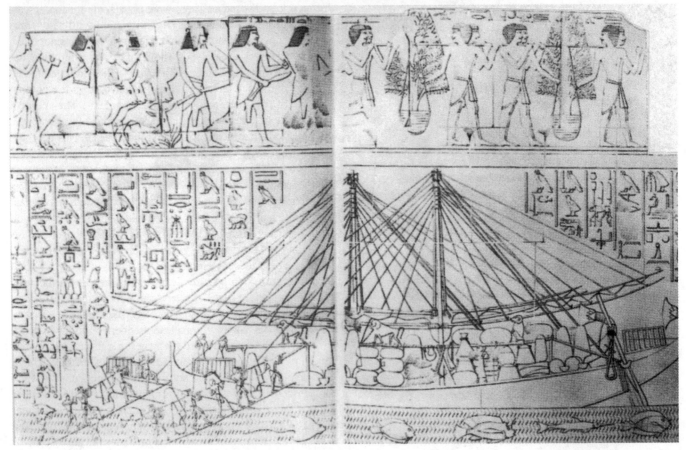

A characteristic of Hatshepsut is her preoccupation with historical context. It is as if she is trying to define her own role in events, to justify her intervention on to the stage and to issue a challenge at the same time. In a deserted valley in Middle Egypt, in the eastern cliffs about 175 miles south of modern

Cairo, is an unusual rock-cut temple known by its classical name of Speos Artemidos, the grotto of Artemis. The goddess in question was known to the Egyptians as Pakhet, an obscure deity with the attributes of a lioness. On the facade of this temple is a long dedication, put there by Hatshepsut and her artists, designed, as she tells us, to 'record the annals of her supremacy for ever'. In this text she announced the theme of her reign, which is no less than a complete rebuilding of the land of Egypt. Solar imagery abounds in the text, and Hatshepsut is described without any attempt at modesty as the one predestined since the moment of creation to restore the ritual purity of the temples, to recapture the perfection of the world's origins:

A touch of the exotic—the 'fat lady' of Punt and her husband—one of the observations of Hatshepsut's artists from the walls of her temple on the expedition sponsored by the queen in years 8-9 of her reign.

> I raised up what was dismembered, even from the time when the Asiatics were in the midst of (the Delta), overthrowing what had been created. They ruled in ignorance of Re (the sun-god), and acted not by divine command, until my august person.

This is a reference both to the resurrection of the god Osiris and to the occupation of Egypt by the alien Hyksos, which had preceded the Eighteenth Dynasty: an episode which was shameful, but by no means as barbaric as Hatshepsut makes out. Nor did it last as long as she pretended. This combination of historical perspective and return to religious purity is characteristic of Hatshepsut. Since her position as Pharaoh was unorthodox, an appeal to fundamentalism was necessary to correct the balance. This may well have corresponded to her own thinking, and need not be merely cynical.

Determination to rewrite history is also seen in the official version of the queens proclamation and accession, where the choice of her as ruler is made, not by inheritance or acclamation, but by the oracle of the god Amun, leader of the Egyptian pantheon and ruler of the royal city of Thebes. An oracle of this sort probably happened, since it is suspiciously convenient and could easily have been arranged by the queen's followers after her seizure of power. What is more important is that the queen

is cutting out any human medium, and going straight for an identification with the divine. As Pharaoh, she had this identification automatically, and there would normally be no need to labour the point. Hatshepsut is not normal, and she labours the point for all it contains, here and in her other inscriptions. The platinum goddess can be seen as the Egyptian equivalent of Gloriana, the mythical transformation of Elizabeth I. This is a comparison to which we will return.

One feature of Hatshepsut's reign is often noted: the apparent lack of military activity. There is evidence for minor campaigns in Nubia, and the period is not a complete blank, but the frantic action of the previous reign is lacking. This is sometimes explained as a deliberate attempt by Hatshepsut to adopt a pacifist and feminine approach to politics. This is so completely out of line with what can be deduced about her character that it cannot convince. Female rulers can be as warlike as any man, especially if they feel that they have something to prove. A more likely reason is that Hatshepsut could not trust the army. If she led a campaign herself, even if this were politically acceptable, what would happen if she lost? A female commander would be the natural thing to blame for defeat. If the army won, it might start agitating for more victories, and for a greater role for the queen's nephew, who would gain status as he grew in years. The whole subject was best avoided, especially if Tuthmosis I had already made the point that Egypt was the leading power in Asia. Some things could be left as they were.

If the army could not be used on a large scale, an outlet must be found elsewhere. This is one of the purposes behind the famous expedition to the land of Punt, which occupied the eighth and ninth years of her reign. The location of Punt is unknown, though it may have been Eritrea or part of Somalia, or somewhere further south, but it was the home of the frankincense-tree. The adventure is recorded on the walls of the queen's masterpiece, the great temple in the cliffs of Deir el-Bahri in western Thebes, the modern Luxor. Exquisite reliefs show the departure of the expedition, the arrival at the exotic land beyond the sea, the lading of Hatshepsut's ships with the produce of Punt, and the preparations for the voyage home.

The event was not simply a foraging mission, since it was accompanied by artists to record the flora and fauna of the Red Sea and of the African coast. It can almost be described as the beginning of comparative anthropology, even if the climax—the appearance of the grossly overweight queen of Punt accompanied by a donkey—has an element of the ridiculous about it. Part of the expedition found its way back to Egypt by way of the upper Nile, while five shiploads, including incense-trees, returned by sea. Walter Raleigh would probably have enjoyed Punt, although the reasons for the voyage are not entirely clear. It may have been imperial prospecting, although this is unlikely at this early stage in the dynasty. Perhaps it was economic, an attempt to corner part of the lucrative incense-trade for Egypt. It was certainly an exercise for an underemployed army, and it was propaganda for the queen as provider of the exotic. Perhaps it was also fun.

The roots of the incense-trees can still be seen before the Deir el-Bahri temple, where they were planted and where they perfumed the night air. The temple has been excavated slowly over

Careful courtier: Senenmut, Hatshepsut's steward and one of the queen's closest advisers, shown here as a tutor cradling her daughter, the princess Nefrure.

showing the slightly austere elegance that is common to Tuthmosid art, the balance between light and shade which is necessary in such an exposed site, and the originality of its design make the building unique. Perhaps to contemporaries it was too unique; certainly the concept was never recreated. Manuals of classical architecture tell us that the Doric column was developed in Greece around the seventh century BC. The north colonnade of Deir el-Bahri was composed of them, eight centuries earlier.

Part of the temple was devoted to the divine birth of Hatshepsut, another piece of mythology which normal Pharaohs did not need to use. The god Amun himself desired to create his living image on earth, to reveal his greatness and to carry out his plans. He disguised himself as Tuthmosis I, went one day to see the queen, and the result, in due course, was Hatshepsut. Amun did not mind that his image was female, so why should anyone else?

Similar themes are explored in a rather strange medium, an inscribed pair of granite obelisks which the queen set up in her sixteenth year before the temple of Amun at Karnak opposite Deir el-Bahri. The entire work, she tells us, took seven months. Obelisks in Egyptian thinking were a representation of the first ray of light which inaugurated the creation, or what we would now call the Big Bang. In the text Hatshepsut knows the mind of God: she was present with the creator at the beginning, she is the luminous seed of the almighty one, and she is 'the fine gold of kings'—another reference to electrum. This metal was even used to coat the obelisks, to make her splendour visible. Her sense of posterity, and the force of her personality, are clear from the words she uses:

> Those who shall see my monument in future years, and shall speak of what I have done, beware of saying, 'I know not, I know not how this has been done, fashioning a mountain of gold throughout, like something of nature'... Nor shall he who hears this say it was a boast, but rather, 'How like her this is, how worthy of her father'.

She also tells us that her obelisks were situated by the gateway of Tuthmosis I, since it was he who began the obelisk habit. This preoccupation with the father is not accidental. Pharaoh was Pharaoh because his father had been Pharaoh; in Egyptian mythology, he was Horus to his predecessor's Osiris, one god ruling on earth while the other reigned over the netherworld. However, this was conventional, and orthodox Pharaohs did not need to make it explicit. Hatshepsut, the female Horus, was not orthodox. Her kingship depended on mythological props, and also on political ones; in fact, she would not have made a distinction between the two. But there may well be a third element at work, a personal one.

Tuthmosis I is prominent in many of her inscriptions, far more than is necessary. His sarcophagus was even discovered in his daughter's tomb, where it had been transferred from his own. Clearly she intended to spend eternity with the man who had been her father on earth. She left her husband, Tuthmosis II, where he was lying in the Valley of the Kings, and her inscrip-

the past century (its scenes were first copied by a young draughtsman named Howard Carter), and its plan is now clear. No one who walks the path over the mountain from the Valley of the Kings and looks down at the other side can ignore the series of terraces below, built into the western cliffs. It is one of the most dramatic sights in Egypt. The variety of its scenes, all

tions never mention him, even though he was presumably the parent of her child. This is a trait which prominent females sometimes show. Anna Freud turned herself into Sigmund's intellectual heir, Benazir Bhutto makes a political platform out of her father's memory, and one is reminded of a recent British prime minister whose entry in *Who's Who* included a father but no mother. Did Tuthmosis I ever call his daughter 'the best man in the dynasty', and is this why Hatshepsut shows no identification with other women? This is not entirely hypothetical: among Hatshepsut's inscriptions is an imaginative reworking of an episode when she was young, in which her father proclaims her his heir before the entire palace. Such a text could have been based on a coming-of-age ceremony, or even a chance remark to an impressionable child.

Hatshepsut was determined to hold on to power, and the way she achieved this is clear. After the gradual disappearance of her father's advisers, almost all her supporters are new men (women she could not have appointed, even if she had had a mind to). They owed nothing to the traditional aristocracy, little to conventional patronage: they were 'one of us'. They were hers, and if she fell, they would fall also. Their tombs are still visible in the cliffs above Deir el-Bahri. They are easily distinguished by the terraced effect of their facades, which resemble the royal temple; even in their architecture they showed whose men they were. This must have been a court where many lesser lights danced attendance on the sun-queen.

The most prominent courtier of Hatshepsut's reign is Senenmut. He dominates the temple of Deir el-Bahri, where he seems to be an overall but ill-defined master of works. His figure even appears in small niches in some of its chapels, worshipping the god Amun and his royal mistress. These niches are hidden behind the doors, but the gods would have known what was in them, and so probably did Hatshepsut. This must have been done with her approval. Senenmut's place in the royal household is confirmed by his position as tutor to the queen's daughter Nefrure, and statues survive showing Senenmut crouching in the guise of a patient client, while the head of the royal infant peeps out from between his knees. Senenmut was given permission to be buried within the precincts of the great temple, an unprecedented honour.

Around the seventh year of the reign Senenmut's mother died, and she too was interred in the temple. Senenmut exhumed the body of his father at the same time, and reburied him in splendour alongside her and other members of his family. The father had no title (otherwise the Egyptians, who were obsessed with titles, would have not failed to mention it), and his original burial was tantamount to a pauper's. Senenmut must have come from a small town along the Nile, and rose to prominence entirely through merit and the queen's patronage. This sheds unexpected light on what could happen in ancient Egypt. Senenmut seems never to have married. Perhaps he did not dare

to; did not Walter Raleigh fall from grace as soon as he married one of Gloriana's maids?

Recently evidence has emerged that the reign of Hatshepsut could inspire distinctly tabloid reactions. Some years ago, in an unfinished tomb above the Deir el-Bahri temple, a series of graffiti were found. One of these is a feeble drawing of Senenmut, but on another wall there is a sketch showing a female Pharaoh undergoing the attentions of a male figure, in a way that implies her passive submission. This may be a contemporary comment on the relationship between Senenmut and the queen, or it may be a later satire on the notion of an impotent female Pharaoh, or it may simply be the fantasy of a little man for something he could never attain, rather on the lines of the stories which later circulated about Cleopatra or Catherine the Great. If the scene is genuine, it is extremely interesting, even if its meaning is less explicit than its drawing.

The queen died on the tenth day of the sixth month of the twenty-second year of her reign (early February 1482 BC). She was perhaps fifty. Tuthmosis III, so long cooped up, became sole Pharaoh and immediately led his army into Syria, where in seventeen campaigns he restored Egyptian overlordship of the Near East. At some point, though not for some years, he began a proscription of his aunt's memory. Probably he chose to wait until Senenmut and her other supporters had passed away. Perhaps he remained in awe of her. Her inscriptions were erased, her obelisks surrounded by a wall, and her monuments forgotten. Her name does not appear in later annals, which is why we refer to Tuthmosis by a Greek transcription, while hers is missing. The bodies of many of the New Kingdom Pharaohs survive, and are now in the Cairo Museum. As far as we know, hers is not among them. What we do know about her has been gained by excavation and careful epigraphy over the past hundred years. Perhaps this is as it should be, since the late twentieth century is a better time than most to think about the meaning of her reign. Will the feminist movement rediscover her, or will she be uncomfortable for us, as she was for some of her contemporaries?

FOR FURTHER READING:

Cambridge Ancient History (3 edn., vol. II, 1973, ch. 9); Peter F. Dorman, *The Monuments of Senenmut* (Kegan Paul International, 1988); Miriam Lichtheim, *Ancient Egyptian Literature II* (California, 1976); Donald B. Redford, *History and Chronology of the Eighteenth Dynasty of Egypt* (Toronto, 1967) and the same author's *Egypt, Canaan, and Israel in Ancient Times* (Princeton, 1992); John Romer, *Romer's Egypt* (Rainbird, 1982); Edward F. Wente, 'Some Graffiti from the Reign of Hatshepsut', *Journal of Near Eastern Studies 43* (1984).

John Ray is Herbert Thompson Reader in Egyptology at Cambridge University.

The Cradle of Cash

*When money arose in the ancient cities of Mesopotamia,
it profoundly and permanently changed civilization.*

By Heather Pringle

The scene in the small, stifling room is not hard to imagine: the scribe frowning, shifting in his seat as he tries to concentrate on the words of the woman in front of him. A member of one of the wealthiest families in Sippar, the young priestess has summoned him to her room to record a business matter. When she entered the temple, she explains, her parents gave her a valuable inheritance, a huge piece of silver in the shape of a ring, worth the equivalent of 60 months' wages for an estate worker. She has decided to buy land with this silver. Now she needs someone to take down a few details. Obediently, the scribe smooths a wet clay tablet and gets out his stylus. Finally, his work done, he takes the tablet down to the archive.

For more than 3,700 years, the tablet languished in obscurity, until late-nineteenth-century collectors unearthed it from Sippar's ruins along the Euphrates River in what is now Iraq. Like similar tablets, it hinted at an ancient and mysterious Near Eastern currency, in the form of silver rings, that started circulating two millennia before the world's first coins were struck. By the time that tablet was inscribed, such rings may have been in use for a thousand years.

When did humans first arrive at the concept of money? What conditions spawned it? And how did it affect the ancient societies that created it? Until recently, researchers thought they had the answers. They believed money was born, as coins, along the coasts of the Mediterranean in the seventh or sixth century B.C., a product of the civilization that later gave the world the Parthenon, Plato, and Aristotle. But few see the matter so simply now. With evidence gleaned from such disparate sources as ancient temple paintings, clay tablets, and buried hoards of uncoined metals, researchers have revealed far more ancient money: silver scraps and bits of gold, massive rings and gleaming ingots.

In the process, they have pushed the origins of cash far beyond the sunny coasts of the Mediterranean, back to the world's oldest cities in Mesopotamia, the fertile plain created by the Tigris and Euphrates rivers. There, they suggest, wealthy citizens were flaunting money at least as early as 2500 B.C. and perhaps a few hundred years before that. "There's just no way to get around it," says Marvin Powell, a historian at Northern Illinois University in De Kalb. "Silver in Mesopotamia functions like

our money today. It's a means of exchange. People use it for a storage of wealth, and they use it for defining value."

Many scholars believe money began even earlier. "My sense is that as far back as the written records go in Mesopotamia and Egypt, some form of money is there," observes Jonathan Williams, curator of Roman and Iron Age coins at the British Museum in London. "That suggests it was probably there beforehand, but we can't tell because we don't have any written records."

Ancient texts show that almost from its first recorded appearance in the ancient Near East, money preoccupied estate owners and scribes, water carriers and slaves.

Just why researchers have had such difficulties in uncovering these ancient moneys has much to do with the practice of archeology and the nature of money itself. Archeologists, after all, are the ultimate Dumpster divers: they spend their careers sifting through the trash of the past, ingeniously reconstructing vanished lives from broken pots and dented knives. But like us, ancient Mesopotamians and Phoenicians seldom made the error of tossing out cash, and only rarely did they bury their most precious liquid assets in the ground. Even when archeologists have found buried cash, though, they've had trouble recognizing it for what it was. Money doesn't always come in the form of dimes and sawbucks, even today. As a means of payment and a way of storing wealth, it assumes many forms, from debit cards and checks to credit cards and mutual funds. The forms it took in the past have been, to say the least, elusive.

From the beginning, money has shaped human society. It greased the wheels of Mesopotamian commerce, spurred the development of mathematics, and helped officials and kings rake in taxes and impose fines. As it evolved in Bronze Age civilizations along the Mediterranean coast, it fostered sea trade, built lucrative cottage industries, and underlay an accumulation

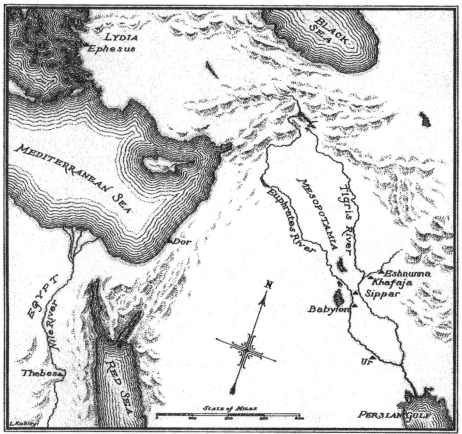

Illustrations by Laszlo Kubinyi

Cash first appeared in Mesopotamia then spread westward to the Mediterranean

of wealth that might have impressed Donald Trump. "If there were never any money, there would never have been prosperity," says Thomas Wyrick, an economist at Southwest Missouri State University in Springfield, who is studying the origins of money and banking. "Money is making all this stuff happen."

Ancient texts show that almost from its first recorded appearance in the ancient Near East, money preoccupied estate owners and scribes, water carriers and slaves. In Mesopotamia, as early as 3000 B.C., scribes devised pictographs suitable for recording simple lists of concrete objects, such as grain consignments. Five hundred years later, the pictographs had evolved into a more supple system of writing, a partially syllabic script known as cuneiform that was capable of recording the vernacular: first Sumerian, a language unrelated to any living tongue, and later Akkadian, an ancient Semitic language. Scribes could write down everything from kingly edicts to proverbs, epics to hymns, private family letters to merchants' contracts. In these ancient texts, says Miguel Civil, a lexicographer at the Oriental Institute of the University of Chicago, "they talk about wealth and gold and silver all the time."

In all likelihood, says Wyrick, human beings first began contemplating cash just about the time that Mesopotamians were slathering mortar on mud bricks to build the world's first cities. Until then, people across the Near East had worked primarily on small farms, cultivating barley, dates, and wheat, hunting ga-

zelles and other wild game, and bartering among themselves for the things they could not produce. But around 3500 B.C., work parties started hauling stones across the plains and raising huge flat-topped platforms, known as ziggurats, on which to found their temples. Around their bases, they built street upon twisted street of small mud-brick houses.

To furnish these new temples and to serve temple officials, many farmers became artisans—stonemasons, silversmiths, tanners, weavers, boatbuilders, furniture makers. And within a few centuries, says Wyrick, the cities became much greater than the sum of their parts. Economic life flourished and grew increasingly complex. "Before, you always had people scattered out on the hillsides," says Wyrick, "and whatever they could produce for their families, that was it. Very little trade occurred because you never had a large concentration of people. But now, in these cities, for the first time ever in one spot, you had lots of different goods, hundreds of goods, and lots of different people trading them."

Just how complex life grew in these early metropolises can be glimpsed in the world's oldest accounting records: 8,162 tiny clay tokens excavated from the floors of village houses and city temples across the Near East and studied in detail by Denise Schmandt-Besserat, an archeologist at the University of Texas at Austin. The tokens served first as counters and perhaps later as promissory notes given to temple tax collectors before the first writing appeared.

Courtesy Denise Schmandt-Besserat

These clay tokens from Susa, Iran, around 3300 b.c., represent (clockwise from top left): one sheep, one jar of oil, one garment, one measure of metal, a mystery item, one measure of honey, and one garment.

By classifying the disparate shapes and markings on the tokens into types and comparing these with the earliest known written symbols, Schmandt-Besserat discovered that each token represented a specified quantity of a particular commodity. And she noticed an intriguing difference between village tokens and city tokens. In the small communities dating from before the rise of cities, Mesopotamians regularly employed just five token types, representing different amounts of three main goods: human labor, grain, and livestock like goats and sheep. But in the cities, they began churning out a multitude of new types, regularly employing 16 in all, with dozens of subcategories representing everything from honey, sheep's milk, and trussed ducks to wool, cloth, rope, garments, mats, beds, perfume, and metals. "It's no longer just farm goods," says Schmandt-Besserat. "There are also finished products, manufactured goods, furniture, bread, and textiles."

Faced with this new profusion, says Wyrick, no one would have had an easy time bartering, even for something as simple as a pair of sandals. "If there were a thousand different goods being traded up and down the street, people could set the price in a thousand different ways, because in a barter economy each good is priced in terms of all other goods. So one pair of sandals equals ten dates, equals one quart of wheat, equals two quarts of bitumen, and so on. Which is the best price? It's so complex that people don't know if they are getting a good deal. For the first time in history, we've got a large number of goods. And for the first time, we have so many prices that it overwhelms the human mind. People needed some standard way of stating value."

In Mesopotamia, silver—a prized ornamental material—became that standard. Supplies didn't vary much from year to year, so its value remained constant, which made it an ideal measuring rod for calculating the value of other things. Mesopotamians were quick to see the advantage, recording the prices of everything from timber to barley in silver by weight in shekels. (One shekel equaled one-third of an ounce, or just a little more than the weight of three pennies.) A slave, for example, cost between 10 and 20 shekels of silver. A month of a freeman's labor was worth 1 shekel. A quart of barley went for three-hundredths of a shekel. Best of all, silver was portable. "You can't carry a shekel of barley on your ass," comments Marvin Powell (referring to the animal). And with a silver standard, kings could attach a price to infractions of the law. In the codes of the city of Eshnunna, which date to around 2000 B.C., a man who bit another man's nose would be fined 60 shekels of silver; one who slapped another in the face paid 10.

How the citizens of Babylon or Ur actually paid their bills, however, depended on who they were. The richest tenth of the population, says Powell, frequently paid in various forms of silver. Some lugged around bags or jars containing bits of the precious metal to be placed one at a time on the pan of a scale until they balanced a small carved stone weight in the other pan. Other members of the upper crust favored a more convenient form of cash: pieces of silver cast in standard weights. These were called *har* in the tablets, translated as "ring" money.

At the Oriental Institute in the early 1970s, Powell studied nearly 100 silver coils—some resembling bedsprings, others slender wire coils—found primarily in the Mesopotamian city of Khafaje. They were not exactly rings, it was true, but they matched other fleeting descriptions of *har*. According to the scribes, ring money ranged from 1 to 60 shekels in weight. Some pieces were cast in special molds. At the Oriental Institute, the nine largest coils all bore a triangular ridge, as if they had been cast and then rolled into spirals while still pliable. The largest coils weighed almost exactly 60 shekels, the smallest from one-twelfth to two and a half shekels. "It's clear that the coils were intended to represent some easily recognizable form of Babylonian stored value," says Powell. "In other words, it's the forerunner of coinage."

The masses in Mesopotamia, however, seldom dealt in such money. It was simply too precious, much as a gold coin would have been for a Kansas dirt farmer in the middle of the Great Depression. To pay their bills, water carriers, estate workers, fishers, and farmers relied on more modest forms of money: copper, tin, lead, and above all, barley. "It's the cheap commodity money," says Powell. "I think barley functions in ancient Mesopotamia like small change in later systems, like the bronze currencies in the Hellenistic period. And essentially that avoids the problem of your being cheated. You measure barley out and it's not as dangerous a thing to try to exchange as silver, given weighing errors. If you lose a little bit, its not going to make that much difference."

Measurable commodity money such as silver and barley both simplified and complicated daily life. No longer did temple officials have to sweat over how to collect a one-sixth tax increase on a farmer who had paid one ox the previous year. Compound interest on loans was now a breeze to calculate. Shekels of silver, after all, lent themselves perfectly to intricate mathematical manipulation; one historian has suggested that Mesopotamian scribes first arrived at logarithms and exponential values from their calculations of compound interest.

"People were constantly falling into debt," says Powell. "We find reference to this in letters where people are writing to one another about someone in the household who has been seized for securing a debt." To remedy these disastrous financial affairs, King Hammurabi decreed in the eighteenth century B.C. that none of his subjects could be enslaved for more than three years for failing to repay a debt. Other Mesopotamian rulers, alarmed at the financial chaos in the cities, tried legislating moratoriums on all outstanding bills.

While the cities of Mesopotamia were the first to conceive of money, others in the ancient Near East soon took up the torch. As civilization after civilization rose to glory along the coasts of the eastern Mediterranean, from Egypt to Syria, their citizens began abandoning the old ways of pure barter. Adopting local standards of value, often silver by weight, they began buying and selling with their own local versions of commodity moneys: linen, perfume, wine, olive oil, wheat, barley, precious metals—things that could be easily divided into smaller portions and that resisted decay.

And as commerce became smoother in the ancient world, people became increasingly selective about what they accepted as money, says Wyrick. "Of all the different media of exchange, one commodity finally broke out of the pack. It began to get more popular than the others, and I think the merchants probably said to themselves, 'Hey, this is great. Half my customers have this form of money. I'm going to start demanding it.' And the customers were happy, too, because there's more than just one merchant coming around, and they didn't know what to hold on to, because each merchant was different. If everyone asked for barley or everyone asked for silver, that would be very convenient. So as one of these media of exchange becomes more popular, everyone just rushes toward that."

What most ancient Near Easterners rushed toward around 1500 B.C. was silver. In the Old Testament, for example, rulers of the Philistines, a seafaring people who settled on the Palestine coast in the twelfth century B.C., each offer Delilah 1,100 pieces of silver for her treachery in betraying the secret of Samson's immense strength. And in a well-known Egyptian tale from the eleventh century B.C., the wandering hero Wen-Amon journeys to Lebanon to buy lumber to build a barge. As payment, he carries jars and sacks of gold and silver, each weighed in the traditional Egyptian measure, the deben. (One deben equals 3 ounces.) Whether these stories are based on history or myth, they reflect the commercial transactions of their time.

To expedite commerce, Mediterranean metalsmiths also devised ways of conveniently packaging money. Coils and rings seem to have caught on in some parts of Egypt: a mural painted during the fourteenth century B.C. in the royal city of Thebes depicts a man weighing a stack of doughnut-size golden rings. Elsewhere, metalsmiths cast cash in other forms. In the Egyptian city of el-Amarna, built and briefly occupied during the fourteenth century B.C., archeologists stumbled upon what they fondly referred to as a crock of gold. Inside, among bits of gold and silver, were several slender rod-shaped ingots of gold and silver. When researchers weighed them, they discovered that some were in multiples or fractions of the Egyptian deben, suggesting different denominations of an ancient currency.

All these developments, says Wyrick, transformed Mediterranean life. Before, in the days of pure barter, people produced a little bit of everything themselves, eking out a subsistence. But with the emergence of money along the eastern Mediterranean, people in remote coastal communities found themselves in a new and enviable position. For the first time, they could trade easily with Phoenician or Syrian merchants stopping at their harbors. They no longer had to be self-sufficient. "They could specialize in producing one thing," says Wyrick. "Someone could just graze cattle. Or they could mine gold or silver. And when you specialize, you become more productive. And then more and more goods start coming your way."

Such wealth did the newly invented coins bring one Lydian king, Croesus, that his name became a byword for prosperity.

The wealth spun by such specialization and trade became the stuff of legend. It armed the fierce Mycenaean warriors of Greece in bronze cuirasses and chariots and won them victories. It outfitted the tomb of Tutankhamen, sending his soul in grandeur to the next world. And it filled the palace of Solomon with such magnificence that even the Queen of Sheba was left breathless.

But the rings, ingots, and scraps of gold and silver that circulated as money in the eastern Mediterranean were still a far cry from today's money. They lacked a key ingredient of modern cash—a visible guarantee of authenticity. Without such a warranty, many people would never willingly accept them at their face value from a stranger. The lumps of precious metal might be a shade short of a shekel, for example. Or they might not be

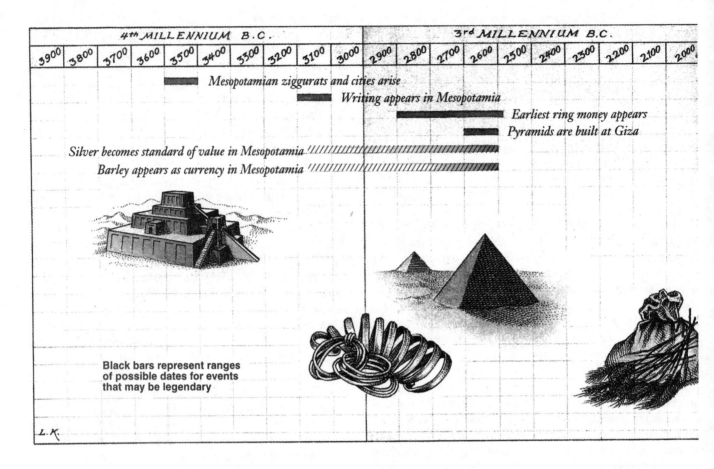

| 4th MILLENNIUM B.C. | 3rd MILLENNIUM B.C. |

Mesopotamian ziggurats and cities arise

Writing appears in Mesopotamia

Earliest ring money appears

Pyramids are built at Giza

Silver becomes standard of value in Mesopotamia

Barley appears as currency in Mesopotamia

Black bars represent ranges
of possible dates for events
that may be legendary

L.K.

MONEYFACT

The Bartering Ape

William Hopkins and Charles Hyatt at Yerkes Regional Primate Center report that chimpanzees were observed swapping items for food from humans. First, a human experimenter knelt down and begged in front of a chimp cage (chimpanzees customarily beg from one another in the wild). At the same time, the experimenter also pointed at an item—an empty food case—in the chimp's cage and held out desirable food, like an apple or half a banana. Of 114 chimpanzees, nearly half caught the trading spirit and pushed the item out. Some even traded much faster for more desirable food—taking just 15 seconds to trade for a banana versus nearly 3 minutes to trade for typical fare. And some chimpanzees negotiated on their own terms, notes Hopkins. He has worked with four who refused to cooperate in experiments for their usual food reward when other, more preferable food was in sight.

utable certified that a coin was both the promised weight and composition.

Balmuth has been trying to trace the origins of this certification. In the ancient Near East, she notes, authority figures—perhaps kings or merchants—attempted to certify money by permitting their names or seals to be inscribed on the official carved stone weights used with scales. That way Mesopotamians would know that at least the weights themselves were the genuine article. But such measures were not enough to deter cheats. Indeed, so prevalent was fraud in the ancient world that no fewer than eight passages in the Old Testament forbid the faithful from tampering with scales or substituting heavier stone weights when measuring out money.

Clearly, better antifraud devices were needed. Under the ruins of the old city of Dor along northern Israel's coast, a team of archeologists found one such early attempt. Ephraim Stern of Hebrew University and his colleagues found a clay jug filled with nearly 22 pounds of silver, mainly pieces of scrap, buried in a section of the city dating from roughly 3,000 years ago. But more fascinating than the contents, says Balmuth, who recently studied this hoard, was the way they had been packaged. The scraps were divided into separate piles. Someone had wrapped each pile in fabric and then attached a bulla, a clay tab imprinted with an official seal. "I have since read that these bullae lasted for centuries," says Balmuth, "and were used to mark jars—or in this case things wrapped in fabric—that were sealed. That was a way of signing something."

pure gold or silver at all, but some cheaper alloy. Confidence, suggests Miriam Balmuth, an archeologist at Tufts University in Medford, Massachusetts, could be won only if someone rep-

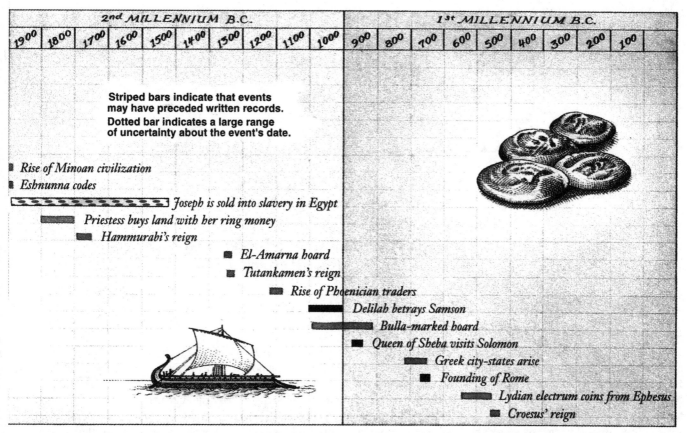

2nd MILLENNIUM B.C.	1st MILLENNIUM B.C.
1900 1800 1700 1600 1500 1400 1300 1200 1100 1000	900 800 700 600 500 400 300 200 100

Striped bars indicate that events
may have preceded written records.
Dotted bar indicates a large range
of uncertainty about the event's date.

Rise of Minoan civilization
Eshnunna codes
Joseph is sold into slavery in Egypt
Priestess buys land with her ring money
Hammurabi's reign
El-Amarna hoard
Tutankamen's reign
Rise of Phoenician traders
Delilah betrays Samson
Bulla-marked hoard
Queen of Sheba visits Solomon
Greek city-states arise
Founding of Rome
Lydian electrum coins from Ephesus
Croesus' reign

All that remained was to impress the design of a seal directly on small rounded pieces of metal—which is precisely what happened by around 600 B.C. in an obscure Turkish kingdom by the sea. There traders and perfume makers known as the Lydians struck the world's first coins. They used electrum, a natural alloy of gold and silver panned from local riverbeds. (Coincidentally, Chinese kings minted their first money at roughly the same time: tiny bronze pieces shaped like knives and spades, bearing inscriptions revealing places of origin or weight. Circular coins in China came later.)

First unearthed by archeologists early this century in the ruins of the Temple of Artemis in Ephesus, one of the Seven Wonders of the ancient world, the Lydian coins bore the essential hallmarks of modern coinage. Made of small, precisely measured pieces of precious metal, they were stamped with the figures of lions and other mighty beasts—the seal designs, it seems, of prominent Lydians. And such wealth did they bring one Lydian king, Croesus, that his name became a byword for prosperity.

Struck in denominations as small as .006 ounce of electrum—one-fifteenth the weight of a penny—Lydia's coinage could be used by people in various walks of life. The idea soon caught on in the neighboring Greek city-states. Within a few decades, rulers across Greece began churning out beautiful coins of varied denominations in unalloyed gold and silver, stamped with the faces of their gods and goddesses.

These new Greek coins became fundamental building blocks for European civilization. With such small change jingling in their purses, Greek merchants plied the western Mediterranean, buying all that was rare and beautiful from coastal dwellers, leaving behind Greek colonies from Sicily to Spain and spreading their ideas of art, government, politics, and philosophy. By the fourth century B.C., Alexander the Great was acquiring huge amounts of gold and silver through his conquests and issuing coins bearing his image far and wide, which Wyrick calls "ads for empire building."

Indeed, says Wyrick, the small change in our pockets literally made the Western world what it is today. "I tell my students that if money had never developed, we would all still be bartering. We would have been stuck with that. Money opened the door to trade, which opened the door for specialization. And that made possible a modern society."

The Coming of the Sea Peoples— *Primarily warriors*

started showing up by 13th century

A low-tech revolution in Bronze Age battlefield tactics changed the history of the Western world.

by Neil Asher Silberman

In the long annals of Western military history, one important group of battle-field innovators—whose archaeological traces have been uncovered from mainland Greece to the coasts of Lebanon and Israel—has often been overlooked. Around 1200 B.C., a wave of sword-wielding warriors streamed southward across the Aegean and eastward toward Asia Minor, Cyprus, and Canaan. By around 1175, some of them had reached the borders of Egypt, where they were finally repulsed by the land and sea forces of Pharaoh Ramesses III. Yet in their stunning military successes throughout the region, these warriors exerted an enormous impact on the development of ancient warfare and proved instrumental in the transformation of Mediterranean society. In subsequent centuries, the rising kingdoms of Israel and Phoenicia and the city-states of Classical Greece all adopted their tactics, arms, and strategic mentality.

Who were these invading forces and where did they come from? What was it about their weapons and tactics that proved to be so deadly to the great Late Bronze Age empires—and so influential in shaping the societies that succeeded them? For the past 150 years, historians have recognized that the twelfth century B.C. was a time of great upheaval, in which ancient empires were toppled and new societies were born. They have as-

cribed this dramatic transformation not to innovations in warfare but to vast population movements, spearheaded by a coalition of northern tribes and ethnic groups who are mentioned repeatedly in ancient Egyptian inscriptions—and whom nineteenth-century scholars dubbed the "Sea Peoples" or the "Peoples of the Sea." These Sea Peoples were not simply Bronze Age Vikings but were a haphazard collection of farmers, warriors, and craftspeople, as well as sailors who originated in the highlands of the Balkans and the coastlands of Asia Minor. Their only common trait seems to have been their movement across the Mediterranean toward the centers of trade and agriculture of the Near East.

Their impact on the Near Eastern empires was dramatic, though scholars are deeply divided on the reasons. Some maintain that the Sea Peoples were displaced from their homelands by famine, natural disasters, or political breakdown and were able to overcome the sophisticated, cosmopolitan empires of the Mediterranean by their sheer barbarian savagery. Others suggest that a closer analysis of the historical records and archaeological remains from this period can pinpoint a more specific agent of change connected to the era's vast population movements. There is reason to believe that only a small, specialized class of professional warriors, in the midst of

the much more massive migratory waves, was responsible for the military attacks of the Sea Peoples. As a skilled caste of mercenary foot soldiers who drifted southward to find employment in kingdoms throughout the region, this group of Sea Peoples had both the tactical know-how and the weaponry to recognize—and demonstrate—just how pitifully vulnerable the great Late Bronze Age powers had become. The civilization of the Late Bronze Age (c. 1550 to c. 1200 B.C.), to which these northern mercenary contingents gravitated, was typified by grand monuments, opulent palace cultures, and some of the most complex administrative and accounting systems the Mediterranean world had ever seen. In Egypt, the powerful pharaohs of the New Kingdom resided amid the splendor of Thebes in Upper Egypt. There they prospered from the rich agricultural produce of the Nile valley and enjoyed the luxury goods acquired from a far-flung trade network reaching from Africa and the southern coast of Arabia to the islands of the Aegean Sea. To the north of Egypt, in the city-states of Canaan, on the island of Cyprus, and at the cosmopolitan port of Ugarit, local dynasties ruled over docile peasant populations and vied with one another for diplomatic or commercial advantage. In the vast continental expanse of Asia Minor, the Hittite empire

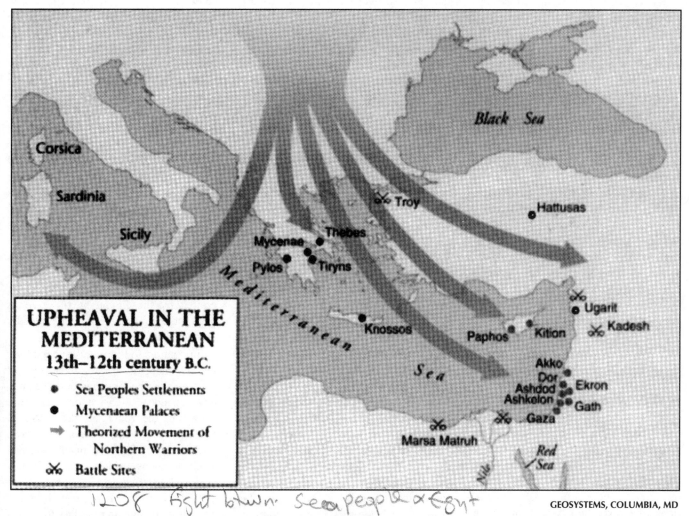

UPHEAVAL IN THE MEDITERRANEAN
13th–12th century B.C.

- Sea Peoples Settlements
- Mycenaean Palaces
- Theorized Movement of Northern Warriors
- Battle Sites

1208 fight btwn. Sea people & Egypt

GEOSYSTEMS, COLUMBIA, MD

Not long after appearing in Egypt, Sea People warriors fought for the Egyptians at Kadesh (c. 1275 B.C.). They would become agents of radical change, likely bringing down Mycenaean civilization and enfeebling the great empires of the ancient world.

maintained its feudal rule from the stronghold of Hattusas. And across the Aegean Sea, on mainland Greece, Crete, and the islands, a unique palace-based civilization of regional rulers, with their coteries of servants, craftsmen, priests, and mercenary forces, comprised the chivalric society that was at least partially reflected in the physical details of Homer's *Iliad*.

Despite these differences in styles and traditions, all the empires of the Late Bronze Age were united in their dependence on a single military technology. No self-respecting kingdom could exist for long without attack forces based on the light battle chariot, which was then the most sophisticated and reliable vehicle of war. The chariots of this period were constructed with considerable skill—and at considerable cost—from sturdy yet highly flexible laminates of wood and bone that enabled them to travel at high speed and with great maneuverability. Propelled by a specially bred and trained two-horse team, the chariot was manned by a professional driver and a combat archer, whose composite bow, also constructed of laminated materials, could launch arrows with extraordinary accuracy and force. These factors all added up to make the light chariot a high-powered, highly mobile weapons delivery system that could swoop down on static infantry forces with frightening speed and velocity.

The figure of the charioteer—as an embodiment of individual skill and courage—became, in many respects, a symbol for the age. The firepower of the new-style chariots was so overwhelming on the battlefield that no ruler who hoped to maintain his throne against his local or regional rivals could afford to be without them—any more than any truly modern nation can afford to be without an effective air force. As a result, Bronze Age kings, pharaohs, and princes scrambled to assemble chariot forces. And just as the kings and potentates of other eras strutted in the guise of knights-errant, cavalry officers, or naval commanders, Late Bronze Age Egyptian pharaohs and Mycenaean, Hittite, and Canaanite kings were all grandly depicted on their monuments in the pose of triumphant charioteers. Yet as the chariot buildup continued through the fourteenth and thirteenth centuries B.C., and as chariot formations gradually rendered infantry battles obsolete in conflicts between rival city-states or empires, a costly arms race began to get out of control.

By the time of the Hittite-Egyptian confrontation at the battle of Kadesh in Syria in 1275 B.C., relatively modest chariot corps of a few dozen vehicles had expanded to enormous contingents. At Kadesh, the Hittite chariot corps alone numbered at least 3,500 vehicles. This placed a strain on even the wealthiest kingdoms. The cost of chariots and horses was substantial. And the skilled craftsmen, chariot drivers, archers, and horse trainers required to maintain the battle-readiness of a kingdom's chariot force could—and did—demand lavish personal support, generous land grants, and conspicuously privileged status at each court they served. Thus, at times of shortage brought about by drought, flood, disease, or poor crop yields, the demands of the charioteers and their staffs could force individual kingdoms toward the breaking point. And yet the Late Bronze Age powers had all become dangerously dependent on this method of warfare. Little wonder, then, that when its tactical vulnerability was discovered, the whole edifice came tumbling down. The result was one of the great turning points in history dubbed by some the Great Catastrophe. Within the span of just a few decades before and after 1200 B.C., the Bronze Age civilizations of Greece and Asia Minor were shattered, and Egypt gradually lost its role as a regional superpower. At the same time, the sudden arrival and settlement of new peoples on Cyprus and along the coast of Canaan ushered in a new era of small kingdoms and city-states.

J ust beyond the confines of the civilized regions of the Mediterranean world, in the mountainous areas of the Balkan peninsula and in the rugged hinterlands of western and southern Asia Minor, the chariot had no power. It was suited only to action on the relatively level battlefields of the lowlands and the plains. On the occasions when the great empires felt the need to mount punitive expeditions against the inhabitants of the highlands, they dispatched infantry forces for brief, brutal demonstrations of force. For the most part, however, the highlanders were left alone as long as

they handed over the demanded tribute and did nothing to interfere with the main routes of trade. Among the tribal societies of these regions, internal disputes were settled in contests of single combat between experienced professional warriors. Archaeological finds from warriors' tombs across western and central Europe, from Scandinavia to the Black Sea, have provided evidence of this mobile, deadly kind of hand-to-hand warfare, waged with long, two-edged swords that could be swung with enough momentum to decapitate an opponent or cut off a limb. Small round shields seem also to have been used to deflect rapid parries. Helmets of various designs and light body armor of many shapes and materials were also common in this individualistic style of war. In terms of weaponry and personal aggressiveness, the warriors of the frontier areas were much more formidable than the typical infantries of the Mediterranean empires, whose members were usually conscripted from the local peasantry, poorly trained, and armed only with short daggers, spears, or clubs.

The reason for the neglect of the infantry by the Mediterranean empires was the overwhelming importance accorded to chariot forces, which comprised the main tactical elements. Lines of chariots would charge against each other like modern tank forces, and, having penetrated or outflanked the opposing formation, would wheel around quickly and charge against the opposing chariots again. Foot soldiers were used in the decidedly secondary capacities of guard duty, road escort, frontier patrols, and routine police work. The only battlefield function reserved for foot soldiers was as "runners" who raced behind and among the chariots, snatching up fallen enemy booty and finishing off wounded enemy chariot crews. This mopping-up function was of little tactical significance. But by the time of the battle of Kadesh, the appearance of a new kind of runner proved to be an omen of the way that subsequent wars in the Mediterranean region would be waged—and won.

In a provocative new book entitled *The End of the Bronze Age: Changes in Warfare and the Catastrophe, ca. 1200 B.C.*, Robert Drews, a professor of an-

cient history at Vanderbilt University, argues that the arrival of northern-style warriors in the Mediterranean upset the unquestioned domination of the chariot. By so doing, it undermined the foundations of the regimes the chariots were meant to defend. Drews notes that barely ten years before the battle of Kadesh, Egyptian hieroglyphic reliefs recorded the ominous movements of a people named the "Sherden," who had arrived "in their warships from the midst of the sea." Wearing trademark horned helmets and armed with long swords and small round shields, they obviously made a profound impression on the Egyptians. By the time the Egyptian chariot forces moved north to confront the Hittites, contingents of Sherden had been recruited by the Egyptians to serve as bodyguards and particularly deadly "runners" among the chariots.

In contrast to the usual runners, who merely mopped up after the chariot charges, the Sherden apparently became an independent offensive force. They are shown in the reliefs of the battle of Kadesh using their weapons to slash, hack, and dismember enemy charioteers. Their weapons, which were originally designed for individual combat, made Sherden warriors far more mobile and adaptable to changing battlefield conditions than the traditional formations of infantry. And with significant numbers of aggressive, northern-style warriors swarming among the chariots, deflecting arrows with their shields and pouncing on disabled vehicles with long swords swinging, they would have posed a sudden, unexpected threat to the firepower and mobility of even the most impressive concentrations of chariotry. While the traditional Bronze Age foot soldiers marched together in relatively slow-moving formations and used weapons such as clubs and spears, which had only a limited radius of effectiveness, the Sherden seem to have ranged widely, pouncing on vulnerable chariot crews.

No less important, they possessed weapons far more effective in combat than those of standard Bronze Age foot soldiers. Ancient pictorial representations of Sherden runners suggest that they were also skilled in the use of the hunting javelin, commonly used in this period for felling wild game. In combination with the long sword, the hunting javelin would have been especially deadly. Drews makes a persuasive—if admittedly speculative—case for suggesting that these new weapons could transform units of runners into an effective battlefield strike force. "For the 'hunting' of chariot horses the javelin must have been ideal," Drews writes, "although it seldom would have killed the horse that it hit, the javelin would have surely brought it to a stop, thus immobilizing the other horse, the vehicle and the crew."

The battle of Kadesh ended in a stalemate between the Egyptians and the Hittites, ushering in a brief period of military balance between the two powers. But by the middle of the thirteenth century B.C., new groups of northern warriors armed with long swords and javelins were drawn in increasing numbers toward the centers of the Late Bronze Age empires, where they were destined to upset the delicate geopolitical balance. Initially, they found employment as mercenaries just as the Sherden had done. Among the names mentioned in Egyptian records and in the archives of Ugarit and the Hittite empire were—in addition to the Sherden—groups known as the Shekelesh, Tursha, Lukka, Shardana, and Ekwesh. Linguistic analysis of these names has enabled scholars to identify them with peoples mentioned in classical and biblical literature: Sicilians, Tyrrhenians, Lycians, and Achaean Greeks. The Sherden have been identified as a group originating on the island of Sardinia, or, according to some scholars, as its eventual conquerors.

It is important to recognize, however, that these Sea Peoples mentioned in the ancient records were not entire nations displaced from their homelands, but a particular military caste represented by warriors from many ethnic groups. Like the pirates and freebooters of the seventeenth-century Caribbean, their many separate nationalities were as conspicuous as the threatening uniformity of their weapons and hand-to-hand fighting techniques.

Archaeologists are generally agreed that the relative tranquility of the Late Bronze Age world following the battle of Kadesh was rocked sometime after 1250

B.C. by a great wave of destructions and upheavals that seems to have begun in the Aegean basin. The Mycenaean palace of Thebes in Boeotia was destroyed and abandoned. The flourishing city of Troy, guarding the trade routes to the Black Sea, was likewise destroyed in a great conflagration, to be succeeded by a much more modest settlement. There is suggestive evidence that these destructions may not have resulted from normal clashes between chariot forces. The hasty construction of a great fortification wall across the Isthmus of Corinth and the strengthening of the defenses around other Mycenaean palace complexes may reflect apprehensions about a far more pervasive danger, perhaps a threat by potential attackers that Bronze Age chariotry would have been unable to withstand. And those apparent fears of attack and conquest seem to have been justified, for by the middle of the next century, the destruction of all the Mycenaean palace complexes was virtually complete.

There may, of course, have been many specific, local reasons for this wave of upheaval. In some places, rivalries between regional centers could have led to the violence. In others, widespread social unrest caused by growing inequalities in late Bronze Age society may have led to local uprisings and the overthrow of the palace elite. Yet in a thought-provoking hypothesis that has already aroused considerable scholarly discussion, Drews pulls together tactical analysis, archaeological evidence, and the colorful testimony of heroic Greek myth to offer a novel reconstruction of the events. He suggests that the legendary accounts of the attacks against Thebes by a coalition of champions (immortalized by Aeschylus in his play *Seven Against Thebes*) and Homer's epic poem about the sack of Troy by Agamemnon's forces preserve memories of the first dramatic triumphs of free-lance northern infantry concentrations, fighting in the new style.

The gradually increasing scope of such encounters may suggest that news of the vulnerability of chariot forces spread among northern mercenary contingents. And in this very period, a wave of northern warriors now made their way

southward in search of plunder, not employment. In looking anew at Homer's poetic metaphors about the epic battle between Achaeans and Trojans, it may well be—as Drews suggested—that the repeated description of the Achaean hero Achilles as "fleet-footed," and the characteristic description of the Trojans as "horse-taming," preserve memories of an epic clash between foot soldiers and horse-powered troops. Even though the *Iliad* was set down in writing several centuries later, at a time when chariot warfare had long been abandoned, the vivid image of Achaean soldiers streaming from the Trojan Horse may eloquently express, at least in mythic language, the sudden emergence of a new style of infantrymen—whose hidden power was revealed in an age of horse-based warfare. In their conquest of Troy, the Achaean foot soldiers departed from the empty wooden horse, thereby symbolically leaving behind the horse (and chariot) as the preferred weapons platforms of the age.

The violent events in the Aegean do not seem to have affected the great capitals and emporia of the Near East—at least not immediately. International commerce continued throughout the thirteenth century B.C., and a certain measure of prosperity was enjoyed in the royal courts of the Near East. New Kingdom Egypt (where at least some Sea People had gone to find work as mercenary runners) therefore beckoned as a tempting target for plundering attacks. The aging pharaoh Ramesses II (c. 1279–c. 1212 B.C.), after having emerged from the battle of Kadesh in a military stalemate with the Hittites, still presided over a vast territory and trade network extending from Canaan, south to Nubia, and as far west as Libya. Excavations at Late Bronze Age port cities and recovered cargoes from sunken merchant ships of this period throughout the eastern Mediterranean have emphasized the volume of international trade—and the extent of interaction between nations, cultures, and ethnic groups during this cosmopolitan age. Only recently have excavations uncovered the ruins of a once busy Late Bronze Age trade depot—littered with sherds of pottery from Mycenaean Greece, Egypt, Cyprus, and Canaan—on a sandy island known as Bates's Island off the coast of Egypt's western desert, about 120 miles east of the modern border with Libya.

It was surely no coincidence or accident that the first major attack by northern warriors on Egypt was launched from this direction. Far from being an isolated wilderness, Libya was connected to Egypt by land and sea trade routes. At a time of reported famine, it was a Libyan leader named "Meryre, Son of Did," who instigated the first major operation in which a coalition of northern warriors played a prominent role. Scholars have always puzzled over how and why Libyans forged a coalition with the various Sea Peoples. Yet the archaeological evidence of an offshore trade depot so close to Libya indicates that it was not a cultural backwater but on one of the main routes in the movement of people and goods. It is entirely conceivable that Meryre was aware of events going on elsewhere in the eastern Mediterranean, possibly through the contact his subjects had with the polyglot gangs of sailors, stevedores, and workers who were drawn into the networks of long-distance trade. More important, he seems to have been keenly aware of the recent—one might even say revolutionary—developments in the art of warfare. Indeed if Meryre had heard about recent successes achieved by northern warriors in direct assaults on chariot forces in Greece and Asia Minor, his subsequent actions in recruiting Sea People warriors for his own campaign would suddenly be understandable.

Why else would he contemplate an invasion of Egypt with only foot soldiers? If he were planning a less organized infiltration of the border lands, he would not have needed to form the grand coalition he did. Yet soon after the death of Ramesses II around 1212 B.C., Meryre began to organize a campaign against the western Nile Delta, for which he gained the cooperation of a number of warrior bands. Later Egyptian records note that they came from "the northern lands"—which could indicate an origin in any of the territories along the northern shores of the Mediterranean. The specific mention of Ekwesh, Lukka, Sherden, Shekelesh, and Tursha (identified as Achaeans, Lycians, Sardinians, Sicilians, and Tyrrhenians) suggests that Meryre's appeal attracted recruits from many lands. He promised them a share of the fertile territory and booty to be gained in attacking the forces of the new pharaoh, Merneptah, the long-lived Ramesses' already elderly son. Seen in the context of the times, Meryre thus made an audacious tactical gamble: in recruiting tens of thousands of northern-style foot soldiers along with his own sizable infantry contingents, he was confident that he could overcome the Egyptian chariotry.

As things turned out, Meryre lost his gamble but proved to be a strategist ahead of his time. Merneptah's chariots met the advancing Libyan-Sea People coalition in midsummer 1208 B.C. in the western desert, at a site probably not far from the later and also fateful battlefield of El Alamein. The Egyptian forces reportedly slew 6,000 Libyans and more than 2,200 of the invading Ekwesh, with significant casualties suffered by the other Sea Peoples as well. Yet the list of spoils taken in the battle by the Egyptians gives a clear indication of the novel nature of the encounter: more than 9,000 long swords were captured from the invaders—with only an utterly insignificant twelve Libyan chariots being seized. For the time being, the pharaoh's chariots had prevailed over massed formations of swordsmen and javelineers. But new troubles were not long in coming for the pharaoh. Frontier populations in other regions were growing restless, and Merneptah soon had to undertake a punitive campaign into Canaan, where he was forced to reassert his control over some important cities and pacify the highlands. In typically bombastic prose he reported one of the most gratifying outcomes of the encounter: "Israel is laid waste; his seed is not!" The clear, if mistaken, implication was that this people had been so thoroughly defeated that they or their descendants would never appear on the stage of history again.

The quotation, which comes from Merneptah's so-called Victory Stele at the Temple of Karnak, contains this earliest mention of the people of Israel outside the Bible, and it may also indicate the extent of the tactical revolution spreading throughout the Mediterranean world. For in the hill country of Canaan at precisely this period, c. 1250–c. 1200 B.C., archaeologists have discovered the sudden establishment of scores of hilltop villages throughout the modern area of the West Bank. Being far from the lowland Canaanite urban centers and outposts of Egyptian presence in fortresses along the coast and major trade routes, they represent the earliest settlements of the Israelites. Their defense against outside powers was not based on chariot warfare but most likely on coordinated militia campaigns. Certainly the biblical books of Joshua and Judges are filled with references to the defeat of the Canaanite kings and the destruction of their chariot forces. Although many historians have come to question the historical reliability of the story of the Israelite Exodus from Egypt, the vivid scriptural account of the drowning in the Red Sea of the pharaoh's pursuing army— and its great chariot corps—might preserve in dreamlike narrative an indelible historical memory of an era of great victories over chariotry.

The threats by northern-style raiders against Egypt and the other great centers of the Bronze Age civilization continued to intensify in this period, with port cities, fortresses, temples, and trade depots throughout the region put to the torch, and in some cases never fully reoccupied again. It is likely that in the spreading chaos, movements of people grew more frequent. Warriors and mercenaries were on the move, of course, but so were other groups formerly serving as craftsmen, servants, or functionaries in the palace centers that had been destroyed by hostile attacks. All of these groups were the "Sea Peoples," both the victims and the perpetrators of the spreading wave of violence. In certain places on Cyprus and along the coast of Canaan, settlers from the Aegean world arrived to establish new communities in the ruins of destroyed Late Bronze Age cities. And the characteristic Mycenaean-style pottery they produced at sites such as Ashkelon, Ekron, and Ashdod in Canaan clearly indicates that whether they themselves were marauders or refugee craftsmen and officials from the destroyed palace centers of the Aegean, the course of their lives and communities had been disrupted by upheavals throughout the Mediterranean world.

Although it is impossible to follow precisely the sequence of raids, conquests, and refugee colonizations in Greece, Cyprus Egypt, and Canaan, there is suggestive evidence that the use of new weapons and tactics by the invaders continued to play a crucial role. In the rubble of the great trading emporium of Ugarit on the coast of modern Syria, for example, excavators have found a number of hunting javelins scattered in the destruction ruins. And the discovery of several newly cast long swords (one even bearing the royal cartouche of Merneptah!) hidden away in hoards at the time of the city's destruction may reflect a desperate, last-ditch effort by some local commanders to equip their forces with the same deadly weapons borne by the marauding Peoples of the Sea.

The last and greatest of attacks by contingents of northern warriors against the centers of Bronze Age civilization is memorialized in exacting detail on the outer walls of the Egyptian temple of Medinet Habu in Upper Egypt, built by Pharaoh Ramesses III, who ruled from c. 1186 to c. 1155 B.C. The Medinet reliefs depict what was one of the most notable events of Ramesses' reign: thousands of Egyptian foot soldiers, sailors, and archers are shown engaged in battles on land and sea against a bizarrely costumed coalition of invaders, who include—in addition to the Sherden and the Shekelesh of the earlier invasions—people known as the Tjekker, Denyen, Weshesh, and Peleset (whom scholars have identified as the biblical Philistines).

This invasion was apparently different and far more threatening than earlier actions. The tone of Ramesses III's official inscription accompanying the pictorial representations conveys an atmosphere of deep crisis that gripped Egypt when word arrived that seaborne and overland coalitions of northern warriors "who had made a conspiracy in their islands" were approaching. Although the precise origin of these warrior bands has never been pinpointed, the mention of "islands" suggests that the threat came from the direction of the Aegean Sea. Ramesses' chronicle goes on to trace the progress of the invaders across the region, in which many separate actions seem to have been combined for rhetorical purposes to heighten the drama of the events.

"All at once the lands were removed and scattered in the fray," reported the inscription in tracing the path of the invaders southward from the Hittite empire, through the cities of Cilicia, Cyprus, and Syria, toward Canaan, which was also known as Amor. "No land could stand before their arms from Hatti, Kode, Carchemish, Arzawa, Alayshia on, being cut off at one time. A camp was set up in one place in Amor. They desolated its people, and its land was like that which has never come into being. They were coming forward to Egypt, while the flame was being prepared before them," the inscription continued. "They laid their hands upon lands as far as the circuit of the earth, their hearts confident and trusting, 'Our plans will succeed!'"

In retrospect, we can see that Pharaoh Ramesses III was placed in an impossible situation in the Great Land and Sea Battles of 1175 B.C. When this last and greatest wave of Sea Peoples' invasions burst upon Egypt, Ramesses was forced to confront forces that had proved they could successfully overcome chariots—which remained the backbone of the Egyptian defense. In response, he apparently tried to change radically the fighting capabilities of his forces—as many desperate, doomed warlords have attempted to do throughout history. Indeed, as analysis of the Medinet Habu reliefs suggests, the vaunted Egyptian chariotry played almost no role in the fighting. Ramesses III's inscriptions can be seen as a commemoration of the heroism of his own infantry. He boasted that the Egyptian foot soldiers—once scorned as insignificant tactical factors—had fought "like bulls ready on the field of battle" and that the militiamen who engaged the enemy in hand-to-hand fighting aboard their ships "were like lions roaring on the mountaintops." No less significant is the fact that in one scene Ramesses himself is depicted as an unmounted archer—not a charioteer—with his two royal feet firmly planted on the bodies of fallen Sea People enemies.

Yet in discarding the ethos and discipline of chariot warfare on which his empire had become so dependent—and in mobilizing his foot soldiers to fight on the same terms and with the same weapons as the invaders—Ramesses sealed the fate of New Kingdom Egypt as surely as a defeat at the hands of the Sea Peoples would have done. For even though the Sea Peoples' invasion was repulsed, and some of the Sea Peoples, like the Philistines, were permitted to settle peacefully in colonies along the nearby coast of Canaan, Egypt would never regain its former strength. The Egyptian Empire—like all other Late Bronze Age kingdoms—had been built and maintained over hundreds of years as a towering social pyramid in which the king, his court, officers, and chariot forces reserved the pinnacle for themselves. The new method of marshaling units of highly mobile, highly motivated infantry against chariot forces required unprecedentedly large numbers of trained fighters. Egypt was never a society that viewed its general population as much more than beasts of burden; to accord peasant recruits respect and intensive training within the armed forces was something that the highly stratified society of New Kingdom Egypt found extremely difficult to do. The strict hierarchy began to crumble, and the growing power of mercenary units and local infantry bands caused widespread social unrest. By the end of the twelfth century, the power of New Kingdom Egypt was ended, and the country entered a new dark age. In contrast, the new world that unfolded in the centuries after the appearance of the Sea Peoples in Greece, Cyprus, Asia Minor, and Canaan drew its strength from the new cultural pattern, which was based on the solidarity and military might of local levies of foot soldiers, not elite units of courtly charioteers.

Chariot forces would again be used on the field of battle—as in the later campaigns of the Assyrian empire in the ninth and eighth centuries B.C.—but only in a supporting role to the infantry. And with the development of effective tack and stirrups during the subsequent centuries, the chariot could be dispensed with altogether, except perhaps as a battlefield conveyance for generals and kings. The Sea People warriors themselves were eventually assimilated into the general populations of the refugees from the great upheavals. Along the coast of Canaan and on Cyprus, new societies derived from Mycenaean models and led by descendants of refugees were born. Even in the rising kingdoms of Israel, Phoenicia, Aramea, Cilicia, Phrygia, and the city-states of Greece, where new forms of military and social organization emerged after the end of the Bronze Age, the legacy of the Sea Peoples—though dramatically transformed—could still be perceived. Just as the fleet-footed Achaean warrior Achilles became the role model for the citizen soldier of the archaic Greek polis, the image of the young David, surrounded by his band of mighty men of war, remained a cherished biblical symbol of national solidarity. And there were to be even more far-reaching developments in the use of large infantry formations as the kingdoms of Assyria and Babylonia swelled into great empires with enormous populations. Eventually, the massive formations of infantry units evolved into the Macedonian phalanx and the Roman legion.

The sweeping scenario of scattered contingents of Sea People warriors streaming together from their distant islands and hill country homes to overcome the elite chariot forces of the Bronze Age Mediterranean has not been without its critics. Scholars who still favor explanations such as natural disasters, generalized social breakdown, or the gradual cultural shift from Bronze Age chariot empires to Iron Age infantry kingdoms are skeptical of a single military cause. But without minimizing the possibility that natural or economic crises may indeed have undermined the political order and intensified social tensions, there is much to be said for the contention that only something as dramatic as the introduction of new weapons and tactics could have triggered violent upheavals on such a massive scale.

And there is, even beyond the specific questions of this remote period, a far more basic historical point. We must not merely see the episode of the "Sea Peoples" as a bizarre and bloody episode that took place in a far-off region more than 3,000 years ago. The long swords, javelins, and body armor of the invading Sea Peoples may seem quaintly rustic to us in a day of Stealth fighter-bombers and Tomahawk missiles. Yet they offer an important object lesson in the way that complacent dependency by great powers on expensive and complex military technology can suddenly be undermined. The grand catastrophe of the end of the Bronze Age and the role of the Sea Peoples in it should show us how unexpectedly simple weapons in the hands of committed warriors can topple great empires. Societies in any age can become dangerously presumptuous about the invulnerability of their advanced military technologies. Over centuries or even decades the society molds itself, in its religion, political order, and social hierarchy, to conform to the dominant technology. If that technology is undermined by groups with little stake in preserving the existing system, the results can be catastrophic. Today we speak of terrorists with homemade bombs and shoulder-fired missiles, but at the end of the Late Bronze Age in the eastern Mediterranean, it was northern warriors with long swords and hunting javelins who laid the groundwork for a dramatic transformation of society.

Neil Asher Silberman is an author and historian specializing in the ancient history of the Near East. He is a contributing editor to Archaeology *magazine.*

This article is reprinted from the Winter 1998 issue of *Military History Quarterly* magazine, pp. 6-13, with permission of Cowles Enthusiast Media, Inc. (History Group), A PRIMEDIA Publication. © 1998, Military History Quarterly magazine.

Grisly Assyrian Record of Torture and Death

Erika Bleibtreu

Assyrian national history, as it has been preserved for us in inscriptions and pictures, consists almost solely of military campaigns and battles. It is as gory and bloodcurdling a history as we know.

Assyria emerged as a territorial state in the 14th century B.C. Its territory covered approximately the northern part of modern Iraq. The first capital of Assyria was Assur, located about 150 miles north of modern Baghdad on the west bank of the Tigris River. The city was named for its national god, Assur, from which the name Assyria is also derived.

From the outset, Assyria projected itself as a strong military power bent on conquest. Countries and peoples that opposed Assyrian rule were punished by the destruction of their cites and the devastation of their fields and orchards.

By the ninth century B.C., Assyria had consolidated its hegemony over northern Mesopotamia. It was then that Assyrian armies marched beyond their own borders to expand their empire, seeking booty to finance their plans for still more conquest and power. By the mid-ninth century B.C., the Assyrian menace posed a direct threat to the small Syro-Palestine states to the west, including Israel and Judah.

The period from the ninth century to the end of the seventh century B.C. is known as the Neo-Assyrian period, during which the empire reached its zenith. The Babylonian destruction of their cap-

ital city Nineveh in 612 B.C. marks the end of the Neo-Assyrian empire, although a last Assyrian king, Ashur-uballit II, attempted to rescue the rest of the Assyrian state, by then only a small territory around Harran. However, the Babylonian king Nabopolassar (625–605 B.C.) invaded Harran in 610 B.C. and conquered it. In the following year, a final attempt was made by Ashur-uballit II to regain Harran with the help of troops from Egypt, but he did not succeed. Thereafter, Assyria disappears from history.

We will focus here principally on the records of seven Neo-Assyrian kings, most of whom ruled successively. Because the kings left behind pictorial, as well as written, records, our knowledge of their military activities is unusually well documented:

1. Ashurnasirpal II—883–859 B.C.
2. Shalmaneser III—858–824 B.C.
3. Tiglath-pileser III—744–727 B.C.
4. Sargon II—721–705 B.C.
5. Sennacherib—704–681 B.C.
6. Esarhaddon—680–669 B.C.
7. Ashurbanipal—668–627 B.C.

Incidentally, Assyrian records, as well as the Bible, mention the military contracts between the Neo-Assyrian empire and the small states of Israel and Judah.

An inscription of Shalmaneser III records a clash between his army and a coalition of enemies that included Ahab, king of Israel (c. 859–853 B.C.). Indeed, Ahab, according to Shalmaneser, mustered more chariots (2,000) than any of the other allies arrayed against the Assyrian ruler at the battle of Qarqar on the Orontes (853 B.C.). For a time, at least, the Assyrian advance was checked.

An inscription on a stela from Tell al Rimah in northern Iraq, erected in 806 B.C. by Assyrian king Adad-nirari III, informs us that Jehoahaz, king of Israel (814–793 B.C.), paid tribute to the Assyrian king: "He [Adad-nirari III of Assyria] received the tribute of Ia'asu the Samarian [Jehcahaz, king of Israel], of the Tyrian (ruler) and the Sidonian (ruler)."[1]

From the inscriptions of Tiglath-pileser III and from some representations on the reliefs that decorated the walls of his palace at Nimrud, we learn that he too conducted a military campaign to the west and invaded Israel. Tiglath-pileser III received tribute from Menahem of Samaria (744–738 B.C.), as the Bible tells us; the Assyrian king is there called Pulu (2 Kings 15:19–20).

In another episode recorded in the Bible, Pekah, king of Israel (737–732 B.C.), joined forces with Rezin of Damascus against King Ahaz of Judah (2 Kings 16:5–10). The Assyrian king Tiglath-pileser III successfully intervened against Pekah, who was then deposed. The Assyrian king then placed Hoshea on the Israelite throne. By then Israel's northern provinces were devastated and part of her population was deported to Assyria (2 Kings 15:29).

At one point, Israel, already but a shadow of its former self and crushed by the burden of the annual tribute to Assyria, decided to revolt. Shalmaneser V (726–722 B.C.), who reigned after Tiglath-pileser III, marched into Israel, besieged its capital at Samaria and, after three years of fighting, destroyed it (2 Kings 18:10). This probably occurred in the last year of Shalmaneser V's reign (722 B.C.). However, his successor, Sargon II, later claimed credit for the victory. In any event, this defeat ended the national identity of the northern kingdom of Israel. Sargon II deported, according to his own records, 27,290 Israelites, settling them, according to the Bible, near Harran on the Habur River and in the mountains of eastern Assyria (2 Kings 17:6, 18:11).

Later, in 701 B.C., when King Hezekiah of Judah withheld Assyrian tribute, Sargon II's successor, Sennacherib, marched into Judah, destroying, according to his claim, 46 cities and besieging Jerusalem. Although Sennacherib failed to capture Jerusalem (2 Kings 19:32–36), Hezekiah no doubt continued to pay tribute to Assyria.

The two principal tasks of an Assyrian king were to engage in military exploits and to erect public buildings. Both of these tasks were regarded as religious duties. They were, in effect, acts of obedience toward the principal gods of Assyria.

The historical records of ancient Assyria consist of tablets, prisms and cylinders of clay and alabaster. They bear inscriptions in cuneiform—wedge-shaped impressions representing, for the most part, syllables. In addition, we have inscribed obelisks and stelae as well as inscriptions on stone slabs that lined the walls and covered the floors of Assyrian palaces and temples.

In all of these inscriptions, the king stands at the top of the hierarchy—the most powerful person; he himself represents the state. All public acts are recorded as his achievements. All acts worthy of being recorded are attributed only to the Assyrian king, the focus of the ancient world.

The annals of the kings describe not only their military exploits, but also their building activities. This suggests that the spoil and booty taken during the military campaigns formed the financial foundation for the building activities of palaces, temples, canals and other public structures. The booty—property and people—probably provided not only precious building materials, but also artists and workmen deported from conquered territories.

The inscriptional records are vividly supplemented by pictorial representations. These include reliefs on bronze bands that decorated important gates, reliefs carved on obelisks and some engravings on cylinder seals. But the largest and most informative group of monuments are the reliefs sculpted into the stone slabs that lined the palaces' walls in the empire's capital cities—Nimrud (ancient Kalah), Khorsabad (ancient Dur Sharrukin) and Kuyunjik (ancient Nineveh).

According to the narrative representations on these reliefs, the Assyrians never lost a battle. Indeed, no Assyrian soldier is ever shown wounded or killed. The benevolence of the gods is always bestowed on the Assyrian king and his troops.

Like the official written records, the scenes and figures are selected and arranged to record the kings' heroic deeds and to describe him as "beloved of the gods":

"The king, who acts with the support of the great gods his lords and has conquered all lands, gained dominion over all highlands and received their tribute, captures of hostages, he who is victorious over all countries."[2]

The inscriptions and the pictorial evidence both provide detailed information regarding the Assyrian treatment of conquered peoples, their armies and their rulers. In his official royal inscriptions, Ashurnasirpal II calls himself the "trampler of all enemies... who defeated all his enemies [and] hung the corpses of his enemies on posts."[3] The treatment of captured enemies often depended on their readiness to submit themselves to the will of the Assyrian king:

"The nobles [and] elders of the city came out to me to save their lives. They seized my feet and said: 'If it pleases you, kill! If it pleases you, spare! If it pleases you, do what you will!' "[4]

In one case when a city resisted as long as possible instead of immediately submitting. Ashurnasirpal proudly records his punishment:

"I flayed as many nobles as had rebelled against me [and] draped their skins over the pile [of corpses]; some I spread out within the pile, some I erected on stakes upon the pile... I flayed many right through my land [and] draped their skins over the walls."[5]

The account was probably intended not only to describe what had happened, but also to frighten anyone who might dare to resist. To suppress his enemies was the king's divine task. Supported by the gods, he always had to be victorious in battle and to punish disobedient people:

"I felled 50 of their fighting men with the sword, burnt 200 captives from them, [and] defeated in a battle on the plain 332 troops.... With their blood I dyed the mountain red like red wool, [and] the rest of them the ravines [and] torrents of the mountain swallowed. I carried off captives [and] possessions from them. I cut off the heads of their fighters [and] built [therewith] a tower before their city. I burnt their adolescent boys [and] girls."[6]

A description of another conquest is even worse:

"In strife and conflict I besieged [and] conquered the city. I felled 3,000 of their fighting men with the sword... I captured many troops alive: I cut off of some their arms [and] hands; I cut off of others their noses, ears, [and] extremities. I gouged out the eyes of many troops. I made one pile of the living [and] one of heads. I hung their heads on trees around the city."[7]

The palace of Ashurnasirpal II at Nimrud is the first, so far as we know, in which carved stone slabs were used in addition to the usual wall paintings. These carvings portray many of the scenes described in words in the annals.

From the reign of Shalmaneser III, Ashurnasirpal II's son, we also have some bronze bands that decorated a massive pair of wooden gates of a temple (and possibly a palace) at Balawat, near modern Mosul. These bronze bands display unusually fine examples of bronze repoussé (a relief created by hammering on the opposite side). In a detail, we see an Assyrian soldier grasping the hand and arm of a captured enemy whose other hand and both feet have already been cut off. Dismembered hands and feet fly through the scene. Severed enemy heads hang from the conquered city's walls. Another captive is impaled on a stake, his hands and feet already having been cut off. In another detail, we see three stakes, each driven through eight severed heads, set up outside the conquered city. A third detail shows a row of impaled captives lined up on stakes set up on a hill outside the captured city. In an inscription from Shalmaneser III's father, Ashurnasirpal II, the latter tells us, "I captured soldiers alive [and] erected [them] on stakes before their cities."[8]

Shalmaneser III's written records supplement his pictorial archive: "I filled the wide plain with the corpses of his warriors.... These [rebels] I impaled on stakes.[9]... A pyramid (pillar) of heads I erected in front of the city."[10]

In the eighth century B.C., Tiglath-pileser III held center stage. Of one city he conquered, he says:

"Nabû-ushabshi, their king, I hung up in front of the gate of his city on a stake. His land, his wife, his sons, his daughters, his property, the treasure of his palace, I carried off. Bit-Amukâni, I trampled down like a threshing (sledge). All of its people, (and) its goods, I took to Assyria."[11]

Such actions are illustrated several times in the reliefs at Tiglath-pileser's palace at Nimrud. These reliefs display an individual style in the execution of details that is of special importance in tracing the development of military techniques.

Perhaps realizing what defeat meant, a king of Urartu, threatened by Sargon II, committed suicide: "The splendor of Assur, my lord, overwhelmed him [the king of Urartu] and with his own iron dagger he stabbed himself through the heart, like a pig, and ended his life."[12]

Sargon II started a new Assyrian dynasty that lasted to the end of the empire. Sargon built a new capital named after himself—Dur Sharrukin, meaning "Stronghold of the righteous king." His palace walls were decorated with especially large stone slabs, carved with extraordinarily large figures.

Sargon's son and successor, Sennacherib, again moved the Assyrian capital, this time to Nineveh, where he built his own palace. According to the excavator of Ninneveh, Austen Henry Layard, the reliefs in Sennacherib's palace, if lined up in a row, would stretch almost two miles. If anything, Sennacherib surpassed his predecessors in the grisly detail of his descriptions:

"I cut their throats like lambs. I cut off their precious lives (as one cuts) a string. Like the many waters of a storm, I made (the contents of) their gullets and entrails run down upon the wide earth. My prancing steeds harnessed for my riding, plunged into the streams of their blood as (into) a river. The wheels of my war chariot, which brings low the wicked and the evil, were bespattered with blood and filth. With the bodies of their warriors I filled the plain, like grass. (Their) testicles I cut off, and tore out the privates like the seeds of cucumbers."[13]

In several rooms of Sennacherib's Southwest Palace at Nineveh, severed heads are represented; deportation scenes are frequently depicted. Among the deportees depicted, there are long lines of prisoners from the Judahite city of Lachish; they are shown pulling a rope fastened to a colossal entrance figure for Sennacherib's palace at Nineveh; above this line of deportees is an overseer whose hand holds a truncheon.

Sennacherib was murdered by his own sons. Another son, Esarhaddon, became his successor. As the following examples show, Esarhaddon treated his enemies just as his father and grandfather had treated theirs: "Like a fish I caught him up out of the sea and cut off his head,"[14] he said of the king of Sidon; "Their blood, like a broken dam, I caused to flow down the mountain gullies";[15] and "I hung the heads of Sanduarri [king of the cities of Kundi and Sizu] and Abdimilkutti [king of Sidon] on the shoulders of their nobles and with singing and music I paraded through the public square of Nineveh."[16]

Ashurbanipal, Esarhaddon's son, boasted:

"Their dismembered bodies I fed to the dogs, swine, wolves, and eagles, to the birds of heaven and the fish in the deep.... What was left of the feast of the dogs and swine, of their members which blocked the streets and filled the squares, I ordered them to remove from Babylon, Kutha and Sippar, and to cast them upon heaps."[17]

When Ashurbanipal didn't kill his captives he "pierced the lips (and) took them to Assyria as a spectacle for the people of my land."[18]

The enemy to the southeast of Assyria, the people of Elam, underwent a special punishment that did not spare even their dead:

"The sepulchers of their earlier and later kings, who did not fear Assur and Ishtar, my lords, (and) who) had plagued the kings, my fathers, I destroyed, I devastated, I exposed to the sun. Their bones (members) I carried off to Assyria. I laid restlessness upon their shades. I deprived them of food-offerings and libations of water."[19]

Among the reliefs carved by Ashsur-banipal were pictures of the mass deportation of the Elamites, together with severed heads assembled in heaps. Two Elamites are seen fastened to the ground while their skin is flayed, while others are having their tongues pulled out.

There is no reason to doubt the historical accuracy of these portrayals and descriptions. Such punishments no doubt helped to secure the payment of tribute—silver, gold, tin, copper, bronze, and iron, as well as building materials including wood, all of which was neces-sary for the economic survival of the Assyrian empire.

In our day, these depictions, verbal and visual, give a new reality to the Assyrian conquest of the northern kingdom of Israel in 721 B.C. and to Sennacherib's subsequent campaign into Judah in 701 B.C.

NOTES

1. Stephanie Page, "A Stela of Adad-nirari III and Nergal-eres from Tell al Rimah," *Iraq* 30 (1968), p. 143.
2. Albert Kirk Grayson, *Assyrian Royal Inscriptions*, Part 2: *From Tiglath-pileser I to Ashur-nasir-apli II* (Wiesbaden, Germ.: Otto Harrassowitz, 1976), p. 165.
3. Ibid., p. 120.
4. Ibid., p. 124.
5. Ibid.
6. Ibid., pp. 126–127.
7. Ibid., p. 126.
8. Ibid., p. 143.
9. Daniel David Luckenbill, *Ancient Records of Assyria and Babylonia*, 2 vols. (Chicago: Univ. of Chicago Press, 1926–1927), vol. 1, secs. 584–585.
10. Ibid., vol. 1, sec. 599.
11. Ibid., vol. 1, sec. 783.
12. Ibid., vol. 2, sec. 22.
13. Ibid., vol. 2, sec. 254.
14. Ibid., vol. 2, sec. 511.
15. Ibid., vol. 2, sec. 521.
16. Ibid., vol. 2, sec. 528.
17. Ibid., vol. 2, secs. 795–796.
18. Ibid., vol. 2, sec. 800.
19. Ibid., vol. 2, sec. 810.

Courtesy of the *Biblical Archaeology Review*, January/February 1991, pp. 52–61. © 1991 by the Biblical Archaeology Society, 3000 Connecticut Avenue, NW, Suite 300, Washington, DC 20008.

Scythian Gold

An exhibition of treasures from ancient Ukraine illuminates a great warrior culture,
notable for its relentless ferocity and remarkable art

By Doug Stewart

SOMEWHERE UP IN THE SWEET HEREAFTER, a grave gobber is cursing his eternal rotten luck for having plied his trade before the days of metal detectors. When he tunneled into a fifth-century B.C. Scythian burial chamber near a tributary of Ukraine's Dnieper River, he pocketed a goodly trove of gold artifacts scattered about the bones of a one-time Scythian strongman. But how was he to know that hidden under just a few inches of dirt next to the deceased were priceless masterpieces of solid gold: an ornate finial covered with a furious orgy of snarling, thrashing animals, a braided-gold necklace and an exquisite drinking cup with six horse heads patterned in a tight, whirling hexagon, their gold reins radiating from a disk of Baltic amber?

The owners of these treasures were violent, hard-living horsemen who dominated the European steppe from the seventh to the third century B.C. Like the Huns and the Mongols, who thundered across the same open grasslands centuries later, the Scythians lived in the saddle and traveled light. At the same time, oddly enough, they were among the ancient world's most extravagant art patrons. Nearly all their treasure, most of it finely wrought gold, was small enough to wear, befitting a people on the move.

"The elite within this nomadic culture were able to amass an incredible amount of wealth," says Gerry D. Scott III, curator of ancient art at the San Antonio Museum of Art, "and I guess, like the Egyptians, they believed they could take it with them, so fortunately we've been

BRUCE WHITE

The charmingly rendered golden boar (above) likely served as the handle of a wooden cup.

able to learn about their culture from their burials."

The three objects near the Dnieper that the looter missed remained hidden until 1990, when a team of Ukrainian archaeologists uncovered them. They are now highlights of a sumptuous new traveling exhibition, "Gold of the Nomads: Scythian Treasures from Ancient Ukraine," at Baltimore's Walters Art Gallery from March 7 to May 28. The show includes a number of other recently unearthed pieces, many of which have never before left Ukraine. With more than 170 artifacts—fanciful and attention-getting jewelry, weapons and ritual objects—this is the most comprehensive exhibition of Scythian gold ever assembled. It opened last fall at the San Antonio Museum of Art and will move from Baltimore to the Los Angeles County Museum of Art on July 2 and to the Brooklyn Museum of Art on October 29. Next year, it travels to Toronto's Royal Ontario Museum, Kansas City's Nelson

Atkins Museum of Art and the Grand Palais in Paris.

Neither Greek nor Asian, Scythian art arose from the creative interplay of nomadic Central Asia and the classical Mediterranean world, says archaeologist Ellen D. Reeder. Now deputy director for art at the Brooklyn Museum, Reeder curated the exhibition while at the Walters Art Gallery, in collaboration with Gerry Scott in San Antonio and experts on Scythian culture in Ukraine. Reeder also has edited the companion volume from Harry N. Abrams, Inc., *Scythian Gold: Treasures from Ancient Ukraine*. "There's a common idea that nomads are longhaired and unwashed, so they must be primitive, but that's not true," she says. The Scythians had a discriminating eye for good design, and the wealth to indulge it. By the fifth century B.C., the steppe-dwelling horsemen were important patrons of master goldsmiths living in Greek cities on the northern shores of the Black Sea. "It was a symbiotic relationship. The Greeks, who didn't want to leave their cities on the Black Sea, were happy to work with the Scythians, who didn't want to abandon their nomadic life." The result, she says, was "a wonderful new artistic amalgamation."

To traditional art historians, the Scythians are little more than a footnote. The neglect is due in part to the Scythians' lack of a written language and in part to their disdain for building houses, fortresses, temples, or monuments other than graves. The few eyewitness reports on the Scythians' ways were usually

Top: A disk of hammered gold bearing a spotted leopard attacking a stag adorns the top of a fifth-century B.C. finial; Bottom: the life-size limestone stele of a warrior once marked a Scythian burial mound. Right: This modern reconstruction of a Scythian warrior's battle dress, complete with iron-plated armor, is based on remains found in fifth- and fourth-century B.C. tombs.

written by Greeks, who tended to be condescending if not hostile. The fifth-century B.C. physician Hippocrates reported that Scythians were "bloated" and "sweaty." His contemporary Aristophanes wrote them into his plays as stock comic characters who dressed outlandishly, spoke mangled Greek and drank to excess. More charitable was the fourth-century B.C. historian Ephorus. Some of the Scythians, he maintained, "excel all men in justice.... They not only are orderly towards one another... but also remain invincible and unconquered by outsiders."

Scythia was less a nation than a group of related, warring nomadic tribes. During the first millennium B.C., what was sometimes called Greater Scythia stretched from the Carpathian Mountains in eastern Europe to Mongolia, more than 4,000 miles away. The Scythians who roamed this vast sweep of grasslands were probably of Indo-European stock and may have spoken a language related to Persian. The new exhibition focuses on finds from tombs of the most powerful and sophisticated of these nomad groups, which the ancient Greeks called the Royal Scythians. Having swept into present-day Ukraine from Central Asia sometime after 700 B.C., they soon dominated the flat, fertile pastures from the Danube to the Don and viewed all other Scythians as their slaves.

Suddenly, wild-eyed horsemen broke ranks and galloped recklessly across the plain.

These nomads had a fearsome reputation throughout the ancient world. At a time when the horse had not been domesticated for very long, the Scythians fielded the first truly effective mounted cavalry. The sight of Scythian warriors on horseback could have inspired the Greek myth of the centaur. And a biblical allusion to a horde threatening Babylon, in the Book of Jeremiah, possibly referred to a Scythian penetration into the Near East in the seventh century B.C.: "Behold, a people comes from the north.... They lay hold of bow and spear; they are cruel, and have no mercy. The sound of them is like the roaring of the sea; they ride upon horses, arrayed as a man for battle against you, O daughter of Babylon!"

Following a fact-finding mission to the northern Black Sea coast in the fifth century B.C., Herodotus devoted much of Book IV of his *Histories* to tabloid-worthy tales of the Scythians' gruesome exploits. Wealthy Scythians, he reported, gilded the insides of their enemies' skulls and used them as drinking cups. "They treat the skulls of their kinsmen in the same way, in cases where quarrels have occurred." Though Herodotus professed not to admire the Scythians, he saluted their military success. "A people without fortified towns, living, as the Scythians do, in wagons which they take with them wherever they go, accustomed, one and all, to fight on horseback

A scene from a hammered gold gorytos cover reflects the interplay of Greek and Scythian artistry.

with bows and arrows, and dependent for their food not upon agriculture but upon their cattle: how can such a people fail to defeat the attempt of an invader not only to subdue them, but even to make contact with them?"

Darius the Great of Persia learned this to his regret when he invaded the Scythian heartland in 513 B.C. at the head of a 700,000-man army. The Scythians' use of "tactical retreat"—staying tauntingly just out of reach, while poisoning wells and burning fields as they withdrew—confounded the king and exhausted his troops. After several weeks, the Scythian army at last approached the Persian camp, ready to do battle. Suddenly, reported Herodotus, boisterous whoops arose from the Scythian lines as wild-eyed horsemen broke ranks and galloped recklessly across the plain—in pursuit of

One of the 16 Greek-made bronze vessels found in a peat bog with the remains of a ship-wrecked trader, this fifth-century B.C. hydria bears the image of a siren.

a hare. "These fellows have a hearty contempt for us," Darius was said to mutter to an aide. Humiliated, the Persians began their retreat under cover of darkness that night.

On their home ground, the Scythians were invincible for four centuries. "Using the speed of their horses, these people in essence practiced an ancient form of blitzkrieg," Gerry Scott tells me as he and Ellen Reeder take me around the exhibition at the San Antonio Museum of Art. On display is a suit of reconstructed armor—leather covered with tiny, scale-like iron plates—based on archaeological finds. Nearby is a lavish gold cover for a gorytos, a combination bow-and-arrow holder that the Scythians apparently invented; its intricate gilded design suggests it was either ceremonial or belonged to a paramount chieftain. Next to

BRUCE WHITE

Gold boat-shaped earrings were derived from Greek prototypes, but modified to respond to Scythian taste.

it is an impressive array of arrowheads, used in hunting as well as combat.

"The Scythians were incredible archers," Scott says, "and they chose their weapons depending on what they were hunting. If they were after birds, they'd choose a delicate arrowhead because they aimed for the eye." Warriors might carry more than 200 needle-sharp arrows into battle. Several of the arrowheads, I notice, are barbed. "These were designed to do as much damage coming out as going in," Scott explains. Morever, wrote Ovid of the Scythians' favored weapon, "a poisonous juice clings to the flying metal"—a juice brewed from snake venom, putrefied human blood and dung (to hasten infection). The Greeks dubbed the mixture "scythicon." Could there be any doubt that these people reveled in warfare?

Other than the weapons on display, however, most of the pieces in the exhibition exude a sense not of violence but of ostentatious refinement and even charm. There are hammered-gold headdresses, decorative gold scabbards, elaborately wrought jewelry and embossed gold plaques the size of postage stamps that were sewn onto their clothing.

Though they were technically homeless nomads, the Scythians of the European steppe were nonetheless at the top of their world's pecking order. "The area north of the Black Sea was a breadbasket of the ancient Mediterranean world," Reeder says. "Grain exported from this region kept ancient Greece alive." The Scythians who ruled the area weren't farming the grain; more likely, they exacted tribute from those who did. They also commandeered a lively north-south trade in fur, timber and, perhaps, slaves. "They went from a pastoral culture to a military culture to the international import-export business," Reeder continues. "You have to admire their adaptability." In the process, they grew immensely wealthy, which allowed them to buy caravans' worth of gold (probably from the Urals or Central Asia) and to pay for artisans to shape it to their taste.

Scythians were fond of three pictorial motifs, which recur obsessively in their artwork: the leopard, the eagle and the stag. Most likely, these animals were cherished memories from the Scythians' origins in the mountainous wilds of Central Asia. Burial sites in the Altai Mountains, near Mongolia, have yielded artifacts with much the same imagery. The three animals, along with other beasts, appear as stylized, almost abstract forms. Worn on a gorytos or tunic, images of predators and prey might have served as good-luck charms for a hunter or a fighter. Often, the antlers and hooves of stags mutate fancifully into bird heads or spiral motifs. On one plaque, a tiny spotted leopard munches on a severed human head.

Oddly, horses rarely figure in the Scythians' animal-style art. Perhaps horses were too ordinary and too tame to merit immortality in art. One important exception is a pair of sixth-century B.C. cheekpieces carved in bone, with a horse head at one end and a single hoof at the other. The Scythians themselves are also notably absent from most of the objects on display, but here, too, there are exceptions. One is a fourth-century B.C. solid-gold helmet on which long-haired warriors with embroidered tunics, tight-fitting leggings and tasseled scabbards menace one another with swords and spears. That all the combatants are dressed Scythian-style suggests a bit of internecine strife. "Herodotus records that these people did take scalps," Scott says, referring to one scene on the helmet. "The fact that the man on the ground is being grabbed by the hair is probably significant here."

Gold being a soft metal, this extravagant headgear was no doubt intended for show, not protection. Indeed, showiness seems central to the Scythian aesthetic. Nomads or no, these bold horsemen must have prided themselves on the lavishness as well as the sheer volume of their goldwork. "This makes sense," Scott says, "when you consider they were living in yurtlike structures that they took down and moved along with their livestock. In that situation, you can't put in a swimming pool to show you're elite." Better, he says, to concentrate on personal displays. One buried Scythian male was found wearing a gold earring, a heavy bronze torque, and gold beads, buttons and plaques on his clothing. Both men and women were buried with mirrors, possibly to admire themselves in the afterlife.

"The sunlight would have jumped off all of this gold—it would have been fabulous."

I take in a pair of earrings that would make a belly dancer blush, each an exaggerated boat hull from which dense clusters of golden ducks dangle on gold chains. Yes, Reeder says, .an Athenian aesthete would have sneered at these as tacky gewgaws for nouveau riche barbarians. "The Scythians took a Greek design and made it bigger, made it fatter, made it louder," she explains.

Louder in more ways than one. Noise-making pendants were a favorite of well-to-do Scythian women. A particularly elaborate pair of cascading headdress pendants would have jingled distractingly next to the wearer's ears. "When you move these, the pendants make a mesmerizing tinkle and rattle," Reeder

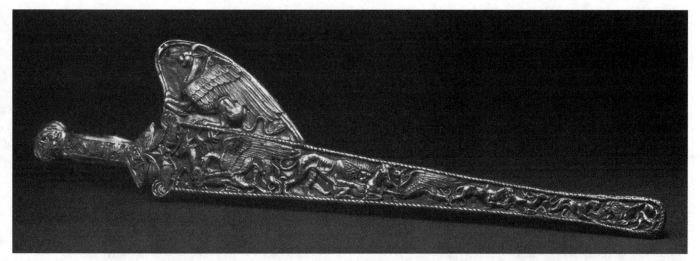

The imposing image of a horned lion-griffin and a frieze of battling animals enliven a fourth-century B.C. sword and scabbard.

says. "And when a woman walked through an encampment, the sunlight would have jumped off all of this gold—it would have been fabulous."

One of the show's centerpieces is a very different kind of noisemaker. A mysterious bronze ornament, possibly a cap for a tent pole or a staff, consists of a set of curved branches with a nude goateed male (most likely a deity) in the center. Perched on his head, or maybe carrying him off, is an eagle with wings outstretched. "This was probably an important ritual object," Reeder says. "The sound it makes when it moves is just magical." A ritual use would help explain its jarringly different feel from the more refined, clearly secular objects in the show. Its form may hark back to homegrown Asian archetypes.

Later objects increasingly show the influence of Greek and Near Eastern figurative art. A golden scabbard from the late fourth century B.C. features a winged griffin. Another boasts a boar with a tightly curled mane, calling to mind the almost heraldic figures on Assyrian reliefs. Both these and a spectacular gorytos cover include the Scythians' favorite motif, animals in deadly combat. The gorytos, however, also offers a rare tableau of human figures interacting in some long-forgotten drama. The figures are Greek in style, but aspects of the scene are decidedly un-Greek. "Notice that each of the nude males has some strategically placed drapery," says Scott.

Scythians were evidently prudes. And everyone's hands are almost comically busy, Reeder points out, unlike the classic Greek poses of effortless ease. Moreover, for reasons unknown, two of the women are perched on overturned stools.

Archaeologists have found the remains of a number of heavily armed Scythian women.

The routines of a dusty, windswept Scythian camp were certainly a world apart from the existence of a well-heeled urbanite in Athens or Babylon. Scythians spent their days and nights amid cattle, sheep, goats and, above all, horses. They drank fermented mare's milk, made mare's-milk cheese and ate horsemeat, along with other meat, domestic and wild. In lieu of bathing, Herodotus reported, Scythians crowded into tightly sealed woolen tents and tossed hemp seeds onto red-hot stones inside: "The Scythians enjoy it so much that they howl with pleasure." The historian seems to have been unfamiliar with the mood-altering properties of cannabis. The nomads also consumed huge quantities of wine, drinking it uncut with water (which the disapproving Greeks called "Scythian style").

The role of women and family is largely a mystery. A tale passed on by

Herodotus recounted how a marauding band of Amazons clashed repeatedly with a Scythian contingent near the Sea of Azov. Discovering their foes were female, the Scythians dispatched their most virile young horsemen to make love, not war. The goal, according to Herodotus, was to breed new warriors. The women were easily seduced but not so easily domesticated. Rebuffing the Scythians' marriage proposals, the Amazons explained: "We are riders; our business is with the bow and the spear... but in your country... women stay at home in their wagons occupied with feminine tasks, and never go out to hunt, or for any other purpose." Ultimately, Herodotus reported, the two groups rode off together and founded their own tribe. The women continued to dress as men and to hunt and fight. Although Herodotus' tale has long been taken as fiction, archaeologists in recent years have found the remains of a number of heavily armed Scythian women. Their weapons could be ceremonial, yet the graves are numerous enough, writes Esther Jacobson of the University of Oregon, a leading expert on Scythian art, "to allow one to conclude that there was in Scythian society a place for women to take up a warrior's role."

In any case, woman's work in a Scythian encampment held its own challenges. Herodotus wrote in amazement of the nomads' approach to cooking a feast on the steppe. "This has called for a

LYNTON GARDINER

This ritualistic staff ornament with pendant bells was designed to appeal to the Scythians' predilection for sound and movement.

little inventiveness, because there is no wood in Scythia to make a fire with." Thus a butchered animal would be simmered using its own paunch as a pot and its bones as fuel.

The Scythians didn't always travel so light, especially in later years. As early as the fifth century B.C., Greek traders were venturing far into the steppe north of the Black Sea. The exhibition includes eight of the large bronze vessels uncovered by chance in 1961 in a peat bog along a tributary of the Dnieper. Greek in form and superbly ornamented, the containers were found with the remains of a capsized boat, hewn from the trunk of a massive oak, along with the bones of the boatman or trader. "These say a lot about the extensiveness of the Greek trade and the affluence of the Scythian customers," Reeder says. "You don't sail expensive things like these 300 treacherous miles

upstream unless you're fairly confident they're going to be sold."

The Scythians' ever-growing possessions eventually undercut their mobile lifestyle. Inevitably, they began to settle down and intermarry with other groups. In the second century B.C. a new tribe of ruthless horsemen, the Sarmatians, swept across the steppe. In time, the displaced Scythians faded from history.

Although the Scythians' culture disappeared, their burial mounds, or kurhans, remained in Ukraine for millennia as mysterious holy sites. In place of grave markers, crudely carved stone figures stood at the top. Though the European steppe has now been sliced by canals, factories and farms, thousands of these mounds still punctuate the table-flat Ukrainian landscape. The largest are the height of a six-story building and more than 300 feet across.

"The Scythians didn't just heap up whatever was around," Scott says. "They had layers of sod brought in, maybe to provide pasturage in the afterlife for the horses that were buried with their owners." Equine sacrifice was a staple of Scythian funerals. In one kurhan in 1898, archaeologists found the remains of more than 400 horses arrayed geometrically around the fallen warrior. The outside perimeter of another tomb yielded enough bones and amphora shards to suggest a knockout wake for about 1,000 people. Some mourners suffered more than hangovers. Herodotus reported that the funeral of important Scythians included the strangling and co-burial of consorts and retainers. Though the Father of History's credibility has often been challenged— Aristotle himself called him a "legend-monger"—archaeologists have dug up support for many of his claims, including evidence of human sacrifice.

Many kurhans were looted almost immediately, perhaps by local peasants who'd been recruited to build them. Burial chambers, however, are hazardous sites. "Some of the tomb robbers weren't too clever and ended up part of the archaeological record," says Scott. With Scythian grave robbing a cottage industry by the early 1700s, Peter the Great ordered that looters be arrested and that the gold and other finds be added to the Russian imperial collections.

Methodical investigation of Scythian kurhans began only in the 19th century. The tombs have yielded not only gold but also pottery, wagons, remnants of clothes, even residues of cosmetics. With independence in 1991, Ukraine is looking to Scythian history, and that of the new nation's other legendary horsemen, the Cossacks, as it seeks to flesh out its own national heritage. These days, though, the government has little money for archaeological digs. "In Soviet times, there were more than 50 teams working in Ukraine on Scythian archaeology," says Denis Kozak, deputy director of the country's national archaeological institute. "For now, there are only two teams still working."

Wonderful finds continue to surface, nonetheless; a spectacular gold necklace and a pair of headdress pendants in the exhibition were unearthed only in 1998. Kozak and others in Ukraine and the United States hope the current tour will spark new interest in Ukrainian history and new support for Scythian archaeology. Herodotus wrote of a remote place called Gerrhi, where the richest Scythian tombs were said to be clustered. Some scholars believe Herodotus was misinformed. Others believe Gerrhi can be found. If the optimists are right, and the looters haven't gotten there first, look for a grander and even more dazzling exhibition of Scythian gold a few years hence.

The author, a regular contributor, wrote about American designers Charles and Ray Eames in the May 1999 SMITHSONIAN.

From *Smithsonian* magazine, March 2000, pp. 89, 90-94. © 2000 by Doug Stewart.

UNIT 2

Greece and Rome: The Classical Tradition

Unit Selections

Key Points to Consider

- How were the ancient Olympic games different from those of today?

- What were the charges brought against Socrates? Was he what we could call a democrat?

- What happened when Alexander died? What is the mystery surrounding Alexander's tomb?

- What was life like for Athenian women? How could the husband make a defense of his actions?

- How did Cleopatra influence Roman history? What were some of the views about Cleopatra?

- What kinds of things did the pirates do that angered the Romans? How were the pirates finally dealt with?

- Who were among the gladiators? Why were they very popular figures in Roman history?

 **Links: www.dushkin.com/online/**
These sites are annotated in the World Wide Web pages.

Diotima/Women and Gender in the Ancient World
http://www.stoa.org/diotima/
Exploring Ancient World Cultures
http://eawc.evansville.edu
WWW: Classical Archaeology
http://www.archaeology.org/wwwarky/classical.html

It has been conventional to say that, for the West, civilization began in Mesopotamia and Egypt, but that civilization became distinctly Western in Greece. These matters no longer go undisputed: witness recent academic debates over Martin Bernal's thesis that Greek civilization derived from the older cultures of Egypt and the eastern Mediterranean.

Those disputes aside, the Greek ideals of order, proportion, harmony, balance, and structure—so pervasive in classical thought and art—inspired Western culture for centuries, even into the modern era. Their humanism, which made humans "the measure of all things," not only liberated Greek citizens from the despotic collectivism of the Near East, but also encouraged them, and us, to attain higher levels of creativity and excellence. In "Olympic Self-Sacrfice," Paul Cartledge recounts how the games were interwined with religion.

Though the Greeks did not entirely escape from the ancient traditions of miracle, mystery, and authority, they nevertheless elevated reason and science to new levels of importance in human affairs, and they invented history as we know it. It was their unique social-political system, the polis, that provided scope and incentives for Greek culture. Each polis was an experiment in local self-government. But to many moderns the Greek order was tainted because it rested on slavery and excluded women from the political process. The essay "Was Socrates a Democrat?" offers perspectives on the Greek social and political order. Kenneth Cavander discusses the place of Greek women in "Love and Death in Ancient Greece."

Yet for all its greatness and originality, classical Greek civilization flowered only briefly. After the great Athenian victory over the Persians at Marathon, the weaknesses of the polis system surfaced during the Peloponnesian Wars. After the long conflict between Athens and Sparta, the polis ceased to fulfill the lives of its citizens as it had in the past. The Greeks'confidence was shaken by the war and subsequent events.

But it was not the war alone that undermined the civic order. The Greek way of life depended upon unique and transitory circumstances—trust, smallness, simplicity, and a willingness to subordinate private interests to public concerns. The postwar period saw the spread of disruptive forms of individualism and the privatization of life.

Eventually, Alexander the Great's conquests and the geographical unity of the Mediterranean enabled the non-Greek world to share Greek civilization. Indeed, a distinctive stage of Western civilization, the Hellenistic age, emerged from the fusion of Greek and Oriental elements. At best the Hellenistic period was a time when new cities were built on the Greek model, a time of intellectual ferment and cultural exchange, travel and exploration, scholarship and research. At worst it was an era of amoral opportunism in politics and derivative styles in the arts. It may be argued that "Cleopatra: What Kind of a Woman Was

She, Anyway?" came to represent the best and worst of these ideals.

Later, the Greek idea survived Rome's domination of the Mediterranean. The Romans themselves acknowledged their debt to "conquered Greece." Modern scholars continue that theme, often depicting Roman culture as nothing more than the practical application of Greek ideals to Roman life. The popularity of gladitorial contests shows how the Romans differed in their view of the sports from the Greeks as reported in "Sudden Death." In addition, the Roman Republic invented an effective system of imperial government and a unique conception of law.

The Romans bequeathed their language and law to Europe and preserved and disseminated Greek thought and values. The Greeks had provided the basis for the cultural unity of the Mediterranean; the Romans provided the political unity. Between them they forged and preserved many of the standards and assumptions upon which our tradition of civilization is built—the classical ideal.

Olympic Self-Sacrifice

*With the Sydney Olympics up and running, **Paul Cartledge** explores the radical cultural differences between our present-day interpretation of the Games and their significance in the ancient world.*

The modern Olympics seem so much part and parcel of our modern world—all those accusations of drug-taking and financial chicanery—that it is hard to remember they are only just over a hundred years old. Their founder, Baron Pierre de Coubertin, wished to foster both athletic excellence and international harmony, and as a conventionally educated French aristocrat he looked back to the ancient Greek Olympic Games for inspiration, believing fondly that that was exactly what they too had done, and why they had been founded. In fact, de Coubertin was wildly wrong: not only about the peaceful diplomatic mission of the ancient Games, but also, and more crucially, about their essential nature. The original Olympics, as we shall see, were desperately alien to what we understand by competitive sports today.

First, however, a brief recapitulation of what the ancient Games actually consisted of by the time they were definitively reorganised in the aftermath of the Persian Wars (490–479 BC). They were held then, as always, before and since, at Olympia, in the north-west Peloponnese, a relatively insignificant and inaccessible location. They were under the presidency of the local city-state of Elis, again not one of the major players in the ancient Greek league. So far as the sports component went, there were by then nine main events, all for male competitors only: the *stadion* or one-lap sprint (about

200 metres); *diaulos* or 400 metres; dolichos or 'long' distance (24 laps); *pentathlon*; boxing; four-horse chariot race; *pankration*; horse race; and race-in-armour. But the sports component was only one part, and not the most important, of the five-day festival, held at the second full moon after the summer solstice. The festival began with a swearing-in and oath-taking. It was punctuated by religious rituals and communal singing of victory hymns. And it ended with a religious procession to the Temple of Olympian Zeus, where the victors were crowned, followed by the sacrifice of many animals, feasting and celebrations.

It was indeed the Greeks who invented the idea of competitive games or sports. Their word *agon*, meaning 'competition', gives us our word 'agony', which is a fair indication of the spirit of ancient Greek competitiveness. But they did so within a specifically religious context. We sometimes say today, metaphorically, that for some, sport is a religion. But for the ancient Greeks the sport of the Olympic Games was quite literally a religious exercise—a display of religious devotion and worship. The Olympic Games, the grand-daddy of all the many hundreds of regular and irregular athletic festivals held throughout the Greek world, were in origin part of the worship of Zeus Olympios (Zeus, the mighty overlord of Mt Olympos), far away to the north in Thessaly.

Parallels in this respect can be drawn with the development of the theatre. It was the ancient Greeks, and more especially the Athenians, who invented what is recognisably our idea of theatre, but they did so within the context of religious festivals in honour of the wine-god Dionysos. 'Theatre' at, for example, our Edinburgh 'Festival', bears little obvious trace of its origins in the festivals of Dionysos at Athens (apart perhaps from the consumption of alcohol).

To show how heavily the Games impacted on the Greeks' everyday consciousness, mentality and behaviour, I shall consider four allegedly historical examples, three of them taken from the not (to us) so obviously religious fields of war and politics away from the sanctuary of Zeus at Olympia. It does not matter whether the incidents happened exactly as reported. The point is that the Greeks unquestioningly assumed they could have done, since they fitted in with their established, conventional outlook. They help us to understand the nature of the religious atmosphere and ritual that the Games enshrined, and to answer the question of in what sense and to what extent they remained a religious festival, despite a certain process of secularisation.

The first example concerns a man from the island of Rhodes, who was given the nationalistic name of Dorieus, 'the Dorian'; something akin to our calling a Scottish boy Scott, or an Irish-American girl Erin. This Dorieus came from a family of extraordinarily successful gamesmen. His own speciality was the *pankration*, a notoriously gruelling mixture of judo, boxing and all-in wrestling, with practically no holds barred. In 432, 428 and 424 BC, as we learn from contemporary documents, he won no fewer than three Olympic crowns in a row. These were in addition to eight victories at the Isthmian Games, another Panhellenic (all-Greek) games festival which was held every two years; seven at the Nemean Games (also biennial); and one, by a walkover—the Greek for which was 'without dust'—since no one would challenge him, at the Pythian Games, which were held every four years at Delphi. The fact that he won at all four of the so-called 'Circuit' Games entitled him to claim the special accolade of 'Circuit Victor'.

Dorieus, as his name suggests, was fanatically pro- the Dorian Spartans and anti- the Ionian Athenians. Towards the end of the Peloponnesian War (431–404 BC) between Sparta and Athens, when Athens had almost lost its control of the east Mediterranean, Dorieus fought on the Spartan side with his own ships. But the Athenians captured him and brought him alive to Athens. They were about to put him to death as an enemy, when it became known to the Assembly who he was. Whereupon 'they changed their minds and let him go without doing him the least ungracious action,' as one Athenian source puts it. Would we have treated a captured German athlete in 1944 in quite so gracious a manner, I wonder?

My second example also concerns the Athenian treatment of a successful Olympic competitor, but this time one of its own citizens, the pin-up glamour-boy Alcibiades. In 415 BC he was the leading spirit behind the imperialist gamble of invading and, ideally, conquering all of Sicily. The gamble, we know, ended in total disaster two years later, but at the time, when Alcibiades stood up in the Assembly to speak in its favour, he was on a high and Athens was on a bit of a roll. In addition to the more practical political and military reasons Alcibiades gave for the Athenians to vote in favour

of his proposal, he threw in an extraordinary argument based on his recent success in the Olympic Games.

Can we imagine Tony Blair arguing in favour of war in Kosovo on the grounds that he owned a horse that had won the Derby?

He was, he said, the sort of man who had achieved the unprecedented feat of not only winning the four-horse chariot race at the Olympics, probably in 416, but also of entering no fewer than seven chariot teams in all, which between them gained second, fourth and seventh places as well as the crown itself. Alcibiades had not, of course, personally driven the winning team; as in the Palio, the horse race held at Siena since the Middle Ages, professionals were hired to act as drivers. But he had put up the money—an enormous amount. He even persuaded Euripides to write a commemorative ode about it. Can we imagine Tony Blair or Bill Clinton arguing in favour of war in Kosovo, say, on the grounds that a horse of theirs had won the Epsom or Kentucky Derby?

My third example is not an individual, but rather a city, namely Sparta, which was Athens' major rival or enemy for much of the Classical period. In 480 the Persian Great King Xerxes had led a mighty expedition into Greece by land and sea from the north and east. It was not quite as mighty as Herodotus would have us believe (1,700,000 land troops; 1,207 ships), but it was nevertheless a huge armament to pit against the relatively puny and very disunited Greek resistance. Early in 480 the handful of Greek cities that could actually agree to co-operate, up to a point anyway, decided their first land strategy should be to defend the passes from Thessaly into central Greece. One of these ran through Thermopylai, the 'Hot Gates'. Yet Leonidas, the Spartan king appointed to defend Thermopylai, set off from Sparta with a mere 300 men, champion fighters all, of course, but still only a tiny task

force. Why so? Because the Spartans were an exceptionally religious people, and it happened to be the Dorians' sacred month *Karneios* (in honour of ram-god Apollo), so they felt unable to send out a full force until the *Karneia* festival was over. The other allies found this a completely convincing explanation, since they too had a religious reason for sending out no more than advance forces of their own—as Herodotus put it, 'there was the Olympic festival, which fell in at just the same time as this outbreak of war.' When Herodotus came later to offer a definition of Greekness, it is no surprise to find that central to it was the Greeks' common religious outlook and practice.

Finally, we come to Kleomedes from the tiny Aegean island of Astypalaia, who was victor in the boxing at the Olympics of 484. Let me quote the relevant passage of Pausanias, a religious travel-writer of the second century AD, but one who used much earlier sources:

They say Kleomedes of Astypalaia killed a man called Hikkos of Epidauros; he was condemned by the judges and lost his victory, and went out of his mind from grief. He went home to Astypalaia and attacked a school there where there were sixty boys. He overturned the pillar that held up the roof, and the roof fell in on them. The people stoned him and he took refuge in the sanctuary of Athene, where he climbed inside a chest and pulled down the lid. The Astypalaians struggled in vain to get it open, and in the end smashed in its wooden sides. But they found no trace of Kleomedes either alive or dead. So they sent to the Delphic oracle to ask what had become of Kleomedes, and they say the Pythian priestess gave them this oracle: 'Astypalaian Kleomedes is the last of the heroes. Worship him—he is no longer mortal.'

I have listed these four incidents in reverse chronological order, because I want to show the religious content increasing with each instance. For the ancient Greeks, however, religion was so intimately intertwined with every other aspect of their lives that they did not actually have a word corresponding to our 'religion' (which we have taken from Latin). The nearest they got was a circumlocution meaning, literally, 'the things of the gods'.

A victor in the Olympic Games, in other words, whether or not he actually won in person, and whether or not he had to kill his opponent to win, was regarded as having been touched by divinity, as being raised above the station of a mere mortal. He might even, as in the case of the Houdini-like Kleomedes, receive hero-cult, a form of religious worship, after his death. I stress too the gendered 'he'. This was strictly men-only sport. In fact, women, apart from a priestess, were banned even from watching the Olympic sports. A doubtless apocryphal tale had it that a female relative of Dorieus tried to sneak in to watch her male relations carrying off all those crowns. She was forced to go in male disguise, but alas tripped over, her *chiton* (tunic) rode up, and all—or all that mattered—was revealed.

Gender-disguise and bodily revelation offer an appropriate point of departure for our enquiry into the precise religious nature of the Games. They probably did begin, chiefly as a local Peloponnesian festival, some time around their alleged starting date of 776 BC. But their ultimate origins are lost in the mists of time. All athletes competed at Olympia entirely naked, *gumnos*, whence our word 'gymnastics'. Aetiological stories to account for this practice differed; according to one, in 720 the eventual winner of the *stadion* race (hence 'stadium') or 200-metre dash, then still the only event, crossed the finishing line wearing rather less than when he left the starting sill. In other words, his kit unravelled and fell off, but he won, and ever after all competitors, whatever the event, ran or boxed or threw, or whatever, stark naked (apart from a truss).

In reality, this literally gymnastic practice was not adopted because it was ergonomically more efficient, nor because the ancient Greeks were devoted naturists. Nor, I suspect, was it a survival from those far-off Palaeolithic days

when 'Man the Hunter' allegedly hunted in the nude. This was, rather, a case of ritual nudity, marking the sacredness of Olympic space and time, a crucial part of the religious ritual within which the running and (later) other events were enfolded.

The Olympic truce was simply a practical device for ensuring that competitors and spectators could attend the Games in safety.

Another sign that the Olympic Games were religious, and indeed specially religious, was that the prizes awarded were always symbolic tokens—simple crowns made of olive leaves taken from trees growing wild in the Altis, or sacred precinct of Zeus. Olympic competitors did not compete for money nor for other intrinsically valuable objects. (In contrast, bronze tripods were awarded at the games in honour of Hera at Argos, and oil-filled decorated jars donated at the Athenian Panathenaia.) Competitors at Olympia were therefore technically amateurs, although they could earn a fortune at other, value-prize games, so perhaps we should rather say they were shamateurs. At any rate, the ideology of amateurism and religious devotion was crucial to the ancient Games. Pierre de Coubertin was not then completely off-beam in insisting that his new, revived Olympics should be for amateur as opposed to professional athletes ('athletes' comes from Greek *athlon* meaning 'prize').

He was, on the other hand, totally wrong in his interpretation of the spirit in which the ancient Greeks competed. What seems to have especially misled him was the sacred Olympic truce which ran for a month on either side of the five-day festival. This was not a symbol of the amity then reigning among the comity of Greek nations, but a severely practical device for ensuring that the competitors and spectators could get to the Games safely, and that the Games could then be held without interruption from the other-

wise endemic Greek inter-state warfare. This explains the precise name given to the truce: *ekekheiria*—'a staying of hands' or armistice. Actually, even the declaration of the truce was not always foolproof. In 364, warfare spilled over into the Altis itself.

Furthermore, despite the wishful imaginings of the anglophile de Coubertin, the events at the ancient Olympics were not conducted in any 'gentlemanly' British spirit of 'fair play'. They were more like a paramilitary exercise, 'war minus the shooting', as George Orwell once described modern professional sport. From the gender point of view, moreover, they were in the fullest sense a display of *andreia*. This literally meant 'manliness', but it was also the general Greek word for 'courage' in the sense of martial pugnaciousness. The unintended death of Hikkos in 484 at the hands, or rather fists, of Kleomedes was, predictably, not a one-off occurrence.

To conclude, let me focus briefly on why this article is entitled 'Olympic self-sacrifice'. Sacrifice, derived from the Latin, means in general a 'making-sacred'. Specifically, it is a term used by scholars of ancient religions to describe those acts of ritual dedication and devotion whereby something is given up or offered up by mankind to a god or the gods in exchange for an expected return. It refers to an act of communication or communion between human and super-human, mortal and divine, but also an act that marks the unbridgeable gap between the two. Almost anything could in principle be sacrificed in this way—even bodily sweat, if you believe David Sansone's theory explaining the origins and meaning of the *stadion* race at the Olympics as a ritual expenditure, or sacrifice, of sweat as the runners dashed towards their goal, the altar of Zeus, in a ritual designed to ensure the goodwill of the Father of Gods and Men.

Less fanciful, and historically better attested, is the religious significance of the undoubted climax of the ancient Olympic festival. This was not in fact any of the athletic events, but the concluding grand procession to the altar of Zeus outside his temple by all participants and spectators, led by the winner of the *stadion* race (who gave his name to the whole Games—thus 720 BC was the Games of Orsippos of Megara). This ritual procession was followed by a great blood-sacrifice of a *hekatomb*, 100 oxen, provided by the organising city of Elis. Such was the antiquity of the festival, and so numerous were the cattle slaughtered ritually over the years, that the great altar of Zeus was not built as usual out of stone, but composed simply of the burnt animals' ashes congealed with blood and fat.

That is perhaps not a very enticing thought, but then ancient religion is often desperately alien to our way of thinking. To the Greeks, however, it all seemed the most natural thing in the world. And they had the texts to back them up—above all the poems of Hesiod (*Theogony* and *Works and Days*) in which they had heard, no doubt many times, the origins-myth of how the Titan Prometheus had once tricked the younger (that is, more recently created) god Zeus on behalf of

mankind in the matter of animal blood-sacrifice. Thereafter, the Olympian gods were entitled to receive only the smell of the animal sacrifice, which rose up to them from the burning of the animal bones wrapped in fat, whereas men got to eat the meat and innards, which thanks to Prometheus's theft of fire they were able to cook to a turn. They then ate the cooked meat in a communion meal which reinforced their sense of common identity as sharers in the ritual feast. In the very special case of the Panhellenic Olympics, it also reinforced their sense of national identity as Greeks.

FOR FURTHER READING

Exhibition Catalogues of the Olympic Museum, Lausanne: D. Vanhove (ed.) *Olympism in Antiquity* vols. 1–3 (1993, 1996, 1998); Pausanias (ed. & tr. Peter Levi), *Description of Greece,* 2 vols. (Penguin 1971); Paul Cartledge, *The Greeks* (revised edition OUP, 1997);

M.I. Finley and H.W. Pleket, *The Olympic Games: the first thousand years* (Chatto & Windus 1976); Mark Golden, *Sport and Society in Ancient Greece* (CUP, 1998); Michael Poliakoff, *Combat Sports in the Ancient World* (Yale UP, 1987); David Sansone, *Greek Athletics and the Genesis of Sport* (University of California Press, 1988); Judith Swaddling, *The Ancient Olympic Games*, 2nd edition (British Museum Press, 1999); A. and N. Yalouris, *Olympia: the Museum and the Sanctuary* (Ekdotike Athenon, 1987); CD-Rom: 'Olympia, 2,800 Years of Athletic Games'—Finatec Multimedia (Athens) media@athena.compulink.gr

Paul Cartledge is Professor of Greek History at the University of Cambridge and the author of *The Greeks: Crucible of Civilization* (BBC Books, 2001).

Was Socrates a Democrat?

Melissa Lane looks at the reputation of Socrates, both at the time
of his death and in subsequent debates about democracy.

CORBIS/FRANCIS G. MEYER

'The Death of Socrates' by Jacques Louis David, 1787. Responses to Socrates through the ages have been coloured by the dramatic circumstances of his death.

Born to a humble artisan family in fifth-century democratic Athens, Socrates (469–399 BC) attracted a circle of prominent disciples, with whom he pursued the question of how to live well. His conversations with all-comers in search of knowledge, on the grounds that 'the unexamined life is not worth living' (Plato, *Apology* 38a); his ugly face, which concealed the beauty of his soul; his legendary self-control, which enabled him to stand for hours in the cold while meditating; his rejection of the commitment to retaliation which was central to Greek ethics: these are among the characteristics ascribed to him by his closest disciples.

But the life of Socrates might never have become resonant were it not for the manner of his death. Indicted in 399 BC at the age of seventy on the charges of neglecting the Athenian gods, introducing new gods, and corrupting the young, Socrates was tried before a popular jury, convicted and sentenced to death. When ordered to do so, he obediently drank a cup of poisonous hemlock and calmly died, having declared that he did not fear death since he could not know it to be an evil (Plato, *Apology* 29a).

The fact that Socrates lived and died at the behest of the pre-eminent democracy of the ancient world has posed an enigmatic challenge to every generation since. Was Socrates a democratic patriot, or a justly condemned traitor to democracy? Must reason and democracy—philosophy and the city—be at odds? For centuries, the issue seems to have been settled in Socrates' favour. Roman Stoics, Christian Fathers, Enlightenment anti-clericalists—all concurred that Athens had been in the wrong, though they differed as to the merit and nature of Socrates' beliefs. But modern admiration for Athens and affection for its democracy as a precursor of our own has made the status of its most famous judicial victim newly problematic. If we now consider ourselves to be democrats, and imaginatively ally ourselves with democrats 'then', must we too condemn Socrates? How have changing historical perspectives about Athens coloured our view of Socrates?

It is best to begin by asking why the Athenians convicted Socrates. Our evidence from the trial comes almost exclusively from Plato (c. 429–347 BC) in his *Apologia of Socrates*, which literally meant in Greek 'defence speech'. Plato's *Apology* describes the charges and the accusers, gives the results of the two votes taken (the first to decide guilt, the second to decide the punishment), and gives a version of the two defence speeches given by Socrates. That this was a version is made very likely by the existence of a rival *Apology* by Xenophon (c.428–354 BC), which agrees with Plato about the charges and accusers and some elements in Socrates' speech, but not others. We know that writing Socrates' 'apology' became a popular literary pastime after his death, so that Plato's version of it cannot be taken to be (or perhaps even to have been intended as) a verbatim transcription; on the other

hand, it is the most extensive source we have and is generally trusted with regard to the nature of the charges and the results of the votes.

Each of the charges, brought by three citizens (Meletus, Anytus and Lycon), is salient. 'Not worshipping the city's gods' is a rough translation of *asebeia*, impiety; the civic centrality of religious festivals and sacrifice counted as a political offence. According to Plato, Socrates protests that he did carry out the sacrifices, so the best way to understand this first charge is in light of the second: introducing new gods. This was itself a common practice, given the syncretic shifting deities of the Greek cities. But the idea that Socrates introduced a 'new god' was probably a reference to his *daimon*, an internal individual guiding spirit which he claimed always stopped him when he was about to do something wrong. Appeals to this *daimon* may have struck his fellow citizens as dangerously individualistic in contrast to the public gods of the city. Viewed together, these two charges suggest that Socrates was seen as failing to follow accepted traditions. Twenty-four years earlier, Aristophanes in his play *Clouds* had lampooned Socrates as a sophist who taught his pupils to scorn parental authority and subvert civic justice for their own gains. The idea of Socrates representing a dangerous wave of intellectual gamesmanship may have lingered in Athenian minds.

A sense of paternal, religious and civic subversion is also expressed in the third allegation of 'corrupting the young'. But there was an explosive political dimension here. Five years before the trial in 399, Athens had lost the Peloponnesian War, and the victorious Spartans had encouraged a bloody oligarchical coup led by the Thirty Tyrants who had briefly seized control of Athens. They had killed, exiled and expropriated thousands until democratic loyalists succeeded in re-conquering the city and re-establishing its democratic regime. Two of the Thirty, Charmides and Critias, were close friends of Socrates. Charmides, who was Plato's uncle, features in one of his nephew's Socratic dialogues. Moreover, the most notorious traitor of the whole preceding war with

Sparta had been Alcibiades: the self-proclaimed lover of Socrates in Plato's *Symposium*.

Was this association with tyranny and treachery the cause of Socrates' trial and conviction? Officially, it could not be so, as a general amnesty for crimes committed during the reign of the Thirty had been passed. But several seemingly political trials were brought under cover of other charges, and some evidence suggests that the case against Socrates was one of them. Consider the orator Aeschines (c.398/7–c.322 BC), who in the next generation declared:

> Gentlemen of Athens, you executed Socrates the sophist because he was clearly responsible for the education of Critias, one of the Thirty antidemocratic leaders... (*Against Timarchus*)

The Roman historian Plutarch (c. AD 50–120) in his *Lives* reported a similar condemnation from the conservative Roman moralist Cato the Censor some hundred and fifty years later: Socrates had 'attempted... to be his country's tyrant, by abolishing its customs, and by enticing fellow citizens into opinions contrary to the laws'. This was clearly not a universal view in Athens—Socrates was found guilty by 281 votes to 220—and there was also evidence against it. Socrates had carried out the minimally required democratic duties as council member and soldier faithfully throughout his life. But in the way of ancient Greek trials, what mattered was whether a case could be made convincing to the jury, and a majority of the democratic jury in question was persuaded that Socrates had indeed introduced new gods (and perhaps failed to worship the existing gods) and corrupted the young—both crimes against the democratic order of the city.

Perhaps the best evidence to suggest that many of Socrates' contemporaries believed him to be no democrat, is the fact that his admirers, in particular Plato and Xenophon, later worked so hard to argue that he had been. In their surviving writings both seek to show that Socrates not only never harmed the city, but also—in a new and unorthodox sense—

served the democratic regime itself. Such a defence forced the authors to expand the meaning of the notion 'serving the democracy'. Both Plato and Xenophon conceded that Socrates did not behave in the manner conventionally expected of a good democratic citizen. He did not voluntarily take part in the Assembly's debates (though he took his turn on the Council when required to do so); he did not flock to the popular law-courts to act as prosecutor or to sit on juries. Instead, they suggest, his seemingly 'private' pursuit of conversational enquiry into the nature of virtue and how to live was in fact a 'public' benefit, even a public 'necessity'. Xenophon suggested that although not himself engaged in political life, the philosopher was educating others to be good politicians: he has Socrates saying,

> Should I play a more important part in politics, by engaging in it alone or by taking pains to turn out as many competent politicians as possible? (*Memorabilia* I.6.15).

Similarly, in Plato's *Gorgias* Socrates calls himself the only true politician. More subtly, in Plato's *Apology*, Socrates declares that he has been a necessary 'gadfly' to the 'great and noble' but 'sluggish' horse of Athens, performing a necessary function by his provocative questioning. Plato's Socrates even proposes that his 'punishment' should consist of free meals and housing like those given to the Olympic victors. Thus the city should be brought to recognise his contribution to civic welfare. (This *hubris* seems, according to Plato, to have alienated many of those jurors who initially found him innocent: the second vote, on whether he should suffer the death penalty, swung to 361–140 against Socrates.)

For both Plato and Xenophon, Socrates' way of living had been a boon to his native city and its democracy, and Athens' murderous ingratitude had been an unconscionable mistake. But Aeschines' observation as quoted above, assuming that Socrates was executed for having taught the anti-democrat Critias, implied that their rehabilitation (some would say 'whitewash') of Socrates re-

mained a defensive manoeuvre for as long as the democratic regime continued in Athens.

Alexander the Great changed all that. One consequence of the fall of Athens in 322 BC was the demise of the whole debate. With the end of Athenian independence, there was no one left to argue the standard view of Socrates as a traitor to democracy, and no need, therefore, for the Platonic-Xenophontic response defending him as a true, though unconventional, democrat. For the Hellenistic period that followed, Socrates became a model not of 'the only true politician' in Athens but of the true philosopher (whether interpreted as Stoic sage, Cynical dog-man, or Academic Skeptic). And for some of the Christian writers after this, Athens was herself simply to be condemned for having condemned the model philosopher. Meanwhile, liberty came to be modelled on 'Roman virtue' rather than Athenian 'mob rule'. From the fall of Athens to the fall of the Bastille, the prevailing assumption was that if Athens' condemnation of Socrates proved that Socrates was no democrat, so much the worse for democracy. Socrates was seen as a hero, as a martyr or as a sage; democracy was seen as merely a nasty, pernicious and mainly defunct political regime.

Nietzsche went so far as to suggest that Socrates had deliberately sought his own death.

Two major upheavals in political and intellectual life converged to overturn this assumption. The first, taking sides in the pan-European 'quarrel of the ancients and the moderns', was the tidal wave of enthusiasm for the art and culture of ancient Greece unleashed by the German critic J.J. Winckelmann (1717–68). His passion for Greek sculpture inspired the Romantic poets and philosophers. It also informed the German philosopher G.W.F. Hegel (1770–1831) in his admiration for the Greeks as the beautiful 'children' of the human race, noble in their bearing and their ethical

particularity, though doomed to fall before the universalising empire of Alexander, Rome and then Christianity in the forward march of the world-spirit. But if what mattered about the Athenians was not their peculiar democratic institutions so much as their embodiment of Greek culture, then as a dissenter from that culture, Socrates became a suspicious character.

Such suspicion of Socrates was developed unforgettably by the German philosopher and classical philologist, Friedrich Nietzsche (1844–1900) who despite rejecting Hegel's dialectical scheme of historical progress, only heightened his predecessor's elegiac love for the Greeks as the best of all human types. Nietzsche saw the pinnacle of Greek culture in tragedy and the pre-Socratic philosophers. To Nietzsche, by the time Socrates came along, the intuitive balance of his predecessors' 'pessimism of strength' had begun to erode. To replace the crumbling tragic sense of the irrational, Socrates proposed a new and optimistic equation between reason, virtue and happiness. Reason alone could tell one how to live, giving a prescription that was inherently universal in claiming authority over everyone. In this way, Socrates was the ancestor of the Enlightenment, the 'theoretical man' *par excellence*. In the words of Nietzsche:

> Socrates believed that he was obliged to correct existence... he, the individual, the forerunner of a completely different culture, art and morality steps with a look of disrespect and superiority into a world where we would count ourselves supremely happy if we could even touch the hem of its cloak in awe.

Thus Socrates was 'the nub and turning-point of so-called world history'. Nietzsche went so far as to suggest that Socrates had deliberately sought his own death, either to become a martyr to the cause of reason, or (in a later account) because he realised that his own rationality had only served to make himself sick of life. In either case, Socrates' relation to Athenian democracy was cast aside in favour of his relation to Greek culture as a whole.

Led by Hegel and Nietzsche, many nineteenth-century continental thinkers such as Georges Sorel applauded not 'Athenian democracy' but 'Greek culture', and most often condemned Socrates for destroying the latter. In contrast, the gradual and bitterly contested British transition to a democratic franchise put the issue of Athenian democracy squarely at the centre of intellectual and political life. The old dismissal of Athenian democracy as mob rule—coupled with a comfortingly simple picture of Socrates as hero—would no longer do if democracy were to be intellectually legitimated. That old stereotype had had new life breathed into it briefly by the French Revolution; Robespierre's outspoken admiration for Athens had provoked British historians such as William Mitford (1744–1827) to condemn Athenian democracy ever more strongly. But the political developments which led to the Reform Acts of 1832 and 1867 made such responses look hackneyed and out of date. As the political climate slowly thawed toward democracy, the path was open for a thawing of the intellectual climate as well.

The ice was broken most decisively by the radical, liberal-utilitarian banker and sometime MP, George Grote (1794–1871), in his monumental *History of Greece* (1845–56). Athenian democrats had long been condemned as fickle in their allegiances, emotional and volatile in their decisions. Grote argued that the democrats had been cool and reflective judges, changing their minds only when new evidence or arguments gave them good reason to do so. Ancient democracy had been condemned as a cover for class rule by the poor. Grote defended the poor sailors of the Athenian fleet as the backbone of the democracy and, moreover, as having forced the rich to accept the 'constitutional morality' which was the condition of free government in England, the United States and the Swiss cantons in his own day. Appealing to English pride in the jury system, he urged that Athenian juries had been run along the same principles. Theirs was not a form of mob rule, rather a system of constitutional

self-government of which modern liberals could and should approve. Yet Grote refrained from converting his defence of Athens into an attack on Plato and Socrates. Far from it: his next major work was a critical but admiring evaluation, *Plato, and the Other Companions of Sokrates* (1865).

Here Grote defined philosophers as 'individual reasoners' who 'dissent from the unreasoning belief which reigns authoritative in the social atmosphere around them'. Though the Athenians were politically capable, they were, like any other society, entangled in a tissue of prejudices enforced by the drastic sanctions of public opinion. 'The community hate, despise, or deride, any individual member who proclaims his dissent from their social creed, or even openly calls it in question': with these words Grote indicted his fellow Victorians along with the ancient Athenians, and ranged himself and his utilitarian comrades with the dissenter *par excellence*—Socrates. The latter's death had been due to the sheer suspicious stupidity that infects every community. Society, not democracy, was to blame. Democracy as such was (or should be) friendly to the free thought and conscientious dissent that Socrates had pioneered. But all democracies had to learn to resist their own worst instincts. To borrow an expression from Grote's friend John Stuart Mill, it was the tyranny of the majority—usurping the legitimate concerns and methods of democracy—that killed Socrates.

There is a sense in which Grote adopted the Platonic-Xenophonic solution to the problem of Socrates and democracy, by arguing that democracy needs and should embrace dissent, and that the Athenians were mistaken in failing to recognise this. Yet, while adopting Plato's solution to the problem of Socrates, Grote coped with the antidemocratic elements in Plato's dialogues by ascribing them not to 'Socrates' but to Plato himself. In other words, Grote partially sacrificed his admiration for Plato in order to save the democratic face of Socrates. His claim was that Plato in the *Republic* committed a 'great betrayal' of Socrates by establishing his character 'Socrates' as no longer a dissenter, but as

the 'infallible authority' himself. As Grote wrote:

> Neither the Sokrates [sic] of the Platonic Apology, nor his negative Dialectic, could be allowed to exist in the Platonic Republic.

With these words Grote inaugurated a peculiarly British tradition, in which the democratic celebration of Socrates has gone hand in hand with the democratic vilification of Plato. Whereas the ancient democrats had attacked Socrates for questioning the *mores* of the city and its political regime, modern democrats celebrated him for contributing a culture of critical self-awareness to democratic politics. On the other hand, these liberals seemed loath to give up the sense of a great contest between democracy and philosophy that Athens had witnessed. As a result they transferred the anti-democratic stain from Socrates to Plato. Despite the fact that much of what we know of Socrates—and most of what scholars since the nineteenth century have taken most seriously—comes from Plato, they discerned a pure and unsullied figure behind the ambitious machinations of his pupil and scribe. Thus Plato was seen as the villain, the evil prophet of metaphysics or totalitarianism, so that Socrates could remain pure, the hero whose faith in reason could still inspire.

Not everyone after Grote adopted this position; some scholars stuck to the older view that Socrates had been a straightforward opponent of the democracy. However, two powerful books published just before and during the Second World War reinforced Grote's stance in the minds of twentieth-century readers of Plato. One was by the Austrian Jew Karl Popper, who wrote his passionate denunciation of Plato in the first volume of *The Open Society and Its Enemies*, as a wartime refugee in New Zealand. Popper declared his credo thus:

> It is hard… to conceive of a greater contrast than that between the Socratic and the Platonic ideal of a philosopher. It is the contrast between two worlds—the world of a modest, rational individualist and that of a totalitarian demi-god.

George Grote transferred the anti-democratic stain from Socrates to Plato.

Popper himself had been influenced by an earlier heir of Grote, the liberal Oxford don Richard Crossman, who would become a Labour MP and eventual minister.

In *Plato Today* (originally delivered on the radio and published in 1937), Crossman described Plato as a dangerous partisan of what would inevitably become 'a polite form of fascism'. Plato was the real enemy of democracy. Socrates, in contrast, was the victim of a tragic misunderstanding. He was himself democracy's friend—critical, undoubtedly, but then criticism was the life-blood of democracy. For Crossman, Socrates was an independent-minded liberal, committed to free enquiry and social progress: 'Socrates showed that philosophy is nothing else than conscientious objection to prejudiced unreason'. He had been tragically misunderstood by the Athenian democrats whom he sought to serve, and then betrayed by his student Plato, the self-deluded would-be architect of an illiberal regime.

In light of so many conflicting views, how should one judge the chequered history of Socrates and democracy? The best way to characterise the ancient evidence is to understand that it is inherently and irresolubly divided. Some friends of Socrates turned democratic traitors (though Plato tries to suggest that Alcibiades at least did not adequately understand or follow Socrates), others remained loyal democrats. Socrates played his part in the democratic institutions but did not actively defend them when threatened. The jury itself was not unanimous but was deeply divided. In other words, the question, was Socrates a democrat?, has been opaque from the moment it was first posed. With no writings of his own to go by, with only the memories created by bitter opponents to help us decide, we find ourselves swayed by our own ideological commitments in judging his.

What seems clear is that the complex and painful nature of the relationship between Socrates and Athens should not be oversimplified to serve our own ideological needs. The effort to show that Socrates' intellectual commitments constituted a healthy and useful criticism of democracy, rather than a challenge to it, came about only after his death, first by his ancient followers and then by their modern descendants. But ancient Athenians did not hold such a functionally differentiated view of democratic virtue. For them, commitment to democracy involved commitment to the fundamental value of the equality of citizens to rule, and this is something that Socrates questioned in discussion, although he did not challenge Athenian institutions in practice. The modern notion that dissent is valuable for democracy is not something that the ancients would have recognised. In their terms, Socrates may have abided by the rule of a democratic city, but he showed himself to be rather a critic of democratic presuppositions than a champion of them, and some of his students radicalised that criticism into outright opposition. To claim Socrates as a democrat is to apply an anachronistic standard to the democracy of his day. It makes better historical sense to affirm that democracy is not the only thing we value from the Greek inheritance, and to value the Socratic life of philosophy not as a backhanded contribution to democracy but as an independent good in itself.

FOR FURTHER READING

George Grote, *A History of Greece: From the Time of Solon to 403 BC*, condensed and edited by J.M. Mitchell and M.O.B. Caspari, with introduction by Paul Cartledge (Routledge, 2001); I.F. Stone, *The Trial of Socrates* (Jonathan Cape, 1988).

Melissa Lane is a University Lecturer in History and Fellow of King's College at Cambridge University. She is the author of *Plato's Progeny: how Socrates and Plato still captivate the modern mind* (Duckworth, 2001, £9.99 , ISBN: 0-7156-2892-5).

This article first appeared in *History Today*, January 2002, pp. 42-47. © 2002 by History Today, Ltd. Reprinted by permission.

Alexander

The Great Mystery

Written by T. Peter Limber

Alexander's Macedonian veterans—the hard men he had led to victory after victory, the nucleus of his forces—could not believe that their beloved young leader was dying. They demanded, with an insistence that verged on mutiny, to see him themselves.

All day long, grief-stricken soldiers shuffled past in an endless line as Alexander, barely alive, lay on his cot in Nebuchadrezzar's already-ancient palace in Babylon. A slight nod of his head, a movement of his hand or eyes, was all he could manage to acknowledge them, but "he greeted them all," wrote a chronicler.

Alexander died at sunset on June 10, in the year we today know as 323 BC. He was 32 years old.

For 12 years Alexander had personally led his men from rugged highland Macedonia, in the north of the Greek peninsula, first destroying rebellious Thebes, then crossing the Hellespont—today's Dardanelles—to begin his revenge on Persia. His troops fought their way across Anatolia, subjugating the great Persian Empire, defeating even the Bactrian armored cavalry, and winning onward, undefeated, as far as the Beas River in India. Alexander had been wounded many times, but nothing, it seemed, could overcome his boundless energy, his iron constitution, and his capacity for quick recovery. Yet now came this fever, which modern doctors believe was typhoid, "complicated by bowel perforation and ascending paralysis." His own doctors had tried every remedy they knew, but without success. During the last 10 days Alexander had grown steadily weaker.

Finally he assembled his closest companions, his eight chief officers, to hear his answer to the inevitable question: To whom would he leave what was now a Macedonian empire? His answer is still debated. Arrian quotes it as "Hoti to kratisto"—

which can mean "to the strongest," "to the best" or "to the most able." If Alexander meant "to the strongest of my generals," he was almost predicting the succession wars that followed. Yet he had already handed his royal ring to Perdiccas, his second-in-command, thus appointing him regent—and certainly Alexander's Bactrian wife, Roxane, was pregnant at the time.

A final ambiguity is that, instead of "Hoti to kratisto," the dying man—he was probably also suffering from pneumonia by then—may well have simply gasped the name "Cratero," referring to his most trusted general, Craterus, whom he had already appointed regent of Macedonia.

Alexander died at sunset on June 10, in the year we today know as 323 BC. He was 32 years old.

Alexander's eight senior generals agreed to divide his empire among them, each to govern his respective territory as a vassal of the ruling house of Macedonia. As to who would be king of Macedonia, and Alexander's heir, they also agreed that it could only be a blood relative of the conqueror's—which meant, regrettably, either Alexander's mentally handicapped half-brother, Philip Arrhidaeus, or Roxane's half-Macedonian child, if it should be male. (It was.) Perdicca's regency did not much please those strong-minded leaders, but no other solution was even tolerable to them.

Aristander, Alexander's chief soothsayer, had said that the country in which Alexander was buried would have good fortune, a prediction that increased the rivalry developing among the generals. Alexander himself had made known his wish to be buried at the well-known temple of the supreme Egyptian god Ammon Ra in the remote oasis of Siwa, in the Egyptian-Libyan desert. Alexander had made a crucial visit to this oracular shrine in 331, when he had taken Egypt from the Persians. The temple priests, who said they had foreseen his arrival, had welcomed him as the son of Ammon—a designation that certified his divinity—and, apparently more important, they had given him the answer "that his soul desired" to a personal question, its content never divulged, that he had put to them when he spoke to them alone.

Mindful of Aristander's prediction, Perdiccas, whose long record of loyal service ran back to the days of Alexander's father, Philip II, defied Alexander's wish. Instead of Siwa, he ordered the body transported to Macedonia for burial at Aegae, in the company of Alexander's royal ancestors. While thus seeming to honor his dead king and his country, Perdicca's true objective may well have been to settle this politically unstable moment by sending into Macedonia an army which he controlled, under the guise of an escort of honor. He knew that several Greek leaders and generals who opposed the authority conferred upon him had been meeting there.

None of this happened quickly, of course. The preparations for Alexander's entombment had to be appropriate not only for an incomparable military leader and emperor, but in fact for a "god." A funeral pyre in the old style was not for Alexander, whose body was, to his followers, both a sacred relic and a political token of the greatest importance. It was to be preserved. Diodorus Siculus, a Roman historian who wrote during the first century BC, gives the most detailed description. First, Egyptian and Chaldean embalmers worked their skills "to make the body sweet-smelling and incorruptible." Then, further following Egyptian custom, the body, clothed and in armor, was sealed in beautifully formed, close-fitting, heavy sheets of beaten gold, which were shaped so that even the features of Alexander's face were recognizable. None of the ancient historians mentions the use of a stone sarcophagus, though the body had to be safely transported over more than 3000 kilometers (nearly 2000 mi) of rough terrain.

The funeral cart, or catafalque, that was to bear Alexander's body was beautifully designed, sculptured and decorated, a gold- and jewel-covered extravagance that surpassed anything known in history or legend. It took two years and may skilled craftsmen to prepare it, with cost no object. Sparkling brilliantly in the sunlight, the heavy, roofed funeral carriage was pulled by teams of 64 matched mules. An army of honor guards accompanied it, under the command of a distinguished Macedonian nobleman, one of Alexander's staff officers.

Departing from Babylon, the funeral cortege traveled north a short distance along the Euphrates River, then east toward the ancient Persian city of Opis, then northwest along the banks of the Tigris. Ahead of the procession, road-builders smoothed the way, and thousands of people traveled to gather all along the route to see the magnificent spectacle pass. The cortege proceeded slowly, probably no more than 15 kilometers (9 mi) a day. Its route then skirted the northern edge of the Syrian desert, and headed toward the coast at Alexandria ad Issum (now Iskenderun, Turkey), a city founded by Alexander in 333 to consolidate his victory over the Persians at nearby Issus.

At this point, the procession reached a crossroads of sorts. If it were to proceed to Macedonia, it would have to continue west along Turkey's southern coast, either overland or by ship. If Siwa were the destination, then it would either sail southwest across the Mediterranean to Paraetonium (now Marsa Matruh) on the Egyptian coast, or travel by land down the Palestinian coast to Gaza and then turn west. Travel by sea was easier, but

if the intent were to allow the largest possible number of people to see the funeral procession pass, then a land route would be preferable.

Ptolemy wanted the body for Alexandria, the better to bring honor to his own domain.

Whatever the aim, it was another of Alexander's generals who determined the direction of the next leg of the long journey. Ptolemy, who had been made governor of Egypt, arrived with a sizable army to meet the funeral procession. In what biographer Mary Renault called "a reverent hijack," he forced it to take the overland route south toward Egypt. And though he may have appeared to be acting to fulfill Alexander's personal wish, Ptolemy had no intention of burying Alexander at Siwa. He wanted the body for his own capital of Alexandria in Egypt, the better to bring honor to his own domain. But as these events took place before a suitable mausoleum—prominently located in the center of the city—could be constructed in Alexandria, Ptolemy brought the body first to the old pharaonic capital of Memphis, where it was to remain for some years.

In Babylon, the reaction of Perdiccas was predictable: When he learned of Ptolemy's coup, he set out for Egypt with an army to punish the hijacker and recover the body. But on the way, some of his officers, bribed by Ptolemy, stabbed him to death. No other attempt was made by any of the other generals to remove Alexander's body from Egypt, and eventually it was transported to the site in Alexandria that Ptolemy had designated as the location of the future royal cemetery of the Ptolemaic line. Within a few years Ptolemy, like each of Alexander's successors, had declared himself king in his own right, and over the next three centuries Ptolemy's descendants succeeded each other. As each died he was buried in the royal cemetery in an opulent mausoleum, near the central tomb of Alexander. Local residents and travelers to Alexandria visited the site, and Alexander's tomb, especially, was treated as a shrine. But it was not to be left untouched.

Octavian visited the tomb in 30 BC. By AD 397, it was gone, most likely demolished by anti-pagan Christians.

One of the kings, Ptolemy X Alexander I, who ruled from 107 to 88 BC, was an extremely unpopular monarch whose people revolted and forced him to flee into Syria. Organizing a mercenary army there, he reentered Egypt to regain his throne. But to help pay for these forces, he ordered the gold sheathing to be stripped from the body of Alexander the Great and melted down. The embalmed body itself was not otherwise harmed, and remained in its tomb, but public outrage was great.

Alexander's body had been, in A. B. Bosworth's phrase, "the talisman of the Ptolemaic house." As Rome's imperial power grew, its leaders too had not hesitated to invoke Alexander's name and legend for their own purposes, and their admiration of his greatest accomplishment: empire from the Danube to the Ganges. While most of this immense territory remained in the control of Alexander's successors and their descendants for three centuries or so, parts were gradually lost to belligerents to the east. The Romans had taken possession of some areas of western Asia Minor beginning in 133 BC, but their only eastward success came with the annexation of Armenia by the East Roman ruler, Mark Antony, who was subverted by, and finally married, the last of the Ptolemies, Queen Cleopatra VII. In 30 BC, facing defeat by the West Roman emperor, Octavian, the two lovers committed western history's most famous double suicide, Egypt became a Roman province, and Octavian entered Alexandria.

On his first tour of the newly won capital, Octavian, who now carried the title of Augustus, visited the tomb of Alexander and left an imperial standard in tribute. Julius Caesar and, very probably, Marc Antony had paid homage there before him. Alexander's body must not have been covered, for Dio Cassius, in his 80-book history of Rome, reports that during his close inspection, Augustus touched or bumped the nose of the mummified corpse and broke off part of it. The tale, however, is somewhat hard to believe. It may have been after this that the coffin was said to have been covered by a kind of crystal—possibly fine, translucent alabaster—to protect it.

In subsequent times, successive Roman emperors likewise traveled to Alexandria, and a visit to the tomb to pay homage to the great conqueror and pagan god became virtually a sacred duty. Though Caligula, who ruled from AD 37 to 41, did not visit Egypt himself, his officers went to the tomb, and as they departed they removed a breast-plate from Alexander's armor. This was brought to Caligula, who wore it on ceremonial occasions. Finally, near the turn of the third century, Septimus Severus ordered the mausoleum of Alexander sealed to prevent further damage to the famous tomb and corpse. Even so, his son and successor, Caracalla, had it opened again for a look at the remains. In admiration and respect, Caracalla is said to have removed his own purple imperial robe from his shoulders and spread it over the body, and he also left many other precious gifts.

Reverence for the dead Alexander and the safekeeping of his remains might have survived the fourth century if he had been looked upon not as a god, but only as the great mortal leader he had been. By this time paganism was giving way to rising Christianity, which the East Roman emperor Theodosius I (379–395) finally declared the state religion in 392, banning public pagan rites throughout the empire. Alexandria was fast becoming a key Christian center, and though the many pagan temples and shrines in the city were not at first affected, zealots among both groups clashed with increasing frequency. The patriarch of Al-

exandria at the time was Theophilus, a hierarch of great faith, energy and anti-pagan passion. He enthusiastically directed the conversion of pagan institutions into churches, was instrumental in the destruction, in 391, of Alexandria's great Temple of Sarapis, a pagan shrine which dated back to early Ptolemaic times, and took other steps to speed the conversion of the city to an entirely Christian metropolis.

A number of historians hypothesize that the anti-pagan forces had demolished the tomb of Alexander and destroyed his corpse by 397. There are no direct accounts, and the tomb of Alexander is not mentioned in any of the sources of the time, which are otherwise often quite detailed. Yet we may draw inferences from such documents as the writings of John Chrysostom, bishop of Constantinople from 398 to 404. Drawing a contrast with the veneration paid the sepulchers of the Christian martyrs, he challenges, "Where is now the tomb of Alexander? Show me! Tell me the day of his death!"

The tombs of the Ptolemies that had surrounded Alexander's were destroyed as well, for they too had been regarded as "gods." On the site, a large church was built dedicated to St. Athanasius, an earlier Alexandrian bishop; in 640, when the Muslim Arabs captured Alexandria, they converted the church into a mosque. In modern times, the building, in a ruinous condition, was demolished, and the Mosque of the Prophet Daniel was constructed in its place, which still stands today. Under it is a series of catacombs which are said to have been thoroughly and officially explored early in the 20th century, and which were probably even more thoroughly and quite unofficially explored over many earlier centuries. The monuments themselves having been pulled down, it is possible—but far from certain—that these catacombs include parts of the foundations of the Ptolemaic and Alexander tombs.

Napoleon, looking for reflected glory, took what he thought was Alexander's sarcophagus, and the British stole it from him—but it wasn't Alexander's after all.

A more recent episode associated with the mysterious fate of Alexander's remains took place in 1798, when Napoleon Bonaparte's armies invaded Egypt through Alexandria. In the courtyard of the mosque that had once been the church of St. Athanasius, standing inside a small open building, was a handsome, heavy sarcophagus carved from a single block of rare, beautiful, dark green breccia. It was decorated, inside and out, with Egyptian hieroglyphics. Although it was being used as a cistern for worshipers' ablutions before prayers, locals referred to it as "the tomb of Alexander." French troops removed it and transported it to the hold of a French hospital ship. It was said that they intended to bring it to Paris, where a monument to Napoleon would be built around it, thus associating the latter with

DEAD KINGS Are Hard To Find

Written By Frank L. Holt

Why may not imagination trace the noble dust of Alexander till he find it stopping a bunghole?
WILLIAM SHAKESPEARE
Hamlet (Act V, Scene I)

>> *Dead kings are hard to find.* It is strange that this should be an immutable law of modern archeology. After all, when you consider all the generations of dead kings out there, whole dynasties waiting to be dug up, you would think it virtually impossible to put a shovel in the ground without hitting a royal grave. Since the earliest *lugals* of Babylon and the first pharaohs of Egypt, they lived and died by the thousands, each one burying his predecessor in a millennial procession of mounds and pyramids, crypts and coffins. Even in Egypt, the burial ground of more than 30 dynasties across 30 centuries, a dead king is downright hard to find: Fewer than one percent of all pharaonic burials have been found intact. As if by a writ of non-habeas corpus, they all seem to have disappeared.

To find *any* dead king is an archeologist's dream. Think not only of Howard Carter's 1922 discovery of King Tut, but also of Heinrich Schliemann and his find in 1876 of the so-called grave of King Agamemnon. And think, too, of Manolis Andronikos, who found the royal tombs of Macedonia in northern Greece in 1977. One of these extraordinary tombs may actually be the grave of King Philip II, the mighty unifier of Greece in the fourth century BC—and yet this discovery served only to remind us of the search for the tomb of Philip's son, the vastly more famous Alexander the Great.

Everyone from William Shakespeare to a self-professed psychic archeologist named Stephen Schwartz has wondered where Alexander is, or was. In the 20th century alone there were some 150 officially sanctioned archeological expeditions that searched for his tomb. Since 1805, there have been at least seven announcements of the grave's discovery, two of them in the 1990's. But dead kings, as ever, are hard to find.

One of the seven "finds" occurred in 1850, when an interpreter for the Russian Consulate in Alexandria, one Ambrose Schilizzi, explored the subterranean chambers of the Mosque of the Prophet Daniel. He claimed to have found a regalbody with a diadem, surrounded by a papyrus library; unfortunately, no one else ever saw it.

In 1888, Heinrich Schliemann received permission from the Egyptian prime minister to try his luck in the search for Alexander. Local Muslims, however, refused to let Schliemann dig beneath the Mosque of the Prophet Daniel, so the great archeologist had to leave empty-handed.

In 1960, a Polish archeological team excavated to a depth of about 15 meters (48') alongside the mosque, but found no tomb. Another expedition dug beneath the mosque in 1991, but rival archeologists persuaded religious authorities that every millimeter of the area had already been investigated.

One legend from the Ferghana Valley of Central Asia maintains that Alexander's body never even made it to Egypt. Three time zones east of Alexandria lies the ancient Silk Road town of Marghilon, where locals claim Alexander was in fact buried, all other evidence to the contrary notwithstanding. There are also persistent rumors that Alexander's body actually lies hidden in a secret cave somewhere in the southern Illinois heartland.

At the risk of losing count of Alexander's supposed coffins, crypts, and corpses, I must add one allegedly found in Egypt by a Greek in 1893, another by a Canadian in 1966, a third by a respectable Italian scholar, and of course the "psychic discovery" of 1979. This last was the achievement of a hapless group led by Stephen Schwartz. In the desert monastery of Saint Makarios they were shown a bag of old bones, and since the skeletons seemed to be short one skull, they concluded that one of the dead must be John the Baptist. They then concluded that Alexander "might" be in the bag, too.

Others have simply claimed special knowledge of Alexander's whereabouts. One such person was Howard Carter, the discoverer of King Tut's tomb. As an old man, in 1936, Carter gave the future King Farouk a personal tour of the Valley of the Kings. Carter concluded with an odd reference to the long-sought tomb of Alexander, whose precise location he insisted that he knew, but he vowed never to tell a soul.

"The secret will die with me," he said. Three years later, it apparently did.

Professor Achille Adriani, for many years the head of the Greco-Roman Museum in Alexandria, died before he could publish his conclusion that the tomb was "right under our noses all the time" in the city's Latin Cemetery. After working on Adriani's notes for two decades, a colleague this year published his theory.

Equally strange is the story of Stelios Comoutsos, a Greek waiter who has spent his life—when not at work at the Élite Café in Alexandria—searching for Alexander's tomb in Egypt. Comoutsos gained notoriety for his clandestine excavations, inspired by a treasure map inherited from his ancestors. He persisted in his obsession for more than 30 years before retiring to Athens, but he too never found Alexander.

Others have found him more than once. Archeologist Liani Souvaltze and her husband announced her *second* discovery of Alexander's tomb at the oasis of Siwa in January 1995. The news hit networks and the Internet like a Saharan sandstorm, with television reports and front-page coverage in newspapers the next day. The Souvaltzes won the immediate support of the chairman of the Egyptian antiquities organization, who visited the site and deemed it the true tomb of Alexander.

Within days, however, he began to have his doubts. The Souvaltzes, after all, had already cried "wolf" in 1991 when they announced their first discovery of Alexander's tomb at an international archeological congress. That turned out to be a Greco-Roman temple already known to other archeologists. In 1995, a team of Greek archeologists journeyed to Siwa to review Souvaltze's evidence. The archeologist refused to show the scholars all her finds, and what she did show them was clearly Roman, not Ptolemaic. So far, there is no reliable information to confirm her claims.

Dead kings are still hard to find.<<

Dr. Frank Holt, professor of history at the University of Houston, has published numerous books and articles on the life and legacy of Alexander the Great.

Alexander the Great in much the same way rulers had done since Ptolemy first hijacked the funeral cortege in southern Turkey.

But in 1801, the British invaded Egypt and expelled the French. Antiquaries attached to the British forces knew about the so-called "Alexander sarcophagus" from travelers' writings. They searched for it specifically, removed it from the French ship, and today the sarcophagus is not in Paris, but in London, on display in the British Museum. At first, British scholars rationalized that the hieroglyphic text covering its inner and outer surfaces was attributable to Alexander's role as an Egyptian god, but the decipherment of hieroglyphics a few decades later—thanks to the Rosetta Stone, which had been carried off by the British at the same time as the sarcophagus—made it obvious that it had been carved for the last native Egyptian pharaoh, Nectanebo II, who had ruled from 360 to 343 BC. Historians and archeologists concluded that this sarcophagus had never contained the body of Alexander; that it came to be called "Alexander's tomb" is an example of the great flourishing of legend and false attribution about the conqueror that began even during his lifetime.

One branch of this thicket of association connects the breccia sarcophagus, Nectanebo II and Alexander himself. Alexander's mother, Queen Olympias, had been devoted to the rites of Orpheus and Dionysus, which sometimes featured the presence of large snakes that were believed to represent or embody the gods. It is known that Olympias kept one such snake in her chamber, and after Alexander's birth Olympias was said to have declared that her son had not been sired by his mortal father, King Philip, but by the Egyptian god Ammon, who had taken the form of the snake. For his part, Philip apparently believed this tale and considered his wife an adulteress.

Beginning shortly after Alexander's death, a more fantastic tale began to circulate. According to this story, when Nectanebo II, now said to be an adept of the magic arts, fled the Persian occupation of his country in 343 BC, he went not to southern Egypt but to Macedonia, there to beget an avenger of his country's defeat. Olympias gave him refuge in Philip's court, and, casting her horoscope, Nectanebo predicted that she would give birth to a son, a hero, fathered by Ammon. The pharaoh, who could indeed claim to represent Ammon, fulfilled his own prophesy by seducing the then childless Olympias, and the offspring of their union was none other than Alexander! This is, of course, largely pharaonic propaganda, designed after the fact to bolster the Egyptian spiritual claim to Alexander, for in reality it is not only well documented that Nectanebo never set foot in Macedonia, or anywhere else in Greece, but in 343, when he supposedly went there, Alexander was already 13 years old. Nonetheless, the story may have inspired the connection of the breccia sarcophagus of Nectanebo II with the memory of Alexander.

There exists yet another "Alexander Sarcophagus," a magnificent, monumental work of marble discovered by accident in 1887, in what turned out to be a royal necropolis in Sidon, a city on the Mediterranean in what is today Lebanon. This extraordinary monument, still in nearly perfect condition and now in the Istanbul Archaeological Museum, is the work of an unknown Greek master sculptor, carved in the classic Hellenic style from a pure white marble quarried in the Pentelic mountains northeast of Athens—the same material used to build the Parthenon and other famous works of the classical period. Around its perimeter are animated scenes of Alexander himself hunting, and battling the Persians. It has been estimated to date from the last quarter of the fourth century BC, and its intended purpose is unknown. Is it possible it was made to receive Alexander's remains? As a work of art, it is certainly worthy to have been used for this purpose.

But as tempting it is to make the connection, archeologists and historians have concluded that this sarcophagus was more than likely carved for the body of a king of Sidon, Abdalonymos, a few years after Alexander's death. Abdalonymos was a Phoenecian who ordered it made to commemorate his close friendship with Alexander, who had had him appointed ruler of the region. In fact, historians now believe that the use of any sarcophagus to carry Alexander's body on that long last trip was unlikely. As the remains were originally to be sent to Siwa, Alexander's body was prepared in the Egyptian manner by Egyptian embalmers. Also, the close-fitted gold sheathing surrounding the body was a style used for royalty, and designed to be seen, not hidden by stone, however beautifully carved.

Few figures in history have been studied more, written about more, or spoken of more than Alexander the Great, whether seriously by scholars, fantastically by unknown compilers of legends, or personally by tirbesmen who, even today, claim descent from his Macedonian troops. Some still dream and hope that, somewhere in the catacombs under the Mosque of Prophet Daniel, his remains might yet be discovered. But extensive explorations and excavations have been made in Alexandria, under the mosque and elsewhere, and no trace has been found either of the royal Ptolemaic necropolis or of Alexander's tomb.

The story of what happened to Alexander's remains remains a mystery.

T. Peter Limber (limberis@att.net) specializes in Greek history. He is working on a historical novel about Alexander and the years after his death, to be called *The Chronicle of Hexadoros*.

From *Aramco World,* May/June 2001, pp. 2-13. © 2001 by Saudi Arama World. Reprinted by permission.

Love and Death in Ancient Greece

Catching him in the act, an obscure citizen of Athens slew his wife's lover. But was it a crime of passion—or premeditated murder?

Kenneth Cavander

Euphiletos was tired. He had been out in the country all day attending to business, and now he was home trying to get some sleep, and the baby was crying. His house was on two floors; the baby slept with a maid on the first floor; above, there was a combined living-dining-sleeping area for him and his wife. Euphiletos told his wife to go downstairs and nurse the baby. She protested that she wanted to be with him; she'd missed him while he was in the country—or did he just want to get rid of her so that he could make a pass at the maid, as he had the time he got drunk? Euphiletos laughed at that and at last his wife agreed to go downstairs and hush the child, but she insisted on locking the door to their room. Euphiletos turned over and went back to sleep. It never occurred to him to ask why his wife had gone through the charade of keeping him away from the maid, or why she had spent the rest of the night downstairs. But a few days later something happened that made him ask these questions, and by the end of the month a man was dead, killed in full view of a crowd of neighbors and friends.

This drama took place nearly two thousand five hundred years ago in ancient Athens. The characters were none of the brilliant and celebrated figures of the times—Socrates, Plato, Euripides, Aristophanes, Alcibiades—but members of the Athenian lower-middle class, obscure people who receded into the shadows of history. Their story is a soap opera compared to the grander tragedies being played out at the festivals of Dionysos in the theater cut into the slopes of the Acropolis.

By a quirk of fate and an accident of politics the speech written for the murder trial that climaxes this story was the work of a man named Lysias. As a boy, Lysias sat in the company of Plato and Socrates, who often visited his father's house. As an adult, he was active in politics, and when a coup by the opposition party sent his family into exile, his property was confiscated and he narrowly escaped with his life. But a countercoup soon allowed him to return to Athens, and Lysias, now without a livelihood, had to find a profession.

He found one in the Athenian legal system. Athenian law was complex and attorneys were unknown; every citizen had to prosecute or defend himself in person. As a result, a class of professional legal advisers emerged that made a living supplying litigants with cogent, legally sound briefs. In time, Lysias became one of the most sought-after of these speech writers and several examples of his elegant and literate Greek style have been preserved, including the speech written for the defendant in this case.

Euphiletos, like many Athenians of modest means, lived in a small house in the city and commuted to the country to attend to his farm or market garden. He cannot have been well-off, for his house had the minimum number of slaves—one. Even a sausage seller or baker had at least one slave. Euphiletos had recently married and he was a trusting husband, so he said, giving his wife anything she asked for, never questioning her movements, trying to please her in every possible way. The most exciting event in the marriage was the birth of their child, whom his wife nursed herself. But the most significant event was the death of his mother: the whole family attended the funeral and, although Euphiletos did not know it at the time, his marriage was laid to rest that day along with his mother.

After the birth of their child Euphiletos and his wife had rearranged their living quarters. It was too dangerous to carry the baby up and down the steep ladder to the upper floor every time the child needed to be washed or changed, so the family was split up. Euphiletos and his wife moved into the upper part of the house, while the baby, with the slave girl to look after it, stayed downstairs.

The arrangement worked well, and Euphiletos's wife often went down in the middle of the night to be with the baby when it was cranky. But on the evening of the day Euphiletos came back tired from the country, two things in addition to the little drama of the locked door struck him as unusual. One was his wife's makeup: it was only a month since her brother had died—yet he noticed that she had put powder on her face. And there were noises in the night that sounded like a hinge creaking. When his wife awakened him by unlocking the bedroom door the next morning, Euphiletos asked her about these sounds. She said she had gone next door to a neighbor's house to borrow some oil for the baby's night light, which had gone out. As for the makeup, when Euphiletos thought about it he remembered his wife saying how much she had missed him and how reluctantly she had left him to go down and take care of the baby. Reassured, he dismissed the whole episode from his mind and thought no more about it—until something happened to shatter this comforting domestic picture and rearrange all the pieces of the puzzle in quite a different way.

One morning, a few days later, Euphiletos was leaving his house when he was stopped in the street by an old woman. She apologized for taking his time. "I'm not trying to make trouble," she said, "but we have an enemy in common." The old woman was a slave. Her mistress, she said, had been having an affair, but her lover had grown tired of her and left her for another woman. The other woman was Euphiletos's wife.

"The man is called Eratosthenes," said the old slave. "Ask your maid about him. He's seduced several women. He's got it down to a fine art."

In the midst of his shock and anger Euphiletos revealed a streak of something methodical, almost detached, in his character. Instead of going straight to his wife or her lover, he proceeded like an accountant investigating an error in the books.

He retraced his steps to his house and ordered the maidservant to come with him to the market. His wife would see

nothing unusual in this, for respectable married women did not go out shopping in fifth-century Athens. That was left to the men and the slaves. Halfway to the market Euphiletos turned aside and marched the girl to the house of a friend, where he confronted her with the old woman's story. The girl denied it. Euphiletos threatened to beat her. She told him to go ahead and do what he liked. He talked of prison. She still denied it. Then Euphiletos mentioned Eratosthenes' name, and she broke down. In return for a promise that she would not be harmed, she told Euphiletos everything.

Her story was bizarre as well as comic and macabre. It began at the funeral of Euphiletos's mother. Eratosthenes had seen Euphiletos's wife among the mourners and had taken a fancy to her. He got in touch with the maid and persuaded her to act as go-between. Whether it was a difficult or an easy seduction we don't know; but, as the old woman had said, Eratosthenes was a practiced hand.

This love affair, first planned at a funeral and then set in motion by proxy, was carried on mostly at Euphileto's house when he was away in the country. On one occasion his wife may have contrived to meet her lover away from the house, for she had gone with Eratosthenes' mother to the festival of the Thesmophoria, one of several festivals celebrated in honor of feminine deities. During these festivals a woman could leave the seclusion of her own house without arousing suspicious comment.

The slave girl also told Euphiletos that on the night he came back tired from the country, her mistress had told her to pinch the baby to make it cry, which gave her an excuse to go downstairs. His wife's parade of jealousy, Euphiletos now realized, was an act, designed to provide her with a reason to lock the door on him. So while he was a temporary prisoner in his own bedroom, his wife was downstairs in the nursery with her lover, and the maid was keeping the baby quiet somewhere else.

In a crisis, a person will often revert to archetypal behavior. For the Greeks of the fifth century B.C. the Homeric poems provided a mythological blueprint for almost any life situation, and it is in-

teresting to see how Euphileto's next move re-created a scene out of the legends. In *The Odyssey* Homer tells the story of what happened when Hephaistos, the god of fire, found out that his wife, Aphrodite, had been sleeping with the war god, Ares. Hephaistos decided not to face Aphrodite with her infidelity; instead, he wove a magical net that was sprung by the two lovers when they climbed into bed together. Then, as they lay there trapped, Hephaistos invited the other Olympians to come and view the guilty pair, "and the unquenchable laughter of the gods rose into the sky." In his own mundane way, but without the magic net, Euphiletos would follow the example of Hephaistos. He made his slave promise to keep everything she had told him a secret; then, pretending to his wife that he suspected nothing, he went about his business as usual and waited for a chance to spring his trap.

The part of cuckold is a mortifying one to play, and it was particularly so in ancient Athens where the relative status of men and women was so unequal. A freeborn Athenian woman was free in little more than name. She could not vote, make contracts, or conduct any business involving more than a certain sum of money; legally she was little more than a medium for the transmission of property from grandfather to grandchildren through the dowry she brought with her to her husband. Her husband, of course, was invariably chosen for her by her father or by the nearest male relative if her father was dead. Almost the only thing she could call her own was her reputation, which depended on good behavior, an unassertive demeanor, a life spent dutifully spinning, weaving, dyeing clothes, cooking, bearing and raising children, and, above all, on not interfering in the serious business of life as conducted by the men. In a famous speech in praise of the Athenian men who died during the Peloponnesian War, Pericles makes only one reference to women: according to Thucydides, who reports the speech in his history of the war, Pericles said that women should never give rise to any comment by a man, favorable or unfavorable. In the tragic dramas, moreover, women who offer their opinions unasked or who go about alone in public usually feel they have to apologize for behaving in such a brazen and immodest way.

Such was the official status of women. Unofficially, the women of ancient Athens found ways, as their sisters have done in every age and culture, to undermine the barriers of male prejudice. In Euripides' play *Iphigeneia at Aulis* (written within a year or two of Euphiletos's marriage), Agamemnon tries to assert his authority over his wife, Clytemnestra, in order to get her out of the way while he sacrifices his own daughter, Iphigeneia, to Artemis. Clytemnestra, with a show of wifely stubbornness that surely came out of the playwright's contemporary observation, refuses to be dismissed and finally cuts the conversation short by sending her husband about his business. In another play by Euripides, *Hippolytos*, there are some lines that might have been written specifically for Euphiletos himself to speak. Hippolytos, told that his stepmother, Phaidra, is in love with him, remarks scathingly: "I would have no servants near a woman, just beasts with teeth and no voice, [for] servants are the agents in the world outside for the wickedness women do."

Drink and sex are the traditional outlets for the oppressed. The comedies of Aristophanes are studded with snide references to the excessive drinking habits of women. According to Aristophanes, festivals such as the Thesmophoria were excuses for massive alcoholic sprees. More likely, these mystery cults were the safety valve for pent-up emotions, a chance to transcend the cruelly narrow boundaries imposed on women by their roles in a rigidly male society.

As for sex, women were the weaker vessel when it came to this human urge. In *Lysistrata* Aristophanes has the women wondering whether they can hold out long enough to bring the men to their knees. And in the legends that canonized popular wisdom on the subject there is a story about Zeus and Hera squabbling over who gets the greater pleasure out of sex—the man or the woman. When they finally appeal to Teiresias, the blind seer and prophet, who, as part man and part woman, ought to be able to settle the question for them, he duly reports that in the sexual act the

woman, in fact, gets nine-tenths of the pleasure, and the man only one-tenth.

These scraps of myth and folklore, however, filtered through male fantasy as they are, reveal a sense of unease about women. In the Orestes myth, for instance, it is Clytemnestra who takes over the reins of government in the absence of Agamemnon, then murders him when he returns; and it is her daughter Electra who pushes a faltering Orestes into taking revenge for the slain king. A whole army of formidable heroines—Electra, Clytemnestra, Antigone, Hecuba, Andromache, Medea—marches through the pages of Greek drama. The Fates, the Muses, and the Furies are all women. None of these female figures is anything like the meek and passive drudge that the Greek woman of the fifth century was expected to be.

But were they real types, these mythological heroines, or were they phantom projections of male fears and desires, mother imagoes, castration anxieties dressed up as gods, embodiments of the part of a man he most wants to repress—his own irrational and emotional side, his moon-bound, lunatic aspects—thrust onto women because he dare not admit them in himself?

It is possible. Every mythologized figure embodies inner and outer worlds. We see what we wish to see, and the picture we perceive turns into a mirror. Were there actual women in Athens capable of organizing a fully functioning communistic state and pushing it through the assembly, like the Praxagora of Aristophanes' play *Ekklesiazousai?* Were there Electras and Clytemnestras and Medeas? If there were, they never reached the pages of the history books. We hear of Aspasia, Pericles' "companion" (the Greek word is *hetaira*, meaning "woman friend"), for whom he divorced his legal wife. But Aspasia was a member of the demimonde of "liberated" women who lived outside the social order, not necessarily slaves, but not full citizens either. They were often prostitutes, but some of them were cultured and educated, better traveled and more interesting to Athenian men than their own wives. Custom permitted one or more relationships with *hetairai* outside the marriage, but a *hetaira* had no legal

claim on a man, and he could sell her or dispose of her any time he liked. Meanwhile, for the trueborn Athenian woman who wanted a more varied life than the one prescribed by convention, what was there? Gossip with the neighbors. The bottle. A festival now and then. A clandestine love affair.

Four or five days passed while Euphiletos brooded over the wrong done to him. Suppose a child was born from this liaison: who could tell whether it was his or Eratosthenes'? All kinds of complications might follow. But whatever he was feeling, Euphiletos managed to hide it from his wife. She never suspected that he knew anything at all.

Euphiletos had a good friend named Sostratos. Less than a week after his interview with the maid Euphiletos met Sostratos coming home from the country, and since it was late Euphiletos invited his friend to his house for supper. This casual meeting was to become important later at the trial. The two men went upstairs, ate and drank well, and had a pleasant evening together. By custom Euphiletos's wife was not present. After Sostratos had gone home Euphiletos went to sleep.

Some time in the middle of the night there was a knock on his door. It was the maid. Eratosthenes had arrived.

Leaving the maid to keep watch, Euphiletos slipped out a back way and went around the neighborhood waking up his friends. Some of them were out of town, but he managed to collect a small group who went to a nearby store and bought torches. Then they all trooped off to Euphiletos's house where they stood outside in the street holding the lighted torches while Euphiletos tapped on the door. Quietly the maid let him into the courtyard. He pushed past her into the room where his wife was supposed to be asleep with the baby. A few of Euphiletos's friends managed to crowd in behind him.

For a split second the scene must have been like a tableau out of Homer: Eratosthenes naked in bed, Euphiletos's wife in his arms, the two lovers trapped in the light of torches held by the neighbors.

Then Eratosthenes, still naked, sprang up. Euphiletos shouted at him, "What are you doing in my house?" and knocked him off the bed, pulled his wrists behind his back, and tied them.

Eratosthenes offered to pay Euphiletos any sum he named. Euphiletos had a choice: he could accept the bribe, or he could take a form of revenge allowed by law—brutalizing and humiliating Eratosthenes by such methods as the insertion of tough thistles up his rectum. There was also a third option open to him under the circumstances: since he had caught Eratosthenes in the act, and there were witnesses present, Euphiletos could kill him.

Euphiletos interrupted the other man's pleas. "I won't kill you," he said, and then, in the kind of logical twist the Greeks loved, he added, "but the law will."

And in the name of the law he killed Eratosthenes.

Athenian homicide law required the dead man's family, not the state, to bring charges of murder. Eratosthenes' family undertook the task, and approximately three months later Euphiletos found himself facing a jury of fifty-one Athenians in the court known as the Delphinion, located in the southeast corner of Athens, where cases of justifiable homicide were tried. Eratosthenes' family charged Euphiletos with premeditated murder on the grounds that he had sent his maid to lure Eratosthenes to the house; they may also have tried to prove that Eratosthenes was dragged into the building by force, or took refuge at the hearth before he was killed. In the speech he writes for Euphiletos, Lysias sets out to rebut all these charges.

Lysias puts into Euphiletos's mouth some ingenious legal arguments. The law (of which a copy is read to the court) says that a seducer caught in the act may be killed. "If you make it a crime to kill a seducer in this way," he argues, "you will have a situation in which a thief, caught burglarizing your house, will pretend that he is an adulterer in order to get away with a lesser crime." Lysias also

refers the jury to the law on rape. Rape carries a lower penalty than seduction. Why? Because, theorizes Lysias, the rapist simply takes the woman's body, while the seducer steals her soul.

Nevertheless, in spite of Lysias's able and sophisticated defense, there is a flaw in Euphiletos's argument: His defense rests on the assumption that his action was unpremeditated, committed in the heat of the moment, under the shock and stress of finding his wife in bed with another man. That is surely the intent of the law, and Euphiletos goes to great lengths to prove he had not planned the encounter. He cites the dinner invitation to Sostratos, which, he says, is not the behavior of a man planning murder. But the rest of his story contradicts this. The signals by which the maid warned him that Eratosthenes had arrived and by which he let her know that he was waiting at the front door; the rounding up of friends to act as witnesses; the presence of the murder weapon on his person—all point to prior preparation. Euphiletos may prove to the jury's satisfaction that he did not lure Eratosthenes deliberately to his house that night, but he fails to prove that he was taken totally by surprise or that he tried to do anything to stop the affair before it reached that point. His action looks suspiciously like cold-blooded revenge executed under color of a law that forgives even violent crimes if they are committed in the heat of passion.

Neither the speech for the prosecution nor the testimony of witnesses has survived, so we do not know if the wife or the maid gave evidence. Though women were not allowed to appear as witnesses in court cases, the rules for murder trials may have been different. A slave could not testify at all, but a deposition could have been taken from her under torture and read to the court. On the other hand, Euphiletos may have wanted to avoid bringing the women into it: after all, they had been in league against him throughout the whole unhappy affair.

There is something touching in the alliance between the slave, an object without rights or status, and the wife, legally a free citizen but in reality a kind of slave too. The maidservant probably accepted a bribe from Eratosthenes, but all the same she had a moment of heroism when, threatened with a beating and prison, she refused to incriminate her mistress. Afterward, when she became Euphiletos's accomplice, there is an eerie reversal of the situation: the slave admits her master to the house in the same stealthy way that she had opened the door for her mistress's lover a few minutes earlier. But still, there was a moment when Euphiletos was the outsider, barred from his own house and his wife's arms, with only his rage and his group of male friends for company.

Finally there is the wife herself, the center of the drama and its most shadowy character. Apart from his grudging admission that she was thrifty and capable and a good housekeeper, Euphiletos tells us little about her. From what we know of Athenian marriage customs, we can guess that she was probably married at fourteen or fifteen to a virtual stranger and expected to keep house for this man who spent much of his time away from home on business. Was she satisfied with the trinkets that Euphiletos says he let her buy, and with all of the household duties and her young baby?

A small fragment survives from a lost play by Aristophanes in which a character says, "A woman needs a lover the way a dinner needs dessert." Euphiletos's wife was no Lysistrata, able to express her frustration and rebellion in some dramatic act of revolutionary will, but she did find a way to rebel all the same. It cost her dear. By Athenian law, if a man discovered that his wife had been raped or seduced, he was expected to divorce her. And from what we know of Euphiletos's character, we can be sure that he obeyed the law.

From *Horizon*, Spring 1974. © 1974 by Forbes, Inc. Reprinted by permission of *Horizon* magazine, a division of Forbes, Inc.

Cleopatra: What Kind of a Woman Was She, Anyway?

Serpent of the Nile? Learned ruler? Sex kitten?
Ambitious mom? African queen? History
is still toying with the poor lady's reputation

Barbara Holland

Until now, everyone has had pretty much the same fix on Cleopatra: passion's plaything, sultry queen, a woman so beautiful she turned the very air around her sick with desire, a tragic figure whose bared bosom made an asp gasp when she died for love. Inevitably, the best-known incarnation of her is Hollywood's: Theda Bara, Claudette Colbert, Elizabeth Taylor, telling us what fun it was to be filthy rich in the first century B.C., spending days in enormous bathtubs and nights in scented sheets. Drinking pearls dissolved in vinegar. (Do not try this at home; it doesn't work.) Lounging around on a barge, being waited on hand and foot. Sometimes the asp looks like a small price to pay.

Hollywood's queen rests less on George Bernard Shaw's Cleopatra, who is a clever sex kitten, than on William Shakespeare's; in the Bard's *Antony and Cleopatra* she's a fiercer soul, downright

unhinged by love for Mark Antony. Of course, they both had to leave out her children. Everyone does. It's tough being the world's top tragic lover with four kids underfoot. Even if you can get a sitter, it doesn't look right.

The latest version, part of the current debate about the possible influences of Africa on Greek and Roman culture, suggests that she was black. The last time we looked she was a Macedonian Greek, but the black-Cleopatra advocates like to point out that since nobody knows anything about her paternal grandmother except that she wasn't legally married to Ptolemy IX, it is possible that she was black.

Most classical scholars disagree. Some note that though Ptolemy II, more than a century earlier, had an Egyptian mistress, the Ptolemies were wicked snobs, so proud of their bloodline, not to mention the line of succession to their

throne, that they tended to marry their brothers and sisters to keep it untainted. When they picked mistresses, they customarily chose upper-class Greeks. They felt so superior to the Egyptians, in fact, that after 300 years in Alexandria, they couldn't say much more than "good morning" to the locals in their native tongue; Cleopatra was the first in her family to learn the language.

Nobody should be surprised at such claims, however. For the fact is that for purposes political and otherwise, people have been fooling around with Cleopatra's image to suit themselves for centuries. In *All for Love* John Dryden gives us a traditional Cleo less a queen and a ruler than an addictive substance. Shaw made her stand for everything unBritish and thus deplorable. In the course of his *Caesar and Cleopatra* she evolves from a superstitious, cowardly little girl into a vengeful, bloodthirsty little girl. To underline his point he lops five years off her actual age and leaves her under the thumb of a sturdy Roman governor, forerunner of the wise and kindly British administrators of later colonies full of childish foreigners.

Of course, nearly everyone's story goes back to Plutarch, the first-century Greek biographer, who included two versions of Cleo. He knew the writings and stories of people in her part of the world who remembered her as a scholar in their own refined tradition, so unlike the ignorant, loutish Romans; a mothering goddess; a messiah sent to liberate the East from under the jackboots of Rome. On the other hand, he had the Roman story, largely attributed to her enemy in war, and conqueror, Octavian (who later became the emperor Augustus—portrayed as the clueless husband of the evil Livia in the television series *I, Claudius*). Octavian worked hard to set her up as everything scheming, treacherous, female, foreign and, most of all, sexually rapacious. His Queen Cleopatra was a drunken harlot, the wickedest woman in the world.

Actually, where we can reasonably deduce them, the facts are more interesting than these exotic scenarios.

Cleopatra VII was born in 69 B.C, the third child of Ptolemy XII, called Auletes, known as the Flute Player. Egypt was still rich, then, but its ancient empire had been nibbled away, and the natives, unfond of their Macedonian masters, were restless. The Flute Player kept going to Rome to get help in holding onto his throne. He may have taken Cleopatra along when she was 12; she may have watched the Roman loan sharks charge him 10,000 talents, or nearly twice Egypt's annual revenue, for services to be rendered.

Not only couldn't he control his subjects, he couldn't do a thing with his children. While he was away his eldest daughter, Tryphaena, grabbed the throne. After she got assassinated, second daughter Berenice grabbed it next—until Ptolemy came back with Roman help and executed her. Cleopatra, now the eldest, had cause to ponder. She knew Egypt needed Roman help, but paying cash for help was beggaring the state. She knew she had to watch her

back around her family. I suppose you could call it dysfunctional.

She seems to have found herself an education. Cicero, like most Romans, couldn't stand her, but he grudgingly admits she was literary and involved like him in "things that had to do with learning." The Arab historian Al-Masudi tells us she was the author of learned works, "a princess well versed in the sciences, disposed to the study of philosophy." According to Plutarch she spoke at least seven languages.

Cleopatra's looks are one of the burning issues of the ages.

In 51 B.C., when Cleopatra was 18, the Flute Player died and left the kingdom to her and her 10-year-old brother (and fiancé) Ptolemy XIII. The reign got off on the wrong foot because the Nile refused to flood its banks to irrigate the yearly harvest. A court eunuch named Pothinus reared his ugly head; he'd got himself appointed regent for little Ptolemy, squeezed Cleopatra clear out of town and began giving orders himself.

Rome, meanwhile, was in the process of shedding its republican privileges to become an empire. An early phase involved the uneasy power-sharing device called the First Triumvirate, with Caesar, Pompey and Crassus (a money man) jointly in charge. It wasn't Rome's brightest idea. Caesar and Pompey quarreled, Caesar defeated Pompey in Greece, Pompey took refuge in Egypt. Not wanting to harbor a loser, the Egyptians had him murdered and cut off his head and presented it to victorious Caesar when he sailed into Alexandria to collect the defunct Flute Player's debts. Pothinus had reason to hate and fear Rome. He was very likely plotting to do in Caesar, too, who took over the palace and stayed on with a guard of 3,000 Roman soldiers. He couldn't take his ships and go home; the winds were unfavorable.

Cleopatra needed a secret word with him, so as we've all heard, she got her-

self rolled up in some bedding and had herself delivered to Caesar as merchandise. According to Plutarch, Caesar was first captivated by this proof of Cleopatra's bold wit, and afterward so overcome by the charm of her society that he made a reconciliation between her and her brother. Then he killed Pothinus. So there was Cleopatra, at the price of being briefly half-smothered in bedding, with her throne back. And of course, sleeping with Caesar, who was in his 50s and losing his hair.

How did she do it? Cleopatra's looks are one of the burning issues of the ages. European painters tend to see her as a languishing blue-eyed blonde with nothing to wear but that asp. However, there's a coin in the British Museum with her profile on it, and she looks more like Abraham Lincoln than a voluptuous queen. Most people who have written about her agree that she commissioned the coins herself and, being a woman, was vain of her looks, so even this profile could have been downright flattering. In any case, it launched a lot of cracks about her proboscis. Had Cleopatra's nose been shorter, according to 17th-century French writer Blaise Pascal, the whole face of the world would have been changed. However, there's no evidence that Antony was unhappy with her nose the way it was.

Or maybe it wasn't so long. Maybe she thought more of her kingdom than her vanity and wanted to scare off possible enemies by looking fierce. Considering the speed with which she corrupted Rome's top commanders—both of them widely traveled, experienced married men—it's possible she looked more like a woman and less like Mount Rushmore than she does on the coins. Besides, the second-century Greek historian Dio Cassius says Cleopatra seduced Caesar because she was "brilliant to look upon... with the power to subjugate everyone." (She knew a few things about fixing herself up, too, and wrote a book on cosmetics full of ingredients unknown to Estee Lauder, like burnt mice.) And Plutarch reports that "It was a pleasure merely to hear the sound of her voice, with which, like an instrument of many strings, she could pass from one language to another...."

She bowled Caesar over, anyway, and when reinforcements came he squelched the rebellious Egyptian army for her. In the process he had to burn his own ships, and the fire spread and took out part of Alexandria's famous library, which housed most of what had been learned up to the time—Shaw called it "the memory of mankind." When the smoke cleared they found Ptolemy XIII drowned in the Nile in a full suit of golden armor, but as far as we know, his sister hadn't pushed him. Caesar then married her to her youngest brother, Ptolemy XIV, age 12, whom she ignored. When Caesar left, she was pregnant. Anti-Cleopatrans scoff at the notion that Caesar was the father, claiming he never admitted it himself, but there was plenty he never admitted, including his whole Egyptian fling, and somehow it seems likely. Giving the childless Caesar a son was a much shrewder move than getting pregnant by your 12-year-old brother; as policy it might have done wonders for Egypt. She named her son Ptolemy Caesar, always referred to him as Caesarion, and took him with her to Rome in 46 B.C. Mindful of her father's mistake, she took Ptolemy XIV, too, so she could keep an eye on him.

In Rome she was Caesar's guest. They gave fabulous parties together. He put up a golden statue of her in the temple of Venus Genetrix, causing a scandal that made him more vulnerable to the people who were plotting to kill him, as they did in March of 44. After he got stabbed, it turned out that he hadn't named Caesarion as his heir, but his great-nephew Octavian, so Cleopatra had to pack up and go home. When brother Ptolemy XIV conveniently died, she appointed the toddler Caesarion as coruler.

Here the record loses interest in her for several years, between lovers, but she must have been busy. She'd inherited a country plagued by civil wars, Egypt was broke, and twice more the Nile floods misfired. Somehow, though, by the time the West began to notice her again, peace reigned even in fractious Alexandria. She'd played her cards deftly with Rome and her subjects loved her. According to the first-century A.D. Jewish historian Josephus, she'd negotiated a sweetheart real estate deal with the Arabs and in general managed the economy so well that Egypt was the richest state in the eastern Mediterranean. So rich that Mark Antony came calling in 41 B.C. in search of funds to finance an attack on the Parthians.

By then the Romans were pigheadedly pursuing the triumvirate notion again, this time with Octavian, Lepidus and Antony. If you believe Plutarch, Antony was simple, generous and easygoing, though a bit of a slob. Cicero says his orgies made him "odious," and there's a story that, after an all-night party, he rose to give a speech and threw up into the skirt of his toga while a kindly friend held it for him. Still, he was doing all right until Cleopatra came along, when he was, as Dryden laments, "unbent, unsinewed, made a woman's toy."

...like any Washington lobbyist with a pocketful of Redskins tickets, she was putting her time and money where they mattered most.

Plutarch's description of their meeting on her barge makes poets and movie producers salivate. Who could resist those silver oars and purple sails, those flutes and harps, the wafting perfumes, the costumed maidens, and the queen herself dressed as Venus under a canopy spangled with gold? Not Antony, certainly. She knew what he'd come for and planned to drive a hard bargain. Naturally, they became lovers; they also sat down to deal; she would pay for his Parthian campaign, he would help fight her enemies and, for good measure, kill her sister Arsinoe, her last ambitious sibling.

Antony came for money and stayed to play. A sound relationship with Rome was tops on the whole world's agenda at the time. So, like a perfect hostess, Cleopatra lowered her standards of decorum and encouraged her guest in rowdy revels that have shocked the ages. The ages feel that all that frivoling means she was a frivolous woman, and not that, like any Washington lobbyist with a pocketful of Redskins tickets, she was putting her time and money where they mattered most.

She drank and gambled and hunted and fished with him. Sometimes they dressed as servants and roamed the town teasing the natives. Plutarch's grandfather knew a man who knew one of her cooks and reported that each night a series of banquets was prepared. If Antony wanted another round of drinks before dinner, the first banquet was thrown out and a second was served up, and so on. Anyone standing outside the kitchen door must have been half-buried in delicacies.

Back in Rome, Antony's third wife, Fulvia, and his brother raised an army against Octavian. (Lepidus, like Crassus, fizzled out early.) She got whipped, and Antony had to bid the fleshpots farewell and go patch things up. Then Fulvia died, and Antony sealed a temporary peace by marrying Octavian's sister, Octavia. Within weeks of that ceremony in Rome, Cleopatra had twins, Alexander Helios and Cleopatra Selene.

At the news of Antony's marriage, Shakespeare's queen has hysterics and tries to stab the messenger, but the Bard is guessing. The real queen probably took it in stride. She could recognize a political move when she saw it; she had Antony's alliance and a son to prove it, and a country to run besides.

SHE HAD NO TIME TO LOLL IN ASS'S MILK

No one suggests that she had a prime minister, and after Ponthinus, who would? No one denies, either, that Egypt was in apple-pie order. So there sits our drunken harlot, with Caesarion and the twins in bed, working late by oil light, signing papyri, meeting with advisers, approving plans for aqueducts, adjusting taxes. Distributing free grain during hard times. Receiving ambassadors and haggling over trade agreements. She may hardly have had time to put eyeliner on, let alone loll in ass's milk, and apparently she slept alone.

Antony finally got it together enough to invade Parthia. He needed help again, so he sent for Cleopatra to meet him at Antioch and she brought the children. Some see this as strictly business, but Plutarch insists his passion had "gathered strength again, and broke out into a flame." Anyway, they were rapturously reunited, and she agreed to build him a Mediterranean fleet and feed his army in exchange for a good deal of what is now Lebanon, Syria, Jordan and southern Turkey.

Did she really love him, or was it pure ambition? Ambition certainly didn't hurt, but it seems she was fond of him, though he probably snored after parties. Sources say she tried to introduce him to the finer things in life and dragged him to learned discussions, which at least sounds affectionate.

After a happy winter in Antioch, he went off to attack Parthia and she was pregnant again. The Parthian campaign was a disaster, ending with the loss or surrender of nearly half his army.

But for Cleopatra it was another boy, Ptolemy Philadelphus. When she'd recovered, she went to Antony's rescue with pay and warm clothes for the survivors. Presently Octavia announced that she, too, was coming to bring supplies. Antony told her to forget it and stay home. Octavian felt his sister had been dissed and suggested to the Romans that Antony was a deserter who planned to move the capital of the empire to Alexandria and rule jointly with his queen from there.

You could see it that way. In a public ceremony in Alexandria, Antony assembled the children, dressed to the teeth and sitting on thrones, and proclaimed Cleopatra "Queen of Kings" and Caesarion "King of Kings." He made his own three kids royalty, too, and gave them considerable realms that weren't, strictly speaking, his to give. Worst of all, he announced that Caesarion, not Octavian, was Julius Caesar's real son and the real heir to Rome.

Then he divorced Octavia.

All hands prepared for war. If the lovers had been quick off the mark, they might have invaded Italy at once and won, but instead they retired to Greece to assemble their forces, including Cleopatra's fleet. She insisted on sailing with it, too; her national treasury was stowed in the flagship. The upshot was that in 31 B.C. they found themselves bottled up at Actium, facing Octavian across the Ambracian Gulf. The standard version of the Battle of Actium is that while the fight hung in the balance, Cleopatra took her ships and left, because, being a woman, she was a coward and deserted in battle. The besotted Antony, we're told, followed her like a dog, and the fight turned into a rout.

With battles, the winner gets to tell the tale. Octavian was the winner, and he saw Cleopatra as a threat to Rome, a lascivious creature, and himself as a noble Roman able to resist her Eastern blandishments. All we really know is that it was a bloody mess, from which she managed to retreat with the treasury intact, enough to build another fleet with change left over. Octavian wanted that money to pay his troops. She wanted Egypt for her children. Perhaps deals could be made. Antony even suggested killing himself in trade for Cleopatra's life, but Octavian was bound for Egypt and he wouldn't deal.

...she and her ladies dressed up in their best finery and killed themselves. Octavian did the handsome thing and had her buried with Antony.

Thus threatened, the queen swiftly stuffed a big mausoleum with treasure, along with fuel enough to burn it down if all else failed, and locked herself in with her serving maids. It's unclear whether Antony was told she was dead or he just felt depressed, but anyway he disemboweled himself. He botched the job—it's harder than you'd think—and lingered long enough to be hauled to the mausoleum and hoisted through the upstairs window, where presumably he expired in Cleopatra's arms. Victorious

Octavian marched into town. He sent his henchmen to the queen, and they tricked their way in, snatched away her dagger, taking her—and her treasure—prisoner.

According to Plutarch, at 39 "her old charm, and the boldness of her youthful beauty had not wholly left her and, in spite of her present condition, still sparkled from within." It didn't help, so she and her ladies dressed up in their best finery and killed themselves. Octavian did the handsome thing and had her buried with Antony. Then he tracked down and killed Caesarion and annexed Egypt as his own personal colony.

The best-remembered Cleo story is the asp smuggled in with the basket of figs. Plutarch, who saw the medical record, mentions it as a rumor, wrestles with the evidence and concludes that "what really took place is known to no one, since it was also said that she carried poison in a hollow comb... yet there was not so much as a spot found, or any symptom of poison upon her body, nor was the asp seen within the monument...."

Later it was suggested—probably by Octavian—that she'd tried various substances on her slaves and, so the story usually goes, opted for the asp, but in truth its bite is even less fun than disemboweling. Maybe she used a cobra, whose effects are less visible. But where did it go? Some people claimed there were two faint marks on her arm, but they sound like mosquito bites to me. Others insist they saw a snake's trail on the sand outside; fat chance, with all those guards and soldiers and distressed citizens milling around shouting and trampling the evidence.

It looks likelier that she'd brewed up a little something to keep handy. She was clever that way; remember the second brother. Octavian's men had patted her down—"shook out her dress," Plutarch says—but she was smarter than they were. And why gamble on the availability of snakes and smugglers when you could bring your own stuff in your suitcase? When Octavian led his triumph through Rome, lacking the actual queen, he paraded an effigy of her with her arm wreathed in snakes, and the asp theory slithered into history. Maybe he'd heard the rumor and believed it, or maybe he started it himself. It would have played well in Rome. In Egypt the snake was a symbol of royalty and a pet of the goddess Isis, but in Rome it was strictly a sinuous, sinister reptile, typical of those Easterners, compared with a forthright Roman whacking out his innards.

History has always mixed itself with politics and advertising, and in all three the best story always carries the day. But why did the man who was now undisputed ruler of the known world work so hard to ruin a dead lady's reputation? Maybe she'd been more formidable than any of our surviving stories tell. We do know she was the last great power of the Hellenistic world, "sovereign queen of many nations" and the last major threat to Rome for a long time. She might have ruled half the known world or even, through her children, the whole thing, and ushered in the golden age of peace that she believed the gods had sent her to bring to the Mediterranean.

At least she would have left us her own version of who she was, and maybe it would be closer to the truth than the others. And then again, given the human urge to tell good stories, maybe not.

Barbara Holland, who often writes wryly about history and politics for the magazine, is the author of several books, including Endangered Pleasures *(Little, Brown).*

Ancient Rome and the Pirates

Philip de Souza considers the impact of piracy on Roman economic and political life.

T HE GREEK HISTORIAN and geographer Strabo, writing around the time of the death of Augustus in AD14, divided the known world into two parts. The better part was that which was subject to the Romans. Here they had installed order and people were prosperous, using the sea for the peaceful and civilised purpose of trading with each other. The rest of world, in his view, was the home of uncivilised, barbarian peoples who practised piracy and did not deserve the benefits of Roman rule.

The stable conditions which prevailed in the Mediterranean and surrounding areas under the Roman emperors were a relatively recent development. In the preceding century, to judge from literary evidence and inscriptions, pirates were a serious problem in the waters which the Romans liked to refer to as 'our sea' (*mare nostrum*).

For merchants piracy was more than just an economic hazard. It was not only the cargo that would be vulnerable to pirates, they might easily kill the crew and any passengers, or sell them as slaves, or if they were wealthy or important ransom them. Similar perils faced the inhabitants of the many coastal communities of the Mediterranean. A ruler with the power to suppress the menace of piracy, therefore, deserved to be honoured alongside the gods, as Roman emperors frequently were.

The idea that powerful rulers should keep the seas safe had a long history in the classical world. Many states and rulers claimed to be suppressing piracy for the common good, although often they seem to have been acting more out of self-interest. Yet not all those whom the ancient sources called pirates were mere armed robbers using ships. The term 'pirate' was a useful label which could be applied to political opponents in order to illegitimise them. Suppression of piracy was also used from time to time by Greek city-states as a justification for acts of imperialism.

Although true piracy was a form of armed robbery, like banditry, the use of ships by pirates made them more of a problem for ancient societies than bandits. Piratical raids could be larger in scale, range over far greater distances and were much harder to anticipate and defend against than those of bandits. The lack of a single, stable political authority made it easier for piracy to flourish, as did the frequent wars between the kingdoms and city-states of the Mediterranean, which tended to encourage piracy at their margins. Pirates could base themselves in the territory of one state and attack the inhabitants of another with little fear of being chastised or evicted. Many maritime communities seem to have been content to trade with or even host groups of 'pirates'. The sale of the booty taken on pirate raids, whether it was slaves, luxury goods, or basic commodities, could contribute significantly to local economies.

The independent island state of Rhodes, which was heavily dependent on maritime trade, earned widespread praise for her long-running conflict with the piratical Cretans in the third and second centuries BC, but the Rhodians had limited resources. By the end of the second century BC Rome was the leading political power in the Mediterranean.

Recent scholarship has stressed the extent to which the Romans' militaristic culture and highly competitive political system encouraged the senatorial aristocracy to seek overseas wars and the conquest of new enemies. The Romans are generally viewed as an aggressive, acquisitive people whose leaders depended heavily on the fruits of war to maintain their dominance.

Yet they liked to portray themselves as the benefactors and protectors of weaker communities, only embarking on wars with a just cause. They claimed, for example, to have gone to war with the Illyrians in the latter part of the third century BC in part to protect Italian traders and the smaller Greek cities of the Adriatic from Illyrian attacks. The Roman conquest of the Balearic islands in 123–22 BC also seems to have been presented as the suppression of piracy, although it is hard to see how the islanders, whom the historian Livy described as 'spending the summer lying around naked', could have posed a serious threat to anyone. It is not surprising, however, that the Romans were put under pressure to do something about piracy in the Eastern Mediterranean by their subjects and allies, especially the Rhodians whose very existence was dependent on maritime commerce.

Although the main priority for Roman armies at the end of the second century BC was combating the incursions of Germanic tribes into northern Italy, the pressure from allied communities, combined with the Roman aristocracy's hunger for military glory, produced an expedition, led by Marcus Antonius the Orator, to the area of southern Turkey known as Cilicia. The Cilicians had acquired a reputation for piracy since they were recruited as allies in the 140s BC by Diodotus Tryphon, a pretender to the Syrian throne. Their raids against the prosperous Levantine cities had not done much to help his cause, but they encouraged the Cilicians to plunder the coastal communities and shipping of the eastern Mediterranean.

Marcus Antonius had completed a year in office in 103 BC as one of the middle-ranking city magistrates of Rome, called *praetors*, and he was assigned the war against the Cilicians as his 'province' (*provincia*), or area of responsibility, for the next year. He was anxious for military success on a scale that would allow him to celebrate a formal triumph and give a major boost to his candidacy for the consulship, Rome's highest magistracy. With a force made up largely of contingents supplied by Rome's Greek allies, particularly the Rhodians, Antonius attacked cities on the southern coast of Turkey which were identified as pirate bases. No detailed account of his campaign survives, but at least one Roman officer, an uncle of Marcus Tullius Cicero, the famous Roman orator, was killed in action. Antonius earned his triumph, and he was elected to the consulship in 99 BC.

In 100 BC a statute was passed by the Roman citizen assembly concerning the assignment and administration of provinces for magistrates of praetorian rank. Among other things that this statute, the *lex de provinciis praetoriis* (statute concerning the praetorian provinces), announces is the decision to make Cilicia into a praetorian province by referring to the need to deny bases to pirates and to enable the citizens and friends of Rome to sail the sea in safety. It instructs the senior consul to write to these allies, notably the kings of Cyprus, Syria, Egypt and Cyrene, inviting them to do their utmost to assist the Romans. The sections of the *lex de provinciis praetoriis* relating to piracy seem to have been framed as a response to the demands of the Rhodians, whose ambassadors were given special treatment by the terms of the statute. The Romans seem to have decided to take a leading role in the suppression of piracy.

There is another interpretation of the statute, however, which is to see it as a manifestation of Roman imperialism. By claiming to be interested in suppressing piracy the Romans were justifying the expansion of their empire in southern Turkey in a way that would both encourage their allies to fight for, or supply them, and at the same time present their opponents unfavourably as pirates, or the supporters of pirates.

After 100 BC there was plenty of Roman military activity in the eastern Mediterranean, but there is little evidence that it was directed against pirates. From 78 to 74 BC Publius Servilius Vatia, one of the consuls of 79 BC, campaigned strenuously in a province designated 'Cilicia'. Servilius is credited with defeating pirates but, while it is clear that he captured some coastal cities which were used as bases for piracy, his main priorities were to enhance his own prestige and to assert Roman control over a strategically important area. The same was true of other Roman aristocrats who campaigned in the region in the 80s and 70s BC.

Many of those designated as 'pirates' by sources for this period were allied to, or in some way associated with, Mithridates VI, King of Pontos. Mithridates was a long-standing enemy of the Romans who fought a series of wars against them from 89 to 63 BC. At times he controlled most of Anatolia and parts of mainland Greece. He used a variety of mercenaries and military allies, and was often accused by the Romans of recruiting Cilician and Cretan pirates to his cause and promoting piracy, in much the same way as Diodotus Tryphon. It made sense for the Romans to exploit the fear piracy engendered among citizens of the Greek cities by presenting Mithridates as an ally of pirates.

Cretan pirates were blamed for many incidents of piracy. Another commander, Quintus Caecilius Metellus, was sent in 69 BC, with orders to bring the whole island under Roman control. The official reasons for his expedition were the suppression of piracy and the punishment of the Cretans for helping Mithridates, but in fact the Senate had been on the verge of clearing the Cretans of these charges and declaring them allies of the Roman people. It was only at the last moment that an ambitious politician, Lentulus Spinther, intervened and forced the Senate to declare war. The conquest of Crete should not, therefore, be seen simply as a further measure to suppress piracy. An extended campaign of this kind offered numerous opportunities to obtain booty and, for the victorious general, prestige and influence in Rome. The Romans had recently annexed the wealthy kingdom of Cyrenaica and an expedition against Crete had already been attempted in 72 BC by the son of Marcus Antonius the Orator. It is reasonable to surmise that many Romans saw Crete as a profitable addition to their growing empire.

Historical sources provide evidence of continuing attacks and spectacular cases of kidnap and ransom by pirates in the 70s and 60s BC. The story of one famous victim illustrates the extent to which most Roman provincial governors were indifferent to the problem. In late 75 or early 74 BC, an aspiring Roman aristocrat called Gaius Julius Caesar was sailing to Rhodes, where he was to study rhetoric, when he was captured by pirates who held him for about forty days until he was ransomed. Having been released, he collected together a small fleet in Miletos and went after the pirates, and captured them. He took them to the Roman governor of the province of Asia, Juncus, to demand that he deal with them, but got no satisfaction. Juncus appears to have been more interested in obtaining the pirates' loot than in punishing them, so Caesar had to organise the executions himself. We are not told what became of the plunder, but my guess is that it may have been used to fund Caesar's rhetoric lessons.

A similar lack of enthusiasm for dealing with pirates was displayed by Gaius Verres, the Roman governor of Sicily between

73 and 71 BC. Verres was put on trial for extortion when he returned to Rome. He had made himself so wealthy, through corruption, extortion and even murder, during his period as a governor that he expected to have little difficulty in bribing the jury to acquit him, but he had to give in to a vigorous prosecution mounted by Cicero (106–43 BC). A recurrent theme of Cicero's case against Verres was his neglect of his duty to protect the province from pirates. During his governorship, Cicero claimed:

> Well fortified harbours and the securest of cities lay open to pirates and bandits; Sicilian sailors and troops, our allies and friends, were starved to death; the finest and most excellently turned out fleets were lost and destroyed, bringing great disgrace to the Roman people.

Verres pocketed the money which the Sicilian cities had set aside for a fleet of warships to deal with pirates, and he had accepted bribes to discharge most of the sailors. When one of the remaining ships eventually did manage to seize a pirate vessel ('laden with booty and sinking under its own weight', according to Cicero) Verres could not restrain himself. Cicero described what followed in his published version of the prosecution speeches:

> The whole night is taken up with emptying out the ship. The pirate captain himself, who ought to be executed, is seen by no one. To this day everyone believes—you may judge for yourselves what truth there is in this conjecture—that Verres secretly accepted money from the pirates in exchange for their captain.

Piratical attacks continued to be widespread and the Romans, for all their claims to be concerned to protect their allies, were more interested in increasing their own wealth and power. Yet in 67 BC, one of Rome's most ambitious generals, Gnaeus Pompeius Magnus (Pompey the Great), was given a special, Mediterranean-wide command to rid the seas of pirates. He was allotted huge resources for three years and, despite the enormous opposition it provoked from within the Senate, he was given overriding authority in all provinces for up to fifty miles inland. Piracy was a serious problem in 67 BC, but it had been so five or ten, or even twenty, years earlier. So why were the Romans prepared to take such drastic action now?

The main explanation seems to be sheer self-interest. While pirates regularly harassed their provincial subjects and allies, but left Rome and Italy relatively untroubled, the Romans were content to profess concern but take little action. In the early 60s BC, however, pirates were striking at targets on the Italian coast. Places like Brundisium, Caieta and even Ostia, at the mouth of the river Tiber, were attacked. The harbours, cities, roads and villas of Italy were easy pickings. Cicero, describing with a rhetorical flourish the background to Pompey's commisssion in a speech of 66 BC, said:

> We used to guarantee not just the safety of Italy, but were able, through the prestige of our imperial power,
> to preserve unharmed all our far-flung allies… yet we are now not only kept out of our provinces, away from the coasts of Italy and its harbours, but we are even driven off the Appian Way!

The Greek biographer Plutarch, whose *Life of Pompey* was written in the second century AD, pinpoints what the Romans perceived as the most urgent problem:

> The pirates' power was felt in all parts of the Mediterranean, so that it was impossible to sail anywhere and all trade was brought to a halt. It was this which really made the Romans sit up and take notice. With their markets short of food and a great famine looming, they commissioned Pompey to clear the seas of pirates.

One thing which no one could ignore in Rome was a threat to the grain supply. The masses of poorer Romans living in the crowded city, whose approval made Senatorial proposals into law in the citizens' assembly, were delighted to vote for a statute putting a popular commander in charge of restoring their main sources of food. Pompey's strategy confirms that securing the grain supply was his first priority. He gathered his naval forces and concentrated them in the western Mediterranean, securing the regions on which Rome depended for her food supply, namely North Africa, Sardinia, Sicily, and Corsica. Plutarch continues:

> He divided up the coasts and seas into thirteen regions, assigning a number of ships to each one, with a commander. His forces were spread out, threatening the pirate hordes from all sides so that they were swiftly caught and brought to land. The more elusive ones were driven together towards Cilicia, like bees swarming to their hive. Pompey made ready to move against them with sixty of his best ships.

The sources are remarkably brief in what they say about the Cilician part of the campaign. Cicero sums it up in one sentence:

> He himself, however, set out from Brundisium and in 49 days he had brought Cilicia into the Roman Empire.

A few more details are given by later sources, like Plutarch and the historians Appian and Cassius Dio, but they do not suggest that there was a hard struggle, or even much fighting. The conquest of Cilicia and the removal of the threat of piracy in forty-nine days seems incredible, especially in the light of the long campaigns fought by previous Roman magistrates in this area, such as Publius Servilius Vatia Isauricus.

Close scrutiny of the sources leaves the distinct impression that Pompey was in a hurry and not at all concerned about doing a thorough job. The main contemporary source, Cicero, was the Roman equivalent of a 'spin doctor', able to take any Roman aristocrat's public career and present him as either the embodiment of corruption and incompetence, as with Verres, or the model of virtue and military excellence, as with Pompey. In his speech delivered in support of Pompey in 66 BC, Cicero argued before the Roman citizen assembly that Pompey was the only man capable of ending the war with Mithridates, and that the secret of Pompey's success was his reputation, which caused most of the enemy to give up without a fight:

> All pirates, wherever they were, suffered capture and death, or handed themselves over to this singularly powerful commander. Even the Cretans, when they sent emissaries to him in Pamphylia to plead their case, learned that there was hope for their surrender, and were ordered to give hostages.

The Greek senator and historian Cassius Dio, writing in the third century AD, elaborates further:

> For he had at his disposal great forces, both in his fleet and his army, so that at sea and on land he was irresistible. Just as great was his clemency towards those who made terms with him, so that he won over many of them by this policy. For those men who were beaten by his forces and experienced his great benevolence, put themselves at his disposal most readily.

The policy of clemency which Cassius Dio refers to meant that all any supposed pirates had to do was surrender at once and they would be treated leniently instead of being executed or sold into slavery, which were the traditional punishments for piracy. It was clearly aimed at allowing Pompey to subdue Cilicia with the minimum of fighting. He would still have the prestige of victory and be well placed to assume the prize of command in the war against Mithridates. The Cretans were still trying to resist another Roman commander, Quintus Caecilius Metellus, when they got news of Pompey's amnesty. Their attempt to surrender to him resulted in the absurd situation of one Roman general ordering his forces to engage those of another so that he could claim the honour of defeating the Cretans.

Pompey's next step was to 'resettle' the former pirates. He supposedly chose places which would be suitable for agriculture, rather than piracy, but some of the sites chosen for the resettlements seem more like ideal pirate bases. In particular Soli on the coast of Cilicia, which was renamed Pompeiopolis, and Dyme at the mouth of the Gulf of Corinth were perfectly positioned for attacking shipping and vulnerable coastal settlements. No wonder the Cretans were so anxious to surrender to him.

Even Cicero was forced to admit that Pompey's war against the pirates in 67 BC had been less than entirely successful. In a speech of 59 BC he defended the actions of Gaius Valerius Flaccus, governor of the Roman province of Asia (western Turkey) in 62 BC. One of the accusations against Flaccus was that he had extorted money from the Greek cities of the coastal region in order to maintain a fleet to guard against pirates. Since Pompey had supposedly ended the pirate menace, the prosecution argued, this fleet was unnecessary. Cicero had to defend Flaccus's policy without seeming to criticise Pompey, the most powerful man in Rome since his victory over Mithridates. He explained the fleet was part of Pompey's grand plan:

> He bestowed peace upon the maritime world through his great courage and incredible speed. But he never undertook, nor should he have undertaken, to be held responsible if a single pirate ship should happen to appear somewhere. Therefore he himself, when he had already brought an end to all the wars on land and sea, nevertheless ordered those same cities to provide a fleet.

Cicero goes on to justify Flaccus's levies as a response to the continued problem of piracy in the Eastern Mediterranean:

> Should Flaccus still be censured for his conscription of rowers? Even if a member of the aristocracy of Adramyttium was killed by pirates, someone whose name is familiar to almost all of us, Atyanas the Olympic boxing champion?

In reply to the point that no pirates were ever captured by Flaccus's fleet, Cicero reminds the court that such things are a matter of luck, for it is a difficult job to find and pursue pirates across the sea. In this way he maintains the reputation of Pompey, whose luck in 67 BC must have been outstandingly good. Other Roman governors also had to deal with piracy in the eastern Mediterreanean in the 50s BC, demonstrating still further the limitations of Pompey's supposed eradication of the problem.

Even Cicero was forced to admit that Pompey's war against the pirates in 67 BC had been less than entirely successful.

In 44 BC, long after Pompey had perished in his struggle for political supremacy with Julius Caesar, Cicero was again faced with the inadequacy of Pompey's measures to suppress piracy. In a letter to his friend Atticus, written when he was contemplating travelling from Italy to Greece after the assassination of Caesar, Cicero remarks:

> It is not surprising that the Dymaeans, having been driven out of their land, are making the sea unsafe. There should be some protection in a joint voyage with Brutus, but I imagine it will only be a matter of very small craft.

The Dymaeans he refers to were the pirates whom Pompey had sent to Dyme, in the northern Peloponnese as part of his resettlement programme. Having been deprived of their land by new colonists, installed by Caesar, they seem to have reverted to their former piratical practices, although it may be that they had never entirely abandoned them.

There is evidence of continued piracy in the 40s and 30s BC. For example, an inscription from the Cycladic island of Syros honours Onesandros, a man from nearby Siphnos, for the assistance he gave to a slave from Syros who had been the victim of a recent pirate raid. Furthermore, the civil wars which followed Caesar's assassination and resulted in the establishment of Augustus as Rome's first emperor promoted the kind of political instability in which piracy often flourished.

As rival aristocrats raised armies and fought each other for control of the Roman empire, the label 'pirate' or 'friend of pirates' was employed to illegitimise political opponents and justify protracted civil wars. From 43 to 36 BC Pompey's surviving son, Sextus Pompeius, waged a campaign against Caesar's heir Octavian, the future emperor Augustus. In a twist of fate, his strategy of blockading Rome and raiding the coast of Italy from bases in Sardinia and Sicily earned him the accusation of being a pirate. In a monumental inscription listing his achievements, which was copied all over the Roman empire on his death, Augustus summarised his defeat of Sextus Pompeius with the words 'I made the sea peaceful and freed it of pirates'.

In a sense it was Augustus's victories over Sextus Pompeius and his other main rival, Mark Antony, that eventually made possible the effective Roman suppression of piracy in the Mediterranean. The creation of a monarchy and the subordination of aristocratic rivalry under Augustus enabled the emperor to maintain a permanant, professional army and navy which could turn Rome's claim to be the guarantor of maritime security into a reality. Pirates could not find anywhere to base themselves beyond reach of the armed might of Rome.

Piracy still did not vanish entirely. While the Mediterranean became relatively pirate-free under the benign despotism of the Roman emperors, pirates found a literary home in ancient novels. They feature briefly in Petronius' *Satyrica*, but they invade the pastoral idyll of Longus's *Daphnis and Chloe*, Xenophon's *Ephesian Tale*, or Achilles Tatius's *Klitophon and Leukippe*, temporarily separating the young couple as they begin to discover the delights of love.

FOR FURTHER READING

Philip de Souza, *Piracy in the Graeco-Roman World* (Cambridge UP, 1999); Michael Crawford, *The Roman Republic* (Fontana, 1992); William V. Harris, *War and Imperialism in Republican Rome 327–70 BC* (Oxford UP, 1979); Robert Kallett-Marx, *Hegemony to Empire: the Development of the Roman Imperium in the East from 148 to 62 BC* (University of California Press, 1995); John Rich and Graham Shipley, eds., *War and Society in the Roman World* (Routledge, 1993); J.A. Crook and others, eds., *The Cambridge Ancient History vol IX* (Cambridge UP, 1994); Alan K. Bowman and others, eds., *The Cambridge Ancient History vol X* (Cambridge UP, 1996).

Philip de Souza is Senior Lecturer in classical studies at St Mary's College, Strawberry Hill.

This article first appeared in *History Today*, July 2001, pp. 48-53. © 2001 by History Today, Ltd. Reprinted by permission.

Sudden Death

Gladiators were sport's first superstars, providing thrills, chills and occasional kills.

by Franz Lidz

THE RUINS OF CARTHAGE, that great city-state crushed by the Romans in 146 B.C., rise from the Tunisian steppes like a mouthful of bad teeth. It was from here that North Africa's Three-H Club—Hamilcar, Hasdrubal and Hannibal—invaded Europe and challenged the Roman Empire in the Punic Wars. Hulking over the few bleak tombs that still stand is El Djem, a coliseum almost as massive as the one in Rome. Few monuments better embody humanity's inhumanity. Over two centuries, El Djem provided an enormous venue for satisfying the Roman appetite for gory spectacle. From dawn until after nightfall, fatal encounters between men and men, men and beasts, and beasts and beasts were staged in this arena, whose wooden floor was covered with sand that soaked up the blood spilled in combat.

> ## "The Romans believed it was beneficial to watch people being slain."

That floor is now collapsed, exposing the narrow corridors below, where an intricate rope-and-pulley system hoisted gladiators, condemned prisoners and wild animals to the surface. You can stand down there and gaze upward, much like the poor souls funneled through there once did, awaiting their fate. The extravagant butchery that was the gladiatorial games—snuff theater, if you will—seems like something out of Monty Python, a point not lost on Flying Circus alumnus Terry Jones, an Oxford don in history who cowrote and narrated a four-part series on the Crusades for the BBC and also did a documentary for the network on gladiators. While scouting locations for *Monty Python's Life of Brian* in 1978, Jones padded though El Djem's underground passageways in awed silence. "I shuddered with gleeful disgust," he recalls, "and tried to imagine how the fighters must have felt sprinting into the sunlight, surrounded by mobs baying for blood."

For seven centuries the Romans celebrated murder as public sport. "A gladiator fight was something between a modern bullfight and a prizefight," says Jones. "It was like bullfighting in that the spectators appreciated the competitors' technique and applauded their skill and courage. It was like boxing in that you went to see people mashing each other into the ground. The games weren't decadent; they were an antidote to decadence. The Romans believed it was beneficial to watch people being slain—you learned how to meet death bravely. In the ancient city, where compassion was regarded as a moral defect, the savage killings weren't just good entertainment, but morally valuable."

The origins of the sport may lie in Etruscan slave fights, which were fought to the death to please the gods and to enhance the reputations of the slaves' owners. The Romans incorporated the tradition into their funeral ceremonies, beginning in 264 B.C. with that of Junius Brutus Pera's. Gradually, the spectacles became more lurid and more frequent—and more necessary for each ruler to provide in order to retain power and sustain the goodwill of a mostly unemployed populace. Before long, just about every Roman city had its own amphitheater. The most majestic, the Colosseum, held 50,000 spectators and offered every sort of diversion from circus acts to reenactments of historic naval battles on the flooded arena floor. Roman emperors spent vast sums on bread and circuses, entertaining the urban masses. Much like the dictators of today, emperors well understood the benefits of athletic triumphs, in propaganda and as a distraction from misery at home. The games that commemorated the emperor Trajan's victories on the Dacian frontier in 107 A.D. featured 10,000 gladiators and lasted 123 days.

Being a gladiator was a job first thought fit only for slaves, convicts or prisoners of war. But under the Republic, many freeborn citizens became gladiators, seeking a kind of macabre glamour. Under the Empire, noblemen, emperors and even women fought. As the games became more popular, criminals were sometimes remanded to gladiator schools. "In general, a sentence to the schools meant three years of training and combat in the arena followed by two years teaching in the schools," wrote Richard Watkins in *Gladiator*. Among the earliest training schools was the one near Capua from which Spartacus and 78 other gladiators made their historic escape in 73 B.C. Eluding the Roman garrison, they stole weapons, pillaged estates and freed thousands of slaves. Within a year, the bandit and his guerrilla band of 90,000 engaged the Roman legions in the Revolt of Spartacus, one of history's more forlorn campaigns. Emboldened by victories all over Southern Italy, the gladiators took on the main body of the Roman army. Its commander, Marcus Licinius Crassus, routed the rebels and cut Spartacus to pieces, celebrating his triumphal return by crucifying 6,000 of his captives along the Appian Way.

Some of Caligula's gladiators supposedly trained themselves not to blink

---

Most of the schools were run by "stable masters" who either bought and maintained gladiators for rental, or trained them for other owners. These overseers were called *lanistae*, which derives from the Etruscan word for butcher. Ranked and housed on the basis of experience, the four grades of trainees honed their swordsmanship on straw men or fencing posts. Instructors taught them conditioning, toughness and the proper postures to assume when falling and dying. They were well-fed (barley porridge was the andro of its day) and pampered with massages and baths. In Rome, however, gladiator schools were in imperial hands. Gladiators owned by Caligula, the Empire's quintessential mad despot, supposedly trained themselves not to blink. The emperor sometimes sparred with them. "To be his partner might prove a dubious honour," wrote Anthony Barrett in *Caligula*. "It is said that when practising with a gladiator from the training school [who was armed] with [a] wooden sword, Caligula ran his partner through with a real one." (Caligula lived out every modern team owner's dream: He once ordered an entire section of gladiator fans thrown to the beasts for laughing at him.)

Every gladiator was a specialist: Spartacus was a Thracian, a class named for and outfitted in the equipment of one of Rome's vanquished enemies. Armored in shin guards and a crested helmet, and armed with a small, round shield and a dagger curved like a scythe, Thracians were generally matched against the *mirmillones*, who protected themselves with short Gallic swords, large oblong shields and fish-crowned helmets. The heavily armored *secutor* was often pitted against the practically bare-skinned *retiarius*, whose strategy was to entangle his opponent in a net and spear his legs with a trident. Then there were the lance-brandishing *andabatae*, believed to have fought on horseback in closed visors that left them more or less blind; the two-knife wielding *dimachaeri*; the lasso-twirling *laqueari*; the chariot-riding *essedarii*; and the befeathered *Samnites*, who

lugged large, rectangular shields and a straight sword called a *gladius*, from which the word *gladiator* comes.

Not all gladiators were eager participants. "In Caligula's day," says Jones, "a dozen gladiators decided not to fight. They laid down their arms, figuring the emperor wouldn't want to waste 12 gladiators. It didn't work. Caligula was so infuriated by this early trade union thing that he ordered them all to be killed. Whereupon one of them jumped up, grabbed a weapon and slew all his unarmed ex-colleagues. Then Caligula stood up and said a very strange thing: 'I've never seen anything so cruel.'"

Cruelty, of course, was the sine qua non of the gladiatorial games. During a typical day out at the amphitheater, you could expect men stalking and killing beasts in the morning, execution of convicts at midday, gladiator bouts in the afternoon. The brutal truths: Mankind trumps the wild, law punishes criminality, valor vanquishes death. "The arena was… a symbol of the ordered world, the cosmos," Thomas Wiedemann wrote in *Emperors and Gladiators*. "It was a place where the civilized world confronted lawless nature."

Morning sessions at the Colosseum were devoted to anti-social Darwinism. In *venationes*, wild game was hunted amid elaborate scenery depicting, say, mountains or glades; in *bestiarii*, ferocious predators faced off in bizarre combinations: bears against lions, lions against leopards, leopards against crocodiles. The scale of the slaughter could be staggering. A *venatio* put on by Pompey in 55 B.C. included the slaughter of 20 elephants, 600 lions, 410 leopards, numerous apes and Rome's first rhinoceros. At a hunt held by Augustus, the score was 420 leopards, dozens of elephants, and as many as 400 bears and 300 lions—a total later matched by Nero. Roughly nine thousand animal carcasses were dragged out of the Colosseum during the opening ceremonies in 80 A.D.; 11,000 more over Trajan's four-month shindig. The Romans were so efficient at keeping their arenas stocked that entire animal populations were wiped out: Elephants disappeared from Libya, lions from Mesopotamia and hippos from Nubia. "All sorts of exotic animals were trapped in African deserts and the forests of India," Jones says. "Fans must have sat in the stands thinking, 'Ooh, what's that? I've never seen one of them before.' A lot of ostriches would come out and the hunters would chase them around a bit, and then you'd get some tigers. 'Ooh, tigers! They're interesting!' Then the tigers would be set on the ostriches. It was kind of a zoo in action."

A dying gladiator was finished off in the arena by having his skull smashed with a mallet

---

Around noon, in an Empirical version of a halftime show, it was mankind's turn to be massacred. While spectators snacked on fried chickpeas and were misted with perfume to mask the stench of carnage, pairs of *meridiani*—arsonists, murderers, Christians—were sometimes subjected to what the philosopher Seneca called "sheer murder… a round-robin of death." One prisoner was handed a sword and ordered to kill the other. His job complete, he was disarmed and killed by the next armed captive. This went on until the last prisoner was whacked by an arena guard. Chariots were then wheeled out bearing men and women chained to posts. At a signal, trapdoors opened and leopards sprang out. In Rome, Christians really were fed to the lions. And leopards.

Still, the lowlight of most games was *professional* gladiatorial combat. The show opened with a procession heralded by trumpets. Dressed in purple and gold cloaks, gladiators circled the arena on foot, shadowed by slaves bearing their weapons. When the combatants reached the royal box, they supposedly thrust their right arms forward and shouted, "*Ave, Imperator, morituri te salutant*!" (Hail, Emperor, those who are about to die salute thee!)

Fight School

Today's homework assignment: Chop off his head!

By Franz Lidz

"If I catch you, I will make your face like an old saint!" It's Day One of gladiator school, and my teacher, Vates, is trying to get me to fight, egging me on with some choice Latin insults, but his taunts are lost in English translations looser than togas and syntax as mangled as felled legionnaires. "Your armpits ride to 100 miles!" he yells. "Screw you and three quarters of your building!"

Here, in an open field behind a bus station on the outskirts of Rome, under a murky December sky, a half-dozen novices and I stand shivering in sandals and short white tunics. We are simulating savagery and trying to get in touch with our inner warrior, which, in my case, has been hibernating since a fourth-grade snowball fight.

Gladiator classes are offered two nights a week by the Gruppo Storico Romano, a fledgling historical society whose 200 or so members love to dress up like *Animal House* frat boys and reenact Roman revels for pageants and town fairs. The society has been inundated with applicants since *Gladiator* splattered the silver screen with its gore last year. Classes are held in a makeshift arena just off the Appian Way, where Spartacus and his rebel army were hung out to dry. The Roman physician Galen described gladiators as massive and overfed. Not much has changed in two millennia. The assembled irregulars—bank clerks, sales managers, traffic cops—tend to be weightier than Umberto Eco novels. We all work at drills designed to teach us agility, tactics and swordplay, thrusting and parrying with wooden practice swords that resemble outsized tongue depressors. Never swing your *gladius* in an arc, Vates tells us, lead with your stronger leg, present as small a target as possible.

The intricate etiquette that prevents our hacking from degenerating into mayhem is vigorously enforced by Vates, a 23-year-old history major known outside the ring as Alessandro Rizzo. He moves through the six-blow sequence of sword thrusts with the sure economy of a veteran dancer. The first maneuver, an overhand thwack to the skull, looks something like a Pete Sampras smash. The second, a low sweep at the legs, suggests an Andre Agassi backhand. The sixth, a swift thrust to the navel, is not unlike John McEnroe spearing a line judge with his racquet.

By the second session I am ready for what Vates calls "virtual killing." Points are awarded for whacking various parts of your opponent's body. The first gladiator to rack up 10 points wins. (Decapitation is worth only three). Swaggering into the armory, I spy dozens of pikes, brooms and blunt-edged metal swords stacked against the walls. What are the brooms for? I ask Vates. "Blood and severed limbs," he says.

He and I pair off for combat. Vates enters the arena bareheaded, armed with a net and a trident; I wear scaly iron armor and a helmet. The claustrophobic headgear tunnels my vision and pinches my cheeks. Already, I have the face of an old saint. We recite the frightful gladiator oath and touch swords. Then the sound of metal clanging against metal echoes in the air as sword meets trident, trident meets shield. While circling each other like gunfighters in a spaghetti western, Vates hisses, "I give you a kick on your bottom that it goes to your shoulders." *Ouch!* "I cut your ass in four halves." *Yow!*.

Quickly, I launch my own Roman riposte: "At whom it touches, it does not grunt." I'm not sure what that means, but Vates seems to know—his eyes narrow and his fingers tighten on the trident as he heaves his fishnet, snags the fin on my helmet and fillets me. I flop in the cords, nicking my shield hand with my sword. I untangle myself. I lick the blood from my wound with gladiatorial gusto. I lunge forward and take a wild swipe at Vates, leaving myself wide open. He charges. I freeze… and become an exceedingly dead gladiator. "Good gladiators try not to die," Vates says with a pained sigh. "Die, and your career is over."

Supposedly, because much of what we think we know about the games is in dispute, or evolved from Hollywood sword 'n' sandal sagas. No one is quite sure if "thumbs down" meant death and "thumbs up" a reprieve. Some scholars believe spectators would turn their thumbs toward their chests as a sign for the winner to stab the loser and that those in favor of mercy turned their thumbs down as a sign for the winner to drop his sword. Which would mean the best review a fallen fighter could hope for was "one enthusiastic thumb down."

After the procession and their salutation to the emperor, weapons were tested for sharpness and combatants paired off by lot. A typical show featured between 10 and 20 bouts, each lasting about 15 minutes. A horn was blown and timid fighters were prodded into the arena with whips and red-hot brands. Each fight was supervised by two referees. Coaches stood nearby, lashing reluctant fighters with leather straps. Just like at the ballpark, the house organist would rally the betting crowd. Cries of "*Verbera!*" (Strike!), "*Iugula!*" (Slay!) and "*Habe!*" (That's got him!) swept the stadium. If a Roman fan yelled "Kill the umpire!" he really meant it. The first gladiator to draw blood or knock his opponent down was the victor. A beaten gladiator could appeal for clemency by casting aside his weapon and raising his left hand. His fate was left to the spectators, those early Roger Eberts. The prevailing notion that most gladiators dueled to the death is no more likely than the idea that most died in the arena. Only about one in 10 bouts were lethal, and many of those fatalities can be blamed on overzealousness. "Gladiators were very, very expensive characters," says Jones. "It cost a great deal to keep them fed and exercised and comfortable. Unless you were Caesar and wanted to impress somebody, you tended not to squander them."

When a gladiator was mortally wounded, an attendant costumed as Charon, the mythical ferryman of the River Styx, finished the job (in a pure Pythonian moment) by smashing his skull with a mallet. After the body was carried off on a stretcher, sand was raked over the bloodstained ground to ready it for the next bout. The festivities ended at sunset, although sometimes, as under Emperor Domitian (81–96 A.D.), contests were held by torchlight—night games.

Victors became instant heroes. They were crowned with a laurel wreath and given gold. Those who survived their term of service were awarded a *rudis*, the wooden sword signifying honorable discharge. Some so liked the gladiator life that they signed on for another tour. The Pompeiian fighter Flamma had four *rudii* in his trophy case.

Gladiator sweat was an aphrodisiac used in facial creams for Roman women

---

Gladiator sweat was considered such an aphrodisiac that it was used in the facial creams of Roman women, and top gladiators were folk heroes with nicknames, fan clubs and adoring groupies. "We think they were sex symbols," says Jones. "A piece of ancient graffito was found at the gladiatorial barracks in Rome that read SO-AND-SO MAKES THE GIRLS PANT." Gladiators were making Roman girls weak-kneed until the early fourth century A.D. Christian emperor Constantine abolished the games in 325, but without much conviction, or success. In 404, the emperor Honorius banned them again after a Christian monk tried to separate two gladiators and was torn limb from limb by the angry crowd. Despite Honorius' decree, the combat may have continued for another 100 years. "The sad truth is that the Christians of Rome became good Romans and staged their own gladiatorial contests," says Jones. "Popes even hired gladiators as bodyguards. The Christians are given far too much credit—they have a lot to answer for, like being responsible for the Dark Ages.".

It was the barbarian invaders who shut down the sport for good. "Whenever Goths and Vandals moved into a Roman city, the games stopped," Jones says. "The barbarians disapproved of them and found them too disgusting." And, we assume, too barbaric.

UNIT 3

The Judeo-Christian Heritage

Unit Selections

14. **Jews and Christians in a Roman World**, Eric M. Meyers and L. Michael White
15. **The Other Jesus**, Kenneth L. Woodward
16. **Ecstasy in Late Imperial Rome**, Dirk Bennett
17. **Who the Devil Is the Devil?** Robert Wernick

Key Points to Consider

• What are some of the differing views about Israel?

• Describe the relationship that existed among Jews, Christians, and pagans during the Roman era.

• How do the Jews, Buddhists, Hindus, and Muslims view Jesus as opposed to the Christian interpretation?

• What happened to the pagan religions when Christianity arose?

• How is the Devil presented in several of the religions discussed?

 **Links: www.dushkin.com/online/**
These sites are annotated in the World Wide Web pages.

Facets of Religion/Casper Voogt
http://www.bcca.org/~cvoogt/Religion/mainpage.html

Institute for Christian Leadership/ICLnet
http://www.iclnet.org

Introduction to Judaism
http://philo.ucdavis.edu/zope/home/bruce/RST23/rst23homepage.html

Selected Women's Studies Resources/Columbia University
http://www.columbia.edu/cu/libraries/subjects/womenstudies/

Western civilization developed out of the Greco-Roman world, but it is also indebted to the Judeo-Christian tradition. If Western civilization derives humanism and materialism, philosophy, politics, art, literature, and science from the former, it derives its God and forms of worship from the latter. It is perhaps difficult or misguided to separate these traditions, for the Judeo-Christian heritage comes to us through a Hellenistic filter. This angle is explored in "Jews and Christians in a Roman World."

On the surface, the history of the Jews seems similar to that of other small kingdoms of the Near East, closely situated as they were to such powerful neighbors as the Babylonians, Assyrians, and Persians. Yet of all the peoples of that time and place, only the Jews have had a lasting influence. What appears to differentiate the Jews from all the rest, writes historian Crane Brinton, is "the will to persist, to be themselves, to be a people." The appearance of Israel on the map of the modern world 2,000 years after the Romans destroyed the Jewish client-state is a testimonial to their spirit.

The legacy of the Jews is a great one. It includes the rich literary traditions found in their sacred texts. And they have bequeathed to Western civilization their unique view of history: a linear and miraculous God intervenes in history to guide, reward, or punish his Chosen People. They also gave birth to the morality within the Ten Commandments, the moral wisdom of the prophets and a messianic expectation that inspired Christianity and other religions. Their monotheism and their god, Yahweh, formed the model for the Christian and Muslim ideas of God.

A brief comparison of Yahweh and the Greek god Zeus illustrates the originality of the Jewish conception. Both gods began as warrior deities of tribal cultures. But Zeus was chiefly concerned with Olympian affairs rather than human ones. Yahweh, on the other hand, was more purposeful and had few interests except for his people. And unlike Zeus, who was not the creator of the universe, Yahweh had created and ordered the universe, with humans to rule over nature.

Certainly Christianity bears the stamp of Judaism. Jesus himself was a Jew. To his early followers, all of them Jews, he satisfied the prophetic messianic messages inherent in Judaism. The New Testament recounts the growth and spread of Christianity from an obscure Jewish sect in Palestine to a new religion with great appeal in the Roman world. Yet Jesus remains shrouded in mystery, for there is a lack of firsthand evidence. The Gospels, the greatest and most familiar source, contain wide gaps in their account of his life. Nonetheless, they remain a profound record of early Christian faith. The essay, "The Other Jesus" describes the ways in which Jesus is viewed by the Jews, Christians, Hindus, and Buddhists.

As it separated from Judaism, Christianity took on new dimensions, including the promise of private salvation through participation in the sacraments. From the beginning, its theology reflected the teachings of St. Paul, who changed the focus from converting the Jews to spreading the faith among the Gentiles. Then, as it took hold in the Near East, Christianity absorbed some Hellenistic elements, Stoicism, Platonism, and the Roman pantheon. This latter is the subject of Dirk Bennet's essay, "Ecstasy in Late Imperial Rome." This prepared the way for a fusion of classical philosophy and Christianity. The personal God of the

Jews and Christians became the abstract god of the Greek philosophers. Biblical texts were given symbolic meanings that might have confounded an earlier, simpler generation of Christians. The Christian view of sexuality, for instance, became fraught with multiple meanings and complexities. In effect, Christianity was no longer a Jewish sect; it had become Westernized. Eventually it would become a principal agent for Westernization of much of the world.

The last essay in this section deals with the Devil. "Who the Devil Is the Devil?" by Robert Wernick recounts the origins and influence of the Devil from the ancient religions until the modern day.

Jews and Christians in a Roman World

New evidence strongly suggests that both in Roman Palestine and throughout the Diaspora, Judaism, Christianity, and paganism thrived side by side.

Eric M. Meyers and L. Michael White

More than a century ago, archaeologists began to rediscover the ancient world of the Mediterranean: the world of Homer and the Bible. Much of the early fieldwork in the classical world arose from a romantic quest to bring ancient literature to life. One thinks instinctively of Schleimann at Troy, a shovel in one hand and a copy of Homer in the other. In the Holy Land, the first biblical archaeologists were theologians and ministers who sought to identify and explore cities of the biblical world and to authenticate biblical stories and traditions; thus they arrived with preconceived ideas drawn from biblical texts and other literary sources. Because many were Old Testament scholars, New Testament archaeology in the Holy Land took a back seat. Outside the Holy Land, it remained for years in the shadow of classical archaeology.

Since World War II, and especially since the discovery of the Dead Sea scrolls in 1947, archaeology has been more attentive to the world of the New Testament. But the new archaeological knowledge has only slowly begun to have an impact because New Testament scholars have been slow to take archaeology seriously. Some scholars think archaeology is of peripheral concern to early Christian studies, concluding debatably that the "earthly" dimension of early Christianity is irrelevant. New Testament archaeology is also given low priority in Jewish studies, which traditionally have placed far greater emphasis on sacred texts. Many believe New Testament archaeology to be of limited value in the study of ancient Palestine, erroneously assuming that the archaeological time frame is restricted to only two generations, from the time of Jesus to the destruction of Jerusalem in the year 70. In fact, one cannot understand the development of either Judaism or Christianity without looking at the historical context over centuries, beginning with the introduction of Greek culture into the ancient Near East.

THE HOMELAND

Scholarly understanding of Judaism and Christianity in the Roman province of Palestine during the early Common Era (abbreviated C.E. and chronologically the same as A.D.) has long been burdened by some dubious suppositions. One is the belief that after the First Jewish Revolt against Rome in 66–70 C.E., the new Jewish-Christian community fled the Holy Land. Certainly there was significant emigration to the Mediterranean lands, but in light of archaeological evidence from the first two or three centuries C.E., a growing number of scholars have found the idea of wholesale Jewish-Christian migration untenable.

Actually, the first followers of Jesus were basically indistinguishable from their fellow Jews. Although they believed Jesus was the Messiah and professed a radical love ethic that had few parallels in Judaism—for example, love for one's enemies—the first Jewish-Christians observed most of the Jewish laws and revered the Temple in Jerusalem. They apparently got along well with their fellow Jews, contrary to the impression created in the Gospels and other New Testament writings, where the Pharisees, the "mainstream" religious

Surprise Findings From Early Synagogues

The synagogue provides a rare opportunity to study the Jewish people—and Jewish-Christians—as they forged a new religious way in Roman Palestine after the fall of Jerusalem. Even within a given region, we find a great variety of architectural forms and artistic motifs adorning the walls and halls of ancient synagogues. This great divergence of synagogue types suggests great variety within Talmudic Judaism, even though the members of different congregations belonged to a common culture.

Such diversity resulted in part from the catastrophe of 70 C.E., after which many sectarian groups were forced to fend for themselves in a new and often alien environment. Some groups settled in town, others in urban centers; their choices reflected their understanding of how hospitable a setting their beliefs would find in either the sophisticated cities or the agrarian towns.

Synagogue excavations also attest to the primacy of Scripture in Jewish worship and provide a clearer view of the place held by the *bema*, or raised prayer platform, and the Ark of the Law. The Ark is the fixed repository for the biblical scrolls, which were stored in a central place in the synagogue by the third century C.E. Until recently, the dominant view was that the Ark remained portable throughout most of antiquity.

Some synagogue mosaics even suggest that Jewish art played an integral part in the composition of new poetry recited in the synagogue. In late Roman synagogue mosaics, themes based on the zodiac begin to appear. These mosaics are followed in the textual record by poems that name the actual constellations of the zodiac. The setting for reciting such poems, or *pzyyutim*, was undoubtedly the synagogue, where the intelligentsia would have gathered and included the poems in their worship.

Finally, survey and excavation of numerous synagogue sites in the Golan Heights have revealed an astonishingly lively and vigorous Jewish community in Palestine in late Roman, Byzantine, and early Islamic times. The supposed eclipse of Jewish life at the hands of early Christendom—especially after the conversion of Constantine and, later, the establishment of Christianity as the state religion in 383 C.E.—needs to be reexamined. In fact, one of the surprises of recent synagogue studies is the generally high level of Jewish culture in Palestine at the end of the Roman period (third and fourth centuries C.E.) and the continued though sporadic flourishing of synagogue sites in the Byzantine period (from the middle of the third century to 614 C.E., the year of the Persian conquest of Palestine). All the evidence points to a picture of a Judaism in Palestine that was very much alive until the dawn of the medieval period.

party of ancient Judaism, are presented in a negative light. The new Christians, in fact, were at odds mostly with the Sadducees, who were much more rigid in their religious outlook than the Pharisees, and far fewer in number. When the Apostles were persecuted by the Sadducean high priest, it was the Pharisee Rabbi Gamaliel who intervened to save them (Acts 5:17–42); when Paul was called before the Sanhedrin (the High Council) in Jerusalem, he obtained his release by appealing to the Pharisees (Acts 22:30–23:10); and according to the Jewish historian Josephus, when Jesus' brother James was put to death by order of the Sadducean high priest in 62 C.E., the Pharisees appealed to the king to depose the high priest. Jesus' natural constituency was the Pharisees, whose doctrine of love for one's fellow humans must surely have been the foundation for Jesus' ethical teaching.

The belief that all or most of the Jewish-Christians left Palestine after the First Revolt stems partly from the lack of clear material traces of the Christian community in the Holy Land from about 70 to 270 C.E. Early Christianity, however, vigorously sought to win converts both among gentiles and in the

many Jewish communities throughout the Mediterranean. It is exceedingly hard to imagine these efforts bypassing the large Jewish community in Palestine.

Moreover, Jews from Jerusalem and the surrounding area fled in large numbers to Galilee after the revolt was crushed. Would the first Jewish-Christians have ignored Galilee, where Jesus spent his childhood and where he conducted his ministry? Later generations of Christians certainly did not, as evidenced by the numerous churches they built in Galilee. The presence of important Christian centers of worship makes it difficult to imagine a great Christian "repopulation" of Palestine between the third and fifth centuries. Rather, it seems there was a large community of Jewish-Christians in Palestine from the first century onward, a community later augmented by pilgrims in the age of Constantine.

Jerusalem is central in the study of early Christianity. It is there that the new religion received its most compelling moments of inspiration in the death and burial of Jesus; and it is from there that its followers took their message to the other cities and towns of the land. As long as the Temple stood, the first Chris-

tians continued to worship there and in private household meetings. With the destruction of the Temple, however, both Jews and Christians had to establish new patterns of worship. Thus the local synagogue, which was both a meeting place and a center of worship, became the focus of spiritual life for Jew and Jewish-Christian after 70 C.E.

Recent synagogue excavations have revealed that Jewish life enjoyed remarkable vitality in Palestine during the Roman period, and in some localities into the Byzantine period and beyond. In the pre-Constantinian era, the synagogue was quite possibly where Jewish-Christians worshiped as well. Although the archaeological record shows very little definitive evidence of Christianity until the end of the third century, the textual record is quite clear. In a reference that may go back to 100 or 120 C.E., the Jerusalem Talmud implies that Christians are a sect of *minim*, or heretics. Irenaeus, the first Christian theologian to systematize doctrine, speaks of Ebionites, who read only the Gospel of Matthew, reject Paul, and follow the Torah and the Jewish way of life. Epiphanius, another early Christian writer, speaks of Nazarenes, or Elkasaites, as Christians who insist on the validity of the Torah and laws of purity.

Whether one looks at early Christianity or rabbinic Judaism in Roman Palestine, it is clear that this was a period of great cultural and religious pluralism. One finds this pluralism in the Lower Galilee, at Sepphoris, and at the great site of Capernaum on the northwestern shore of the Sea of Galilee. The octagonal Church of St. Peter in Capernaum is built over what some excavators believe is a Jewish-Christian "house-church" dating back to about the third century. The excavators have also found evidence of a first-century house below this church edifice that may have been Peter's residence. It is clear that by the fourth century, Christians venerated the site by erecting churches there. Next to these Christian structures are Jewish buildings, including a reconstructed synagogue. Archaeologists once thought the synagogue was from the first century C.E., the very building in which Jesus would have walked. Today there is universal agreement that it is a later structure, dating to the fourth or fifth century, that survived for hundreds of years into the early medieval period. Excavators have recently claimed finding another synagogue, from the first century, beneath this fourth- or fifth-century synagogue. If they are right, then in Capernaum a Jewish synagogue and a Jewish-Christian church existed side by side from the end of the first century on. The grander structures above both the early synagogue and the house of Peter in Capernaum suggest that Jewish and Christian communities lived in harmony until the seventh century. The continuous Christian presence for six centuries also casts serious doubts on the idea that the early Christians fled Palestine after 70 C.E. Evidence like that found in Capernaum is plentiful in the Beth Shean Valley and in the Golan Heights, although the evidence there begins later, toward the end of the Roman period and into the Byzantine period.

In the middle of the fourth century, pluralism began to suffer as the Roman period in Palestine came to an end and the Byzantine period began. The transition from Roman to Byzantine culture as revealed by the archaeological and textual records was dramatic and coincides with either the so-called Gallus Revolt against Roman occupation in 352 or the great earthquake of 363. In the case of the revolt, the Byzantine emperor might have taken the opportunity to place the unruly province under his direct rule. In the case of the earthquake, the damage to Roman buildings would have presented the opportunity for a Byzantine architectural and cultural style to emerge as cities were rebuilt.

In either case, the revolt and the aftermath of the earthquake mark the beginning of a difficult period for Jews, in which they had little choice but to adjust to Christian rule. The Palestine of the Roman period, when Jewish sages spoke in Greek and when Rabbi Judah the Prince reputedly numbered the Roman emperor among his friends, became a land undergoing thorough and vigorous Christianization after the conversion of Constantine. Money poured into Palestine, and much of it went into building churches.

Nevertheless, archaeological evidence prompts us to exercise caution. Pockets of Judaism and Christianity remained in close contact during the Byzantine period. They may well have continued the harmonious relations established during the period of pluralism, even as Christianity became the dominant religion.

THE DIASPORA

Archaeology has also enriched our understanding of the New Testament world outside Palestine. It is significant to both Jewish and Christian history that the bulk of the New Testament is set outside the Jewish homeland. Jews and Christians alike called their communities outside Palestine the Diaspora, or "dispersion."

While the religious heritage of the New Testament may be Hebrew, its language is Greek. Its cultural heritage is not that of the ancient Near East but that of Greece and Rome. The world of the New Testament was fluid and pluralistic, with an extensive transportation network crisscrossing the Mediterranean. Christians and Jews traveled the highways and seaways, carrying their religion with them. This mobility is vividly reflected in the extensive journeys of Paul.

The New Testament record of Paul's travels provided early investigators with both an itinerary for their archaeological work as well as a "case" to be proved. From the 1880s to the 1920s, for example, the eminent Sir William Ramsay sought to corroborate the account given in the Acts of the Apostles of Paul's activities on his way to Rome, in Ephesus, Athens, Corinth, and Philippi. Shaping Ramsay's approach were attractive images of Paul, such as the one in chapter 17 of Acts, where he is depicted preaching to the philosophers on the Areopagus, or Mars Hill, below the entrance to the Acropolis. The story in Acts, and later Christian legends attributed to Paul's followers, are the only evidence we have for this. Paul left no footprints on the Areopagus for archaeologists to follow. It is also interesting that Paul, in his own letters, never once mentioned his activities or this episode in Athens. Still, this remains a popular tourist spot, and the legacy of early archaeologists like Ramsay lives on.

The work of archaeologists should not be used to prove New Testament stories about Paul. The remains of his day are simply too hard to find.

All over the eastern Mediterranean, tourists play out variations on this theme with local guides. (Though Paul was a tireless traveler, if he had visited every one of these places, he might have died of old age before he got to Rome.) Often the difficulties arise when local legends, which seem to grow like stratigraphic layers, become attached to a site. A prime example of this occurs at Paul's *bema* at Corinth.

Excavations at Corinth have revealed a fifth-century Christian church erected over what appears to be a bema, or speaking platform. The obvious assumption was that this was the site of Paul's defense before the Roman governor Gallio in Acts 18:12 ("But when

Palestine's Sophisticated Cities

In recent decades, a number of important cities besides Jerusalem have undergone major excavation, yielding evidence of a sophisticated life-style in Palestine. These were Roman cities, built for the administrative infrastructure of imperial rule, but they also became conduits through which Greco-Roman culture was introduced into Palestine.

These cities dominated Palestine, except for the upper Galilee and Golan regions in the North, but the level of sophistication dropped steeply when one moved away from these urban cores. In the surrounding areas, the older agrarian lifestyle was still very much dominant, and it was town more than city that ultimately encompassed most of Jewish, and Jewish-Christian, life in Palestine.

Nonetheless, there were some Hellenized centers of Jewish life, mostly along the major roadways, the Lower Galilee, the Rift Valley, and the coastal plain. The primary language here was Greek, and the surrounding Jewish population used Greek for trade and day-to-day discourse. In time, Greek eclipsed Hebrew as the common language, and many of Israel's most important sages buried their loved ones, or were themselves buried, in containers or sarcophagi that bore Greek epigraphs or Greco-Roman decorations. In striking contrast, virtually no Greek is found in the Upper Galilee or the Golan.

Such tombs are exceptionally instructive. For example, the Jewish catacombs of the sages in Beth Shearim, excavated in the late 1920s, attest to the high level of Greek spoken by the sages. They attest as well to the fact that the sages were comfortable with a style of decoration in their tombs that was thought by contemporary scholars to be incompatible with Jewish sensibilities and law, and with the proscription against representational and figural art contained in the Second Commandment. With the discovery in 1987 of the extraordinary Dionysos mosaic at Sepphoris, the heartland of the Jewish sages, an exciting new perspective was provided on the Hellenization of Roman Palestine.

It is not yet clear who commissioned the colorful mosaic stone carpet, found near both the Roman theater and Jewish buildings and homes, but the ramifications of the discovery are most significant. The mosaic dates to about 200 C.E., the time of Rabbi Judah the Prince, who was both a leader in the compilation of the Mishnah (Jewish traditional doctrine) and reputedly a close friend of the Roman emperor Caracalla. The central panel of the carpet shows Herakles/Dionysos in a drinking contest. The 15 panels that surround this scene depict the life and times of Dionysos, god of wine, the afterlife, revelry, fertility, and theater. What is so amazing is that they are all labeled in Greek, either to clarify the contents for those who didn't know Greek mythology—a gap in knowledge probably not uncommon in these eastern provinces—or to jog the memory of those who ate in the hall in which the stone carpet was located.

The implications of this discovery are many, but the three most important may be summarized as follows: the extent of Hellenization in Palestine by the third century C.E. is greater than was previously believed; Jews were more accepting of great pagan centers than was previously believed, and had more access to them; Jewish familiarity with Hellenistic culture in urban centers such as Sepphoris was a positive force affecting Jewish creativity. It hardly seems coincidental that the Mishnah was codified and published at Sepphoris during the very same period when a highly visible Hellenistic culture and presence flourished in Palestine.

Gallio was proconsul of Achaia, the Jews made a united attack upon Paul and brought him before their tribunal"). Indeed, the story is given further credence by the discovery of an inscription from Delphi that bears the name of Gallio as well as his title. This inscription has been very important in dating Paul's stay in Corinth to around the years 51 and 52 C.E. But it is most difficult to place Paul's trial on this particular bema, since the South Stoa of Corinth, where the bema is found, was expanded and rebuilt during the next two centuries. Other evidence found at Corinth does little to clear matters up. A pavement bearing the name of Erastus, the city treasurer named in Romans 16:23, identifies him as an *aedile*, a minor administrative official, not as treasurer ("Erastus, the city treasurer, and our brother Quartus greet you"). Is this a tangible record of a follower of Paul at Corinth? One cannot be sure. As at the Areopagus, the best advice may be *caveat* pilgrim.

Similar problems arise in trying to place Paul or John in Ephesus, since Byzantine and medieval accounts have been overlayed on the biblical stories. Current excavations at Ephesus have revealed an elaborate Roman city of the second to sixth centuries C.E., but evidence of the first-century city remains sparse. Extensive excavations at Philippi, in Macedonia, have uncovered a second-century forum and main roadway, but most of the remains come from churches and basilicas dating from the fourth to the seventh centuries. Once again, the remains of Paul's day are difficult to identify.

In some cases, the connection of a site with Paul is demonstrably wrong. For example, Christian pilgrimage and devotion in Philippi helped to equate a Hellenistic pagan crypt with Paul's "prison," as described in chapter 16 of Acts. In the late fifth century, a basilica was built around this site. In short, the work of archaeologists should not be used to prove such New Testament stories. Instead, archaeological work should be used more as a "backdrop" for the discussion of Paul's letters to Christian congregations living in these cities of the Roman world. The focus of archaeology should be placing the Christians and Jews in a cultural context.

More recent archaeological perspectives shed light on the development of Jewish and Christian institutions of the New Testament world. Originally, "church" (the Greek *ekklesia*) and "synagogue" (the Greek *synagoge*) were synonymous terms for assembly or congregation. Especially in the earliest days of the Diaspora, Christian groups including gentile converts, were considered to be following a form of Jewish practice. Only in the second century would the terms "church" and "synagogue" begin to become specific to Christians and Jews. In fact, distinct architectural differences between them did not begin until the fourth century. In other words, if we were following Paul through Ephesus or Corinth, we would not be able to distinguish Christian or Jewish meeting places from the exteriors of the buildings.

Most of the congregations founded by Paul met in the houses of individual members. Significantly, Diaspora Jewish groups would have met in houses, too; but over time, more formal synagogue buildings appeared. If anything, house-synagogues were in use earlier in the Diaspora than in Palestine (as early as the first century B.C.E.). Of the six early Diaspora synagogues known from excavations—at Delos, Priene, Ostia, Dura-Europos, Stobi, and Sardis—five were originally houses that were renovated and adapted to special religious use. The earliest of these, from Delos, dates to the very beginning of the Common Era, or even slightly earlier.

There is evidence that Jews and Christians worshiped as neighbors in the Diaspora, as in Roman Palestine. One of the most impressive discoveries in this regard comes from Dura-Europos, a Roman garrison on the Euphrates River in what is now Iraq, dating to before 256 C.E. On one street was a house that had been renovated, in three stages, into a sanctuary of Mithras, a Persian god whose cult spread throughout the Roman empire from the second half of the first century C.E. onward. Farther down the same street, another house had been converted, in two stages, into a synagogue. Its assembly hall contained one of the earliest datable Torah niches, and on its walls were elaborate frescoes depicting stories from the Hebrew Scriptures. Farther down the same street was a house that was renovated to become a Christian church, with a small assembly hall and a room set aside for baptism. The baptistry room in particular has attracted considerable attention, since it contains some of the earliest clearly datable Christian art, including representations of Jesus in scenes from the Gospels.

More evidence of religious pluralism in the Diaspora can be seen in Rome. Excavations beneath several basilicas, such as those of St. Clement and SS. John and Paul, reveal earlier buildings—houses or apartment complexes—that were being renovated for religious use as early as the first century. The house-church of St. Clement, for example, is generally identified with the first-century levels below St. Clement's Basilica. Interestingly, the second-century house adjacent to the house-church of St. Clement was used as a Mithraic cult sanctuary. Seven such Mithraic halls are known from Rome, and another 14 from the nearby port of Ostia. In addition, inscriptions from Jewish catacombs suggest at least 11 synagogues existed in Rome during imperial times.

The complex society that sustained such pluralism is now the focus of much research. A new group of biblical archaeologists, using what they refer to as a "social history" approach, are attempting to bring biblical texts and archaeological evidence into a more cohesive historical framework. The basis of their work is the use of archaeological evidence not merely as proof or illustration but as a key to the historical and social context of religion. In the Hellenized Roman cities of Palestine, such as Sepphoris, and in major urban centers of the Diaspora, such as Corinth, the activities of Jews and Christians must be seen as part of a complex culture and viewed over several centuries of development.

The evidence suggests that Jews and Christians were able to live in much closer harmony with one another than has often been assumed.

For example, textual evidence shows the existence of a Jewish community at Sardis in Roman Lydia (western Turkey) since the time of Julius Caesar; however, the first significant archaeological evidence of its activities comes hundreds of years later with the renovation of a public hall, part of the bath-gymnasium complex, to serve as a synagogue. Thus we know that Jews and Christians were both in Sardis for a long time, but apparently with no distinctions by which we can recognize their daily activities. The synagogue was in use from the third century to the sixth century, and its size and opulence attest to the vitality of Jewish life in Sardis. The synagogue was renovated by Jews at least twice after its initial adaptation, and these renovations were extensive and costly. Moreover, its inscriptions give evidence of the social standing and connections of the Jewish community: a total of 12 known donors to the renovations are titled "citizen" or "city councillor," and in some cases both. Other notables, including several Roman bureaucrats, are also named in the roster of donors. Here the archaeological record yields a picture of a Jewish community, over several centuries, that was politically favored and socially "at home" in the civic life of Sardis. To understand the life of the Jews of Sardis, however, one must place them not only in the context of their city but also ask how their local conditions compare to other Jewish groups from the Diaspora.

This same social history approach may be applied to Christian groups as well. At stake are a number of traditional assumptions about Judaism and Christianity in relation to their social and religious environment. It would seem that Jews and Christians were able to live in much closer harmony both with one another and with their pagan neighbors than has often been assumed. To an outsider, both church and synagogue might have resembled foreign social clubs or household cults.

The mobility within the Diaspora produced cultural as well as theological diversity, even within the Jewish and Christian traditions. We should not assume that the Diaspora synagogue communities conformed to Talmudic Judaism. A good case in point is seen in recent archaeological evidence, especially from inscriptions, for active participation and even leadership by women in Diaspora synagogues—something also seen in the homeland. This could eventually shed light on the significant role of women in Paul's churches. To date, however, the main information comes from the New Testament writings, which give evidence of women as house-church patrons, as in Romans 16:2–5.

There are numerous ways in which Jews and Christians of the Diaspora were influenced by their cultural environment. Especially noteworthy are conventions of letter writing drawn from the analysis of papyri, which can enhance our understanding of the letters of Paul. Likewise, conventions of building or donation inscriptions offer a means of understanding many synagogue inscriptions, such as those at Sardis. Still more common are Jewish and Christian burial inscriptions.

Both in burial inscriptions and in funerary art one finds that the earliest Jews and Christians, when one can distinguish them at all, regularly used motifs and language common in the larger pagan environment.

Thus there is a wide array of new and old archaeological data available for students of Judaeo-Christian antiquity. Whether it comes from East or West, whether it is inscribed with letters or decorated with figural art, it constitutes the most significant body of evidence for reconstructing the cultural context in which Jews and early Christians lived.

Of all the human sciences, archaeology is best equipped to deal with such complex matters. When strongly tied to the literary and historical disciplines, it becomes the most reliable tool for reconstructing the ancient societies in which Judaism and Christianity, orphaned from Jerusalem, found new homes.

Reprinted with permission of *Archaeology Magazine,* Vol. 42, No. 2, March/April 1989, pp. 26-33. © 1989 by Archaeological Institute of America.

The Other Jesus

To Christians, he is the Son of God. But the world's other great religions have their own visions of a legendary figure.

By Kenneth L. Woodward

Christ is absolutely original and absolutely unique. If He were only a wise man like Socrates, if He were a prophet like Muhammad, if He were enlightened like the Buddha, without doubt He would not be what He is.
—John Paul II

EVER SINCE HIS ELECTION, JOHN PAUL II has wanted one thing: to walk where Jesus walked, preach where Jesus taught and pray where Jesus was crucified, died and was buried. This week the pope finally gets his chance. Weary in body but ecstatic in spirit, John Paul makes his long-anticipated pilgrimage to the Holy Land. For him it is a personal "journey with God"; there will be no intruding television cameras when, lost in prayer, he communes alone at Christianity's holiest shrines. But the land of his heart's desire is holy to Jews and Muslims as well. And so the pope will visit the Western Wall, Judaism's most sacred site, and the Mosque of El Aqsa atop the Temple Mount. He will also meet with Muslim and Jewish religious leaders and—in one particularly resonant moment—pause to pray at Yad Vashem, Israel's memorial to victims of the Holocaust.

Like his powerful plea for forgiveness a fortnight ago, the pope's trip is also an exercise in religious reconciliation. More than 90 times since he took office, John Paul has acknowledged past faults of the church and begged pardon from others—Muslims and Jews, as well as Protestant and Orthodox Christians—for sins committed in the name of Catholicism. Like the sound of one hand clapping, however, his efforts have brought few echoing responses. Now, at the high point of this jubilee year for the church, he comes to Jerusalem, the city of peace, hoping to erect bridges among the three monotheistic faiths.

There are, of course, important commonalities among these three religious traditions. All three believe in one God who has revealed his will through sacred Scriptures. They all look to an endtimes when God's justice and power will triumph. And they all recognize the figure of Abraham as a father in faith. What is often overlooked, however, is another figure common to the three traditions: Jesus of Nazareth.

The Christ of the Gospels is certainly the best-known Jesus in the world. For Christians, he is utterly unique—the only Son of God and, as the pope puts it, the one "mediator between God and humanity." But alongside this Jesus is another, the Jesus whom Muslims since Muhammad have regarded as a prophet and messenger of Allah. And after centuries of silence about Jesus, many Jews now find him a Jewish teacher and reformer they can accept on their own terms as "one of us."

Jesus has become a familiar, even beloved, figure to adherents of Asian religions as well. Among many contemporary Hindus, Jesus has come to be revered as a self-realized saint who reached the highest level of "God-consciousness." In recent years, Buddhists like the Dalai Lama have recognized in Jesus a figure of great compassion much like the Buddha. "I think as the world grows smaller, Jesus as a figure will grow larger," says Protestant theologian John Cobb, a veteran of interfaith dialogues.

Perhaps. Each of these traditions—Judaism, Islam, Buddhism and Hinduism—is rich in its own right, and each has its own integrity. As the pope calls for better understanding among the world's great religions, it is important to recognize that non-Christian faiths have their own visions of the sacred and their own views of Jesus.

JUDAISM

THAT JESUS WAS A JEW WOULD SEEM to be self-evident from Gospels. But before the first Christian century was out, faith in Jesus as universal Lord and Savior eclipsed his early identity as a Jewish prophet and wonder worker. For long stretches of Western history, Jesus was pictured as a Greek, a Roman, a Dutchman—even, in the Germany of the 1930s, as a blond and burly Aryan made in the image of Nazi anti-Semitism. But for most of Jewish history as well, Jesus was also a deracinated figure: he was *the* apostate, whose name a pious Jew should never utter.

Indeed, the lack of extra-Biblical evidence for the existence of Jesus has led more than one critic to conclude that he is a Christian fiction created by the early church. There were in fact a half dozen brief passages, later excised from Talmudic texts, that some scholars consider indirect references to Jesus. One alludes to a heresy trial of someone named Yeshu (Jesus) but none of them has any independent value for historians of Jesus. The only significant early text of real historical value is a short passage from Flavius Josephus, the first-century Jewish historian. Josephus describes Jesus as a "wise man," a "doer of startling deeds" and a "teacher" who was crucified and attracted a posthumous following called Christians. In short, argues Biblical scholar John P. Meier of Notre Dame, the historical Jesus was "a marginal Jew in a marginal province of the Roman Empire"—and thus unworthy of serious notice by contemporary Roman chroniclers.

Christian persecution of the Jews made dialogue about Jesus impossible in the Middle Ages. Jews were not inclined to contemplate the cross on the Crusaders' shields, nor did they enjoy the forced theological disputations Christians staged for Jewish conversions. To them, the Christian statues and pictures of Jesus represented the idol worship forbidden by the Torah. Some Jews did compile their own versions of a "History of Jesus" ("Toledoth Yeshu") as a parody of the Gospel story. In it, Jesus is depicted as a seduced Mary's bastard child who later gains magical powers and works sorcery. Eventually, he is hanged, his body hidden for three days and then discovered. It was subversive literature culled from the excised Talmudic texts. "Jews were impotent in force of arms," observes Rabbi Michael Meyer, a professor at Hebrew Union Seminary in Cincinnati, "so they reacted with words."

HIS ROOTS: Christian and Jewish scholars accept that much of what Jesus taught can be found in Jewish Scriptures, but Jews still see Christ as an 'admirable Jew,' not the Son of God

When skeptical scholars began to search for the "historical Jesus" behind the Gospel accounts in the 18th century, few Jewish intellectuals felt secure enough to join the quest. One who did was Abraham Geiger, a German rabbi and early exponent of the Reform Jewish movement. He saw that liberal Protestant intellectuals were anxious to get beyond the supernatural Christ of Christian dogma and find the enlightened teacher of morality hidden behind the Gospel texts. From his own research, Geiger concluded that what Jesus believed and taught was actually the Judaism of liberal Pharisees, an important first-century Jewish sect. "Geiger argued that Jesus was a reformist Pharisee whose teachings had been corrupted by his followers and mixed with pagan elements to produce the dogmas of Christianity," says Susannah Heschel, professor of Jewish studies at Dartmouth. Thus, far from being a unique religious genius—as

the liberal Protestants claimed—Geiger's Jesus was a democratizer of his own inherited tradition. It was, he argued, the Pharisees' opponents, the Saducees, who became the first Christians and produced the negative picture of the Pharisees as legalistic hypocrites found in the later Gospel texts. In sum, Geiger—and after him, other Jewish scholars—distinguished between the faith *of* Jesus, which they saw as liberal Judaism, and the faith *in* Jesus, which became Christianity.

The implications of this "Jewish Jesus" were obvious, and quickly put to polemical use. Jews who might be attracted by the figure of Jesus needn't convert to Christianity. Rather, they could find his real teachings faithfully recovered in the burgeoning Reform Jewish movement. Christians, on the other hand, could no longer claim that Jesus was a unique religious figure who inspired a new and universal religion. Indeed, if any religion could claim universality, it was monotheistic Judaism as the progenitor of both Christianity and Islam.

A MAN OF LOVE: Buddhists depersonalize the Jesus who walked this earth and transform him into a figure more like Buddha. Some regard him as a bodhisattva, a perfectly enlightened being who vows to help others

The Holocaust occasioned yet another way of imagining Jesus. If some Jews blamed Christians—or God himself—for allowing the ovens of Auschwitz, a few Jewish artists found a different way to deal with the horror of genocide: they applied the theme of the crucified Christ to the Nazis' Jewish victims. This is particularly evident in harrowing paintings of Marc Chagall, where the dying Jesus is marked by Jewish symbols. And in "Night," his haunting stories of the death camps, Elie Wiesel adopted the Crucifixion motif for his wrenching scene of three Jews hanged from a tree, like Jesus and the two thieves on Golgotha. The central figure is an innocent boy dangling in protracted agony because his body is too light to allow the noose its swift reprieve. When Wiesel hears a fellow inmate cry, "Where is God?" the author says to himself; "Here He is. He has been hanged here, on these gallows." "There's no lack of suffering in Judaism," says Alan Segal, professor of Jewish Studies at Barnard College and Columbia University, "and no reason why Jews shouldn't pick up an image central to Christianity."

Today, the Jewishness of Jesus is no longer a question among scholars. That much of what he taught can be found in the Jewish Scriptures is widely accepted by Christian as well as Jewish students of the Bible. At some seminaries, like Hebrew Union, a course in the New Testament is now required of rabbinical candidates. Outside scholarly circles, there is less focus on Jesus, and most Jews will never read the Christian Bible. And, of course, Jews do not accept the Christ of faith. "They see

SOURCES: CENTRAL BUREAU OF STATISTICS, ISRAEL;
NEWS REPORTS. RESEARCH BY FE CONWAY;
GRAPHIC BY KEVIN HAND/NEWSWEEK.

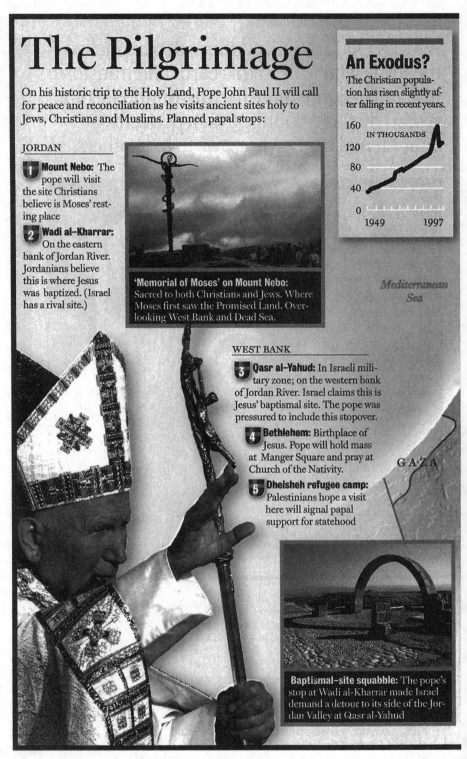

The Pilgrimage

On his historic trip to the Holy Land, Pope John Paul II will call for peace and reconciliation as he visits ancient sites holy to Jews, Christians and Muslims. Planned papal stops:

An Exodus?

The Christian population has risen slightly after falling in recent years.

IN THOUSANDS

160
120
80
40
0

1949   1997

JORDAN

1 Mount Nebo: The pope will visit the site Christians believe is Moses' resting place

2 Wadi al-Kharrar: On the eastern bank of Jordan River. Jordanians believe this is where Jesus was baptized. (Israel has a rival site.)

'Memorial of Moses' on Mount Nebo: Sacred to both Christians and Jews. Where Moses first saw the Promised Land. Overlooking West Bank and Dead Sea.

Mediterranean Sea

WEST BANK

3 Qasr al-Yahud: In Israeli military zone; on the western bank of Jordan River. Israel claims this is Jesus' baptismal site. The pope was pressured to include this stopover.

4 Bethlehem: Birthplace of Jesus. Pope will hold mass at Manger Square and pray at Church of the Nativity.

5 Dheisheh refugee camp: Palestinians hope a visit here will signal papal support for statehood

GAZA

Baptismal-site squabble: The pope's stop at Wadi al-Kharrar made Israel demand a detour to its side of the Jordan Valley at Qasr al-Yahud

Jesus as an admirable Jew," says theologian John Cobb, "but they don't believe that any Jew could be God."

ISLAM

AT THE ONSET OF RAMADAN LAST year, Vatican officials sent greetings to the world's Muslims, inviting them to reflect on Jesus as "a model and permanent message for humanity." But

for Muslims, the Prophet Muhammad is the perfect model for humankind and in the Qur'an (in Arabic only), they believe, the very Word of God dwells among us. Even so, Muslims recognize Jesus as a great prophet and revere him as Isa ibn Maryam—Jesus, the son of Mary, the only woman mentioned by name in the Qur'an. At a time when many Christians deny Jesus' birth to a virgin, Muslims find the story in the Qur'an and affirm that it is true. "It's a very strange situation, where Mus-

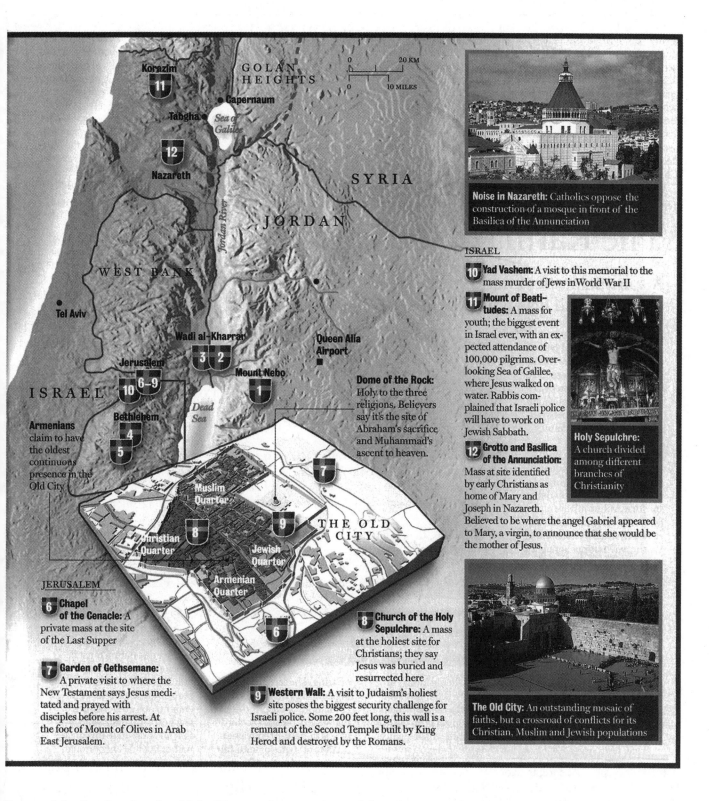

Noise in Nazareth: Catholics oppose the construction of a mosque in front of the Basilica of the Annunciation

ISRAEL

10 Yad Vashem: A visit to this memorial to the mass murder of Jews in World War II

11 Mount of Beatitudes: A mass for youth; the biggest event in Israel ever, with an expected attendance of 100,000 pilgrims. Overlooking Sea of Galilee, where Jesus walked on water. Rabbis complained that Israeli police will have to work on Jewish Sabbath.

12 Grotto and Basilica of the Annunciation: Mass at site identified by early Christians as home of Mary and Joseph in Nazareth. Believed to be where the angel Gabriel appeared to Mary, a virgin, to announce that she would be the mother of Jesus.

Holy Sepulchre: A church divided among different branches of Christianity

Dome of the Rock: Holy to the three religions. Believers say it's the site of Abraham's sacrifice and Muhammad's ascent to heaven.

Armenians claim to have the oldest continuous presence in the Old City

JERUSALEM

6 Chapel of the Cenacle: A private mass at the site of the Last Supper

7 Garden of Gethsemane: A private visit to where the New Testament says Jesus meditated and prayed with disciples before his arrest. At the foot of Mount of Olives in Arab East Jerusalem.

8 Church of the Holy Sepulchre: A mass at the holiest site for Christians; they say Jesus was buried and resurrected here

9 Western Wall: A visit to Judaism's holiest site poses the biggest security challenge for Israeli police. Some 200 feet long, this wall is a remnant of the Second Temple built by King Herod and destroyed by the Romans.

The Old City: An outstanding mosaic of faiths, but a crossroad of conflicts for its Christian, Muslim and Jewish populations

lims are defending the miraculous birth of Jesus against western deniers," says Seyyed Hossein Nasr, professor of Islamic studies at George Washington University. "Many Westerners also do not believe that Jesus ascended into heaven. Muslims do." Indeed, many Muslims see themselves as Christ's true followers.

What Muslims believe about Jesus comes from the Qur'an—not the New Testament, which they consider tainted by human error. They also draw upon their own oral traditions, called *ha-dith*, and on experts' commentaries. In these sources, Jesus is born of Mary under a palm tree by a direct act of God. From the cradle, the infant Jesus announces that he is God's prophet, though not God's son, since Allah is "above having a son" according to the Qur'an.

Nonetheless, the Muslim Jesus enjoys unique spiritual prerogatives that other prophets, including Muhammad, lack. Only Jesus and his mother were born untouched by Satan. Even Mu-

A Rabbi Argues With Jesus

A noted Talmudic scholar insists that Jews must remain faithful to the words of the Torah.

BY JACOB NEUSNER

Imagine walking on a dusty road in Galilee nearly 2,000 years ago and meeting up with a small band of youngsters, led by a young man. The leader's presence catches your attention: he talks, the others listen, respond, argue, obey—care what he says, follow him. You don't know who the man is, but you know he makes a difference to the people with him and to nearly everyone he meets. People respond, some with anger, some with admiration, a few with genuine faith. But no one walks away uninterested in the man and the things he says and does.

I can see myself meeting this man, and, with courtesy, arguing with him. It is my form of respect, the only compliment I crave from others, the only serious tribute I pay to the people I take seriously. I can see myself not only meeting and arguing with Jesus, challenging him on the basis of our shared Torah, the Scriptures Christians would later adopt as the "Old Testament." I can also imagine myself saying, "Friend, you go your way, I'll go mine, I wish you well—without me. Yours is not the Torah of Moses, and all I have from God, and all I ever need from God, is that one Torah of Moses."

We would meet, we would argue, we would part friends—but we would part, He would have gone his way, to Jerusalem and the place he believed God had prepared for him; I would have gone my way, home to my wife and my children, my dog and my garden. He would have gone his way to glory, I my way to my duties and my responsibilities.

Why? Because the Torah teaches that the kingdom that matters is not in heaven, but the one we find ourselves in now: sustaining life, sanctifying life, in the here and the now of home and family, community and society. God's kingdom is in the humble details of what I eat for breakfast and how I love my neighbor.

Can the Kingdom of God come soon, in our day, to where we are? The Torah not only says yes, it shows how. Do I have then to wait for God's Kingdom? Of course I have to wait. But while waiting, there are things I have to do. Jesus demanded that to enter this Kingdom of Heaven I repudiate family and turn my back on home: "Sell all you have and follow me." That is not what the Torah says.

On Sinai Moses told how to organize a kingdom of priests and a holy people, conduct workday affairs, love God—how to build God's kingdom, accepting the yoke of God's commandments. As a faithful Jew, what I do is simply reaffirm the Torah of Sinai over and against the teachings of Jesus. Moses would expect no less of us. So when I say, if I heard those words, I would have offered an argument, my dispute would have been with a mortal man walking among us and talking with us. Only the Torah is the word of God.

I think Christianity, beginning with Jesus, took a wrong turn in abandoning the Torah. By the truth of the Torah, much that Jesus said is wrong. By the criterion of the Torah, Israel's religion in the time of Jesus was authentic and faithful, not requiring reform or renewal, demanding only faith and loyalty to God and the sanctification of life through carrying out God's will. Jesus and his disciples took one path, and we another. I do not believe God would want it any other way.

NEUSNER *has just been named research professor of religion and theology at Bard College. He is the author of "A Rabbi Talks With Jesus."*

---

hammad had to be purified by angels before receiving prophethood. Again, in the Qur'an Muhammad is not presented as a miracle worker, but Jesus miraculously heals the blind, cures lepers and "brings forth the dead by [Allah's] leave." In this way Jesus manifests himself as the Messiah, or "the anointed one." Muslims are not supposed to pray to anyone but Allah. But in popular devotions many ask Jesus or Mary or John the Baptist for favors. (According to one recent estimate, visions of Jesus or Mary have occurred some 70 times in Muslim countries since 1985.)

Although Muhammad supersedes Jesus as the last and greatest of the prophets, he still must die. But in the Qur'an, Jesus does not die, nor is he resurrected. Muslims believe that Jesus asked God to save him from crucifixion, as the Gospels record, and that God answered his prayer by taking him directly up to heaven. "God would not allow one of his prophets to be killed," says Martin Palmer, director of the International Con-

sultancy on Religion, Education and Culture in Manchester, England. "If Jesus had been crucified, it would have meant that God had failed his prophet."

A VIRTUOUS MAN: Many Hindus are drawn to Jesus because of his compassion and his devotion to nonviolence, but they find the notion of a single god unnecessarily restrictive.

When the end of the world approaches, Muslims believe that Jesus will descend to defeat the antichrist—and, incidentally, to set the record straight. His presence will prove the Crucifixion

The Karma of the Gospel

A spiritual leader finds connections between Christian teachings and his own traditions.

BY THE DALAI LAMA

As a buddhist, my attitude toward Jesus Christ is that he was either a fully enlightened being, or a bodhisattva of a very high spiritual realization. I see common notes between Buddhism and Christianity. Here are a few:

Transfiguration. In Buddhism, when an individual practitioner reaches a high degree of realization in his or her spiritual evolution, the transformation can manifest itself at the physical level, as well. We find such stories about the Buddha in the sutras. They begin when Buddha's disciples notice a physical change in his appearance. A radiance shines from his body. Then one of the disciples asks the Buddha, "I see these changes in you. Why are these changes taking place?" These parables are similar to the Gospel passages on the Transfiguration when Jesus' face is suddenly glowing.

Karma. In another Gospel passage, Jesus says: "I have not come to judge the world but to save it.… The word I have spoken will be his judge on the last day." I feel this closely reflects the Buddhist idea of karma. There is not an autonomous being (God) "out there" who arbitrates what you should experience and what you should know; instead, there is the truth contained in the casual principle itself. If you act in an ethical way, desirable consequences will result; if you act in a negative way, then you must face the consequences of that action as well.

Faith. In the Buddhist tradition, we speak of three different types of faith. The first is faith in the form of admiration that you have toward a particular person or a particular state of being. The second is aspiring faith. There is a sense of emulation: you aspire to attain that state of being. The third type is the faith of conviction.

All three types of faith can be explained in the Christian context as well. A practicing Christian can have a very strong devotion to and admiration for Jesus by reading the Gospel. That is the first level of faith, the faith of admiration and devotion. After that, as you strengthen your admiration and faith, it is possible to progress to the second level, which is the faith of aspiration. In the Buddhist tradition, you would aspire to Buddhahood. In the Christian context you may not use the same language, but you can say that you aspire to attain the full perfection of the divine nature, or union with God. Then, once you have developed that sense of aspiration, you can develop the third level of faith, a deep conviction that it is possible to perfect such a state of being.

Empathy. One of the grounds on which the presence of Buddha-nature in all people is argued is the human capacity for empathy. Some people may have a stronger force, others less; but all of us share this natural capacity to empathize. This Buddha-nature, this seed of enlightenment, of perfection, is inherent in all of us. To attain perfection, however, it is not enough that a spiritual practitioner merely possess such a nature; this nature must be developed to its fullest potential. In Buddhist practice, you require the assistance of an enlightened guide, a guru or teacher. Christians believe that all of us share this divine nature but it is only through Jesus that one perfects it. Through Jesus it comes into full bloom and becomes unified, one, with the Father.

THE DALAI LAMA *is the author of "The Good Heart"* (Wisdom Publications, Boston), *from which this is excerpted.*

was a myth and eventually he will die a natural death. "Jesus will return as a Muslim," says Nasr, "in the sense that he will unite all believers in total submission to the one God."

HINDUISM

THE GOSPELS ARE SILENT ABOUT the life of Jesus between his boyhood visit to the Jerusalem Temple with his parents, and the beginning of his public ministry at the age of 30. But in India there is a strong tradition that the teenage Jesus slipped away from his parents, journeyed across Southeast Asia learning yogic meditation and returned home to become a guru to the Jews. This legend reveals just how easily Hinduism absorbs any figure whom others worship as divine. To Hindus, India is the Holy Land, its sacred mountains and rivers enlivened by more than 300,000 local deities. It is only natural, then, that Jesus would come to India to learn the secrets of unlocking his own inherent divinity.

As Gandhi was, many Hindus are drawn to the figure of Jesus by his compassion and nonviolence—virtues taught in their own sacred Scriptures. But also like Gandhi, Hindus find the notion of a single god unnecessarily restrictive. In their perspective, all human beings are sons of God with the innate ability to become divine themselves. Those Hindus who read the Gospels are drawn to the passage in John in which Jesus proclaims that "the Father and I are one." This confirms the basic Hindu belief that everyone is capable through rigorous spiritual practice of realizing his or her own universal "god-consciousness." The great modern Hindu saint Ramakrishna recorded that he meditated on a picture of the Madonna with child and was transported into a state of *samadhi*, a consciousness in which the divine is all that really exists. For that kind of spiritual experience, appeal to any god will do. "Christ-consciousness, God-consciousness, Krishna-consciousness, Buddha-consciousness—it's all the same thing," says Deepak Chopra, an Indian popularizer of Hindu philosophy for New Age Westerners. "Rather than 'love thy neighbor,' this consciousness says, 'You and I are the same beings.'"

BUDDHISM

THE LIFE STORIES OF JESUS AND THE Buddha are strikingly similar. Both are conceived without sexual intercourse and born to chaste women. Both leave home for the wilderness where each is tempted by a Satan figure. Both return enlightened, work miracles and challenge the religious establishment by their teachings. Both attract disciples and both are betrayed by one of them. Both preach compassion, unselfishness and altruism and each creates a movement that bears the founder's name. Thich Nhat Hanh, a Vietnamese Zen Buddhist monk with a large Western following, sees Jesus and Buddha as "brothers" who taught that the highest form of human understanding is "universal love." But there is at least one unbridgeable difference: a Christian can never become Christ, while the aim of every serious Buddhist is to achieve Buddhahood himself.

Thus when Buddhists encounter Christianity they depersonalize the Jesus who walked this earth and transform him into a figure more like Buddha. "Buddhists can think of Jesus Christ as an emanation or 'truth body' [*dharmakaya*] of the Buddha," says Buddhist scholar Robert Thurman of Columbia University. For Tibetan Buddhists, Jesus strongly resembles a bodhisattva—a perfectly enlightened being who vows to help others attain enlightenment. But to reconfigure Jesus as a Buddhist is to turn him into something he was not. Jesus, after all, believed in God, the creator and sustainer of the universe, which Buddhists do not. He believed in sin, which is not a Buddhist concept. Jesus did not teach compassion as a way of removing bad karma, nor did he see life as a cycle of death and rebirth. In short, says the Dalai Lama, trying to meld Jesus into Buddha "is like putting a yak's head on a sheep's body." It doesn't work.

Indeed, nothing shows the difference between the Jesus and the Buddha better than the way that each died. The Buddha's death was serene and controlled—a calm passing out of his final rebirth, like the extinction of a flame. Jesus, on the other hand, suffers an agonizing death on the cross, abandoned by God but obedient to his will.

A TRUE SAVIOR: The Christ of the Gospel is the best-known Jesus in the world. For Christians, he is unique— the only son of God.

Clearly, the cross is what separates the Christ of Christianity from every other Jesus. In Judaism there is no precedent for a Messiah who dies, much less as a criminal as Jesus did. In Islam, the story of Jesus' death is rejected as an affront to Allah himself. Hindus can accept only a Jesus who passes into peaceful samadhi, a yogi who escapes the degradation of death. The figure of the crucified Christ, says Buddhist Thich Nhat Hanh, "is a very painful image to me. It does not contain joy or peace, and this does not do justice to Jesus." There is, in short, no room in other religions for a Christ who experiences the full burden of mortal existence—and hence there is no reason to believe in him as the divine Son whom the Father resurrects from the dead.

Even so, there are lessons all believers can savor by observing Jesus in the mirrors of Jews and Muslims, Hindus and Buddhists. That the image of a benign Jesus has universal appeal should come as no surprise. That most of the world cannot accept the Jesus of the cross should not surprise, either. Thus the idea that Jesus can serve as a bridge uniting the world's religions is inviting but may be ultimately impossible. A mystery to Christians themselves, Jesus remains what he has always been, a sign of contradiction.

With ANNE UNDERWOOD *and* HEATHER WON TESORIERO

Ecstasy in Late Imperial Rome

Dirk Bennett describes the crowded religious calendar of pagan Rome, and the spiritual market place in which Christianity had to fight for domination.

The sacred cry strikes to heaven with the praises of the eternal Lord and the pinnacle of the Capitol totters with the shock. The neglected images in the empty temples tremble when struck by the pious voices, and are overthrown by the name of Christ. Terrified demons abandon their deserted shrines. The envious serpent pale with rage struggles in vain, his lips blood-stained, bemoaning with his hungry throat the redemption of man, and at the same time now, with unavailing groans, the predator writhes around his dry altars cheated of the blood of sacrificial cattle....

(Paulinus of Nola)

This is Rome in the fourth century after Christ. The Church Fathers unanimously drew a picture of an overwhelming triumph of their creed. According to them, with the conversion of Constantine in AD 312 the old and tired heathen religions gave way to a youthful new belief. Victories of Roman emperors were now interpreted as victories of God; the history of mankind equalled the history of His church. They argued that the old gods could not prevent the defeats, plagues and misfortunes of the past and present, and only since the arrival of Jesus Christ had the Empire achieved its vocation: to spread the true faith all over the world.

Contemporaries, though, saw the situation differently. A closer look at these statements reveals them to be wishful thinking and propaganda: pagan culture still had a huge following. Mid-fourth-century Rome had a colourful mix of religions. Christians, Jews, Manichaeans, Neoplatonists, followers of the old gods, of the Great Mother, of Bacchus and of hundreds of domestic gods taken from the conquered nations all populated the city.

Their brotherhoods, chapels, temples, shrines and sanctuaries spread all over the city and their festivals and celebrations added to the Roman year. Of these, the so-called calendar of Filocalus for the year 354 has survived and lists no less than 177 official holy days for a seemingly endless variety of gods and goddesses. Not one Christian celebration is to be found among them.

The highest festival of ancient origin was the Great Roman Games. The pinnacle of the celebrations, which stretched over several days, was September 13th, according to tradition the day the foundations had first been laid for the great temple of Jupiter on the Capitoline Hill. No expense was spared when the highest god of the community was celebrated, together with his wife and daughter, Juno and Minerva. Statues of all three of them were to be found inside the temple. Around the main event there were days of *epulones* (festive meals for the gods), huge processions along the Via Sacra,

markets and, of course, the games in the Circus Maximus.

A special priesthood, appointed for the occasion, prepared the *epulones*. They purified and adorned the statues, prepared rooms and the sacred meal itself. This was shared between a select group of deserving members of society and the gods, who were symbolised by the statues lying on beds. Similar meals were held all over town on a smaller scale by Roman families.

The Plebeian Games also took place, in honour of the gods Ceres, Flora and Apollo. These festivities, as the celebrated deities show, were closely connected to the peasant origins of the town. The most ancient brotherhoods—the Pontifices, the Sacerdotes, the Flamines, Auguri, Vestal Virgins, Epulones, the Salii, the Arval and Luperci—wearing their traditional robes, processed through town to their temples. Each of these offices followed their own specific and often strict codes. The high priest of Jupiter, for example, the *Flamen Dialis* or 'Divine Flame', was forbidden to touch horses, goats, dogs or meat, dead or alive. Ivy, beans, wheat and bread were prohibited. He was not allowed to have any knot tied on him or cut his nails and hair with an iron knife. By the fourth century, these ancient rituals and instructions had lost their meaning to the people and even to the priests themselves.

The 'Divine Flame' was present at another ancient ritual, again connected to the town's rural origins: the Lupercal. Its

Demeter

celebration is documented up to the late fifth century when Pope Gelasius protested against it. On February 15th, at the Lupercal—the cave where according to legend the she-wolf had fed Romulus and Remus—a number of male goats were sacrificed. A priest then touched the foreheads of two young noblemen with the bloody knife. The blood was then wiped away with a lump of wool soaked in milk, the two young men would laugh out loud and, wrapped in the fur of the killed animals, would start a boisterous race around the borders of the ancient town. On their way they lashed bystanders, especially young women, with whips made from the skin of the goats.

Many other ancient holidays survived, including April 21st, official birthday of the city of Rome, 'Eternal City' of the pagan world, as well as countless birthdays of the domestic and state gods. On February 2nd, there was Hercules; on March 1st, Mars; April 3rd, Quirinus; April 8th, the divine twins and protectors of the town, Castor and Pollux; in August, Salus, Sol and Luna (the goddesses of public wealth, the sun and the moon). Other days were reserved for Fortuna, Persephone, Hermes, the Penates, Diana and others.

Former emperors and empresses were considered gods, and membership of their priesthoods was highly sought after. The duties of the Augustales priesthood included the observance of the birth- and death-dates of the former heads of state. In the fourth century these alone amounted to no fewer than ninety-eight days a year.

The celebration of all these cults reflected the ancient polytheistic attitude towards religion, in which sacrificing on one altar did not exclude the believer from prayer at another. Tomb inscriptions of Roman magistrates show how many sacred offices and priesthoods could be taken on:

To the Divine Shades, Vettius Agorius Praetextatus, Augur, Priest of Vesta, Priest of the Sun, Member of the Fifteen, Curial of Hercules, Consecrated to Liber and the deities of Eleusis, Hierophant, Super-

intendent Minister, initiated by the bull's blood Father of Fathers....

Some historians have called late antiquity the age of spirituality, a time when many believers tried to get to the core of things and gain deeper understanding of the meaning of life. In contemporary opinion, there was more than one way of achieving this. Symmachus, probably the most famous exponent of paganism of his time, expressed it thus:

It is reasonable that all the different gods we worship should be thought of as one. We see the same stars, share the same sky, the same earth surrounds us: what does it matter what scheme of thought a man uses in his search for the truth? Man cannot come to so profound a mystery by one road alone....

The idea is typical for the fourth century, but it also corresponded with a practical and very Roman view of religion. The relations between gods and humans resembled a contract in which both sides had to fulfil certain 'mutually agreed' conditions. The gods' entitled rites and instructions had to be thoroughly observed, and they, in return, were expected to provide health and wealth to the people. It therefore followed logically that the more gods you attended, the more goods you would have. As head of state and the human most responsible for mankind playing its part, the emperor had the important role of supervising all cults and religions as a supreme priest, or Pontifex Maximus.

In a frenzy the most faithful castrated themselves, an act which entitled them to enter the priesthood

The mystery religions have over the centuries aroused the interest of academics and the public alike. Arguably, the cult which has attracted the most atten-

tion is that of Demeter—the Great Mother of Earth, also known as Magna Mater and Kybele—and her lover Attis. Soldiers on campaign in the east in the second century BC had first been initiated into the cult's rites and brought it back to Rome. It soon raised the eyebrows of the senatorial elite, for whom its novel ceremonies presented a serious threat to the Roman way of life, undermining the state. It was declared illegal but was re-established under the emperors, and proved to be one of the firmest and most successful religious communities in and beyond the capital.

The highest ceremonies, in March of each year, described the story of the love between Demeter and Attis, his death and resurrection. The main celebrations began on March 22nd. A freshly cut pine tree was solemnly taken into the temple of Demeter on the Capitoline Hill, where it was adorned with ribbons and pennants under prayers and cantations. Violets symbolised the blood shed by the young god, when he committed suicide under the tree. Then a portrait of Attis himself was attached to the trunk. The following day was dedicated to the preparation of the faithful. We read about festive music, trumpets and prayers. The third day was the 'Day of Blood'. The high priest, or Archigallus, cut his arm with a knife and shed his own blood over the tree, followed by the other priests. They then led the whole community in an ecstatic procession of wild dances and flagellation through the streets. In a frenzy the most faithful few, the so-called *fanatici*, even castrated themselves, an act which entitled them to enter the priesthood. The procession ended in tears and sorrow, the community mourning the death of the god and burying his effigy as a symbol of their grief.

Firmicus Maternus, a Christian author, described what happened next:

One night an image is laid face upwards on a couch and lamented with tears and rhythmic chants. Then, when they have glutted themselves with fake mourning, the light is brought in. The throats of all who have lamented are then anointed by the priest and, after the anointing, the priest whispers these words in a soft murmur: 'Take courage, initiates of the mystery of a god now saved. For you will come salvation from suffering.'

The joy and elation about salvation expressed itself in the celebrations extended over the 'Day of Jubilation'. After that, a day of recuperation, fasting and contemplation was necessary. On the 27th, the statue of the goddess was taken out of the temple and put on an ox-drawn cart. Down the steep streets of Capitol Hill it went, through the town to a little river, the Almo, nearby, where the effigy, together with the cart and instruments of worship, were solemnly dropped into the stream and purified. Now, finally, everything was taken back to the temple under heaps of flowers in preparation for the reappearance of the young god.

But these lavish public rituals were but one aspect of the cult, displayed only once a year. There were numerous smaller events like fasts, sacred meals and a peculiar baptising ceremony, the details of which particularly incensed Christian onlookers:

A trench is dug, and the high priest plunges deep underground to be sanctified. He wears a curious headband, fastens fillets for the occasion around his temples, fixes his hair with a crown of gold, holds up his robes of silk with a belt from Gabii. Over his head they lay a plank-platform criss-cross, fixed so that the wood is open not solid; then they cut or bore through the floor and make holes in the wood with an awl at several points till it is plentifully perforated with small openings. A large bull, with grim, shaggy features and garlands of flowers round his neck or entangling his horns, is escorted to the spot. The victim's head is shimmering with gold and the sheen of the goldleafs lends colour to his hair. The animal destined for sacrifice is at the appointed place. They consecrate a spear and with it pierce his breast.... (Prudentius)

The Egyptian cult of Isis was another highly influential community in Rome. The sources quote two main events in the 'Church of Isis': The *'Navigium Isidis'* (or 'Vessel of Isis') and 'Isia'. The first, on March 5th, officially opened the shipping season and consisted of a colourful procession to the harbour. The main ceremonies, however, took place between October 28th and November 3rd, and also described a love story, on this occasion between Isis and her brother Osiris. The latter is killed by his envious brother, Seth, and, after a long and adventurous search, resurrected by his sister.

The symbol of Isis, a golden calf in a black veil, was paraded through the streets of Rome. The procession recreated Isis's search for her vanished husband and brother Osiris, with key figures represented: the soldier, the fisherman, the hunter, the gladiator, the civil servant, the philosopher and the woman. Female worshippers sprinkled perfume, incense and flowers, others carried the toiletries of the goddess, combs and polished mirrors. Singers and torchbearers followed. Only linen and cotton clothes were permitted. The women were veiled, while the heads of the men were shaved. Then came the priests:

First of all is the singer... and after him follows the watcher of the hours; he holds in his hands a clock and palm branch as the symbols of astrology.... Then the divine writer appears; he wears a feather on his head and in his hands a book and a basket, in which there is an inkwell and a magic wand.... After that comes the steward; he carries the hand of justice and a pitcher for libation.... And at last appears the speaker of the words of god and he holds, visible for all, the water pitcher in his lap; he is followed by the men, who carry the bread to be distributed.... (Clemens of Alexandria)

Many early Christian churches were built over caves dedicated to a highly secretive and, quite literally, underground cult: that of Mithras. However, they succeeded only partially in suppressing the

evidence of this thriving community. Numerous inscriptions, altar stones and statues to the cult survive. The cult differed from other mystery religions from the East in one aspect above all. Only men were allowed into the community. Not surprisingly, its biggest following was with the army. In military outposts all over the empire its symbols and caves can be found.

There were seven grades of initiation to the cult of Mithras: raven, bridegroom, soldier, lion, Persian, heliodrome and the father, each standing under the protection of a particular planet and god. Most of the strange symbols that adorn the caves are now meaningless to us and we know little about the mythology. The caves seem to symbolise both the world and the birthplace of the saviour god Mithras.

Underground chapels have been found under the Piazza Navicella, the San Stefano Rotondo and elsewhere. These rooms were small, and only rarely offered space for more than thirty or forty of the faithful. They were furnished with statues of the planet gods, among them Chronos, the lionheaded, half-human half-animal, guardian of time, a snake winding around his body. The ancient scriptures mention atmospheric illuminations, which seems appropriate for a god connected with sun and fire, and is supported by archaeological findings. The grottoes are full of light shafts, openings and hidden niches for lamps or candles. There were benches along the walls for the worshippers and mosaics on the floor depicting the 'Mithras ladder', the climb from one grade to another. Everything was concentrated towards one end of the room where the statue of Mithras stood flanked by his helpers Cautes and Cautophates, sunrise and sunset, slaying the bull and bringing salvation to the world. Reliefs surround the central scene, telling the legend of the god. One Christian author describes a baptism:

Some flap their wings and imitate the cry of a raven, while others roar like lions. Some have their hands bound with fowls' entrails and water is spilled over them, while someone appears with a sword, cuts the ties and calls himself 'the saviour'... (Ps. Augustinus)

How did Christianity overthrow these ancient cults? Some historians have pointed to the organisation of the church, and others to Christian intolerance, which proved an effective weapon against the pagan cults. Its consistent ideology might also have played a part. Opportunism on the part of the emperors is another well-known explanation. The Roman emperors recognised and made use of the unifying potential of Christianity throughout the Empire. A decisive point was reached in AD 392 when Theodosius officially banned the practising of pagan ceremonies.

However, without question, the success of Christianity could not have occurred to such an extent if it had not held huge appeal to the masses in its own right. Perhaps the 'age of spiritualism' had tired of the old beliefs, which contained no notion of an afterlife. Mystery religions were one step closer, but it is doubtful whether their promises and visions were truly focused on the afterlife. They were also aimed at elite societies with no interest in converting the masses or bringing wider salvation.

The genuine appeal of Christianity to people in the fourth century cannot be underestimated. However, it faced a real threat from two very different quarters: from Manichaeism (or Gnosticism) and from the heretic sects. The first resembled Christianity at first glance and offered a seemingly more consistent and logical ideology. The second introduced life-threatening division into the Christian community.

The Manichaean church had an elaborate organisation, and a message which pointed to salvation in the afterlife. Many who later became Christian dignitaries began their religious life as Manichaeans, including St Augustine. Their ascetic priests spread the word of their founder Mani far and wide.

According to Mani, the world was divided between the principles of good and evil linked in a cosmic, predestined battle. For mankind there was no escape and no free will, like angels, demons, gods and prophets—Jesus being one of them—they were participants, messengers or helpers in a war which ultimately would lead to salvation.

In the end, however, this dark and unworldly vision could not match the positive message proclaimed by the great Christian scholars, who from the fourth century sought and gained the initiative. Manichaeism ultimately turned back to its roots in the East. In the years following the Council of Nicaea in 325, the Christian church faced heated arguments between different factions about the nature of Jesus. Splinter groups had their own variations in teaching and ritual—the Judaeo-Christians, Novatians, Paulianists and many more. But so strong was its message, the Christian creed still triumphed.

What happened to the rich world of ancient paganism, to its rituals, symbols, instruments, holy days and holy places? Certainly, paganism survived until long after the fall of the Western Empire to the barbarian king Odoacer in 476. The frequent repetition of laws and numerous complaints from bishops and popes against pagan practices show that it was still very much alive until late into the sixth century.

The Christian church took over many pagan elements, transformed and made them into their own. Even statues like that of Demeter with the small Dionysus were reinterpreted as Mary and Jesus. Pagan ceremonies were transformed into Christian holy days, best known of which is Christmas which replaced the birthday celebrations for the sun god. Incense found its way into Christian liturgy. Symbols like the crescent moon of Isis became a symbol for the Virgin Mary, while Christian churches were erected on the sites of, or sometimes even built into, pagan temples. Priestly robes still resemble their pagan predecessors—especially the papal costume with its extensive use of the imperial purple which directly emphasised the role of its hearer as the new Pontifex Maximus.

FOR FURTHER READING

J. Ferguson, *Greek and Roman Religion. A Sourcebook* (Noyes Classical Studies, 1982); M. R. Salzmann, *On Roman Time, The Codex Calendar of 354 and the Rythms of Urban Life in Late Antiquity* (University of California Press, 1990); B. Cook & J. Harris, *Religious Conflict in 4th Century Rome* (Sydney University Press, 1982); R. Turcan, *The Cults of the Roman Empire* (Oxford University Press, 1996). W. Burkert, *Ancient Mystery Cults* (Cambridge/Mass., London 1987).

Dick Bennett studied ancient history and archaeology at Regensburg University

---

This article first appeared in *History Today*, October 1998, pp. 27-32. © 1998 by History Today, Ltd. Reprinted by permission.

Who the Devil Is the Devil?

BY ROBERT WERNICK

WITH THE RAPID APPROACH of the third millennium, many people can't help wondering what role the Devil will be playing in it. But a cursory examination of the mainstream press of America reveals almost no mention of him, and even using the Internet services that promise to keep track of everything, it's much easier to find information on Monica Lewinsky than on the Devil.

What a humiliating comedown for one the mere mention of whose name was once enough to make the hair of kings stand up in terror; of whom Saint Augustine said, "The human race is the Devil's fruit tree, his own property, from which he may pick his fruit."

To appreciate the full extent of that downfall, try to put yourself someplace in Western Europe in the year 999, as the second millennium was about to bow in.

In the tenth century and for at least half a millennium thereafter, the Devil was everywhere. He leered out of every church door, he capered through castle and church and cottage, and his plots and pranks and temptings of humans were spelled out in sermons, on the stage, in paintings, in pious books, and in stories told in taverns or in homes at bedtime.

No corner or cranny of daily life escaped him. He lurked outside every orifice of the human body, waiting for the chance to get at the human soul inside—one reason why to this day we say "God bless you" when we hear someone sneeze.

The Devil fathered children on sleeping women, he stirred up conspiracies and treasons, he led travelers astray. He caused boils, plagues, tempests, shipwrecks, heresies, barbarian invasions. Whatever he did, his name was on everyone's tongue, and he went by many names: Satan, Lucifer, Beelzebub, Belial, Mastema, the Prince of Darkness, the Lord of Lies. In the Bible he was the Accuser, the Evil One, the Prince of this World.

This suave, sardonic Devil is actually a new kid on the block.

Today, a few scant hundred years later, he has dropped so far out of sight that some believe he is gone for good. It may be true that 48 percent of Americans tell the pollsters they believe in the existence of the Devil and another 20 percent find his existence probable. But though they use him often enough in common lighthearted expressions (give the devil his due, the devil is in the details) and in the privacy of their hearts may put the blame on him when they covet their neighbor's wife or cheat on their income tax, they do very little talking about him

out loud. Reported physical appearances of the Devil are far rarer than sightings of UFOs. In practical terms, people have banished him from public life.

Yet most everyone who discusses moral standards in pulpits or on television talk shows or in the *New York Times* is agreed that morals are lower than ever before. The Devil should be out in the streets and on the airwaves, roaring like a lion about his triumphs. Where has he gone? It all depends on precisely what you mean by "the Devil."

Theologians have been arguing for centuries (and sometimes have gone to the stake for expressing the wrong opinion) to achieve a satisfactory definition. But today the average person with no theological axe to grind is apt to envisage the Devil as a sleek, dark-complexioned male figure, with black chin-whiskers, little horns and cloven hooves, perhaps with a foxy glint in his eye and a trace of a foreign accent, but on the whole handsome, worldly-wise, a persuasive talker, a friendly sort of customer. He may tell you anything, try to talk you into something too good to be true. Only later, when you've taken that risky bet or signed the shady contract, and he comes to collect his due, do you realize you have signed away your immortal soul. He is unquestionably the Lord of Lies.

This suave, sardonic Devil is actually a new kid on the block; he has been around for barely a few hundred years, a mere stutter in the long swell of human misery and woe. And the Devil in general, the Devil with a capital *D*, as opposed to the legions of lowercase devils, demons, imps, satyrs, fiends and so on, first entered human history less than 3,000 years ago.

But humans indistinguishable from us have been around for many thousands of years, and it seems fair to assume that from the very beginning they were all aware of unseen powerful presences affecting their lives and everything around them. Every ancient religion that we know of, as well as many modern religions with hundreds of millions of followers, perceives a bewildering array of such spirits: gods, demigods, angels, devils, demons, sprites, imps, goblins, ghosts, fairies, fauns, nymphs, jinns, poltergeists. Some of them are benevolent, some are malignant, though most of them alternate between the two extremes. The gods of ancient Greece are typical: Zeus was a wise ruler up on Mount Olympus, but he became a serial rapist when he came down to the lowlands; Persephone was goddess of life in spring and goddess of death in autumn. None of these ancient religions ever developed a single Devil concentrating all the essence of evil, any more than they ever concentrated the essence of good in a single God.

The Old Testament, which was composed between the tenth and third centuries B.C., has little trace of the Devil with a capital *D*, and in its earlier books, none at all. God, speaking through the mouth of the prophet Isaiah, says, "I form the light and create darkness, I make peace and create evil, I the LORD do all these things." The serpent who tempted Adam and Eve in the Garden of Eden was later identified by Jewish rabbis and Christian church fathers with the Devil, the principle of Evil; but in the third chapter of Genesis as written, he is only a snake. It took another few hundred years before both snake and Devil were identified with Lucifer ("light-bearer," the Latin translation of the Hebrew and Greek words for the morning star, the planet Venus) who in Isaiah is thrown down from Heaven for having presumed to set his throne high above the stars of God.

Ancient Hebrew had a noun, *satan*, meaning "obstructor" or "accuser," and several satans appear in the Old Testament being sent by God on different errands, such as blocking the path of Balaam's ass or giving King Saul a fit of depression. When the Old Testament was translated into Greek beginning in the third century B.C., *satan* was rendered *diabolos*, "adversary," from which come the Latin *diabolus*, French *diable*, German *Teufel*, English "devil." The first time the word appears with a capital *S*, defining a particular person, is in the Book of Job, where Satan is a sort of celestial J. Edgar Hoover, sent by the Lord to check up on the loyalty of the folks down on earth.

The first Devil, the first concentration of all evil in a single personal form, appears in history some time before the sixth century B.C., in Persia. His name is Ahriman, described by the prophet Zoroaster (Zarathustra) as the Principle of Darkness (evil) engaged in ceaseless conflict for control of the world with Ormazd or Mazda, the Principle of Light (good).

Satan was once an angel who had led a rebellion in Heaven.

The Jews were under Persian domination for almost two centuries, and it is likely that Ahriman had some influence on the formation of the figure of their Satan. He appears for the first time acting independently in the third-century Book of Chronicles, where the text of the much older Book of Samuel is changed from "The LORD incited David," to read "Satan incited David." In the next few centuries of the so-called Intertestamentary Period between the compilation of the Old and New Testaments, when a major subject of theological speculation and literature was the apocalypse—the final struggle between good and evil at the imminent end of the world—this Satan grew in stature as the leader and embodiment of the forces of evil. The Jewish rabbis soon lost interest in him, and though he runs wild through folklore, he

is a very minor figure in modern Judaism. He would be a major figure, however, as the Satan or Lucifer of the Christians or the Iblis or Shaytan of the Muslims. Whatever he does, and however powerful he may be at times, none of these religions have ever followed Zoroaster in allowing the Devil an independent existence apart from God. He is always separate but far from equal, though exactly to what extent separate and unequal has been the subject of perpetual debate on the questions that the postulation of a Devil naturally calls up: Why did a good God create an evil Devil in the first place? And if he had to, why did he give him so much power and let him reign so long? Or, as Friday asked Robinson Crusoe, "If God much strong, much might as the Devil, why God no kill the devil, no make him no more do wicked?" Such questions were being debated in Latin by 12th-century scholars in Paris in almost the same terms as by 12th-century scholars in Baghdad, and they are still being debated by scholars all over the world today.

The Christian Devil, who is the one most familiar in today's literature and art, appears often, but with only sketchy details, in the New Testament. It took three or four centuries of debate and speculation for the church to settle on a unified but not quite consistent picture of his history and functions. He was once an angel—some said the firstborn and chief of all the angels—who had led a rebellion in Heaven (some said out of pride; some said out of envy either of God himself or of the man, Adam, created in God's image; some said out of sexual lust for pretty women) and had been cast down to Hell (some said on the very first day or hour of the creation of the world, others after the creation of Adam, others after the Fall of Man, others during the time of Noah), had tempted humankind into sin, which allowed him to rule the world until the coming of Christ (or until the Second Coming), and would on the Day of Judgment be condemned to perpetual torment along with all the sinners of the race of Adam.

At the beginning there was curiously little interest in the particular features of this Devil, who does not appear at all in the first six or seven centuries of Christian art. Perhaps the early Christians, members of a small persecuted sect faced with the daily possibility of meeting the representatives of the Roman state in the form of gladiators, lions and howling mobs in arenas, did not need to dream up faces for the Devil. After Christianity became the state religion of Rome in the early fourth century, the fight against the enemy changed in character. The heroes were not martyrs in an arena: they were monks who went out into the deserts to meet Satan face-to-face. Satan appeared to all of them to tempt them, and it was then that Satan first acquired a recognizable physical form, appearing variously as lion, bear, leopard, bull, serpent, hyena, scorpion and wolf.

---

*Around the tenth
century, the Devil
began to assume
monstrous forms.*

Still, for hundreds of years no one thought of putting an image of the Devil on paper or a church wall. There is a sixth-century manuscript of the Gospels in Syriac that shows a couple of little black-winged creatures fleeing from the mouth of a man being exorcized. Not till the ninth century, in an illustrated manuscript known as the *Utrecht Psalter*, does a recognizable Devil appear, as a half-naked man holding a three-pronged pitchfork. The Devil would appear often like this in the next couple of centuries, human or at least humanoid in form, sometimes wearing the halo of his old angelic days in Heaven.

Then, some time around the pre-millennial tenth century, the Devil began, all over the Western world, to assume monstrous forms. He appeared on the illustrated pages of books now written for the first time in the vernacular languages, and on the painted walls and ceilings and the carved doors and columns and waterspouts of churches and cathedrals. Everywhere there were scenes from sacred history intended to teach the illiterate

masses the way to salvation, and the Devil played a prominent, sometimes predominant, role in these scenes.

He appeared in a thousand grotesque and horrible guises. His features might be derived from those of old gods of Greece and Rome whose broken images still cluttered the soil of Europe, or the newer gods of the barbarian Germans and Scandinavians, or more ancient supernatural beings from Mesopotamia, Egypt, Persia, even China, who spread their wings on imported silks and tapestries. He borrowed horns and hairy legs with cloven hooves from the Greek god Pan, a hooked nose and grimacing lips from the Etruscan death god Charun, a pitchfork from the Roman sea god Neptune, an animal head from the Egyptian god Anubis. Sometimes he was a furry black monkey with great black bat's wings. Sometimes he was a snake, a wolf, a frog, a bear, a mouse, an owl, a raven, a tortoise, a worm. Often he appeared as a combination of human and animal forms, with a tail, spiky flamelike hair, an apish body, a goat's hairy thighs, an ass's feet, a boar's tusks, a wolfish mouth, an eagle's claws, a monkey's paws, a lizard's skin, a snake's tongue. When he led the revolt of the angels in Heaven, fighting Saint Michael, he was a scaly dragon. Enthroned in Hell, he was a potbellied imbecilic old man, with snakes growing out of his head and limbs, mindlessly chewing on the sterile souls of naked sinners as they dropped down to him on Judgment Day.

He was meant to be both frightening and disgusting, to demonstrate both the horror and the folly of sin. The fright was all the greater because the devices like bone-vices, spine-rollers and red-hot prongs being used to torture sinners down in Hell were copied from those being used to torture heretics in public up on earth.

The static visions on the church walls were regularly brought to life in plays staged in front of churches or in public squares. Surrounded by elaborate scenery and firecrackers, the Devil was always a popular performer when, clothed in snakeskin and with a woman's face, he dangled an apple before our First Parents in Eden, or with fanged mask and hairy goat's body, he grimaced and

grunted and growled as he prodded wailing sinners into a Mouth of Hell that could open and shut and spit flames.

One of the most popular stories throughout the Middle Ages, retold hundreds of times in many European languages, was that of Theophilus of Cilicia, a sixth-century ecclesiastic who signed a pact with the Devil, exchanging his soul for a powerful and profitable position in the church. He was then able to lead a life of unbridled pride and corruption till one day the Devil reappeared and demanded his payment. In terror, Theophilus repented and threw himself on the mercy of the Virgin Mary, who took pity on him, descended into Hell, grabbed the pact from Satan, then interceded for the sinner at the throne of God. He was pardoned, and the Devil was cheated of his due.

---

*Ben Jonson summed
it up in one of
his plays,* The Devil
is an Ass.

This tale played a major role in establishing the cult of the Virgin in Catholic Europe. It had the subsidiary effect of familiarizing everyone with the idea of diabolical pacts. The authorities of church and state took advantage of this when sometime in the 15th century they claimed to discover a vast conspiracy by a confederation of witches dedicated to the subversion of all order. There were, of course, plenty of supposed witches around, mostly old countrywomen who knew the traditional herbs and chants and charms that would attract a handsome lover or stop an unwanted pregnancy or blast the crops in an unfriendly neighbor's field. But for the space of two or three centuries, tens of thousands of accused witches, most of them women, most of them poor illiterates, were hanged or burned after being forced to confess to taking part in secret midnight meetings at which they ate babies, copulated with the Devil and signed blood compacts with him.

The Salem witch trials of 1692 are the most familiar to Americans, having left an indelible stain on the name of our Puritan forebears. Perhaps the most interesting thing about them is that, compared with what had been going on in Europe for the previous three centuries, they were on such a very small scale: 18 women, one man and two dogs put to death in obedience to the biblical command "Thou shalt not suffer a witch to live." And there were no more witch trials in the Colonies after Salem.

For by the year 1700 few educated people really believed in witches anymore, and increasingly they were coming not to believe in the Devil himself. The reason was that Western Europe, followed in more or less short order by the rest of the world, was entering the modern era, the world of exploration, discovery, science, technology, individualism, capitalism, rationalism, materialism, democracy, progress. In such a world the old Devil was getting to seem both embarrassing and superfluous. When he appeared on the stage with his monkey suits and his conjuring tricks, he was only an unsightly clown—Ben Jonson summed it up in the title of one of his plays, *The Devil is an Ass*. And when you got down to the business of explaining what was going on around you, the Devil only got in the way. When Shakespeare's Othello learns too late how he has been tricked into murdering his wife and losing his soul, his first, medieval instinct is to look down at Iago's feet; then he pulls himself together and says, "But that's a fable." Iago doesn't need supernatural cloven hooves; he has all the wickedness he needs stored up in his own human heart. Bit by bit, the Devil's possessions and prerogatives were stripped from him.

When Benjamin Franklin called down a great spark from Heaven with a mere key hanging on a kite, all the army of infernal spirits that had been swarming through the air vanished, and the atmosphere became nothing but a mass of nitrogen and oxygen and other atoms, whirling around according to laws that Satan had never heard of.

Where the 13th-century Cistercian abbot Richalm blamed the Devil for the "wondrous sound that would seem to proceed from some distemper" of his stomach or bowels, a modern monk sends for a gastroenterologist. Great storms are no longer conjured up by the Devil, but by El Niño currents, and no one blames the wreck of the *Titanic* on anything but errors of judgment and faults of design. People are still possessed by devils, and the Roman Catholic church among others provides means of exorcizing them. But their numbers are infinitesimal compared with the number of people who are daily put under the care of psychiatrists.

The old-fashioned horror-show Devil virtually disappeared from the fine arts with the coming of the Renaissance. In 1505 Raphael painted a traditional picture of Saint Michael beating the Devil out of Heaven; the Devil is a kind of outsize science-fiction insect with horns and wings and a madman's gasping face. Thirteen years later he did another painting on the identical theme, but the Devil this time, though a pair of bat wings grows out of his shoulders, is otherwise wholly human, a young man writhing in the despair of defeat, a much more arresting and moving figure than the bland self-satisfied saint who is poking him with a spear.

To adjust to this modern world, the Devil has had to change his ways.

The real gravedigger of the old brutal, terrifying, physically threatening Devil was John Milton, whose *Paradise Lost* was to influence the world's conception of Satan in a way no other work of art has ever done, though not at all in the way the author intended. It was designed to be an epic poem like those of Homer or Virgil, but told to "justify God's ways to Man," and dealing with creation, sin and salvation. In outline, it is a very orthodox story of pride and sin eventually humbled and destroyed by the infinite wisdom and goodness of God. Milton's Satan follows the theologically correct process of transformation from the most radiant of angels to the loathsome crawling serpent of Book Ten. Few readers, however, get to Book Ten of *Paradise Lost*. They are more apt to let themselves be lost in fascination with the Satan of the first books, a heroic figure of the first order, young, proud, self-confident, self-reliant, inventive, ingenious, yielding to no obstacle, defiant, who will not accept defeat even if defeat is inevitable, who values his own freedom more than happiness, who would rather "reign in Hell than serve in Heaven." These might be considered features of the tireless visionary entrepreneurs from Columbus to Bill Gates whose dreams and exploits have shaped so much of modern history, and provided the heroes for so many modern movies and novels.

But to the modern Devil, even more galling than his loss of physical power, his control of earthquakes and unholy wars, must be his loss of respect. The Prince of Darkness has become, in the view of Prof. Andrew Delbanco of Columbia University, in a book called *The Death of Satan*, a superannuated athlete who has gone on the lecture circuit.

He can always get a supporting role in a horror movie like *Rosemary's Baby* or a science-fiction thriller about a professor of comparative literature who carves up and cooks his more attractive students. But no one takes him really seriously. He is toned down, domesticated. Bowdlerized, he has become politically correct. As one of the title characters in John Updike's *Witches of Eastwick* remarks, "Evil is not a word that we like to use. We prefer to say 'unfortunate' or 'lacking' or 'misguided' or 'disadvantaged.'" Even hellfire preachers who make a speciality of describing in detail the horrors of the afterlife no longer say, as the church fathers of a more robust age used to do, that one of the joys of being in Heaven will be to watch sinners writhing in the hands of the Devil.

To adjust to this pallid modern world, the Devil has had to change his ways. Always an expert shape-changer, he now comes on most often in the form of Mephistopheles. The name was made up in a 15th-century German updating of the old Theophilus legend, which has Mephistopheles signing a pact with Dr. Johann Faustus, a professor-turned-magician who is more than willing to trade his soul for 24 years of unbounded knowledge, power and sex. Christopher Marlowe's play of *Doctor Faustus* would launch both the Faust story and the character of Mephistopheles on a fabulously successful career. He was followed two centuries later by Goethe with his epic drama *Faust*. Between them they created the modern Devil, witty, ironic, disillusioned, a much more complex and interesting character than Doctor Faustus himself. Unlike Faust, however, Mephistopheles never *does* anything; he just talks.

He talks very well, of course. He talks very wittily and convincingly in Dostoyevsky's *Brothers Karamazov* and in George Bernard Shaw's *Man and Superman*. He is funny in a sinister kind of way when in C. S. Lewis' *Screwtape Letters* he becomes a conscientious bureaucrat filling reams of paper with instructions to an Englishman on how to get on his mother's nerves. He looks very handsome and winning when he is played by Al Pacino in the movies. But out in the world of commerce, politics, wars and gross national product, he is little more than a joke.

For some observers like Professor Delbanco and Prof. Jeffrey Burton Russell, of the University of California, Santa Barbara, whose five-volume biography of the Devil is the most authoritative, this is a tragic situation; it means that America, like the modern world generally, has lost its sense of evil, and without a sense of evil a civilization must go straight to Hell.

Perhaps, however, he is not dead after all; he may only be in hiding. A 17th-century Englishman, Richard Greenham, was apparently the first to coin the phrase, later borrowed or reinvented by Baudelaire, Dostoyevsky, G. K. Chesterton and Whittaker Chambers, "it is the policy of the Devil to persuade us that there is no Devil." The Devil, after all, if he is anything, is the personification of evil, and no one can deny that there is plenty of evil around even in today's comparative peace and prosperity.

> *Common sense tells us that we will go on performing wicked deeds.*

The psychiatrist Viktor Frankl was a young doctor in Vienna in 1940 when he and his wife were picked up by Nazi thugs and sent off to concentration camps. She was soon murdered, but he managed to survive through all five years of the war. One night, as he climbed up to his wooden bunk, he found the man next to him moaning and roaring and thrashing, in prey to the worst nightmare Frankl had ever seen in his years of medical practice. His every humane instinct as a doctor told him to wake the man up before he hurt himself, but as he reached out to shake him he suddenly remembered that the reality he would be waking the man up to was Auschwitz, with all its stenches and screams and heavy thudding blows, and that was a hundred times worse than anything the mere human imagination could make up in the confines of a narrow human skull. So he let the nightmare gallop on.

There were no devils running Auschwitz, only human beings doing an ill-paid job that they must have found unpleasant at times but which was clearly preferable to being sent to die in the hell of the Russian front. That does not mean the Devil was not there.

Most everyone these days has taken the pledge that there will be no more Auschwitzes. But such pledges have been taken before. Common sense tells us that we will go on performing wicked deeds of one sort or another till an automated virtue machine is patented or (more likely) till the end of the world.

Madame Carmelita, a psychic on the Upper East Side of Manhattan, has assured me that the world will end on or about my 100th birthday, February 18, 2018. And a science-fiction scenario might have the world (meaning human life) come to an end when a giant comet hits the earth, clearing the ground for little polyps that will evolve into creatures much nicer and more spiritual than us mere mammals. A scientist has assured me that the world (meaning life on earth) will come to an end when our sun becomes a red giant in the year 4,000,001,999. If in the meanwhile a sleek gentleman dressed as a prosperous options-and-derivatives salesman offers you fantastic odds on a bet that he will not be around right up to the last second on any or all of those occasions, and you take him up on it, you will probably be making a bad bet.

Robert Wernick reports that he has received many offers from the Devil but thus far has resisted his blandishments.

UNIT 4
Muslims and Byzantines

Unit Selections

Key Points to Consider

- Why were some of the accomplishments of Constantine?

- Why was the Eastern Roman Empire able to survive after the West had fallen? Was this Byzantine civilization merely an extension of late Roman culture, or was it a new departure?

- What are some of the main events in the life of Muhammad? What are the problems today?

 **Links: www.dushkin.com/online/**
These sites are annotated in the World Wide Web pages.

ByzNet: Byzantine Studies on the Net
  http://www.thoughtline.com/byznet/
Islam: A Global Civilization
  http://www.templemount.org/islamiad.html
Middle East Network Information Center
  http://menic.utexas.edu/menic/religion.html

After the western collapse of the Roman Empire, three ethnic/religious entities emerged to fill the vacuum. Germanic kingdoms arose in central and western Europe. In the Balkans and Asia Minor, the eastern remnants of Rome evolved into the Byzantine Empire. The Near East, North Africa, and much of the Iberian Peninsula fell under the control of the Arabs. Each area developed a unique civilization, based in each instance upon a distinctive form of religion—Roman Catholicism in most of Europe, Orthodox Christianity in the Byzantine sphere, and Islam in the Arab world. Each placed its unique stamp upon the classical tradition to which all three fell heir. The articles in this unit concentrate on the Byzantine and Muslim civilizations. The medieval culture of Europe is treated in the next unit.

Western perceptions of Islam and Arabic civilization have been clouded by ignorance and bias. To European observers during the medieval period, Islam seemed a misguided or heretical version of Christianity. In the wake of Arab conquests, Islam increasingly came to represent terror and devastation, a dangerous force loosed upon Christendom. Reacting out of fear and hostility, Christian authors were reluctant to acknowledge the learning and high culture of the Arabs.

Muslim commentators could be equally intolerant. Describing Europeans, one wrote: "They are most like beasts than like men.... Their temperaments are frigid, their humors raw, their bellies gross... they lack keeness of understanding... and are overcome by ignorance and apathy."

The stereotypes formed in the early encounters between Christians and Muslims survived for generations. Centuries of hostility have tended to obscure the extent of cultural exchange between the Arab world and the West. Indeed, as historian William H. McNeil has observed, "Muslims have been written out of European history."

The domain of Islam, however, encroached upon too many points for the two cultures to remain mutually exclusive. In western Europe Islam swept over Spain, crossed the Pyrenees, and penetrated France; in the central Mediterranean, it leaped from Tunis to Sicily and then into southern Italy; in eastern Europe, Islam broke into Asia Minor, the Balkans, and the Caucasus. In its expansion, early Islam was exposed to Jewish, Christian, and classical influences. History and geography determined that there would be much cross-fertilization between Islam and the West.

Yet there is no denying the originality and brilliance of Islamic civilization. There is the religion of Muhammad, unquestionably one of the world's most influential faiths. "In the Beginning, There Were the Holy Books" highlights essentials of that faith. Additional evidence of Arab creativity can be found in the visual arts, particularly in the design and decoration of the great mosques. The Arabs also made significant contributions in philosophy, history, geography, science and medicine.

The medieval West borrowed extensively from the Arabs. The magnificent centers of Islamic culture—Baghdad, Cairo, Cordoba, and Damascus outshone the cities of Christendom. Their administration of Andalusia was a model of successful governance. Islamic scholars surpassed their Christian counterparts in astronomy, mathematics, and medicine—perhaps because the Arab world was more familiar than medieval Europe with the achievements of classical Greece. European scholars eventually regained access to the Greek heritage at least partially through translations from the Arabic.

As for the Byzantine Empire, it was for nearly 1,000 years a Christian bulwark against Persians, Arabs, and Turks. Charles Freeman recounts the great contributions to the Christian faith by Constantine in "The Emperor's State of Grace." It also made important cultural contributions. The beautiful mosaics and icons of Byzantine artists set the pattern for later visualizations of Christ in the West. Byzantine missionaries and statesman spread Orthodox Christianity, with its unique tradition of Caesaro-Papism, to Russia. Byzantine scholars and lawmakers preserved much of the classical heritage. Even hostile Islam was subject to a constant flow of ideas and traditions from the Byzantines.

The Emperor's State of Grace

Charles Freeman considers whether Constantine's famous adoption of Christianity was a spiritual conversion or an act of political expediency.

THE STORY OF CONSTANTINE and Christianity is often simply told. It is AD 312. Constantine, the Augustus or senior emperor of the western Roman empire, confronts the usurper Maxentius who holds Rome and the African provinces. Alerted by a vision that the Christian God is on his side, Constantine decorates the shields of his men with a cross and goes into battle at the Milvian Bridge just north of Rome. The result is a stunning victory, all the western empire falls into Constantine's hands and a conversion of Constantine to Christianity follows. Then with the emperor of the east, Licinius, Constantine issues the Edict of Milan which declares toleration for Christianity throughout the empire and underlines this with massive commitments to the Christian communities. Within twelve years, and now sole emperor, Constantine is presiding at the first empire-wide council of bishops, which produces the earliest version of the Nicene creed and soon to be the badge of Christian orthodoxy.

Many studies of this extraordinary turnaround in Christian affairs (there had been brutal persecutions of Christians under Diocletian only a few years before) make the assumption that Constantine accepted Christianity on its own terms. However, the evidence suggests instead that Constantine treated the God of Christianity as if he were similar to the pagan gods, such as Apollo, to which he had already given allegiance. As he began to grasp the distinctive nature of Christianity, he acted to bring the Church directly under his control, giving himself special roles as a bishop outside the Church and later as 'the thirteenth apostle' in order to maintain his distance from, and dominance over, it.

An early clue to Constantine's beliefs can be found in the Edict of Toleration itself. In it Constantine and Licinius 'grant both to Christians and to all men unrestricted right to follow the form of worship each desired, to the end that whatever divinity there may be on the heavenly seat may be favourably disposed

and propitious to us and all those placed under our authority'. So this was genuinely an Edict of Toleration and a true Christian brought up in the tradition that the polytheistic world was evil could hardly have supported it. One reason for such a wide-ranging decree was that Constantine had to maintain the support of Licinius but it seems clear that he had not appreciated that Christians energetically rejected all other gods.

There is another important theme here: Constantine is suggesting that by giving appropriate honour to the 'divinity on the heavenly seat', he will get that divinity's support. This need remained paramount in the years that followed. But what drew Constantine to Christianity in the first place? A simple answer would be the vision before the Milvian Bridge. Yet the accounts of this vision date from years later and are contradictory. In the earliest account (c.415) Lactantius, himself a convert to Christianity, reported that Constantine had had a dream the night before the battle in which he was commanded to place the 'heavenly sign of god', the Chi-Rho sign, on his soldiers' shields and he did so. Many years later Constantine told his biographer Eusebius—and under oath Eusebius tells us—a somewhat different version of the story. At some moment before the battle a cross of light appeared in the skies above the sun. It was inscribed, 'By this, conquer,' and this command was confirmed in a dream when Christ himself appeared to Constantine and asked him to inscribe a cross on his standards as a safeguard against his enemies.

Yet in Eusebius's *Life of Constantine* another story is developed and it links Constantine's adherence to Christianity directly to his father, Constantius. His father was enormously important to Constantine's legitimacy. When Constantius had been appointed Caesar or junior emperor (in the Tetrarchy set up by Diocletian, there were four emperors: two senior, known as Augusti, and two junior, known as Caesars) in the west in

293, his son Constantine, then about twenty, had remained in the east and cut his teeth on campaigns against the frontier tribes along the Danube. Constantine only rejoined his father some years later, in York where the latter was dying. On Constantius's death in 306, Constantine was immediately proclaimed Augustus in his place by his men, although this elevation was only accepted three or four years later by Galerius, Augustus in the east. Meanwhile the Tetrarchy was disintegrating and the politically astute Constantine set out to establish his legitimacy independently of it. Panegyrics to Constantine which survive from the years immediately after Constantius's death assume the latter is in heaven and Constantine, 'similar to you [Constantius] in appearance, in spirit and in the power of empire,' holds power on earth as a symbol of his father's immortality.

Constantine believed the god of the Christians was on his side, but this did not mean a rejection of other gods.

Next Constantine stretched Constantius's own legitimacy back to an early third-century emperor, Claudius Gothicus (r. AD 268–270), whose victory over the Goths at Naissus (coincidentally Constantine's birthplace, present-day Nish in Yugoslavia) in 269 blunted their strength for over a century. With a line of descent from an earlier emperor and divine support assumed through his father, Constantine now claimed to rule the western empire in his own right. Yet there is another vital ingredient. Constantine came to believe that his father was Christian. The evidence on which he based his belief, as reported by Eusebius, was circumstantial. Constantius had refrained from enforcing the edicts of persecution, he was known to talk of a single God, and his very survival (in comparison to the fates of other emperors in these troubled years) confirmed that he enjoyed his God's favour. The apparent visions before the Battle of the Milvian Bridge, followed by the great victory, were enough to confirm for Constantine that it was the God of the Christians who was on his side.

Yet for Constantine this did not mean a rejection of other gods. The triumphal arch in 315, erected by the senate of Rome in Constantine's honour three years after his 'conversion', makes the point well. The arch is traditional in form and is notable for its use of reliefs from monuments to earlier emperors, Trajan, Hadrian and Marcus Aurelius. There are reliefs of Mars, Jupiter and Hercules and Constantine's victory at the Milvian Bridge is associated with the power of the sun and the goddess Victory, but there is no hint of any Christian symbol and no mention of Christ. (Alistair Kee, in his *Constantine versus Christ*, goes so far as to argue that Christ played no part in the religion of Constantine.) An inscription on the arch credits Constantine's victory to the 'instigation of the Divinity', but the 'Divinity', like the 'Supreme Deity', is a vague term used by pagans and Christians alike. In 313 Licinius had used it in a prayer before his troops when it appears that he was referring to Jupiter. Constantine clearly had no inhibitions about using this phrase alongside traditional pagan symbols.

Whatever Constantine believed the 'Divinity' might be, he desperately needed its support and feared that any form of disunity among Christians might threaten it. Toleration was followed by the granting of special favours to the clergy, in particular exemption from the heavy burden of holding civic office, so that, in Constantine's words, the clergy 'shall not be drawn away by any deviation and sacrifice from the worship that is due to the divinity, but shall devote themselves without interference to their own law… *for it seems that, rendering the greatest possible service to the deity, they most benefit the state.*' (My italics). When, for instance the Donatist dispute broke out over whether a bishop who had surrendered the scriptures at a time of persecution was legitimate, Constantine supported those who said he was, but in a letter to an official he expressed his real concerns, particularly his fear that his own position as the ruler favoured by God would be jeopardised by internal squabbles. 'I consider it absolutely contrary to the divine law that we should overlook such quarrels and contentions,' he wrote, 'whereby the Supreme Divinity may perhaps be roused not only against the human race but also against myself, to whose care he has by his celestial will committed the government of all earthly things.'

By 324 Constantine had defeated Licinius and was sole ruler of the empire. In view of his concern that the Christian churches should be unified he must have been shocked by what he found. The Greek speaking east had always been a hotbed of lively debate, theological controversy and rivalry between the great bishoprics. Constantine's victories would have made him more convinced that the god of the Christians was on his side, yet this relationship was threatened by the endemic political and theological disunity of the east.

Almost immediately he was confronted by a major dispute between a bishop, Alexander of the important see of Alexandria, and a presbyter in the diocese, one Arius. It concerned a central problem of Christian doctrine, the relationship between God the Father, and Jesus Christ the Son. Arius claimed that Jesus, though fully divine, was a subsequent creation of God the Father and hence subordinate to him. An alternative, monotheistic, view was to suggest that Jesus had been part of the Godhead since the beginning of time. The dispute erupted when Arius, who had a well-developed sense of drama, loudly interrupted one of Alexander's sermons and Alexander, with the backing of other bishops, excommunicated him. Constantine was irritated by the dispute and wrote to Alexander and Arius urging them to stop their idle and trivial speculations. By this time, however, the controversy had spread as other bishops had associated themselves with one side or the other and Constantine realised that only by summoning a council of bishops could he hope to enforce a solution. The bishops were to assemble at Nicaea in Asia Minor, where there was an imperial palace with an audience hall. Constantine would pay their travel expenses and preside himself.

By now the Emperor's aura and reputation were overwhelming. When he arrived at the Council he was described by Eusebius as 'like some heavenly messenger of God, clothed in a shining raiment, which flashed as if with glittering rays of light… and adorned with the lustrous brilliance of gold and precious stones'. Those who beheld him were 'stunned and amazed at the sight—like children who have seen a frightening apparition'. Later Byzantine mosaics and frescos (as in the refectory of the Great Lavra on Mount Athos) show Constantine as the central figure of the council, larger than the bishops assembled around him.

It is impossible to know what went on at Nicaea because the accounts are so fragmentary. The assumption has to be that the determination of Constantine to resolve the issue, his dominating presence, and the growing dependency of the Church on him for patronage combined to give him an overwhelming position. Eusebius describes him working assiduously to get an agreement. The Creed which emerged declared that Christ 'is of the substance [ousia] of the Father,… true God of true God,… consubstantial [homoousios] with the Father…'. Then, at the end, it contained a number of anathemas condemning specific Arian beliefs, notably that there was a time that Jesus had never existed or that Jesus was of a different substance from the Father. What had happened in effect was that Christ had been brought into the Godhead, and was no longer subordinate to it as in previous Church tradition. It was, as Hanson in his *The Search for the Origins of Christian Doctrine* puts it; 'a startling innovation' but a united Godhead, of one substance, provided a more effective theological backing for an autocratic political order than one whose powers were divided between God and Jesus as a lesser divine figure.

Constantine enforced the creed by excommunicating those attending the Council who refused to sign it. 'Thus,' wrote Eusebius, 'the Faith prevailed in a unanimous form…' and he concludes '…When these things were finished, the Emperor said that this was the second victory he had won over the enemy of the Church, and held a victory-feast to God.' Constantine later came to realise that he had created a false unity, and he accepted Arius back into the Church, and received his own baptism at the hands of an Arian bishop, before his death.

Constantine's allegiance to his God was backed by massive patronage. Emperors had always honoured their favoured gods with benefactions and buildings. Constantine's patronage was so lavish that he had to strip resources from temples to fund it. One of his early foundations in Rome was the church of St John Lateran, whose apse was to be coated in gold. Around 500 pounds weight of it were needed at a cost of some 36,000 *solidi*. This sum, which might be translated into approximately £60 million today, could have fed about 12,000 poor for a year (according to calculations from Dominic Janes' *God and Gold in Late Antiquity)*. Another 22,200 *solidi* worth of silver (3,700 lbs was required for light fittings and another 400 pounds of gold for fifty gold vessels. The costs of lighting were to be met by estates specifically granted for the purpose which brought in 4,390 *solidi* a year. Everything in these new churches had to be of the highest quality. While early Christian decoration, in the catacombs or house churches, for instance, had been painted walls, now nothing less than mosaic was appropriate. In order to make the effect more brilliant the mosaics were made of gold, silver or precious stones set within glass. It was an enormously

delicate and costly business. Studies of the original floor mosaics at the Church of the Nativity in Bethlehem, one of Constantine's foundations in the Holy Land, reveal the care and cost lavished on decoration. While the normal pattern of high-quality mosaics in Palestine is 150 tesserae per 10cm square, the ratio in the nave is 200 and in the Octagon at the end of the nave, some 400. In their size and opulent decoration, the basilicas echoed the great audience halls of the emperors. The transformation in a religion whose founder had been so committed to the poor was shocking to many. 'Parchments are dyed purple, gold is melted into lettering, manuscripts are dressed up in jewels, while Christ lies at the door naked and dying,' wrote the horrified Jerome. But by the end of the century the Church had accepted its buildings and the scriptures had been reinterpreted to justify the fortunes spent on them.

There were, of course, tensions with the pagan senatorial aristocracy over these transformations, particularly in Rome (where Constantine's two major churches, St John Lateran and St Peter's on the Vatican Hill, were build outside the city centre). There was also deep shock in the city over the mysterious execution of Constantine's son Crispus and Crispus's stepmother, Constantine's second wife Fausta, in 326, on suspicion of treason. The pagan writer Zosimus even suggested that the pilgrimage of the Emperor's mother Helena to the Holy Land had been ordered as a Christian penance for her part in allegedly drowning Fausta in a bath.

Such opprobrium, and a desire to celebrate his own glory, must have been one reason why Constantine was so determined to create a city where he could be personally supreme. He chose an ancient Greek foundation, Byzantium, which occupied a stunning and well defended site overlooking the southern end of the Bosphorus and which was well placed on the main routes between east and west. As its name suggests Constantinople was Constantine's city. Eusebius, in his attempt to assert the Christian commitment of Constantine, went so far as to claim, misleadingly, that Constantinople was always a wholly Christian city without a single pagan temple. For its founder, however, this was the city of Constantine, not of Christ.

Many elements of the foundation were traditional. Constantine traced the line of the future walls of the city with a spear just as a Greek founder would have done. Statues and classical monuments were brought from all over the world to grace the public spaces. The protecting goddesses Rhea, the mother of Olympian gods, and Tyche, the personification of good fortune, were honoured with new temples. Constantine's most ambitious plants, however, were to create a central complex of forum, hippodrome and imperial palace as a setting for his own majesty. In the circular forum, on one of the highest hills of the city, Constantine erected a great porphyry column twenty-five metres high, topped with a gold statue of himself.

All this was dedicated on a great day of celebration in May 300 and it was as much a celebration of Constantine as of his city. A gold coin was struck to mark the occasion showing Constantine gazing upwards in a pose made famous by Alexander the Great, his head crowned by an opulent diadem. The ceremonies began in the presence of the Emperor with the lifting of the great gold statue onto its column. Dressed in magnificent robes and wearing a diadem encrusted with jewels (another spiritual allegiance of Constantine's, to the sun, a symbol of Apollo, first known from 310 was expressed through rays coming from the diadem). Constantine processed to the imperial box. Among the events that followed one stood out: the arrival in the hippodrome of a golden chariot carrying a gilded statue of the emperor. In his hands was a smaller statue of Tyche. For the next two hundred years the ritual drawing of the statue and chariot through the hippodrome was to be re-enacted on the anniversary of the dedication.

He built a circular mausoleum with a tomb surrounded by twelve sepulchres, symbolic burial places for the apostles.

Where did Christianity fit into all this? In the original celebrations hardly at all. Space was put aside for churches in the centre of the city but their titles, Hagia Sophia, Holy Wisdom, Hagia Eirene, Holy Peace and Hagia Dynamis, Holy Power, suggest that Constantine was still using epithets which were as comprehensible to the pagan world as to the Christian. The only saints honoured with churches were local martyrs. The pagan elements of the city were not erased until later in the century, under Theodosius I, when Rhea and Tyche were absorbed into the cult of the Virgin Mary, the new protectress of the city.

In April 337 Constantine realised he was dying. Then, and only then, did he allow himself to be baptised. In the last weeks of his life (he died on May 22nd) he discarded the imperial purple and dressed himself in the white of the newly baptised Christian. He had already built his final resting place within Constantinople and it provided a fitting testimonial to how he saw himself in relation to God and Christ. It was a circular mausoleum with a tomb left for the emperor under the central dome. Placed around the tomb were twelve sepulchres—each a symbolic burial place of one of the original apostles. Constantine was to be the thirteenth apostle. To orthodox Christians this might seem blasphemous but it made sense in terms of Constantine's own perception of himself in relation to the god who had given him such support.

After his death his sons issued a coin to commemorate their own *consecratio* (being made sacred as emperors). On one side it bore Constantine's veiled head and an inscription, 'The deified Constantine, father of the Augusti', on the other Constantine is seen ascending to heaven in a chariot with God's hand reaching out to welcome him. The evidence suggests that Constantine was using the Christian god as an adjunct to his own power, much as earlier Roman emperors had done with their gods. Every victory was simply a confirmation that the relationship was intact and that the emperor was justified in maintaining his power and magnificence. Constantine kept himself at arm's length from the institutional structure of the Church. He once told the bishops, 'You are bishops of those within the Church, but I am perhaps a bishop appointed by God over those outside.' For Constantine his policy was justified by his continuing victories:

> While God was close at hand to make him Lord and Despot, the only Conqueror among the Emperors of all time to remain Irresistible and Unconquered, Ever-conquering and always brilliant with triumphs over enemies, so great an Emperor... so God beloved and Thrice blessed,... that with utter ease he governed more nations than those before him, and kept his dominion unimpaired to the very end.

When the papacy and the Roman Catholic Church came under sustained attack in the Reformation, the Medici Pope Leo X (r. 1513–21) ordered a great room to be built in the Vatican. Known as the *Sala di Constantino*, it had unashamedly propagandist aims. It frescoes, planned by Raphael, show the early popes, from Peter onwards, and then, in four great scenes, the achievement of Constantine. One fresco shows the vision of the Cross, another the battle of the Milvian Bridge itself. Leo associated himself with the victory. The *palle* from the Medici coat of arms are on Constantine's tent and lions, a reference to Leo's name, are also found on the tend with another on a standard. At a moment of crisis and confrontation, this was the event the pope chose to highlight. It was more than toleration that Constantine gave to Christianity, it was transformation. By tying in his victories to the support of the Christian God, and associating his allegiance with massive patronage, Constantine had shifted the nature of Christianity itself.

FOR FURTHER READING

D. Bowder, *The Age of Constantine and Julian* (London, 1978); Averil Cameron, *The Late Roman Empire* (London, 1993); G. Bowersock, and others, eds, *Late Antiquity: A Guide to the Postclassical World* (London, 1999); H. Pohlsander, *Constantine the Emperor* (London, 1997); Eusebius's *Life of Constantine*, trans. Averil Cameron and Stuart Hall (Oxford, 1999); Dominic Janes, *God and Gold in Late Antiquity* (Cambridge, 1998); R. Hanson, *The Search for the Christian Doctrine of God* (Edinburgh, 1988); Sabine MacCormack, *Art and Ceremony in Late Antiquity* (London, 1981); Alistair Kee, *Constantine versus Christ* (SCM Press, 1982).

Charles Freeman is author of *The Greek Achievement* (Penguin 1999) and is working on a study of the transition from the Greek to the Christian world.

This article first appeared in *History Today*, January 2001, pp. 9-15. © 2001 by History Today, Ltd. Reprinted by permission.

The Survival of the Eastern Roman Empire

Stephen Williams *and* **Gerard Friell** *analyse why Constantinople survived the barbarian onslaughts in the fifth century, whereas Rome fell*

THE OLD ATTITUDE still prevails in some quarters that what we know of as the Roman Empire was dismembered in the fifth century, and that what survived in the East was something different—Byzantium, Greek and Christian; fascinating, no doubt, but no longer the real Rome. This quite misleading picture is often accompanied by another: that the survival of the Eastern half in the terrible fifth century, when the West went under, was a more or less natural development—even unconsciously anticipated by Constantine's wise foundation of his new capital in the wealthier, more urbanised East.

The reality of course was very different. Despite the administrative division into East and West, which predated Constantine, the empire was everywhere seen as one and indivisible. At the beginnings of the fifth century both halves faced similar chronic problems: immature or inept emperors, rebellious armies, external barbarian invaders and the large and dangerous settlements of barbarian 'allies' within imperial territories. By difficult expedients and innovations the East was eventually able to overcome these problems, while the West was not. After several attempts, Constantinople accepted that it had not the strength to save the West, but it still treated it as a group of temporarily lost provinces to be recovered when the situation permitted—a view that the emperor Justinian in the sixth century took entirely literally.

After the disastrous defeat by the immigrant Visigoths at Adrianople (Edirne) in 378, the new Eastern emperor, Theodosius, was eventually able to fight and manoeuvre them into signing a treaty in 382, settling them in the Balkans as 'allies' (*foederati*), since they could not possibly be expelled. They were obliged to support the emperor, militarily, on request, but this was nonetheless a radically new departure in foreign policy, the result of Roman weakness. Instead of mere farmer-settlers under Roman administration, this was an entire armed Germanic nation established deep within Roman territory under its own tribal leaders. It could not help but be a precedent for other land-hungry barbarians. Theodosius, however, had no option but to hope that in time the Goths could be assimilated as others had been.

After Theodosius's death in 395, his two young sons, Arcadius (377–408) and Honorius (384–423), inherited the thrones of East and West respectively. Both boy-emperors were immature and incapable (Honorius was practically retarded), and although strong loyalty to the dynasty kept them on their thrones, they were entirely managed by individuals or factions within the two courts. Instead of the cooperation that was badly needed, the two governments of East and West intrigued and manoeuvred against each other like hostile states for over ten years, with damaging consequences.

On Theodosius's death the Visigoths immediately broke out of their assigned territories and ravaged the Eastern provinces, under their leader Alaric, who now declared himself king. Temporarily without their main army, the Eastern government, dominated by the eunuch chamberlain Eutropius, was able to deflect Alaric westwards by granting him a top military command in Illyricum (Yugoslavia). The combined status of Roman general and tribal warlord created yet another dangerous precedent. Alaric was able to exploit the deep hostility between the two governments, becoming a destabilising force over the next fifteen years.

In the West, real power was legitimately in the hands of the commander-in-chief Stilicho, of Vandal origin, who had been appointed guardian of the boy-emperor Honorius. He was resented and feared by the ruling circles at Constantinople, who had him declared a public enemy. Stilicho, hoping in vain to force Alaric back into his former alliance, was able to defeat him several times but not destroy him. He had to crush a revolt in Africa (encouraged by Constantinople) and then defeat an Ostrogothic invasion of Italy itself. He was by now forced to buy barbarian fighting men from any source and on any terms, often with personal promises, and even grants of land.

To defend Italy, Stilicho had to strip Britain and the Rhine frontier of troops, and at New Year 407 multiple barbarian invaders crossed the frozen Rhine into Gaul virtually unopposed, never to be expelled again. For this, Stilicho's political enemies in the Senate contrived to have him condemned and executed on the weak emperor's orders, whereupon thousands of his loyal barbarian troops, fearing for themselves and their families, fled over to join Alaric. With Stilicho removed, nothing could prevent Alaric from besieging and finally sacking Rome in 410.

The East had rid itself of the menace of Alaric by propelling him westwards, but this did not free it from other barbarian dangers. What Alaric's Visigoths could do, others could imitate. A new revolt broke out in 399 among the recently-settled Ostrogothic federates. Gainas, the general sent to suppress it, mistrusted the government and was himself of Gothic origin and the commander of other Gothic federate troops. The two Gothic groups joined forces, marched on Constantinople and occupied it, with Gainas dictating his terms to the emperor. However, he was met by a violent anti-Gothic, popular backlash and total hostility from the civil government. Having achieved nothing, he attempted a clumsy withdrawal from the capital in which many Goths and their families were massacred by the mob. Those that escaped were later defeated by loyal units (also commanded by a Goth).

These events had a profound effect on the civilian ruling circles in Constantinople. Henceforth they were determined to keep a firm grip on imperial power and curb ambitious generals, especially those of Gothic origin, even though many were entirely loyal. For several years Goths were excluded from top commands, armies were thinned in numbers, and care was taken to avoid any new settlements of barbarian federates. The Praetorian Prefect, Anthemius, the acknowledged leader of the state, invested instead in strengthening the defences on the Danube frontier, building a new and massive belt of land walls to protect Constantinople, its emperor and government, from both barbarian invasions and its own potentially dangerous armies.

The exclusion of Gothic generals did not last long. With the federate crises past, and a growing external threat from the Huns, able professional commanders such as Plinta, Aspar and Areobindus once again rose to the top *Magister* posts. The fact that they were divorced from any federate or tribal power base (unlike Alaric and Gainas) made them acceptable. They remained what they had been in the previous century—loyal members of the Roman ruling class. *6/21*

The really farsighted achievement of the Eastern empire during this period was not so much the weakening of the power of the army, as the institutionalising of it within a central ruling establishment at Constantinople, which included the palace and civil bureaucracy. The Eastern field army, about 100,000 strong, was already divided into five regional mobile groups, and the commands carefully balanced between men of Gothic and Roman origin. Two of these groups—the Praesental armies—were stationed in the vicinity of Constantinople and their commanders, of whatever background, were senior members of the senate and members of the emperor's inner council of state, the Consistory. *6/21*

Any successful, ambitious general was faced with a choice and a temptation. He could use external military violence to try to dominate the emperor at Constantinople, perhaps even making himself emperor, or at least military dictator. Or he could use the army's indispensability and natural leverage within the legitimate, established power structure where there was a place for him at the top table.

Gainas had attempted the first option and had been ruined. Other military leaders overwhelmingly chose the second. Though politically powerful, the army was only one of several competing, but also interlocking, forces around the throne. To break out of this careful web of power risked losing everything. Certainly, there were bitter conflicts within the Constantinople establishment. For many years the deficiencies of the pious and bookish emperor Theodosius II (408–450) were heavily compensated by his dominating sister Pulcheria, who did everything possible to keep power within the palace and the imperial family rather than the civil ministers and generals. But even she had to negotiate with these other power centres.

The solidarity of the inner establishment was strikingly demonstrated when confronted by the end of an imperial dynasty, *6/21* when all the old threats of factional coup, military violence and even civil war reared their heads in the struggle to place a new emperor on the throne. Aware of what each stood to lose, *Pwr. /structure* palace, bureaucracy, army and, later, church found ways to fight their conflicts behind closed doors and then present an agreed imperial choice to be acclaimed by the senate, the troops, the people and the wider world.

This orderly transmission of imperial power was achieved in the elevation of Marcian in 450, Leo in 457 and Anastasius in 491, all of them dynastic breaks. Through these precedents, buttressed by an increasingly elaborate ceremony of emperor-making, violent coups and civil wars became the exception. Even if a declared rebel succeeded in gaining wide support outside, he still had to cash in his imperial claims in the capital itself, in the face of the central establishment and the city's virtually impregnable defences: if he did not already enjoy powerful allies within the city this was a daunting task. *6/21*

Thus, an important factor in the durability of the establishment was simply the acknowledged geographical concentration of power and authority in a single capital, Constantinople, which was in every sense what Rome had once been. The emergence of a viable, rival power base was made very difficult, and this, as much as the city's strategic position and fortifications, contributed heavily to the stability and survival of the Eastern state. *6/21*

Of all the elements in the establishment, stability was most steadfastly provided by the civil bureaucracy, which provided experience, statecraft and continuity. They kept the impersonal, administrative machine functioning even during violent conflicts within the palace, or purges of this or that faction. These senatorial mandarins, in fact, represented a new service aristocracy created by Constantine. Frequently of modest origins, they owed their power and status not to birth or landed wealth, but entirely to government service. Consequently, regardless of

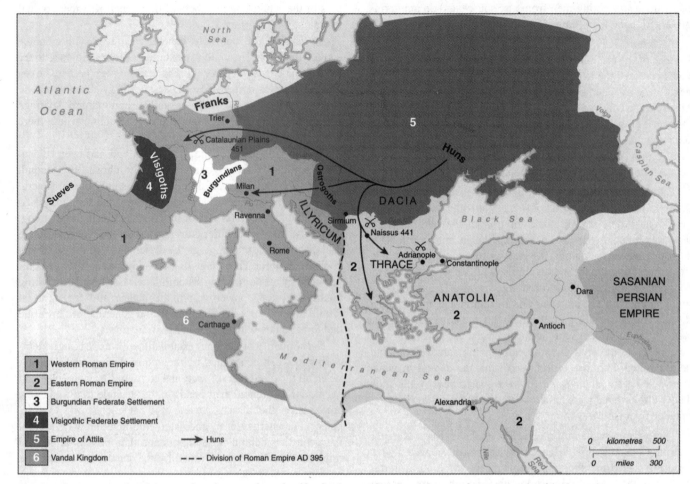

By 450, the Western empire was already a patchwork of barbarian settlements whereas the East retained its integrity.

whether a particular emperor was strong or weak, they took great care to uphold and strengthen the imperial authority itself, since their careers, and hence their prosperity, completely depended on it.

In contrast, the great Western senatorial clans such as the Anicii and Scipiones were only concerned to husband their already huge accumulated family wealth, and treated high state positions as no more than honorific perquisites. Part of the East's undoubtedly greater financial muscle, therefore, was due not just to its inherently greater wealth but also to these mandarins' more honest management of the tax machine, even when it bore on their own aspiring social order.

In the West, the response to the problem of a weak unmilitary emperor was quite different. Real power was concentrated in a military strongman such as Stilicho who ruled on his behalf and enjoyed extraordinary authority, making appointments and issuing laws in the emperor's name. The long reign of the feeble Honorius, the multiple military emergencies and the need to raise and move armies rapidly made this new ruling figure indispensable. After a few years of turmoil the general Constantius stepped into this new position, now vaguely designated 'Patrician' and perhaps better described as military dictator or *generalissimo*. After him came Aetius. Both were patriotic and energetic rulers but had no legally acknowledged position beyond their monopoly of military force, and no regular way of

transferring their power to a successor. Each had to intrigue or fight his way to dominant power, which was destructive and destabilising.

Inevitably they came to depend more on their personal popularity and prestige among the troops, whom they recruited and paid. A gulf steadily grew up between the real power of the warlord with his army, and the symbolic, legal authority with the emperor in his palace. During the invasion of Italy, Stilicho had persuaded Honorius to shift the imperial capital from Milan to the safe refuge of Ravenna, creating a geographical split in addition to the political one.

Constantius achieved a degree of stability in the West, but at enormous cost. Visigoths, Burgundians, Franks, Suevi and Vandals were all settled as federates on large tracts of Gaul and Spain, and were evolving into Germanic kingdoms under only the most nominal Roman overlordship. Constantius and Aetius skillfully exploited their rivalries to maintain some ascendancy. But having relinquished control of so much taxable land and its populations, the regular Roman armies were only one force among many, and no responsible leader could do more than hold the balance, and avoid risking this force if possible.

The Hun menace took on an entirely new dimension with Attila, who had unified them under a single king and subjected all the remaining tribes to Hun rule. His object was not land to settle, but plunder, tribute and glory, and once again the blow fell initially on the East. His hordes ravaged the Balkans three times in the 440s, sacking and ruining many major cities and enslaving their populations. The Roman armies that met him in the field were repeatedly beaten by his cavalry, but he was always deterred by Constantinople whose defences he could not storm. After each invasion he had to be bought off by an increasingly ignominious 'treaty' and larger annual payments, involving heavier taxation of the senatorial classes. In all, the East paid him about nine tons of gold, until the new emperor Marcian finally tore up the treaties and defied him.

Yet here, the two great resources of the East came to the rescue: the impassable fortifications of Constantinople and the enormous taxable wealth of the Asiatic provinces—Anatolia, Syria, Palestine, Egypt. So long as this great land gate was kept shut and so long as these provinces remained secure—meaning peaceful relations with Persia—Attila could always be bought off and much of the Balkan territories temporarily lost without mortal damage to the empire.

Relations with Persia were always a crucial consideration if the empire was to avoid the perils of fighting on two frontiers simultaneously. Unlike other potential enemies, Persia was a centralised, sophisticated state, and both empires were continually involved in a chess game of military and diplomatic manoeuvres which at intervals broke down into open war. In set battle the Romans could usually win, but at quite huge logistical costs. The 1,400-mile frontier zone along the Euphrates was already the most expensive in terms of providing troops and resources. The danger was not so much that Persia would conquer the Roman provinces, as that they would disrupt the whole delicate defensive system of Arab alliances and force the empire to a great commitment of forces, imperilling other frontiers.

But, although Persia tried to take advantage of the empire's difficulties elsewhere, its war aims were limited and it was usually amenable to negotiation. After nearly twenty years of peace, a brief Persian attack in 441 was halted and led to a new treaty involving Roman payments. At the same time, Persia's ambitions were severely checked by pressure from their own northern enemies, the Ephthalite horse peoples, akin to the Huns, who were tacitly encouraged by Constantinople. Whatever martial propaganda they still broadcast to their peoples, the two empires gradually came to accept the advantages of avoiding costly and unrewarding wars, and sought if possible to resolve conflicts by other means. As a result, a mature and structured diplomacy became as important as the military strategy.

Finally, after suffering heavier casualties in battle for diminishing returns of plunder, Attila decided to cut his losses and invade westward. Here Aetius, with all his carefully cultivated barbarian friendships, performed a diplomatic miracle in uniting and commanding the mutually hostile Germanic kingdoms in a great coalition to stop Attila in 451. After a huge and bloody battle on the Catalaunian plains of northern Gaul, Attila was forced for the first time to retreat. The next year he mounted an abortive invasion of Italy. Soon afterwards, he died suddenly in a drunken stupor. Within a short time his always personal and charismatic 'empire' collapsed.

In the West, Aetius was immediately concerned to disperse the more numerous and powerful Germanic armies as quickly as possible. But now that the main barbarian threat seemed removed, he was treacherously murdered by the emperor Valentinian III (425–455) who had long hated him. In revenge, Aetius's partisans assassinated Valentinian shortly afterwards, ending the Theodosian dynasty.

The next *generalissimo* figure, Ricimer, was himself a barbarian and naturally well-qualified to deal with the overwhelmingly barbarian army and allies. He was related both to the Visigoth and Sueve royal houses, and very willing to allow more federate settlements. Ricimer was a leader spanning two worlds. He saw the Roman empire more as a prestigious, unifying symbol than a political reality, and he set up and deposed puppet emperors at will. In the end it was only logical that a barbarian king should step into the ruling role of patrician and *generalissimo*. When that happened there was no need to retain even a figurehead emperor in the West. In 476 the barbarian king Odovacer forced the emperor Romulus Augustulus to abdicate, and sent an embassy to Constantinople declaring that he would henceforth rule as the viceroy of the Eastern emperor. The fiction of a single united Roman empire was still retained.

The East had tried, and partially succeeded, in arranging the fragments of Attila's old empire to its advantage, but it had been forced to accept two large blocs of Ostrogoths, formerly subjects of Attila, as federates in Illyricum (Yugoslavia) and Thrace (Bulgaria-Romania). These were a destabilising element, each too strong to be defeated by a single Roman field army. In the confused reign of Zeno (474–491) all the dangerous elements erupted again: open conflict in the imperial family, civil wars for the throne, rebellion by the Gothic federates. At one point there was fighting within the capital itself. There seemed a real danger that the Ostrogoths would carve out permanent kingdoms for themselves in the way this had happened in the West.

For a time, the central establishment lost control, but they had several strong advantages. There was always a strong core of regular Roman troops to balance the federates, and they continued to be steadily recruited. All the soldiers, Roman or federate, could only be paid from the central treasuries, which were a potent lever in negotiations, as were timely bribes of gold. The Goths also suffered periodic food shortages which the imperial government, with its network of cities and supply depots, naturally exploited. The two Gothic blocs were often in competition and could easily be played off against each other. Their aims were opportunistic and their long-term goals uncertain. One king, Theoderic (471–526), wanted larger, more secure territories for his people, while the other, Strabo, aimed at a top Roman command and a seat at the centre of government.

By the time Zeno had managed to crush or conciliate his other domestic enemies, by adroit and unscrupulous manoeuvring, Strabo was dead and all the Goths followed Theoderic. In 488, with only one king to deal with, Zeno played the masterstroke. Instead of poor and precarious lands in the Balkans, he invited Theoderic to take Italy from Odovacer. Theoderic did so, finally freeing the East of the federate problem.

It was left to the next emperor Anastasius (491–518) to consolidate these gains. Himself a civil bureaucrat who knew the government machinery intimately, he overhauled and improved the entire fiscal system to produce considerably greater sums for the treasury without injuring the mass of taxpayers. With these funds he expanded the armies by raising pay, built new defences, revived and repopulated much of the Balkans, and fought a successful war against Persia, still leaving a healthy surplus. It was with these great resources that Justinian was soon to embark on his ambitious schemes of reconquest.

The East had certain long-term advantages: a strategically placed capital, shorter vulnerable frontiers, a wealthier agricultural base. But it demanded a high order of statecraft to overcome all the external and internal threats of the fifth century. Individually, its leaders were no more skilful than their Western counterparts, but they managed to evolve institutions and practices which applied these skills and perpetuated them. The Constantinople establishment; the constitutional rituals of imperial succession; the integration of the top army commands; the op- position to federate settlements; the centralised pool of administrative, fiscal and diplomatic experience—all these enabled the East to avoid the unravelling process of diminishing control which occurred in the West.

FOR FURTHER READING

A.H.M. Jones, *The Later Roman Empire* (2 vols, Oxford University Press, 1990); J.B. Bury, *History of The Later Roman Empire*, (Dover paperbacks, 1958); R.C. Blockley, *East Roman Foreign Policy* (ARCA, 1992); J.H.W.G. Liebeschuetz, *From Diocletian to the Arab Conquest*, (Oxford University Press, 1990); J.H. W.G. Liebeschuetz, *Barbarians and Bishops: Army, Church and State in the Age of Arcadius and Chrysostom* (Oxford University Press, 1991); C. Mango, *Byzantium. The Empire of New Rome* (London, 1980).

Stephen Williams and Gerard Friell are also the authors of Theodosius: the Empire at Bay *(Batsford, 1994).*

This article first appeared in *History Today*, November 1998, pp. 40-46. © 1998 by History Today, Ltd. Reprinted by permission.

In the Beginning, There Were the
HOLY BOOKS

The Bible and the Qur'an both reveal the word of God.
Both speak of prophets, redemption, heaven and hell.
So why the violence? Searching the sacred texts for answers.

By Kenneth L. Woodward

He was a pious family man, a trader from Mecca who regularly retreated into the hills above the city to fast and pray. In his 40th year, while he was praying in a cave on Mount Hira, the angel Gabriel spoke to him, saying, "Muhammad, you are the Messenger of God," and commanded him to "Recite!" Muhammad protested that he could not—after all, he was not gifted like the traditional tribal bards of Arabia. Then, according to this tradition, the angel squeezed him so violently that Muhammad thought he'd die. Again Gabriel ordered him to recite, and from his lips came the first verses of what eventually became the Qur'an, regarded as the eternal words of God himself by some 1.3 billion Muslims around the world.

Until that moment, 13 centuries ago, the Arabs were mostly polytheists, worshiping tribal deities. They had no sacred history linking them to one universal god, like other Middle Eastern peoples. They had no sacred text to live by, like the Bible; no sacred language, as Hebrew is to Jews and Sanskrit is to Hindus. Above all, they had no prophet sent to them by God, as Jews and Christians could boast.

Muhammad and the words that he recited until his death in 632 provided all this and more. Like the Bible, the Qur'an is a book of divine revelation. Between them, these two books define the will of God for more than half the world's population. Over centuries, the Bible fashioned the Hebrew tribes into a nation: Israel. But in just a hundred years, the Qur'an created an entire civilization that at its height stretched from northern Africa and southern Europe in the West to the borders of modern India and China in the East. Even today, in streets as distant from each other as those of Tashkent, Khartoum, Qom and Kuala Lumpur, one can hear from dawn to dusk the constant murmur and chant of the Qur'an in melodious Arabic. Indeed, if there were a gospel according to Muhammad, it would begin with these words: in the beginning was the Book.

But since the events of September 11, the Qur'an and the religion it inspired have been on trial. Is Islam an inherently intolerant faith? Does the Qur'an oblige Muslims to wage jihad—holy war—on those who do not share their beliefs? And who are these "infidels" that the Muslim Scriptures find so odious? After all, Jews and Christians are monotheists, too, and most of their own prophets—Abraham, Moses and Jesus especially—are revered by Muslims through their holy book. Listening to the rants of Osama bin Laden and other radical Islamists, Jews and Christians wonder who really speaks for Islam in these perilous times. What common ground—if any—joins these three "Peoples of the Book," as Muslims call their fellow monotheists? What seeds of reconciliation lie within the Qur'an and the Bible and the traditions that they represent? Does the battle of the books, which has endured for centuries between Muslims and believers in the West, ensure a perpetual clash of civilizations?

The Qur'an does contain sporadic calls to violence, sprinkled throughout the text. Islam implies "peace," as Muslims repeatedly insist. Yet the peace promised by Allah to individuals and societies is possible only to those who follow the "straight path" as outlined in the Qur'an. When Muslims run into opposition, especially of the armed variety, the Qur'an counsels bellicose response. "Fight them [nonbelievers] so that Allah may punish them at your hands, and put them to shame," one Qur'anic verse admonishes. Though few in number, these aggressive verses have fired Muslim zealots in every age.

To read the Qur'an is like entering a stream. At any point one may come upon a command of God, a burst of prayer, a theological pronouncement or a description of the final judgment.

The Bible, too, has its stories of violence in the name of the Lord. The God of the early Biblical books is fierce indeed in his support of the Israelite warriors, drowning enemies in the sea. But these stories do not have the force of divine commands. Nor are they considered God's own eternal words, as Muslims believe Qur'anic verses to be. Moreover, Israeli commandos do not cite the Hebrew prophet Joshua as they go into battle, but Muslim insurgents can readily invoke the example of their Prophet, Muhammad, who was a military commander himself. And while the Crusaders may have fought with the cross on their shields, they did not—could not—cite words from Jesus to justify their slaughters. Even so, compared with the few and much quoted verses that call for jihad against the infidels, the Qur'an places far more emphasis on acts of justice, mercy and compassion.

Indeed, the Qur'an is better appreciated as comprehensive guide for those who would know and do the will of God. Like the Bible, the Qur'an defines rules for prayer and religious rituals. It establishes norms governing marriage and divorce, relations between men and women and the way to raise righteous children. More important, both books trace a common lineage back to Abraham, who was neither Jew nor Christian, and beyond that to Adam himself. Theologically, both books profess faith in a single God (Allah means "The God") who creates and sustains the world. Both call humankind to repentance, obedience and purity of life. Both warn of God's punishment and final judgment of the world. Both imagine a hell and a paradise in the hereafter.

DIVINE AUTHORITY

AS SACRED TEXTS, however, the Bible and the Qur'an could not be more different. To read the Qur'an is like entering a stream. At almost any point one may come upon a command of God, a burst of prayer, a theological pronouncement, the story of an earlier prophet or a description of the final judgment. Because Muhammad's revelations were heard, recited and memorized by his converts, the Qur'an is full of repetitions. None of its 114 suras, or chapters, focuses on a single theme. Each sura takes its title from a single word—The Cow, for example, names the

THE ANNUNCIATION

In the Qur'an and the Bible the angel Gabriel is God's announcer. Through Gabriel, Muhammad hears the revelations that, for Muslims, is the Word of God made book. In the Bible, Gabriel tells the Virgin Mary she will give birth to Jesus who, for Christians, is the Word of God made flesh.

CREATION

Both the Qur'an and the Bible tell the story of Adam and Eve in the Garden of Eden. But for Muslims, as for Jews, their 'original sin' of disobedience is not passed on to humankind, so they don't require salvation through the sacrifice of Jesus on the cross—a central doctrine of Christianity.

THE ASCENSION

In one story extrapolated from a verse in the Qur'an, the Prophet Muhammad ascends to the throne of God, the model for the Sufis' flight of the soul to God. In the Bible, Jesus ascends to the Father after he is resurrected from the dead. For Muhammad, it was inconceivable that Allah would allow one of his prophets to be executed as a criminal.

HOLY PLACES

The Temple Mount is the holiest shrine for Jews. At first Muhammad directed his followers also to face Jerusalem when they prayed. But after the Jews of Medina refused him as their prophet, he directed Muslims to bow in the direction of the Kaaba in Mecca, now the holiest shrine in Islam.

PEACE AND WAR

Muhammad was not only a prophet but a military commander who led Muslim armies into battle. Jesus, on the other hand, refused even to defend himself against the Roman soldiers who arrested him in the Garden of Gethsemane after he was betrayed with a kiss by Judas, one of his own disciples. The difference helps explain the contrasting attitudes toward war and violence in the Qur'an and the New Testament.

longest—which appears only in that chapter. When Muhammad's recitations were finally written down (on palm leaves, shoulders of animals, shards of anything that would substitute for paper) and collected after his death, they were organized roughly from the longest to the shortest. Thus there is no chronological organization—this is God speaking, after all, and his words are timeless.

Nonetheless, scholars recognize that the shortest suras were received first, in Muhammad's Meccan period, and the longest in Medina, where he later became a political and military leader of the emerging community of Muslims. As a result, the longer texts take up matters of behavior and organization which are absent in the shorter, more "prophetic" suras that announce the need to submit. ("Muslim" means "submission" to God.) The Qur'an's fluid structure can be confusing, even to Muslims. "That's why one finds in Muslim bookstores such books as 'What the Qur'an says about women' or 'What the Qur'an says about a just society'," observes Jane McAuliffe of Georgetown University, editor of the new Encyclopaedia of the Qur'an.

Like the Bible, the Qur'an asserts its own divine authority. But whereas Jews and Christians regard the Biblical text as the words of divinely inspired human authors, Muslims regard the Qur'an, which means "The Recitation," as the eternal words of Allah himself. Thus, Muhammad is the conduit for God's words, not their composer. Moreover, since Muhammad heard God in Arabic, translations of the Qur'an are considered mere "interpretations" of the language of God's original revelation. "In this very important sense," says Roy Mottahedeh, professor of Middle Eastern history at Harvard, "the Qur'an is *not* the Bible of the Muslims." Rather, he says, it is like the oral Torah first revealed to Moses that was later written down. In gospel terminology, the Qur'an corresponds to Christ himself, as the *logos*, or eternal word of the Father. In short, if Christ is the word made flesh, the Qur'an is the word made book.

Compared with the few and much quoted verses that call for jihad against the 'infidels,' the Qur'an places far more emphasis on acts of justice, mercy and compassion.

The implications of this doctrine are vast—and help to explain the deepest divisions between Muslims and other monotheisms. For Muslims, God is one, indivisible and absolutely transcendent. Because of this, no edition of the Qur'an carries illustrations—even of the Prophet—lest they encourage idolatry *(shirk)*, the worst sin a Muslim can commit. Muslims in the former Persian Empire, however, developed a rich tradition of extra-Qur'anic art depicting episodes in the life of Muhammad, from which the illustrations for this story are taken. But for every Muslim, the presence of Allah can be experienced here and now through the very sounds and syllables of the Arabic Qur'an. Thus, only the original Arabic is used in prayer—even though the vast majority of Muslims do not understand the language. It doesn't matter: the Qur'an was revealed through the Prophet's ears, not his eyes. To hear those same words recited, to take them into yourself through prayer, says Father Patrick Gaffney, an anthropologist specializing in Islam at the University of Notre Dame, "is to experience the presence of God with the same kind of intimacy as Catholics feel when they receive Christ as consecrated bread and wine at mass."

'PEOPLE OF THE BOOK'

WHY THEN, DOES THE Qur'an acknowledge Jews and Christians as fellow "People of the Book," and as such, distinguish them from nonbelievers? Contrary to popular belief, "the Book" in question is not the Bible; it refers to a heavenly text, written by God, of which the Qur'an is the only perfect copy. According to the Qur'an, God mercifully revealed the contents of that book from time to time through the words of previous Biblical prophets and messengers—and also to other obscure figures not mentioned in the Bible. But in every case those who received his revelations—particularly the Jews and Christians—either consciously or inadvertently corrupted the original text, or seriously misinterpreted it. On this view, the Qur'an is not a new version of what is contained in the Bible, but what Jane McAuliffe calls a "rerevelation" that corrects the errors of the Hebrew and Christian Scriptures. Readers of the Bible will find in the Qur'an familiar figures such as Abraham, Moses, David, John the Baptist, Jesus and even the Virgin Mary, who appears much more often than she does in the New Testament, and is the only woman mentioned in the Qur'an by name. But their stories differ radically from those found in the Bible. In the Qur'an all the previous prophets are Muslims.

Abraham (Ibrahim), for example, is recognized as the first Muslim because he chose to surrender to Allah rather than accept the religion of his father, who is not mentioned in the Bible. Neither is the Qur'anic story of how Abraham built the Kaaba in Mecca, Islam's holiest shrine. Abraham's importance in the Qur'an is central: just as the Hebrews trace their lineage to Abraham through Isaac, his son by Sarah, the Qur'an traces Arab genealogy—and Muhammad's prophethood—back through Ishmael, a son Abraham had by Hagar.

The Qur'anic Moses (Musa) looks much like his Biblical counterpart. He confronts the pharaoh, works miracles and in the desert ascends the mountain to receive God's commandments. But in the Qur'an there is no mention of the Passover rituals, and among the commandments one of the most important for Jews—keeping the Sabbath—is absent. Obedience to parents is stressed repeatedly, but as in the Qur'anic story of Abraham, disobedience is required when parents are polytheists.

As a prophet rejected by his own people, the Qur'anic Jesus (Isa) looks a lot like Muhammad, who was at first rejected by the people of Mecca. He preaches the word of God, works miracles, is persecuted and—what is new, foretells his successor: Muhammad. But the Qur'an rejects the Christian claim that he is the son of God as blasphemous and dismisses the doctrine of the Trinity as polytheistic. The Crucifixion is mentioned in passing, but according to the Qur'an Jesus mysteriously does not die. Instead, Allah rescues him to heaven from where he will descend in the last days and, like other prophets, be a witness for his community of believers at the Final Judgment.

What Muhammad may have known about the Bible and its prophets and where he got his information is a purely scholarly debate. The Qur'an itself says that Muhammad met a Jewish clan in Medina. He even had his followers bow to Jerusalem when praying until the Jews rejected him as prophet. Some scholars claim that Muhammad had in-laws who were Christian, and they believe he learned his fasting and other ascetic practices from observing desert monks. But Muslims reject any scholarly efforts to link the contents of the Qur'an to the Prophet's human interactions. They cherish the tradition that Muhammad could not read or write as proof that the Qur'an is pure revelation. It is enough for them that Islam is the perfect religion and the Qur'an the perfect text.

That belief has not prevented Muslim tradition from transforming the Qur'an's many obscure passages into powerful myths. By far the most significant is the story developed from one short verse: "Glory be to Him who carried His servant at night from the Holy Mosque to the Further Mosque, the precincts of which we have blessed, that we might show him some of our signs" (sura 17:1). From this Muslims have elaborated the story of Muhammad's mystical nighttime journey from Mecca to Jerusalem, where he addresses an assembly of all previous prophets from Adam to Jesus. Yet another version of this story tells of his subsequent Ascension *(mi'raj)* from Jerusalem to the throne of Allah, receiving honors along the way from the prophets whom he has superseded. For Sufi mystics, Muhammad's ascension is the paradigmatic story of the soul's flight to God. For many Muslim traditionalists, however, the journey was a physical one. Either way, its geopolitical significance cannot be ignored because the spot where the ascension began is Islam's third holiest shrine: the Dome of the Rock on Jerusalem's Temple Mount.

In Islam's current political conflicts with the West, the major problem is not the Muslims' sacred book but how it is interpreted. Muslims everywhere are plagued by a crippling crisis of authority. The Qur'an envisioned a single Muslim community (the *umma*), but as subsequent history shows, Muslims have never resolved the tension between religious authority and Islamic governments. When Islam was a great medieval civilization, jurists learned in the Qur'an decided how to apply God's words to changed historical circumstances. Their *fatwas* (opinions) settled disputes. But in today's Islamic states, authoritative religious voices do not command widespread respect. Like freewheeling fundamentalists of every religious stripe, any Muslim with an agenda now feels free to cite the Qur'an in his support. Osama bin Laden is only the most dangerous and obvious example.

Bin Laden's Twisted Mission

A bloody misinterpretation of the Qur'an's call to arms

BY CHRISTOPHER DICKEY

WHEN OSAMA BIN Laden proclaimed his "jihad against Crusaders and Jews" in 1998, he new he was on shaky religious ground. This was his declaration of "holy war" to justify bombing U.S. embassies in Africa a few months later and, eventually, the attacks of September 11. It was his theological license "to kill the Americans and plunder their money wherever and whenever they are found." And it was based on a lie: that Islam itself was under attack by the United States, that "crimes and sins committed by the Americans are a clear declaration of war on God, his messenger and Muslims." The fact that Americans defended Muslims against the likes of Saddam Hussein and Slobodan Milosevic was ignored because, for bin Laden's bloody-minded purposes, it had to be.

Without that lie about American aggression, none of the many verses of the Qur'an that bin Laden cites would justify violence, much less the unholy slaughter of civilians. There are many interpretations of jihad—which means, literally, "effort." Often it describes the personal struggle merely to be a better, more pious Muslim. The empire builders of Islam waged military offensives in the name of jihad as late as the 17th century, and not a few turned their righteous doctrines on each other. But according to Gilles Kepel, author of the forthcoming book "Jihad: The Trail of Political Islam," the defensive holy war that bin Laden claims to fight is the most potent and most dangerous form of all. It is seen by many Muslims, if it is justified, as a personal obligation that supersedes all others, and may ultimately challenge all authority. "It's a two-edged sword," says Kepel. "Once you open the gate of defensive jihad, it's very difficult to close it again."

"To those against whom war is made, permission is given to fight," says the 22d chapter of the Qur'an—especially "those who have been expelled from their homes… for no cause except that they say, 'Our Lord is Allah'." Thus in Muslim theology defensive holy war was justified against European Crusaders and conquerors who attacked Muslims in the name of Christ and imposed the Inquisition, with all its horrors. Thus, in more recent times, Afghans could wage their war against the atheistic Soviets with plenty of religious backing. Few if any Muslim scholars will speak out against jihad by Palestinians fighting Israeli occupying troops. But bin Laden, a Saudi, was never persecuted for his faith. The goals he fought for initially were political and personal: to overthrow the Muslim rulers of his own country. And the jihad he declared against the United States, in the eyes of most religious scholars, was never a holy war, it was a blatant fraud.

DECIPHERING MEANINGS

BUT THE QUR'AN HAS ITS moderate interpreters as well. Since September 11, brave voices scattered across the Middle East have condemned the terrorist acts of killing civilians and judged suicide bombing contrary to the teaching of the Qur'an. Returning to the text itself, other scholars have found verses showing that Allah created diverse peoples and cultures for a purpose and therefore intended that the world remain pluralistic in religion as well. "The Qur'an," argues Muslim philosopher Jawat Said of the Al-Azhar Institute in Cairo, "gives support and encouragement to sustain the messengers of reform who face difficult obstacles."

America, too, has a core of immigrant and second-generation Muslim scholars who have experienced firsthand the benefits of democracy, free speech and the Bill of Rights. They think the Qur'an is open to interpretations that can embrace these ideals for Islamic states as well. Islam even has feminists like Azizah Y. al-Hibri of the University of Richmond Law School, who are laying the legal groundwork for women's rights through a careful reconsideration of the Qur'an and its classic commentators.

It is precisely here that the Bible and the Qur'an find their real kinship. As divine revelation, each book says much more than what a literal reading can possibly capture. To say that God is one, as both the Qur'an and the Bible insist, is also to say that God's wisdom is unfathomable. As the Prophet himself insisted, God reveals himself through signs whose meanings need to be deciphered. Here, it would seem, lie the promising seeds of religious reconciliation. Humility, not bravado, is the universal posture of anyone who dares to plumb the mind of God and seek to do his will.

UNIT 5
The Medieval Period

Unit Selections

Key Points to Consider

- Why were the gifts sent to Charlemagne thought to be important in the scheme of international trade?

- Why is King Alfred regarded so highly in English history?

- How is our view of the Vikings changing according to recent investigations?

- Why was Spain to be thought of so highly in the tenth century?

- Who undertook the First Crusade and what did it accomplish?

- Why did the myths about witches arise?

- What do you learn about women in the Middle Ages?

- What was life like for people in England during the fourteenth century?

- Why was the introduction of the Trebuchet important in medieval warfare?

- Why did the Italian governments introduce intramural games?

- What were the effects on medieval civilization as a result of the "Black Death"?

- Where the Knights Templar seen as either "saints or sinners" in medieval Europe?

 **Links: www.dushkin.com/online/**
These sites are annotated in the World Wide Web pages.

EuroDocs: Primary Historical Documents From Western Europe
http://www.lib.byu.edu/~rdh/eurodocs/
Feudalism
http://www.fidnet.com/~weid/feudalism.htm
The Labyrinth: Resources for Medieval Studies
http://www.georgetown.edu/labyrinth/
The World of the Vikings
http://www.pastforward.co.uk/vikings/

In the aftermath of barbarian invasions, Western civilization faced several important challenges: to assimilate Roman and Germanic people and cultures, to reconcile Christian and pagan views, and to create a new social, political, and economic institutions to fill the vacuum left by the disintegration of the Roman order—in sum, to shape a new unity out the of the chaos and diversity of the post-Roman world. The next millennium (550–1500) saw the rise and demise of a distinctive phase of Western experience—medieval civilization.

Medieval culture expressed a uniquely coherent view of life and the world, summarized here by literary scholar C. S Lewis:

> Characteristically, medieval man was not a dreamer, nor a spiritual adventurer; he was an organizer, a codifier, a man of system.... Three things are typical of him. First, small minority of his cathedrals in which the design of the architect was actually achieved (usually, of course, it was overtaken in the next wave of architectural fashion long before it was finished).... Secondly, the *Summa* of Thomas Aquinas. And thirdly, the *Divine Comedy* of Dante. In all these alike we see the tranquil, indefatigable, exultant energy of the mass of heterogeneous details into unity. They desire unity and proportion, all the classical virtues, just as keenly as the Greeks did. But they have a more varied collection of things to fit in. And they delight to do it. (*Studies in Medieval and Renaissance Literature*, Cambridge University Press, 1966)

This outlook also expressed itself in a distinctly medieval social ideal. In theory, medieval society provided a well-ordered and satisfying life. The Church looked after people's souls, the nobility maintained civil order, and a devoted peasantry performed the work of the world. Ideally, as historian Crane Brinton explains, "a beautifully ordered nexus or rights and duties bound each man to each, from swineherd to emperor and pope."

Of course, medieval society, like our own, fell short of its ideal. Feudal barons warred among themselves. Often the clergy was ignorant and corrupt. Peasants were not always content and passive. And medieval civilization had other shortcomings. During much of the Middle Ages there was little interest in nature and how it worked. While experimentation and observation were not unknown, science (or "natural philosophy") was subordinate to theology, which generally attracted the best minds of the day. An economy based on agriculture and a society based on inherited status had little use for innovation. Aspects of medieval society are treated in the articles "Charlemagne's Elephant," "The Most Perfect Man in History?" "Britain 1300," and "Women Pilgrims of the Middle Ages." The articles on the Knights Templar, "Saints or Sinners? The Knights Templar in Medieval Europe" and "Ready, Aim, Fire!" explore facets of medieval warfare.

All this is not to suggest that the medieval period was static and sterile. Crusaders, pilgrims, and merchants enlarged Europe's view of the world. And there were noteworthy mechanical innovations: the horse collar, which enabled beasts of burden to pull heavier loads; the stirrup, which altered mounted combat; mechanical clocks, which made possible more exact measurement of time; the compass, which brought the age of exploration closer; an the papermaking process, which made feasible the print revolution, which in turn played key roles in the Reformation and the scientific revolution. "The Amazing Vikings" demonstrates that during the Dark Ages there existed possibilities for enterprise and progress. "An Iberian Chemistry" discusses the accomplishments made possible by Muslim rule in medieval Spain, while article by John France shows how the Crusades began hostilities between Christians and Muslims. Still, the military encounter between the two faiths produced cross-cultural influences that contributed to fundamental economic, military, and political changes in the West.

The medieval order broke down in the fourteenth and fifteenth centuries. Plague, wars, and famines produced a demographic catastrophe that severely strained the economic and political systems. Charles Mee's article, "How a Mysterious Disease Laid Low Europe's Masses," explains how the Black Death affected many aspects of medieval life. During this period social discontent took the form of peasant uprisings and urban revolts. Dynastic and fiscal problems destablized England and France. The Great Schism and the new heresies divided the Church. Emerging capitalism gradually undermined an economy based on landed property. Yet these crises generated the creative forces that would give birth to the Renaissance and the modern era. The nation-state, the urban way of life, the class structure, and other aspects of modern life existed in embryonic form in the Middle Ages. These aspects are treated in "War-Games of Central Italy" by Raymond E. Role, who recounts Italian urban life. And as historian William McNeill has written, it was in medieval Europe that the West prepared itself for its modern role as "chief disturber and principal upsetter of other people's ways."

Charlemagne's Elephant

On the 1,200th anniversary of Charlemagne's coronation in Rome, **Richard Hodges** reviews the evidence for long-distance trade in his empire.

RELATIONS BETWEEN THE MEDITERRANEAN AND NORTHERN Europe in the age of Charlemagne have puzzled archaeologists and historians. At face value the two parts of Europe appear to have been completely separated, despite Charlemagne's famous coronation in Rome in December 800. Furthermore, relations between Latin Christendom, Byzantium and the Abbasid caliphate (based in Baghdad) appear to have been virtually non-existent. Only intrepid pilgrims bridged the ideological divides that separated these three great regions with their different religions in order to visit the Holy Land. What puzzles archaeologists, in particular, is that while the Christian regions of England, France and Germany apparently had little contact with the South and East, archaeological evidence has long revealed that the Viking-Age communities of the Baltic Sea enjoyed successful commercial partnerships reaching Byzantium and the Orient. Moreover, ninth-century Frankish glass and decorated pottery have been found in excavations of Viking-period settlements as far north as the Lofoten Islands.

Ever since archaeologist Haljmar Stolpe began his excavations in the barrow cemetery surrounding the central Swedish island port at Birka in 1870 (situated in Lake Malaren), it has been evident that the north-south divide in post-Classical Europe was more virtual than real. Stolpe found numerous ninth-century merchants' graves containing Arab silver dirhems, similar to the thousands found in hoards in western Russia and around the shores of the Baltic. Many of these coins were defaced with Scandinavian runes, as if to destroy their ideological power. Other oriental grave-goods include silks and collapsible balances. Notable discoveries included a finger-ring bearing the legend *Allah* in Arabic from grave 515, and a cylindrical glass vessel of likely Syrian manufacture decorated with bird and plant motifs from grave 542. Similar finds have been found at other trading sites around the Baltic. Hedeby, for example, the Danish-planned emporium situated at the base of Jutland, boasts not only Arabic objects, but also a lead seal dated *c*.840 belonging to a certain Theodosius, *patrikos*, imperial *protospatharius* and *chartularius* of the public vestiary, chief of the Byzantine emperor's personal security.

Did such objects occur in Latin Christendom in the age of Charlemagne? Only a handful of ninth-century Arabic dirhems have been discovered to date, and only one hoard of them buried in the bed of the river Reno near Bologna in Central Italy. Silks, Syrian glass and other exotica are similarly scarce. Archaeologists argue whether the dirhems were melted down to make Charlemagne's silver-rich coins, while as yet few places were silk might survive have been excavated. On the other hand, while the written sources rarely describe commerce, special gifts did attract the attention of monkish chroniclers. For example, the Emperor Charlemagne was sent a brass clock by the Abbasid caliph, Harun al-Rashid in Baghdad. According to the Emperor's biographer, it was,

> ... a marvellous mechanical contraption, in which the course of the twelve hours moved according to a water clock, with as many brazen little balls, which fell down on the hour and through their fall made a cymbal ring underneath. On this clock there were also twelve horsemen who at the end of each hour stepped out of twelve windows, closing the previously open windows by their movements.

For Charlemagne, this extraordinary object must have represented learning and progress, much as a Model T Ford did in an isolated town in the early twentieth century. The clock, however, was modest by comparison with Harun's more fabled present to his Frankish peer.

Befitting Charlemagne's image of himself as a Roman emperor, Harun sent Charlemagne an elephant, called Abu l'Abbas, which had originally been owned by an Indian raja before Harun's predecessor, Caliph Al-Mahdi, acquired it. The gift of the elephant did not come out of the blue. The embassy to the Frankish court was led by the governor of Egypt, Ibrahim Ibn al-Aghlab, in response to a mission despatched by Charlemagne to the caliph's court in 797—the first of three embassies sent to the caliphate (the others set out in 802 and 807 respectively). Ibrahim crossed the Mediterranean and disembarked at

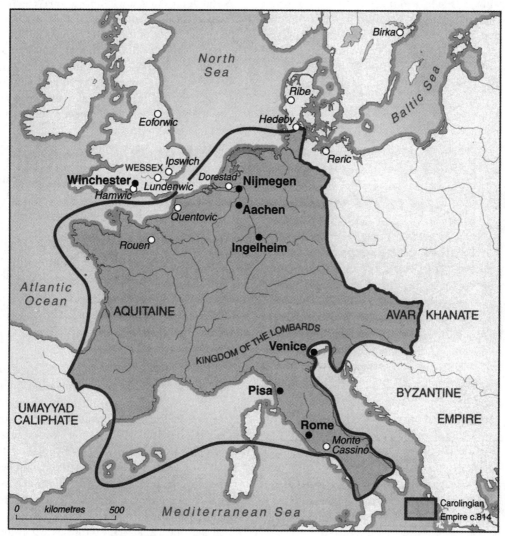

History Today/Tim Aspden

Pisa. From there, in part following the old Via Cassia from Rome to Turin, the embassy journeyed over the Alps to Charlemagne's court in the Rhineland. Once in Germany, Charlemagne presumably built a house for Abu l'-Abbas, where the creature lived for the best part of a decade. We know only one further detail of this creature's colourful life. The Frankish annals record that when King Godfred of the Danes seized traders from a place called Reric—possibly old Lübeck—and installed them at a place that the annalist calls Sliastorp (probably Hedeby near Schleswig in north Germany), Charlemagne took the elephant with him on his march to quell the trouble. The two great casualties of the campaign were Godfred, who was assassinated during a revolt in the Danish camp, and Abu l'-Abbas. The elephant died at Lippeham on Luneburg heath.

The story of the elephant draws the thinnest of historical threads together, forging connections between the Arabs, Latin Christendom and the Vikings: between Muslims, Christians and Nordic pagans, setting in motion a cycle of entangled relations. But we should be cautious of taking the story at face value. Inevitably Harun's gift begs many questions: what kind of boat was used to carry the beast to Pisa? It could not have been ac-

commodated on any of the known late Roman or high medieval wrecks so far discovered in Mediterranean waters. Are we to assume that the deep-draughted cargo vessel could be docked against a quay at Pisa? How did Ibrahim's embassy progress to Germany? Did Charlemagne build elephant houses at his palaces of Ingelheim, Aachen and Nijmegen? How did the elephant, a tangible commodity from another ideology, influence his attitudes to that people and, consequently, to the re-examinations of his own ideology? Was it old Roman imperial vanity that persuaded him to take the creature on the Danish campaign?

The clock and elephant cannot have failed to open Charlemagne's eyes to the expanding horizons of the ninth-century world. Like the Vikings, he must have been aware of the silver-rich mines of the caliphate and perhaps of the harbours in China now open since 792 to foreigners. Quite clearly, he must have known that the Abbasids were a source of silks and spices. Less conspicuous gifts such as these are regularly noted from the later eighth century onwards by the *Liber Pontificalis* (the book of the Pope) in the possession of Rome's churches. Similarly, a rare description of the rich treasury of the Benedictine monastery of Monte Cassino lists silks and exotica. Excavations of Monte Cassino's sister monastery at San Vincenzo al Volturno in Central Italy have produced shards of an Abbasid polychrome dish, glass-making following the Syrian tradition, and a sword-chape made of nephrite jade derived from China. Yet aside from these objects, oriental culture is notably absent.

Courtesy of author

The Swedish site of Birka, regarded as Sweden's oldest town and founded in 800, has yielded many Arabic coins and artefacts.

North of the Alps, town life revived around AD 700 in a few great places on the edges of the North Sea littoral.

Why was this? The prinicpal reason is that this was an agrarian society. The engines of production were royal estate centres and monasteries as towns had not survived beyond the seventh century in Latin Christendom. Rome, of course, never truly died as an urban centre. Recent archaeological excavations in the Forum of Nerva show that north European pilgrims and tourists (such as the retired eighth-century West Saxon king Ina and the young Alfred the Great) would have discovered town life squeezed between the constellation of monasteries that occupied the eternal city in post-Classical times. Yet Rome was not so much a town in the sense that it had been in the age of the Emperor Augustus with streets and public buildings and residences, as a collection of elite centres with thousands of inhabitants that necessitated a bare minimum of production and procurement services. Rome, without doubt, became a town again in the later eighth century when, with Carolingian political support, it entertained a new vigour, situated midway as it was between the centres of occidental power in the Rhineland and East Mediterranean. Many great churches in the city—basilicas such as *SS* Quattro Coronati, and Santa Prassede—remain a testament to this important revival of its post-Classical fortunes.

North of the Alps, town life was revived around AD 700 in a particular and almost quarantined sense in a few great places occupying the edges of the North Sea littoral: Rouen, Quentovic, Dorestad, Hamwic (Southampton), Lundenwic (London), Ipswich, Eoforwic (York), Medemblik, Hedeby and Ribe. These places went largely unnoticed by contemporary chroniclers, yet possessed the hallmarks of later medieval towns: customs, quays, warehouses, gridded streets regularly maintained, tenements and industrial zones.

These *emporia* (trade centres) are archaeology's special contribution to Dark Age history. Like modern shopping malls or airports, these were non-places, in the sense that they were overlooked by contemporary historians. Their rich material culture was first noted in the mid-nineteenth century. Then famished peasants plundered the bonefields of Dorestad (at the mouth of the Rhine), and at the same time Southampton's inquisitive citizens were digging up parts of Hamwic, the eighth- to ninth-century town on the low-lying brick earths in the Itchen-side suburb of St Marys. But only in the last fifty years, following excavation sponsored by the Gestapo at Hedeby on the eve of the Second World War, has the geography of these places become apparent. Hamwic, we now know, was shaped by a rectilinear street grid, not unlike an ancient city, with groups of dwellings clustered in each *insula*. Initially, Hamwic was interpreted as a traders' town, an emporium humming with foreigners. But closer analysis of the rubbish pits shows that it was in fact a centre for regional craft production. Sunk deep into the brickearth, these pits are brimming with refuse as well as rubbish such as animal bones. The first, distinctive English coins known as *sceattas* also occur in striking numbers.

The same features have now been found at the other great centres of this age. Lundenwic, occupying the rising ground west of the deserted Roman walled city, was quite as rich in imported and local material culture as excavations beneath the Royal Opera House and even in the grounds of 10 Downing Street have shown. Ipswich, initially no more than a riverside nucleus, was furnished with a street grid rising well away from the river Gipping. In one sector the distinctive grey burnished pitchers known as Ipswich ware were made in huge quantities. South-east of York's Roman walled city, beside the river Foss, a similar tract of a Northumbrian emporium known as Eoforwic has been excavated. Again it is singularly rich in finds. The pattern is repeated at Quentovic, the great Frankish emporium, now a green field site near Montreuil-sur-Mer, and Dorestad, where in advance of a housing development in the 1960s, a great swathe of the Rhinemouth emporium that served the interests of the Carolingian manufacturers in the Bonn-Cologne region was excavated. In common with the line of later eighth- to ninth-century craft workshops found in the central Italian Benedictine monastery of San Vincenzo al Volturno, these places were awash with material culture much of which has been left for archaeologists to study.

What the emporia lacked distinguishes them as centres. The secular and ecclesiastical elite were absent. Traces of timber or stone palaces like those found at Northampton, for example, simply do not exist in these towns. Churches rarely occur. Hamwic boasts possible examples made of slender posts, as

---

does Dorestad. However, minsters built of stone such as Brixworth (Northamptonshire) or small rural basilicas such as Escomb (Co. Durham) are missing. In a sense, the excavated dwellings, known to archaeologists from the holes vacated by their posts or earthfast beams, follow broadly vernacular forms and reveal only limited variation. Paradoxically, of course, the elite were present in spirit. No archaeologist seriously doubts that the emporia were created by powerful leaders to channel the exchange of prestige goods and to control regional production. Outside Hamwic lay the royal palace of Hamtun; Mercian kings maintained estates at Chelsea near Lundenwic; the Bishop of Utrecht held property in Dorestad. Understated though the ambitions of these places were, we should not underestimate the eagerness of kings and clerics to profit from them.

Hamwic covered more than forty hectares; Lundenwic covered perhaps sixty. As many as 5,000 people lived in these places at their zenith, a figure at least fifty times larger than a large village or royal estate. In each the gravelled streets were regularly repaired, just as the plank-made jetties stretching out into the river at Dorestad were lengthened and maintained as the Rhine bed shifted away from the town.

In contrast to Rome, the northern emporia were places without history or memory, ritual or monuments.

Did such places exist on the north shores of the Mediterranean? Many historians believe that Venice was possibly as ambitious a centre, replacing Marseilles as the conduit leading from the Mediterranean into central Europe. Thousands of traders lived on the islands, if we accept the accounts of Frankish chroniclers of Charlemagne's dogged attempts to conquer the archipelago. As yet, too few archaeological excavations have been possible but the glimpses of the ninth-century levels are intriguing. Several historians believe that Commachio further south, at the mouth of the river Po on the Adriatic, was another emporium.

In complete contrast to Rome, the emporia were without history or memory, ritual or monuments. As such these places could not be central to Charlemagne's vision of a renascent Christendom, with its architecture, art and cultural spirit rooted in the glory of ancient Rome. Convinced of the need to extend the market system beyond these monopolistic centres, Charlemagne promulgated laws intended to introduce regional markets. At the same time laws were issued to encourage the use of a common silver currency based on a closely monitored weight. After 793–94 money brokers, from Naples to Hedeby, minted silver *deniers* to the new euro-standard. It would be foolhardy to suggest that all Europe subscribed to the new economic order, any more than it subscribed to Charlemagne's cultural revolution. It did not. Nevertheless, there was an incremental increase in productivity and trade.

Certainly new towns were created in flourishing regions like Mercia, Wessex, Flanders and central Italy, while extra-mural markets grew up outside the walls of many monasteries. The archaeological remains of these incipient market towns are often fairly vestigial. In Mercian towns like Hereford and Tamworth, at Winchester in Wessex and Norwich in East Anglia, emergent urban nuclei clearly existed, presaging the planned towns of the late ninth or early tenth centuries. The same is true in places like Ghent or Huy, while further south in Italy new towns like Sicopolis, near Capua, and Centocelle near Civitavecchia were laid out rather in the image of the mid ninth-century Leonine city filling the zone between the Vatican and the river Tiber at Rome. These were secular versions of the *vici*, the extra-mural market settlements described by chroniclers outside the holy precincts of monasteries like Monte Cassino (Italy) and St Denys (France) and now identified as clusters of timber buildings in the extensive excavations at San Vincenzo al Volturno, little different from a sector of a north European emporium.

A Chinese jade sword-chape (scabbard-tip) found in the southern Italian monastery of San Vincenzo al Volturno.

Known to King Alfred from his pilgrimage as a youth to Rome, these places must have been in his mind as he instructed the shift around 886 from Lundenwic to Lundenburg, within the old walls of the Roman city. A wall-painting in London's Royal Exchange, painted in 1912, depicts King Alfred on a piebald horse amid the ruins of the Roman city sagely approving an architect's plans for the new capital. The image may be a little far-fetched, but excavations now reveal a block of 30 hectares laid out in a rectilinear grid mirroring, perhaps, the Middle Saxon field system that had existed here, and clearly resembling the earlier town-plan of Lundenwic to the west. Alfred, we may suppose, the quintessential proponent of Charlemagne's ideas on cultural values and government, was locating his premier city in a place that possessed the spirit of antiquity—a place with a memory, as opposed to a non-place. At the same time the Anglo-Scandinavian rulers of Eoforwic abandoned the Foss-side emporium for the security and traditions embedded within the Roman walled town of York; the same happened at Rouen, where its Frankish rulers undoubtedly made the same connection between safety and memory.

The rise of towns, of course, reflected rural productivity and a burgeoning demand for craft production at all levels of society. Excavations of villages from all parts of Carolingian Europe show a growing emphasis upon improved animal husbandry as well as crop management. Villages like Kootwyk, occupying marginal ground in the sparse sandy Veluwe region of the Netherlands, were remodelled, in this case as its iron ore extraction activities lent the community a new significance. Even beyond the bounds of Christendom, the effects of the new order were felt. Recent excavations of the Viking-Age village of Vörbasse (Jutland) brought to light traces of a horizontal-wheel water-mill, a technological device which historians once imagined only to exist in Denmark when it was an established Christian nation in the twelfth century. The archaeological evidence suggests that Carolingian-period Viking magnates were every bit as aware of the new technologies as their Christian contemporaries who possessed similar water-mills on their estates at, for example, Old Windsor in Wessex and Tamworth in Mercia. In a nutshell, ninth-century Scandinavians, it is now clear, were tied in not only to the trade in prestige goods emanating from the Abbasid caliphate but also in new technological information emanating from the heart of Latin Christendom. Nothing better illustrates the integration of Europe as Charlemagne, using new architecture, arts and literacy, promoted a new age of cultural politics.

But precisely who provided the bridge between Christendom and the Orient? As we have seen, much of the evidence is uncomfortably slight. Certainly, after *c*.800 references in the chronicles to pilgrimages to the Holy Land increase as significantly as the references in the *Liber Pontificalis* to gifts of silks to Rome's churches. Is it coincidental that this was the moment that Abbasid silver dirhems first occurred in Swedish towns like Birka, when the clock arrived in Aachen and when the monks in San Vincenzo al Volturno's workshops made lamps using Arabic techniques? Surely not. Whether Charlemagne and his contemporaries were influenced by the pilgrims who had been to Palestine and had seen the great Abbasid cities of the Levant (where townlife persisted uninterrupted in its Arabic reformulation of classical townscapes) is a matter of conjecture. Any contemporary mention of such admiration by a Christian chronicler was heresy. Yet, as the archaeology of the eighth and ninth centuries becomes a little more familiar, we must seriously envisage that, just as the Baltic Sea was regularly in contact with the Abbasid caliphate via the long riverine route passing through western Russia to the Black Sea, so the Carolingian, Byzantine and Arabic worlds were far more interconnected than the media of this Dark Age would have its readers believe. Such contact, as the celebrated Belgian historian Henri Pirenne long ago surmised, was the scaffolding on which the Middle Ages were constructed.

FOR FURTHER READING

Richard Hodges, *Towns and Trade in the Age of Charlemagne*, (Duckworth, 2000); Richard Hodges & David Whitehouse, *Mohammed, Charlemagne and the origins of Europe* (Duckworth, 1983); Philip Grierson & Mark Blackburn, *Medieval European Coinage, vol. 1*, (Cambridge University Press, 1986); G.P. Brogiolo and S. Gelichi, *La Critta nell Alto Medioevo Italiano*, (Laterza, 1998); G.P. Brogiolo and B. Ward-Perkins (eds.) *The Idea and Ideology of the Town between Late Antiquity and the Early Middle Ages*, (E.J. Brill, 1999).

Richard Hodges is Professor of Archaeology at the University of East Anglia and scientific director of the Butrint Foundation. His latest book, *Visions of Rome—The Life and Times of Thomas Ashby*, is published by the British School at Rome.

The Most Perfect Man in History?

Barbara Yorke considers the reputation of King Alfred the Great—and the enduring cult around his life and legend.

King Alfred of Wessex (r.871–99) is probably the best known of all Anglo-Saxon rulers, even if the first thing to come into many people's minds in connection with him is something to do with burnt confectionery. This year sees the 1100th anniversary of his death on October 26th, 899, at the age of about fifty. The occasion is being marked with conferences and exhibitions in Winchester, Southampton and London, but the scale of celebrations will be modest compared with those which commemorated his millenary, and culminated in the unveiling by Lord Rosebery of his statue in Winchester.

Alfred's reputation still stands high with historians, though few would now want to follow Edward Freeman in claiming him as 'the most perfect character in history' (*The History of the Nor-*

man *Conquest of England*, 5 volumes, 1867–79). Alfred is someone who has had greatness thrust upon him. How and why did he acquire his glowing reputation, and how does it stand up today?

There can be no doubt that Alfred's reign was significant, both for the direction of the country's development and for the fortunes of his descendants. After the kingdoms of Northumbria, East Anglia and Mercia had fallen to the Vikings, Wessex under Alfred was the only surviving Anglo-Saxon province. Alfred nearly succumbed to the Vikings as well, but kept his nerve and won a decisive victory at the battle of Edington in 879. Further Viking threats were kept at bay by a reorganisation of military service and particularly through the ringing of Wessex by a regular system of garrisoned fortresses. At the same time Alfred

promoted himself as the defender of all Christian Anglo-Saxons against the pagan Viking threat and began the liberation of neighbouring areas from Viking control. He thus paved the way for the future unity of England, which was brought to fruition under his son and grandsons, who conquered the remaining areas held by the Vikings in the east and north, so that by the mid-tenth century the England we are familiar with was ruled as one country for the first time.

His preservation from the Vikings and unexpected succession as king after the death of four older brothers, seem to have given Alfred a sense that he had been specially destined for high office. With the help of advisers from other areas of England, Wales and Francia, Alfred studied, and even translated from

Latin into Old English, certain works that were regarded at the time as providing models of ideal Christian kingship and 'most necessary for all men to know'.

Alfred tried to put these principles into practice, for instance, in the production of his law-code. He became convinced that those in authority in church or state could not act justly or effectively without the 'wisdom' acquired through study, and set up schools to ensure that future generations of priests and secular administrators would be better trained, as well as encouraging the nobles at his court to emulate his own example in reading and study. Alfred also had the foresight to commission his biography from Bishop Asser of Wales. Asser presented Alfred as the embodiment of the ideal, but practical, Christian ruler. Alfred was the 'truthteller', a brave, resourceful, pious man, who was generous to the church and anxious to rule his people justly. One could say that Asser accentuated the positive, and ignored those elements of ruthless, dictatorial behaviour which any king needed to survive in ninth-century *realpolitik*. Alfred and Asser did such a good job that when later generations looked back at his reign through their works they saw only a ruler apparently more perfect than any before or after. Alfred is often thought to have provided his own epitaph in this passage from his translation of the *Consolation of Philosophy* by Boethius:

I desired to live worthily as long as I lived, and to leave after my life, to the men who should come after me, the memory of me in good works.

Alfred, particularly as presented by Asser, may have had something of a saint in him, but he was never canonised and this put him at something of a disadvantage in the later medieval world. The Normans and their successors were certainly interested in presenting themselves as the legitimate heirs of their Anglo-Saxon predecessors, but favoured the recognised royal saints, especially Edmund of the East Angles, killed by the Danish army which Alfred defeated, and Edward the Confessor, the last ruler of the old West Saxon dynasty. St Edmund and St Edward can be seen supporting Richard II on the Wilton diptych, and members of the later medieval royal houses were named after them. Nor were Alfred's heroic defeats of the pagan Vikings enough to make him the favoured military hero of the post-Conquest period. None of the Anglo-Saxon rulers qualified for this role. After Geoffrey of Monmouth's successful promotion, the British Arthur was preferred—a man whose reputation was not constrained by inconvenient facts, and who proved extremely adaptable to changing literary conventions. However, Alfred was lauded by Anglo-Norman historians, like William of Malmesbury, Gaimar and Matthew Paris, and their presentations, and occasional embellishments, of his achievements would be picked up by later writers. Alfred's well-attested interest in learning made him the obvious choice to be retrospectively chosen as the founder of Oxford University when that institution felt the need to establish its historical credentials in the fourteenth century.

Alfred's lack of a saintly epithet, a disadvantage in the high Middle Ages, was the salvation of his reputation in a post-Reformation world. As a pious king with an interest in promoting the use of English, Alfred was an ideal figurehead for the emerging English Protestant church. The works he had commissioned or translated were interpreted as evidence for the pure Anglo-Saxon church, before it had become tainted by the false Romanism introduced by the Normans. With a bit of selective editing, Anglo-Saxon ecclesiastical provision came to bear an uncanny resemblance to Elizabethan Anglicanism. Archbishop Matthew Parker did an important service to Alfred's reputation by publishing an edition of Asser's *Life of Alfred* in 1574, even if he could not resist adding the story of the burnt cakes which came from a separate, later, Anglo-Saxon source. Perhaps even more significant for getting Alfred's reputation widely known was the enthusiastic notice of him in John Foxe's *Book of Martyrs* (1570 edition), where material derived from sources of Alfred's own time was mixed with stories with a later currency, such as his visit to the Danish camp as a minstrel which was first recorded in a post-Conquest account. It was also writers of the sixteenth century who promoted the designation of Alfred as 'the Great', an epithet that had never been applied to him in the Anglo-Saxon period.

Comparable claims of the contribution of the Anglo-Saxons to English life were used to support radical political change in the seventeenth century, when it was argued, for instance, that the right of all freemen to vote for representatives in Parliament was a lost Anglo-Saxon liberty. The relative abundance of sources from Alfred's reign, including his surviving law-code and Asser's description of his interest in law and administration, naturally meant that attention was drawn to him by those searching for an ancient constitution to serve contemporary needs. Alfred himself was an unlikely champion for the more radical movements, and was more readily adopted by those who wanted to show Stuart, and eventually Hanoverian, rulers, how they could become successful constitutional monarchs by emulating their most famous Anglo-Saxon ancestor. Robert Powell, in his *Life of Alfred*, published in 1634, attempted to draw parallels between the reigns of Alfred and Charles I, something which often called for considerable ingenuity, and his hope that Charles would share the same respect for English law as that apparently shown by Alfred proved misplaced. Rather more impressive as a work of scholarship was Sir John Spelman's *Life of King Alfred*, which drew upon an extensive range of primary material and itself became a source for later biographers. The work was dedicated to the future Charles II when Prince of Wales, and was completed during the Civil War in 1642, in the royalist camp at Oxford. Spelman was to die the following year of camp fever, and publication of the biography was delayed until more propitious times. In fact, any attempts to interest Stuart monarchs in their Saxon forebears had only a limited success. The Stuarts' preferred cultural reference points were from the classical world rather than the history of their own islands.

The common Saxon heritage of the Hanoverians and the Anglo-Saxons provided more fertile ground for the promotion of a cult of King Alfred. His first aristocratic and royal backers came from the circle which gathered around Frederick, Prince of Wales (1707–51), the eldest son of George II, and was united by the opposition of its members to the prime minister Robert Walpole. Walpole's opponents called themselves 'the Patriots', and Alfred was the first 'Patriot King', who had saved his country from tyranny, as it was devoutly hoped Frederick himself would do when he succeeded his father. A number of literary works centred upon Alfred were dedicated to the prince. Sir Richard Blackmore's *Alfred: an Epick Poem in Twelve Books* (1723) enlivened the conventional accounts of Alfred's reign with an extensive description of his imaginary travels in Europe and Africa, in which were concealed many heavy-handed compliments to Prince Frederick. Of much more lasting worth was Thomas Arne's masque *Alfred*, which was first performed in 1740 at the prince's country seat of Cliveden. The main text was provided by two authors already active in Frederick's cause, James Thomson and David Mallett, but included an ode by Viscount Bolingbroke, one of the leaders of the opposition to Walpole who had defined their political philosophy in his essay 'The Idea of a Patriot King' (1738). A visual representation of this political manifesto was provided in Lord Cobham's pleasure grounds at Stowe. Alfred's bust was included alongside those of other Whig heroes in 'The Temple of British Worthies' completed in 1734–35 by William Kent. Alfred is described as 'the mildest, justest, most beneficient of kings' who 'crush'd corruption, guarded liberty, and was the founder of the English constitution', in pointed reference to qualities which George II was felt to lack. Alfred's bust was placed next to that of the Black Prince, a Prince of Wales whose noble qualities were perceived as having been inherited by Frederick, particularly if he followed the example of King Alfred rather than that of his father.

The Stowe landscape gardens also contain a Gothic Temple, in which 'Gothic' should be understood as ancient Germanic. The building was dedicated 'to the Liberty of our Ancestors', and was surrounded by statues of Germanic deities (albeit in Classical pose), while the ceiling of the dome was decorated with the arms of the earls of Mercia from whom Lord Cobham claimed descent. This new interest in the Germanic past began to trickle down to other sectors of society. Those who could not afford to erect their own monuments to Alfred's greatness might nevertheless find remembrances of him in the Wessex landscape. In 1738, the antiquarian Francis Wise, hoping to improve his promotion prospects at the University of Oxford, produced a pamphlet 'concerning some antiquities in Berkshire' in which he argued that the White Horse of Uffington had been cut to commemorate Alfred's victory over the Vikings at the battle of Ashdown, and that all other visible antiquities nearby had some connection with the campaign. His claims were entirely spurious, but helped to publicise the idea that Alfred's influence permeated the very fabric of the country. Those who could not have a Saxon memorial in their grounds or in the nearby countryside could at least own a print of the new genre of History painting. Alfredian topics, especially 'Alfred in the neatherd's cottage' (the cake-burning episode), were among those frequently reproduced.

Alfred at Stowe was also remembered as one 'who drove out the Danes, secur'd the seas', and his role as defender of the country and supposed founder of the British navy ensured him increasing fame as the country found itself embroiled in frequent foreign wars as the reign of Frederick's son, George III, progressed. A series of patriotic Alfred plays, opera and ballets were performed, particularly during the French Wars (1793–1815). More often than not they ended with the rousing anthem which had closed Arne's *Alfred*, 'Rule Britannia', which became increasingly popular as an expression of loyalty to the crown under the threat of foreign attack. It was from this period that 'Alfred' became favoured as a Christian name at all levels of society.

As in other European countries, a new national pride in nineteenth-century England had an important historical dimension, and an accompanying cult of the heroes who had made later success possible. The English, it was believed, could trace language and constitutional continuity back to the fifth century when they had defeated the effete Romans, and it became increasingly felt that other, positive, facets of 'the national character' could be traced back this far as well. These characteristics were felt to have made those of Anglo-Saxon descent uniquely programmed for success, and to rule other less fortunately endowed peoples, and the best of them were represented by King Alfred himself. Alfred was fast being rediscovered as 'the most perfect character in history', and alongside his defence of constitutional liberties, his country and true religion, was added renewed admiration for his Christian morality and sense of duty.

Anglo-Saxonism, and the accompanying Alfredism, could be found on both sides of the Atlantic. Thomas Jefferson had ingeniously argued that, as the Anglo-Saxons who had settled in Britain had ruled themselves independently from their Continental homelands, so the English settlers of America should also be allowed their independence. He believed both countries shared an Anglo-Saxon heritage, and proposed a local government for Virginia based on a division into hundreds, an Anglo-Saxon institution widely believed then to have been instituted by Alfred. A less attractive side of this fascination with Anglo-Saxon roots was that it helped foster a belief in racial superiority, as celebrated in a shortlived periodical called *The Anglo-Saxon* (1849–50), which aimed to demonstrate how 'the whole earth may be called the Fatherland of the Anglo-Saxon. He is a native of every clime—a messenger of heaven to every corner of this Planet.'

One of the chief supporters of *The Anglo-Saxon*, who wrote large segments of it if no other copy was available, was Martin Tupper, the author of several volumes of popular, highly sentimental and moralistic verses. Alfred was one of Tupper's particular heroes, largely because he felt many of the King's writings anticipated his own, and it was through his impetus that the millenary of Alfred's birth at Wantage was celebrated in 1849, one of the earliest of all such jubilees.

The event was not the success for which Tupper had hoped, largely because he left arrangements rather late in the day and had no influential backers. Many of the details were still not fixed on the eve of the event to the indignation of the few local gentry inveigled into attending, but the event still managed to attract crowds estimated at 8,000–10,000 who enjoyed traditional games and an oxroast, as well as Tupper's specially composed Jubilee song:

> Anglo-Saxons!—in love are we met To honour a name we can never forget! Father, and Founder, and King of a race That reigns and rejoices in every place, Root of a tree that o'ershadows the earth First of a Family blest from his birth Blest in this stem of their strength and their state Alfred the Wise, and the Good, and the Great!

During the reign of Victoria, who gave birth to the first Prince Alfred since the Anglo-Saxon period (b.1844), King Alfred was accepted as founder of the nation and its essential institutions to such an extent that one commentator was moved to complain 'it is surely a mistake to make Alfred, as some folks seem to do, into a kind of ninth-century incarnation of a combined School Board and County Council'. Alfred was no longer a mirror for princes, but an exemplar for people at all levels of society and, above all, for children. Charles Dickens's *A Child's History of England* (1851–53) can stand for many such works where Alfred was used to demonstrate the best of the English character:

> The noble king... in his single person, possessed all the Saxon virtues. Whom misfortune could not subdue, whom prosperity could not spoil, whose perseverance, nothing could shake. Who was hopeful in defeat, and generous in success. Who loved justice, freedom, truth and knowledge.

So much had Alfred become the epitome of the ideal Victorian that Walter Besant, in a lecture on Alfred in 1897,

thought it entirely appropriate to apply to him verse that Alfred, Lord Tennyson had written to commemorate Prince Albert.

Alfred was no longer the totem of one political party. In 1877 Robert Loyd-Lindsay, Conservative MP for Berkshire and a perfect exemplar of the paternal landlord of Disraeli's 'Young England' movement, provided Wantage with the statue that Tupper had hoped to raise in 1849, but for which he had failed to get funds. Wantage also got the grand occasion it had missed then as Edward, Prince of Wales, to whom Lindsay had once been an equerry, unveiled the statue carved by Count Gleichen, one of the Prince's German cousins. In 1901, the year of Queen Victoria's death, there were even greater celebrations to commemorate the millenary of that of Alfred. Problems with the calculation of Anglo-Saxon dates meant it was widely believed then that Alfred had died in 901, rather than 899, which is now recognised as the true date of his death, but at the time it seemed particularly apposite to many that the great Queen and her illustrious forebear had died a thousand years apart. On the surface the Alfred millenary appeared to fulfil its aim, as advertised in the National Committee's prospectus, of being 'a National Commemoration of the king to whom this Empire owes so much'. The procession through the heart of Winchester to the site of Hamo Thornycroft's giant statue of the King, included representatives of Learned Societies and Universities 'from all lands where the English speaking-race predominate' (needless to say, they were all white males) and members of the different armed forces. Alfred was further commemorated in the same year by the launching of a new Dreadnought, the HMS *King Alfred*.

But in 1901 Britain was embroiled in the Boer War, and the priority was the reality of the present rather than an imagined past. The National Committee did not raise nearly as much money as it had expected and had to abandon many of its ambitious plans, including one for a Museum of Early English History. Many were worried at the direction Britain's imperial policy was taking. Charles Stubbs, Dean of Ely, took advantage of the millenary year to suggest that Al-

fred's standards were not only in advance of his own age, but in advance of those of many statesman of the present day, especially in their conduct of the Boer War, which had been prompted by 'insolence of pride ... by passion of vengeance... by lust of gold'. But there was also a more positive side to the celebrations when Alfred was used, as he had been in the past, as a cloak for the introduction of change in society. It was not by chance that the statue was unveiled by the Liberal leader Lord Rosebery, for the former Whig support for British Worthies had never completely died away, and Liberals were prominent in the many commemorations of the latter part of the nineteenth century. It was a row over the statue of Oliver Cromwell, commissioned in 1895 by Rosebery from Thornycroft for the House of Commons, that precipitated the former's resignation as Prime Minister. The most active members of the National Committee were leading Liberals and others, like the positivist Frederic Harrison and litterateur Walter Besant, who were associated with them in the promotion of Working Mens' Colleges or the London County Council, formed in 1888 with Lord Rosebery as its first Chairman. Most active of all in the promotion of Alfred was the secretary of the National Committee and mayor of Winchester, Alfred Bowker, who used the millenary as an opportunity to develop the profile and scope of the Corporation of Winchester by, for instance, purchasing the site of Alfred's final resting-place at Hyde Abbey with adjoining land that could be used for public recreation (as it still is today).

Lord Rosebery commented that the statue he was to unveil in Winchester

> can only be an effigy of the imagination, and so the Alfred we reverence may well be an idealised figure.... we have draped round his form... all the highest attributes of manhood and kingship.

Alfred, though no doubt gratified by his posthumous fame, would have trouble recognising himself in some of his later manifestations, and would find it difficult to comprehend, let alone approve, some of the constitutional developments he was supposed to have championed. One hopes that it will not be possible for such a wide divorce between an idealised Alfred and the reality of Anglo-Saxon rule to occur again, but it is possible that Alfred's symbolic career is not over. Now that Britain is relapsing into its regional components, who better than Alfred, the champion of the English language and Anglo-Saxon hegemony, to be a figurehead of the new England?

FOR FURTHER READING:

R. Abels, *Alfred the Great: War, Kingship and Culture in Anglo-Saxon England* (Longman, 1998); J.W. Burrow, *A Liberal Descent: Victorian Historians and the English Past* (Cambridge University Press, 1981); R. Horsman, *Race and Manifest Destiny: The Origins of American Racial Anglo-Saxonism* (Harvard University Press, 1981); S. Keynes and M. Lapidge (eds.), *Alfred the Great: Asser's Life of King Alfred and Other Contemporary Sources* (Penguin, 1983); R. Quinault, 'The Cult of the Centenary, 1789–1914', Historical Research 71 (1998), 303–23; B.A.E. Yorke, *Wessex in the Early Middle Ages* (Leicester University Press, 1995).

Barbara Yorke is Reader in History at King Alfred's College, Winchester. Her latest book is *Anglo-Saxons* (Sutton Pocket Histories, 1999).

The Amazing Vikings

They earned their brutal reputation—
but the Norse were also craftsmen, explorers and believers in democracy

By Michael D. Lemonick and Andrea Dorfman

RAVAGERS, DESPOILERS, PAGANS, HEA-thens—such epithets pretty well summed up the Vikings for those who lived in the British Isles during medieval times. For hundreds of years after their bloody appearance at the end of the 8th century A.D., these ruthless raiders would periodically sweep in from the sea to kill, plunder and destroy, essentially at will. "From the fury of the Northmen, deliver us, O Lord" was a prayer uttered frequently and fervently at the close of the first millennium. Small wonder that the ancient Anglo-Saxons—and their cultural descendants in England, the U.S. and Canada—think of these seafaring Scandinavians as little more than violent brutes.

But that view is wildly skewed. The Vikings were indeed raiders, but they were also traders whose economic network stretched from today's Iraq all the way to the Canadian Arctic. They were democrats who founded the world's oldest surviving parliament while Britain was still mired in feudalism. They were master metalworkers, fashioning exquisite jewelry from silver, gold and bronze. Above all, they were intrepid explorers whose restless hearts brought them to North America some 500 years before Columbus.

The broad outlines of Viking culture and achievement have been known to experts for decades, but a spate of new scholarship, based largely on archaeological excavations in Europe, Iceland, Greenland and Canada, has begun to fill

in the elusive details. And now the rest of us have a chance to share in those discoveries with the opening last week of a wonderfully rich exhibition titled "Vikings: The North Atlantic Saga" at the National Museum of Natural History in Washington.

Timed to commemorate the thousand-year anniversary of Leif Eriksson's arrival in North America, the show examines the Vikings and their Norse descendants from about A.D. 740 to 1450—focusing especially on their westward expansion and on the persistent mysteries of how extensively the Vikings explored North America and why they abandoned their outpost here.

In doing so, the curators have laid to rest a number of popular misconceptions, including one they perpetuate in the show's title. The term Viking (possibly from the Old Norse *vik*, meaning bay) refers properly only to men who went on raids. All Vikings were Norse, but not all Norse were Vikings—and those who were did their viking only part time. Vikings didn't wear horned helmets (a fiction probably created for 19th century opera). And while rape and pillage were part of the agenda, they were a small part of Norse life.

In fact, this mostly blue-eyed, blond or reddish-haired people who originated in what is now Scandinavia were primarily farmers and herdsmen. They grew grains and vegetables during the short summer but depended mostly on livestock—cattle, goats, sheep and pigs.

They weren't Christian until the late 10th century, yet they were not irreligious. Like the ancient Greeks and Romans, they worshiped a pantheon of deities, three of whom—Odin, Thor and Freya—we recall every week, as Wednesday, Thursday and Friday were named after them. (Other Norse words that endure in modern English: berserk and starboard.)

Nor were the Norse any less sophisticated than other Europeans. Their oral literature—epic poems known as *Eddas* as well as their sagas—was Homeric in drama and scope. During the evenings and throughout the long, dark winters, the Norse amused themselves with such challenging board games as backgammon and chess (though they didn't invent them). By day the women cooked, cleaned, sewed and ironed, using whalebone plaques as boards and running a heavy stone or glass smoother over the seams of garments.

The men supplemented their farmwork by smelting iron ore and smithing it into tools and cookware; by shaping soapstone into lamps, bowls and pots; by crafting jewelry; and by carving stone tablets with floral motifs, scenes depicting Norse myths and runic inscriptions (usually to commemorate a notable deed or personage).

Most important, though, they made the finest ships of the age. Thanks to several Viking boats disinterred from burial mounds in Norway, archaeologists know beyond a doubt that the wooden craft were "unbelievable—the best in Europe

BRAVING THE SEAS

Without their superbly designed ships, the Vikings' achievements in exploration, trade and conquest across enormous stretches of Europe and the North Atlantic would never have been possible

THE TRIP WEST

Erik the Red — Bjarni Herjolfsson — Leif Eriksson

Technological breakthrough
The Vikings created a vessel that could operate under a wide variety of conditions. Under sail, the sturdy craft could efficiently traverse hundreds of miles of open sea; powered by oars, the relatively small, shallow-draft vessels could navigate rivers and even be hauled overland for short distances. The ships were ideal for raiding as well as exploration

Have goods, will travel
The Norse trade network spread to continental Europe, Russia, Baghdad, the Caspian Sea and possibly even Africa. The Vikings gathered goods for trade from as far west as Greenland and Canada, and probably bartered with the Inuit

Steering oar
was mounted on the rear right side. "Starboard" comes from *styri*, the Norse word for rudder

Prow ornament
Animal images were used to ward off evil spirits

Sense of direction
Lacking compasses, sextants or any other navigational instruments, the Vikings probably steered by the sun and stars. But when it was cloudy or foggy they may have relied on sightings of wildlife, such as harp seals or sea birds, to tell them land was near

Sails
These were woven from wool. Norse sheep had straighter and larger outer hairs than modern sheep, making the woven material much stronger and lighter. Natural lanolin made the fabric water repellent

Tacking
The ship's rotating sail and steering oar made possible a quick raid and getaway—regardless of wind direction

Rigging
was made from horse-hair (when available) or walrus hide

Strike force
A typical Viking raid probably involved two or three boats, each carrying 40 to 50 men who would hit their targets armed with daggers, swords, bows and arrows, spears and axes, and protected by helmets and chain mail

Shields
were made of wood, covered with cowhide

Oar stowing

Crews
The men could row in calm or opposing winds. They sat on wooden chests containing their effects

CONSTRUCTION
Overlapping planks were laid down and secured with iron rivets

Wool string
was dipped in tar and forced between planks to prevent leaks

Rivets

Oar hole

Wood
Norse craftsmen favored oak trees as a raw material because their branching structure provided natural curves that made it easier to create streamlined shapes

SOURCE: VIKINGS: *THE NORTH ATLANTIC SAGA* (SMITHSONIAN INSTITUTION PRESS)

by far," according to William Fitzhugh, director of the National Museum's Arctic Studies Center and the exhibition's chief curator. Sleek and streamlined, powered by both sails and oars, quick and highly maneuverable, the boats could operate equally well in shallow waterways and on the open seas.

With these magnificent craft, the Norse searched far and wide for goods they couldn't get at home: silk, glass, sword-quality steel, raw silver and silver coins that they could melt down and re-

work. In return they offered furs, grindstones, Baltic amber, walrus ivory, walrus hides and iron.

At first, the Norse traded locally around the Baltic Sea. But from there, says Fitzhugh, "their network expanded to Europe and Britain, and then up the Russian rivers. They reached Rome, Baghdad, the Caspian Sea, probably Africa too. Buddhist artifacts from northern India have been found in a Swedish Viking grave, as has a charcoal brazier from the Middle East." The Hagia Sophia basil-

ica in Istanbul has a Viking inscription in its floor. A Mycenaean lion in Venice is covered with runes of the Norse alphabet.

Sometime in the late 8th century, however, the Vikings realized there was a much easier way to acquire luxury goods. The monasteries they dealt with in Britain, Ireland and mainland Europe were not only extremely wealthy but also situated on isolated coastlines and poorly defended—sitting ducks for men with agile ships. With the raid on England's Lindisfarne monastery in 793, the reign of Viking terror officially began. Says archaeologist Colleen Batey of the Glasgow Museums: "They had a preference for anything that looked pretty," such as bejeweled books or gold, silver and other precious metals that could be recrafted into jewelry for wives and sweethearts. Many monasteries and trading centers were attacked repeatedly, even annually. In some cases the Vikings extorted protection money, known as danegeld, as the price of peace.

Viking Vs. Norse

"Viking" refers only to those among the Norse who went out on raiding parties. Plenty of Norse—including all the women—weren't Vikings at all, and others were Vikings only some of the time

The Vikings didn't just pillage and run; sometimes they came to stay. Dublin became a Viking town; so did Lincoln and York, along with much of the surrounding territory in northern and eastern England. In Scotland, Vikings maintained their language and political links to their homeland well into the 15th century. Says Batey: "The northern regions of Scotland, especially, were essentially a Scandinavian colony up until then." Vikings also created the duchy of Normandy, in what later became France, as well as a dynasty that ruled Kiev, in Ukraine.

Given their hugely profitable forays into Europe, it's not entirely clear why the Vikings chose to strike out across the forbidding Atlantic. One reason might have been a growing population; another might have been political turmoil. The search for such exotic trade goods as furs and walrus ivory might have also been a factor. The timing, in any event, was perfect: during the 9th century, when the expansion began, the climate was unusually warm and stable. Pastures were productive, and the pack ice that often clogged the western North Atlantic was at a minimum.

So westward the Vikings went. Their first stop, in about 860, was the Faeroe Islands, northwest of Scotland. Then,

about a decade later, the Norse reached Iceland. Experts believe as many as 12,000 Viking immigrants ultimately settled there, taking their farm animals with them. (Inadvertently, they also brought along mice, dung beetles, lice, human fleas and a host of animal parasites, whose remains, trapped in soil, are helping archaeologists form a detailed picture of early medieval climate and Viking life. Bugs, for example, show what sort of livestock the Norse kept.)

Agriculture was tough in Iceland; it was too cold, for instance, to grow barley for that all important beverage beer. "They tried to grow barley all over Iceland, but it wasn't economical," says archaeologist Thomas McGovern of New York City's Hunter College. Nevertheless, the colony held on, and in 930 Iceland's ruling families founded a general assembly, known as the Althing, at which representatives of the entire population met annually to discuss matters of importance and settle legal disputes. The institution is still in operation today, more than a thousand years later.

In 982 the Althing considered the case of an ill-tempered immigrant named Erik the Red. Erik, the saga says, had arrived in Iceland several years earlier after being expelled from Norway for murder. He settled down on a farm, married a Christian woman named Thjodhild (the Norse were by now starting to convert) and had three sons, Leif, Thorvald and Thorstein, and one daughter, Freydis. It wasn't long, though, before Erik began feuding with a neighbor—something about a cow and some wallboards—and ended up killing again.

The Althing decided to exile him for three years, so Erik sailed west to explore a land he had heard about from sailors who had been blown off course. Making his way around a desolate coast, he came upon magnificent fjords flanked by lush meadows and forests of dwarf willow and birch, with glacier-strewn mountain ranges towering in the distance. This "green land," he decided (in what might have been a clever bit of salesmanship), would be a perfect place to live. In 985 Erik returned triumphantly to Iceland and enlisted a group of followers to help him establish the first Norse outposts on Greenland. Claiming the

best plot of land for himself, Erik established his base at Brattahlid, a verdant spot at the neck of a fjord on the island's southwestern tip, across from what is now the modern airport at Narsarsuaq. He carved out a farm and built his wife a tiny church, just 8 ft. wide by 12 ft. long. (According to one legend, she refused to sleep with him until it was completed.)

Days of the Week

Wednesday
Odin
Thursday
Thor
Friday
Freya

The remains of this stone-and-turf building were found in 1961. The most spectacular discovery from the Greenland colonies was made in 1990, however, when two Inuit hunters searching for caribou about 55 miles east of Nuuk (the modern capital) noticed several large pieces of wood sticking out of a bluff. Because trees never grew in the area, they reported their discovery to the national museum. The wood turned out to be part of an enormous Norse building, perfectly sealed in permafrost covered by 5 ft. of sand: "definitely one of the best-preserved Norse sites we have," says archaeologist Joel Berglund, vice director of the Greenland National Museum and Archives in Nuuk.

According to Berglund, a leader of the dig at the "Farm Beneath the Sand" from 1991 through 1996, the site was occupied for nearly 300 years, from the mid-11th century to the end of the 13th century. "It went from small to big and then from big to small again," he explains. "They started with a classic longhouse, which later burned down." The place was abandoned for a while and then rebuilt into what became a "centralized farm," a huge, multifunction building with more than 30 rooms housing perhaps 15 or 20 people, plus sheep, goats, cows and horses.

The likeliest reason for this interspecies togetherness was the harsh climate. Observes Berglund: "The temperature to-

Vikings and History

Events in the Viking world (bold) can be seen in parallel with what the rest of the world was doing (italic)

A.D. 793: Viking Age begins with the raid on England's Lindisfarne monastery

800: Charlemagne is crowned Emperor

802: Khmer kingdom is created in Cambodia

841: Vikings found Dublin, in Ireland

845: First Viking assault on Paris

850–900: Maya civilization in Mesoamerica begins to decline

862–82: Viking princes become rulers of Novgorod and Kiev

871: Colonization of Iceland begins

886: Alfred the Great divides England with the Danes under the Danelaw pact

911: Viking chief Rollo founds the duchy of Normandy (now in France)

930: Iceland's parliament, the Althing, is established

969: Fatimids, Muhammad's descendants, sweep across North Africa and make Cairo their capital

982–85: Erik the Red explores Greenland, starts a settlement there

985–86: Icelandic trader Bjarni Herjolfsson sights a lush, forested shore, apparently North America, but opts not to inspect it

c. 1000: Leif Eriksson sets up camp at L'anse aux Meadows, Newfoundland

1000: Iceland adopts Christianity

1042: Accession of Edward the Confessor ends Danish rule in England

1054: Final schism of Roman Catholic Orthodox churches

1066: William the Conqueror, a Norman, defeats England's King Harold at the Battle of Hastings, ending the Viking Age

1077: Completion of the Bayeux tapestry, depicting the Battle of Hastings and showing Viking ships

1095–96: Europe's Christians launch the first Crusades to recapture the Holy Land

1206: Genghis Kahn crowned Emperor of the Mongols, launches wars of conquest

1215: England's King John signs the Magna Carta

1271: Marco Polo sets off for Asia

1337: Beginning of the Hundred Years War between England and France

1347: Plague (Black Death) erupts in Europe

c. 1350: Little Ice Age leads to end of Western Settlement on Greenland

1370: Tamerlane sets out to restore the Mongol empire

1431: Joan of Arc is burned at the stake in Rouen

c. 1450: Last Norse leave Greenland

1492: Christopher Columbus lands in the New World

---

day gets as cold as -50°C [-58°F]." Bones recovered from trash middens in the house indicate that the occupants dined mostly on wild caribou and seals, which were plentiful along the coast. (The domesticated animals were apparently raised for their wool and milk, not meat.) Scientists recovered more than 3,000 artifacts in the ruins, including a wooden loom, children's toys and combs. Along with hair, body lice and animal parasites, these items will be invaluable in determining what each room was used for. Researchers also found bones and other remnants from meals, and even a mummified goat. That means, says Berglund,

"we'll even be able to tell whether there was enough food and whether the people and animals were healthy."

As Greenland's overlord, Erik the Red took a cut of virtually everyone's profits from the export of furs and ivory. Material success apparently did not keep Erik and his family content, though; they undoubtedly heard of a voyage by a captain named Bjarni Herjolfsson, who had been blown off course while en route to Greenland from Iceland. After drifting for many days, Bjarni spotted a forested land. But instead of investigating this unknown territory, he turned back and reached Greenland.

Intrigued by this tale, Erik's eldest son Leif, sometime between 997 and 1003, decided to sail westward to find the new land. First, say the sagas, the crew came to a forbidding land of rocks and glaciers. Then they sailed on to a wooded bay, where they dropped anchor for a while. Eventually they continued south to a place he called Vinland ("wineland," probably for the wild grapes that grew there). Leif and his party made camp for the winter, then sailed home. Members of his family returned in later years, but Leif never did. Erik died shortly after his son returned, and Leif took over the Greenland colony.

Though he retained ownership of the Norse base in North America and received a share of the riches that were brought back, he stopped exploring.

This much had long been known from the Icelandic sagas, but until 1960 there was no proof of Leif's American sojourns. In retrospect, it is astonishing that the evidence took so long to be found. That year Norwegian explorer Helge Ingstad and his wife, archaeologist Anne Stine Ingstad, went to Newfoundland to explore a place identified on an Icelandic map from the 1670s as "Promontorium Winlandiae," near the small fishing village of L'Anse aux Meadows, in the province's northern reaches. They were certain that it marked the location of an ancient Norse settlement.

Finding the settlement turned out to be absurdly easy. When the Ingstads asked the locals if there were any odd ruins in the area, they were taken to a place known as "the Indian camp." They immediately recognized the grass-covered ridges as Viking-era ruins like those in Iceland and Greenland.

During the next seven years, the Ingstads and an international team of archaeologists exposed the foundations of eight separate buildings. Sitting on a narrow terrace between two bogs, the buildings had sod walls and peaked sod roofs laid over a (now decayed) wooden frame; they were evidently meant to be used year-round. The team also unearthed a Celtic-style bronze pin with a ring-shaped head similar to ones the Norse used to fasten their cloaks, a soapstone spindle whorl, a bit of bone needle, a small whetstone for sharpening scissors and needles, lumps of worked iron and iron boat nails. (All these items helped win over detractors, since the artifacts were clearly not native to America.)

Further excavations in the mid-1970s under the auspices of Parks Canada, the site's custodian, made it plain that this was most likely the place where Leif set up camp. Among the artifacts turned up: loom weights, another spindle whorl, a bone needle, jasper fire starters, pollen, seeds, butternuts and, most important, about 2,000 scraps of worked wood that were subsequently radiocarbon dated to between 980 and 1020—just when Leif visited Vinland.

The configuration of the ruined buildings, the paucity of artifacts and garbage compared with those found at other sites, and the absence of a cemetery, stables and holding pens for animals have convinced Birgitta Linderoth Wallace, the site's official archaeologist, that L'Anse aux Meadows wasn't a permanent settlement and was used for perhaps less than 10 years.

Instead, she believes, it served as a base camp for several exploratory expeditions up and down the coast, perhaps as far south as the Gulf of St. Lawrence. "We know this because of the butternuts," she says. "The closest places they grow are east of Quebec near the Gulf of St. Lawrence or in eastern New Brunswick. They are too heavy for birds to carry, and they can't float. And we know the Norse considered them a delicacy."

The National Museum's Fitzhugh notes that the location of the camp was advantageous for various reasons. "L'Anse aux Meadows is rocky and dangerous," he admits. "There are much better places just a few miles away—but there's a good view. They could watch out for danger, and they could bring their boats in and keep an eye on them." What's more, Fitzhugh says, "they would have built where they could easily be found by other people. That's why they chose the tip of a peninsula. All they had to tell people was, 'Cross the Big Water, turn left and keep the land on your right.'" With fair winds, the voyage would have taken about two weeks; a group of men who tried it in the replica Viking ship Snorri (named after the first European born in America) in 1998 were stuck at sea for three months.

Despite all the natural resources, the Norse never secured a foothold in the New World. Within a decade or so after Leif's landing at L'Anse aux Meadows, they were gone. Wallace, for one, believes that there were simply too few people to keep the camp going and that those stationed there got homesick: "You had a very small community that could barely sustain itself. Recent research has shown it had only 500 people, and we know you need that many at a minimum to start a colony in an uninhabited area. They had barely got started in Greenland when they decided to go to North America. It wasn't

practical, and I think they missed their family and friends."

Fitzhugh offers another theory. "I think they recognized that they had found wonderful resources but decided they couldn't defend themselves and were unable to risk their families to stay there," he says. "Imagine 30 Norsemen in a boat on the St. Lawrence meeting a band of Iroquois. They would have been totally freaked out."

As for discovering additional Norse outposts in North America, most experts think the chances are very slim. "These areas were heavily occupied by Native Americans," says archaeologist Patricia Sutherland of the Canadian Museum of Civilization in Hull, "so while there may have been some trade, relations would have been hostile. Maybe someone will find an isolated Norse farm on the coast of Labrador or Baffin Island, but not an outpost."

That's not to say Norse artifacts haven't been discovered south of Newfoundland—but aside from a Norse penny, minted between 1065 and 1080 and found in 1957 at an Indian site near Brooklin, Maine, nearly all of them have turned out to be bogus. The Newport (R.I.) Tower, whose supposed Viking origin was central to Longfellow's epic poem The Skeleton in Armor, was built by an early Governor of Rhode Island. The Kensington Stone, a rune-covered slab unearthed on a Minnesota farm in 1898 that purportedly describes a voyage to Vinland in 1362, is today widely believed to be a modern forgery. So is Yale's Vinland Map, a seemingly antique chart with the marking "Vinilanda Insula" that surfaced in the 1950s bound into a medieval book.

To the north, though, it's a different story. Digs at dozens of ancient Inuit sites in the eastern Canadian Arctic and western Greenland have turned up a wealth of Norse artifacts, indicating that the Europeans and Arctic natives interacted long after Leif Eriksson and his mates left. Says Sutherland: "The contact was more extensive and more complex than we suspected even a couple of months ago."

The Norse referred to the indigenous peoples they encountered in Greenland and the New World as skraeling, a derogatory term meaning wretch or scared weakling, and the sagas make it clear that the Norse considered the natives hostile. But the abundance of Norse items found at Inuit sites—some 80 objects from a single site on Skraeling Island, off the east coast of Ellesmere Island, including a small driftwood carving of a face with European features—suggests that there was a lively trade between the groups (as well as an exchange of Norse goods among the Inuit).

The Vikings held out in their harsh Greenland outposts for several centuries, but by 1450 they were gone. One reason was climate change. Starting about 1350, global temperatures entered a 500-year slump known as the Little Ice Age. Norse hunting techniques and agriculture were inadequate for survival in this long chill, and the Vikings never adapted the Inuit's more effective strategies for the cold.

Another factor was the rapacious overuse of resources. The goats, pigs and sheep brought by the Norse ate or trampled the forests and shrub lands, eventually transforming them into bare ground. Without enough fodder, the farm animals could not survive. The Norse were forced to eat more seal, seabirds and fish—and these too became locally scarce. The depletion of Greenland's meager trees and bushes meant no wood for fuel or for repairing ships.

To make matters worse, demand for the trade goods that Greenlanders exported to Europe plummeted. Not only was African ivory once again available (the supply had been cut off during the Crusades), but the material was falling out of fashion. And Europeans had their own problems: plague, crops failing in the colder conditions and city dwellers rioting in search of food. By the time the last Norse departed Greenland, the colonies had become so marginal that it took several hundred years before some Europeans realized they were gone. The Icelandic colony suffered too, though it managed to hang on.

But the true Vikings—those marauders of monasteries, those fearsome invaders from the north—had long since vanished, except in myth. As Europe's weak feudal fiefs had grown into powerful kingdoms, the Norse raiders had run out of easy victims. In England the victory in 1066 of William the Conqueror—a descendant of Norsemen from Normandy—marked the end of Viking terror.

Indeed, fear of the Vikings had played a pivotal role in reshaping Europe. "They helped develop nations and forced the Europeans to unite and defend themselves," says Fitzhugh. "It was a turning point in European history."

Back in their Scandinavian homeland, the Vikings' descendants also united into kingdoms, ultimately establishing Norway, Sweden and Denmark and pursuing a history no more or less aggressive than that of any other Europeans. The transfer of the Orkney Islands from Danish to Scottish control in 1468, for example, came not as the result of a bloody battle but as part of a royal wedding dowry.

As for the Norse settlements scattered around Britain and Europe, their inhabitants intermarried with the locals and finally disappeared as a distinct people. All that remains of them is their language and genes, spread widely through the Western world. Unlike Columbus, the Vikings may not have established a permanent presence in North America the first time around. But given the millions of Americans who share at least a bit of Viking blood, they are still there—and in considerable force.

An Iberian chemistry

It was a time and place to blend Muslim and Jewish cultures

By Fouad Ajami

Long before the rise of Spain and Spanish culture, before that special run of historical events that took the Iberian Peninsula from the Catholic sovereigns Ferdinand and Isabella to the golden age of Cervantes and El Greco and Velázquez, there was another golden age in the peninsula's southern domains. In Andalusia's splendid and cultured courts and gardens, in its bustling markets, in academies of unusual secular daring, Muslims and Jews came together—if only fitfully and always under stress—to build a world of relative tolerance and enlightenment. In time, decay and political chaos would overwhelm Muslim Spain, but as the first millennium drew to a close, there had arisen in the city of Cordova a Muslim empire to rival its nemesis in the east, the imperial world around Baghdad.

We don't know with confidence the precise population of Cordova in the closing years of the 10th century. The chroniclers and travelers spoke of a large, vibrant city, which could have had a population of some 250,000 people. One 10th-century traveler wrote with awe of a city that had no equal in Syria, Egypt, or Mesopotamia for the "size of its population, its extent, the space occupied by its markets, the cleanliness of its streets, the architecture of its mosques, the number of its baths and caravansaries." Cordova had no urban rival in Western Europe at the time. Its equiva-

lents were the great imperial centers of Baghdad and Constantinople, and cities in remote worlds: Angkor in Indochina, Tchangngan in China, Tollán in Mexico.

LOUVRE, PARIS—GIRAUDON/ART RESOURCE

An age of artistic richness

City life. A Pax Islamica held sway in the Mediterranean region, and Cordova's merchants and scholars took part in the cultural and mercantile traffic of that world. In fact, the city made a bid of its own for a place in the sun in the early

years of the 10th century. One of its great rulers, Abd al-Rahman III, had taken for himself the title of caliph— or successor to the prophet Mohammed—and staked out Cordova's claim to greatness.

In the seven or eight decades that followed, the city would become a metropolis of great diversity. Blessed with a fertile countryside, the city had some 700 mosques, 3,000 public baths, illuminated streets, luxurious villas on the banks of the Guadalquivir River, and countless libraries. Legend has it that the caliph's library stocked some 400,000 volumes.

Andalusia was a polyglot world, inhabited by Arabs, Jews, Berbers from North Africa, blacks, native Christians, and Arabized Christians called Mozarabs, as well as soldiers of fortune drawn from the Christian states of Europe. The Jews did particularly well in this urban world of commerce, philosophy, and secularism. The Jewish documents of that age depict a truly cosmopolitan world in which Jewish merchants traveled between Spain and Sicily, to Aden and the Indian Ocean, from Seville to Alexandria. Jewish academies were launched in Cordova, Granada, Toledo, and Barcelona. By the end of the 10th century, Iberian Jews had declared their independence from the Talmudists of the Babylonian academies in Baghdad. A rich body of Judeo-Arabic literature became the distinctive gift of this age.

VILLAS & MOSQUES

Constructing Andalusia

Andalusia's architects thrived on Cordova's cultural stew, and their work fused myriad regional and cultural styles. The city's villas, built around patios and lined by terraces, are imitated to this day. The Jewish quarter was home to synagogues inspired by the sun-baked edifices of North Africa. But the most spectacular triumphs were the mosques, and chief among them was La Mezquita, or Great Mosque, a 6-acre giant built to hold 35,000.

When the Moors arrived in 711, the existing temples were plain affairs. The newcomers remade mosque interiors with marble columns taken from Roman and Visigothic ruins, creating dense thickets of pillars to support wooden roofs; it is said that one caliph asked his architects to simulate palm tree groves, as a reminder of his native Syria. A vital innovation, adapted from the Visigoths, was the horseshoe arch, a semicircular support that became the Moorish trademark. In the Great Mosque, these arches were made from alternating bands of red brick and white stone, a pattern that tricks the eye into perceiving the interior as limitless in size.

Brendan I. Koerner

A mingling of cultures in Andalusia's golden age

GRANGER COLLECTION

JEWS AND MUSLIMS, though always wary of one another, built a unique world of relative tolerance and enlightenment.

Terror and plunder. Even given these great cultural accomplishments, the success—and the hazards—of the Andalusian world are best seen through the deeds and valor of the Muslim soldier and strongman of Cordova, Almanzor. Cordova's de facto ruler, the first minister of the court in the final years of the 10th century, Almanzor was an able and ambitious ruler descended from the early Arab conquerors of Spain. He had risen to power in 976 and made the caliphate an instrument of his own ambi-tions. By some estimates, Almanzor led more than 50 expeditions against neighboring Christian states. In 997 he undertook his most daring symbolic campaign, sacking Santiago de Compostela, the Christian shrine and pilgrimage center in Galicia. He laid waste to the church and took the church bells for the Great Mosque of Cordova. Three years later, in the year 1000, he cut a swath of terror through much of Castile and plundered Burgos. He died on horseback in 1002, on his way back to Cor-dova from a military campaign in La Rioja.

Almanzor had given Cordova's political center a military vocation but undone its prosperity at the same time. He had brought into this Andalusian setting wholesale contingents of Berber tribesmen from North Africa, and the enmity between Berbers and Arabs would push the Cordovan world into its grave. What unity the Andalusian political structure had once possessed was irretrievably lost. The opening years of the 11th cen-

LIFE ON THE MARGIN

A Zionist in Andalusia's golden age

The Spanish rabbi-poet Judah Halevi lived in a society in which he and other Jews were socially powerless and influenced heavily by the dominant Islamic culture. Still, he used his poetry to explore both conflict and harmony among Arabs and Jews. An outgoing physician and court poet with many friends, he wrote a collection of secular poetry and a huge body of religious verses, some of which have made their way into modern Jewish prayer books. (His famed *Ode to Zion* has been read for centuries in religious services.) The poetry brought forth a deeper sense of Jewish spirituality that had been unheard of in previous generations

With Islam and Christianity locked in a battle of religious giants, the Jewish minority in medieval Spain was left with few privileges. Although some Jews felt at

GRANGER COLLECTION

Some Spanish Jews felt at home in Islamic society.

home in an Islamic society, many, like Halevi, longed for a world in which their own people could rise to the top.

In fact, the years between 900 and 1200 in Spain and North Africa are known as the Hebrew "golden age," a sort of Jewish Renaissance that arose from the fusion of the Arab and Jewish intellectual words. Jews watched their Arab counterparts closely and learned to be astronomers, philosophers, scientists, and poets.

Signs of status. But this was a time of only partial autonomy. Jews were free to live in the Islamic world as long as they paid a special tax to Muslim rulers and submitted to an order forbidding them to own Muslim slaves. Jews had their own legal system and social services, were forbidden to build new synagogues, and were supposed to wear identifying clothing.

These restrictions led to a profound sense of alienation for some Jews. It was, says Raymond Scheindlin, professor of medieval Hebrew literature at New York's Jewish Theological Seminary, a demoralizing daily reminder "that you are part of a losing team." Halevi reacted to that message. To him, life in Spain—though comfortable in between harrowing bouts of persecution—was like slavery compared with the life intended for Jews in Palestine.

Allied neither with the crescent nor the cross, Halevi instead focused on a different destiny. To him, the Jews were a calamitous and wounded people, unsure of their place in human history. He wanted Jews to believe what he was confident of: that Hebrew was superior to Arabic, Palestine to Spain, and they were the chosen people.

When he was 50, Halevi underwent an emotional upheaval and decided to devote himself to God by going on a pilgrimage to the Holy Land. Legend has it that he met his death upon finally arriving in Israel, where he was run over by an Arab horseman. With the vision of Jerusalem set before him, he recited the last verse of his *Ode to Zion*.

—*Lindsay Faber*

tury would be terrible years for Cordova. The city was sacked by Catalan mercenaries in 1010; the Guadalquivir overflowed its banks in the year that followed; and a terrible mass slaughter took place in 1013 when merciless Berber soldiers besieged the city, put a large

number of its scholars to the sword, and torched its elegant villas. Many of the city's notables, Muslims and Jews alike, took to the road.

One of these exiles was a talented Jewish child of Cordova, one Samuel Ibn Neghrela. He was given the gift of Cor-

dova's greatness: He was a poet, learned in Arabic and Hebrew and Latin, the Berber and Romance tongues. But he also inherited the legacy of Cordova's collapse. He fled Cordova's upheaval to the coastal city of Málaga, then made his way to the court of Granada, where he prospered as courtier and chief minister. He saw through the splendor and the hazards of that world. In a poignant poem, entitled "A Curse," he wrote of his wandering and exile: "Heart like a pennant / On a ship's mast, in a storm; / An exile is ink / In God's book. Across my soul, and every shore; / And all on whom wandering is written / Are driven like Jonah, and scavenge like Cain."

Distant memory. It twisted and turned, that world that had risen in the West. Ten years after Neghrela's death, his son and heir, Joseph, was killed by a mob in Granada, in an anti-Jewish riot in which some 1,500 Jewish families perished. By then the unity of the Andalusian world had become a distant memory. The age that followed was dubbed the *mulak al-tawa'if*, a time when warlords and pretenders carved up Muslim Spain into petty, warring turfs. No fewer than 30 ministates claimed what had once been a coherent dominion. The robust mercantile economy eroded.

Calamity soon struck this world. In 1085, Toledo, the ancient capital of the Visigothic kingdom, was conquered by Alfonso VI, King of León. For Christians this was a sign of divine favor, and the conqueror claimed no less than that. "By the hidden judgment of God," a charter of Alfonso read, "this city was for 376 years in the hands of the Moors, blasphemers of the Christian faith.... Inspired by God's grace I moved an army against this city, where my ancestors once reigned in power and wealth." Cordova itself fell in 1236. Its conqueror, Ferdinand III of Castile, claimed the Great Mosque of Cordova in a "purification" ceremony, and his bishops consecrated it for Christian worship as the Catedral de Santa María. The foundations of the Great Mosque had been laid down in the closing years of the eighth century, and successive rulers had adorned and enlarged it. It was the symbol of Andalusian authority, a sublime architectural wonder into which rulers and patrons poured their reverence and ambition, their desire for a new Muslim frontier as grand as the best Baghdad or Damascus could boast. In the peninsula, one people's golden age was always another's decline. What had once been a land of three faiths would in time be cleansed of its Muslims and Jews. A militant new doctrine—called *limpieza de sangre*, or "purity of blood"—would dispense with all that tangled past and its richness.

From the *U.S. News & World Report*, August 16-23, 1999, pp. 44, 48, 50. © 1999 by U.S. News & World Report. Reprinted by permission.

The Capture of Jerusalem

John France recounts the against-the-odds narrative of the capture of the Holy City by the forces of the First Crusade.

On Tuesday, June 7th, 1099, the First Crusade arrived before the city of Jerusalem and began a siege which would end with its capture on Friday July 15th. It was a moment of great rejoicing in the crusader host. because Jerusalem was the Holy Place for whose liberation they had set out on the long and bitter journey some three years before.

After Pope Urban's appeal for a military expedition to the East in November 1095, Western Europe had been swept by a wave of enthusiasm which inspired about 100,000 men, women and children to leave their homes. Many turned back, others died even as they began their journey: Fulcher of Chartres saw 400 drown at Brindisi when a pilgrim ship sank. Even so the group of armies which gathered before Nicaea in June 1097 was some 60,000 strong, including roughly 6–7,000 knights. Not since Roman times had such a host gathered in Europe, though this was not a single army like that of Rome, but a collection of armed bands massively encumbered with non-combatants.

The major armies were commanded by the great princes— Raymond of Toulouse, Godfrey of Bouillon, Robert Duke of Normandy, Robert Count of Flanders, Stephen of Blois, Hugh of Vermandois and Bohemond, son of Robert Guiscard. But there were many others with their own warbands who owed little loyalty to such men, and new leaders emerged during the journey. Bohemond's nephew Tancred enjoyed an independent command at Jerusalem, while Godfrey's younger brother Baldwin seized the principality of Edessa in March 1098.

There were people of so many nationalities on the crusade that they found it difficult to understand one another, and since there was no overall commander the crusade was run by a committee of its most important members, presided over by the papal legate Adhémar of Le Puy who died, however, on August 1st, 1098. The result was a host of quarrelling nationalities presided over by bickering lords: the only unity came from the sense of a common mission reinforced by the dire peril to which they were exposed in the hostile Middle East. But even this mission was a cause of strife. Urban II had wanted his great expedition to aid the Byzantine emperor Alexius Comnenus in his struggle with the Turks who had seized Asia Minor, to rescue

the Christians of the East from their captivity under Islam and to liberate Jerusalem. But many of the crusaders came to regard Alexius as little more than a traitor who had failed to live up to his promises of help: the Count of Toulouse, commander of the biggest army, disagreed and was permanently at odds with his fellows. Few of the crusaders had a high opinion of the native Christians. As a result Jerusalem became the sole focus of their endeavours because it was the one objective on which they could all agree.

Jerusalem had a special place in the religion and culture of medieval Europe for it was the place where Christ had died and his empty tomb in the Church of the Holy Sepulchre was the very symbol of Christian belief. The people of the eleventh century were burdened by a profound sense of their own sinfulness, a perception increased by the confused state of theological ideas about penance. Heaven was a place for which 'Many are called but few are chosen' and the common fate of mankind must have seemed to be eternal punishment. Fear of hell has never prevented men from sinning, but at moments of crisis or illness eternal torment loomed large. In the late eleventh century the church preached peace to an upper class whose *métier* and delight was war—the signs are that the tension engendered by this contradiction was unbearable. Pilgrimage was one deeply satisfying ritual of escape.

Travel in the Middle Ages was hazardous and in such a context to undertake an ordeal voluntarily was admired as a commitment to Christ. The pilgrim took a public vow to complete his journey and assumed a special dress and badges. He left behind his loved ones, submitted to a self-denying discipline and went to a place where heaven and earth met—the shrine of a holy saint—to atone for his sins. Of all pilgrimages the most distant, difficult and therefore respected, was that to the holiest of all places, Jerusalem, which was regarded as wiping a man's slate clean of sin. When Urban launched his crusade he offered to all who participated this special 'remission of sins'. He offered a vision of Jerusalem suffering under the tyranny of Islam and demanded that the military aristocracy avenge Christ for this suffering and recapture His most holy place. This was an

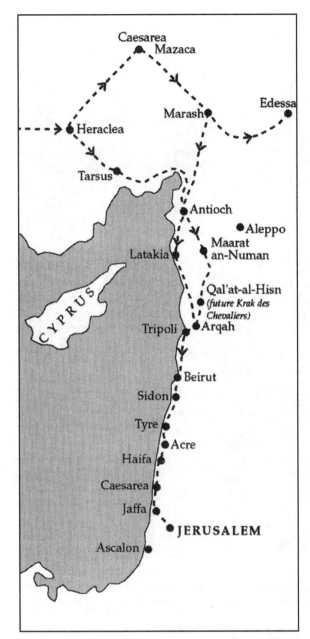

Road to salvation: map showing the final phase of the First Crusade.

even these could have argued that righteous war meant rightful plunder. The army which rejoiced as it reached the gates of Jerusalem on that June day was driven by a heady cocktail of greed and devotion.

In their self-righteousness the crusaders gave little thought to the fact that this same Jerusalem was sacrosanct to Jew and Muslim also. The leaders were not totally ignorant of Islam. The Emperor Alexius had advised them to ally with the Fatimids of Egypt against the Seljuk Turks who dominated Syria and ruled Jerusalem. That alliance served them well, for when they broke it in May 1099 and entered the Fatimid lands of Palestine, the Egyptians were so surprised that they could offer no resistance to their march and even demolished the fortifications of Jaffa, the port of Jerusalem because they could not defend it.

The Fatimids had profited from the Seljuk conflict with the crusaders to seize Jerusalem in August 1098 and now they were faced with defending it against their former allies. For Jerusalem is sacred to Islam: its name al-Kuds, 'the city of the sanctuary', refers to the important shrine we now call the Dome of the Rock, built in 691, whence the angel Gabriel took Mohammed through the heavens. Its great golden dome and the magnificent al-Aksa mosque built nearby in 780 dominate the enormous structure of the Temple Mount which towers over Jerusalem: its western wall is the famous 'Wailing Wall' sacred to Judaism.

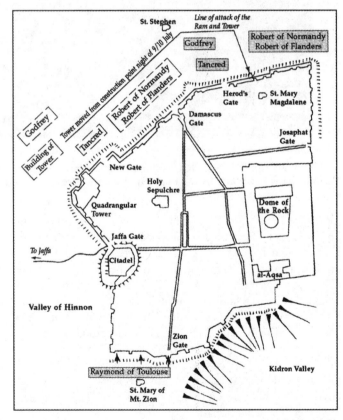

Plan of Jerusalem, showing the final attack of July 13th–15th, 1099.

opportunity for a warlike class to expunge their sins by a single convulsive act of violence.

In this 'new religion' the business of fighting and killing was meritorious, equal to the traditional 'good works', prayer, fasting and charity to the poor. Those who went on this fighting pilgrimage regarded their sufferings as part of a ritual which freed individuals from sin and purified the army as a whole to be the 'chosen of the Lord'—and their ultimate trial was Jerusalem. Of course there were other motives. One eye-witness noted that as they approached the Holy City only 'a few who held God's command dear marched along barefooted, sending up deep sighs to God', while many others indulged in 'a mad scramble caused by our greed to seize castles and villas', but

The Jews had their own quarter in the north-east of the city and they were probably aware that Christian fanatics had mas-

'The chosen of the Lord': Christians and Muslims in mortal combat (from the 14th-century *Romans de Godefroy de Bouillon*); the latter attempting to defend Jerusalem from the warrior pilgrims' bloody sanctioned quest to 'avenge Christ'.

sacred the Jews of the Rhineland cities even before setting out on the crusade, because Jews manned the walls in their own quarter and perished in the great massacre which followed the crusader capture. But the crusaders were not interested in the claims of other religions. Most of those from northern Europe would have known nothing of Islam before their journey to the East and the circumstances of that journey would not have encouraged curiosity. The defenders of the city stood in the way of their path to salvation, loot and land. In later years when they ruled Jerusalem the Dome of the Rock became the Temple of the Lord and the al-Aksa, the Palace of Solomon. History was rewritten to obliterate the memory of Islam, and the despised Jews were excluded from the city.

In attacking Jerusalem the crusaders faced a formidable task. The city is set upon a steep spur dividing the Kidron valley, which falls away southwards towards the Dead Sea. To the east the Valley of Josaphat cuts an enormous gash between the city and the Mount of Olives, while to the west the Valley of Hinnon provides a similar if less dramatic protection. Apart from a level stretch of some 250–300 metres around the Zion Gate, the land before the southern wall falls sharply to the Kidron valley: it was here that the Count of Toulouse chose to mount his attack, but he faced a deep ditch between the wall and his camp. The most vulnerable aspect of the city is the northern wall, about a kilometre long, which is built well below the brow of the hill; here the rest of the army gathered. The whole city was surrounded by a wall, three stories high studded with projecting towers; the relative vulnerability of the northern wall was protected by an outer wall and beyond it a ditch extending from the citadel, called the 'Tower of David' by Jaffa Gate on the west side, to the platform over the Valley of Josaphat at the northeast corner.

War, disease and desertion had reduced the once enormous crusader host to about 1,200 knights and 12,000 on foot.

The end of a bumpy ride: a symbolic image from a 14th-century manuscript shows Godfrey of Bouillon beheading a camel. His own efforts on behalf of the First Crusade were rewarded following the seizure of Jerusalem with his election as Advocate of the Holy Sepulchre.

Through circumstance they had become efficient and seasoned soldiers, but there were not enough of them to surround the city. They were bitterly divided between the Provençals and the rest; only on the eve of the final assault were Raymond of Toulouse and Tancred publicly reconciled. The nearest Christian outpost was 500 kilometres away. The garrison had scorched the land about the city and blocked wells forcing the attackers to bring water from afar; according to Albert of Aachen some of this had leeches in it and when crusaders 'swallowed down the slippery water-worms they were killed by a swollen throat or stomach'. Worst of all the garrison had destroyed or hidden every piece of wood, which was essential for the building of siege machinery. And the whole enterprise was a desperate race against time, for the Egyptians were known to be raising a relief army, a fact which encouraged the garrison recently reinforced by 400 cavalry. They were strong enough to defend the city, but not strong enough to mount sorties against the crusaders, and seem to have relied on forces already at Ascalon to harass the besiegers.

When Tancred, struck by dysentery, sought privacy in a cave and discovered enough wood to build one ladder, the leaders were so anxious about the Egyptian threat that they mounted an attack on the northern wall on June 13th. It failed and Reybold of Chartres, the first on the ladder, had his hand cut off. This forced the crusaders to prepare a more deliberate assault, made possible by the arrival of a Genoese fleet at Jaffa on June 17th, bringing food, timber and above all, skilled labour. The Ascalon garrison attacked the crusader convoy going to Jaffa, but their defeat, near Ramla, ended the harassment of the crusaders. Throughout the crusade sea-power had been a vital factor and never more so than now as siege machinery could be built.

The Count of Toulouse employed the Genoese engineer William Ricau to construct a siege-tower by Zion Gate. At the north-west corner of Jerusalem, Godfrey and the northern French built another, together with a ram to breach the outer wall. These great wooden towers were about four storeys high mounted on wheels or rollers. Brought close to the wall they could clear off the defenders by missiles, enabling others to attack by ladders and mining the walls, though they did not have drawbridges to mount an assault themselves. The defenders on the north wall did not sit idly by. They raised a wooden tower at the anticipated point of attack and brought up beams and padding to protect their defenders. Nine catapults, high-trajectory weapons which hurled stones in a great arc, were deployed against the Provençals, and five against the northern French along with a number of *balistae*, (giant crossbows). The crusaders also built a few catapults and *balistae*, and sent out every man, woman and child to bring light timber for the construction of ladders and mantelets, large shields to cover the attackers' advance to the wall.

In the fever of preparations visions were seen, including one of the dead legate, Adhémar, who commanded that before the assault a solemn procession should be made around the city in the manner of Joshua before Jericho; this duly took place on July 8th, raising morale. But the decisive event in the siege occurred on the night of July 9th–10th, when Godfrey's tower was dismantled and rebuilt at a weak spot on the northeastern corner of the city, almost a kilometre away from where it had been built. The defenders hastened to relocate their forces but they had little time to elaborate their defences before, on Wednesday July 13th, the grand assault began.

By modern standards the whole business must have been painfully slow. The clumsy machines had been assembled as close as possible to the wall, towards which gangs of men pushed and dragged them on wheels or rollers. Before they could be brought into action the northern French had to flatten the ground along the line of attack, while the Provençals faced a large ditch which took three days to fill, with the labourers paid a penny for every three stones moved. Here on Mount Zion there was little room for manoeuvre, for the Provençal camp and the city wall were no more than fifty metres apart. Raymond's mobile tower was severely battered by the nine machines deployed against it, one of which threw blazing balls of pitch and straw not merely at the tower but also into the camp and ultimately set the tower alight: this fire-thrower was dragged off its mounting on the wall when the Provencals improvised a hook mounted on a beam with a chain to drag it. By Friday July 15th, this southern attack was stalled, but it had diverted forces from the north. At the north-east corner of the city

Greed and devotion: the pillage and plunder of Jerusalem, depicted in this 14th-century illustration, did not appear to disturb the consciences of those triumphant at freeing the Holy City from the Infidel.

the ram lumbered up to the outer wall, its crew supported by bowmen and groups with scaling ladders. Godfrey used a crossbow to set fire to the protective padding hung down the wall front. The Egyptians replied with streams of arrows from the wall-head and stones fired from catapults inside the city, and tried to set fire to the ram while the crusaders organised relays of waterbearers.

The fighting at the fore-wall lasted all of Wednesday and into Thursday when the wall was penetrated—and then ensued a pantomime. The tower, slowly dragged up behind, now found its route to the main wall blocked by the ram which could not be cast aside because the outer wall was probably no more than 10 metres from the powerfully defended main curtain. The crusaders set fire to the ram, and now it was the turn of the garrison to throw water from the main wall, but in the end it was burned. Only on Friday, July 15th, did the tower approach the main wall. Wet hides hanging around it defeated enemy fire attack while its osier covering cushioned somewhat the rain of stones. Even so it was badly damaged and the crusaders decided to push the tower right up against the wall. As a counter-measure the defenders hung a great tree blazing with naphtha, pitch and sulphur, on chains down the front of the wall but the crusaders

managed to grapple this down and to manoeuvre the tower against the wall.

Now the defects of the improvised defences were felt. Because of the sudden change in the crusader point of attack, the Egyptians had not had time to build platforms on the wall on which to mount their catapults: they were simply stationed in the streets of the city. These machines had thrown their missiles over the wall, but when the wooden tower moved up to it, their stones, moving slowly at the peak of their arc, merely bounded off onto their own men on, and behind, the wall: lack of time had not permitted demolition of houses to enable them to adjust their range. The crusaders in the siege tower, led by Godfrey with his crossbow, now engaged in a fire-fight with a nearby tower, supported by three catapults and numerous archers and ladder teams, while others tried to mine the wall. Then two Flemish brothers, Ludolf and Engelbert of Tournai, climbed out from the top storey of the siegetower, improvising a bridge by cutting down logs used to reinforce its front, and established a bridgehead on the wall which rapidly expanded.

As news of this breakthrough spread, resistance to the Provençals melted away and the garrison of the Tower of David surrendered in return for their lives. In the north there was a massacre as the crusaders poured through the Jewish quarter where the main synagogue was burned over the heads of those who took refuge there. Muslims fled to the Temple Mount where so many were killed that crusaders 'rode in blood to the knees and bridles of their horses'. Tancred offered quarter to those who took refuge on the al-Aksa roof, doubtless hoping to ransom them, but in the morning, and much to his anger, they too were massacred. After a week in which they cleared the corpses from Jerusalem, the bickering crusader leaders elected Godfrey de Bouillon on July 22nd, as Advocate of the Holy Sepulchre 'so that he might fight against the pagans and protect the Christians'. The conquest, however, remained provisional until, on August 12th, the crusader army surprised the relief force led by the Vizier of Egypt, al-Afdal, at Ascalon and destroyed it. Afterwards, the greater part of the host returned to the West.

In terms of eleventh-century behaviour in war, the massacre at Jerusalem was not unusual. Later in the twelfth century Muslim writers spoke of 70,000 being killed at the al-Aksa alone, but this was propaganda for the holy war, *Jihad*, against the Franks. Not all the Muslims of Jerusalem were killed: many fled to form a suburb of Damascus taking with them the famous Koran of Uthman. Letters from the Cairo synagogue bear witness to the ransoming of Jerusalem Jews in the wake of the fall of the city. Most native Christians had been expelled before the siege, but those left behind welcomed the crusaders into the city.

However horrible it may seem, what happened in Jerusalem was not then exceptional. The city had a strong garrison which could hope for relief—until the last minute they were receiving messages of support from Ascalon. Possibly they had heard exaggerated stories of crusaders' cannibalism at Ma'arrat an Nu'man in Syria, a wholly exceptional event, which may well have stiffened their resistance. The truth was that in the Middle Ages any garrison which held out to the bitter end was liable to bring down massacre on its stronghold. This could hardly be prevented, for armies were poorly disciplined and, in the heat of a breakthrough, impossible to control. In 1057 the Turks massacred or enslaved the whole population of Christian Melitene. William the Conqueror harried the north of England so savagely that a contemporary thought 100,000 had perished, and so ruthlessly did he destroy Mantes in 1087 that many believed his death there was the vengeance of God.

It is not simply the fact of the massacre and its scale which is shocking, but the fact that the crusaders rejoiced in it, as Raymond of Aguilers, who was present at the fall of Jerusalem, describes:

How they rejoiced and exulted and sang a new song to the Lord! For their hearts offered prayers of praise to God, victorious and triumphant, which cannot be told in words. A new day, new joy, new and perpetual gladness, the consummation of our labour and devotion, drew forth from all new words and new songs. This day, I say, marks the justification of all Christianity, the humiliation of paganism, and the renewal of our

faith. 'This is the day which the Lord hath made, let us rejoice and be glad in it', for on this day the Lord revealed Himself to His people and blessed them.

This passage may shock, but it should not surprise us. Each crusader was convinced that every Muslim he cut down represented a step nearer to paradise, for the essence of Urban's message, which was the driving force of the whole expedition, was that killing Muslims was meritorious. To hack down a child, as many must have done in Jerusalem, was an act whose merit was equal to that of the Good Samaritan. These were rational people performing what they believed to be the will of God and certain that it would contribute to their own salvation. Such absolute self-righteousness cloaked much self-interest. Tancred seized Bethlehem as a prize of war as the army neared Jerusalem, and during the sack he plundered the treasures of the Dome of the Rock.

But the real horror of the sack of Jerusalem is its legacy to us all. In the short-run the Christian crusade revived in ever fiercer form the Muslim *jihad*, which soon had plenty of massacres to its credit. Before the crusade most Western Christians had only a vague knowledge of Islam, which was not really relevant to their daily lives. Centuries of crusade propaganda changed that to a latent hatred. Islam and Christianity were in contact in Spain before the crusade, and relations between the two had never been simply characterised by conflict. On July 10th, 1099, as the crusaders prepared to attack Jerusalem, *El Cid*, Rodrigo Diaz de Vivar, died. He was well-versed in Islamic law and culture and had carved out a great career for himself in the service of Muslim and Christian alike. In the twelfth century his life had to be rewritten to make him a champion of Christendom and a worthy hero of the Spanish *Reconquista* in the new age. For the spirit of crusade, symbolised by the fall of Jerusalem, insisted on an absolute hatred of Islam.

The inheritance of the crusades in the West is one of deep suspicion, very evident in our media's portrayal of 'Islamic Fundamentalism'. The inheritance of the capture of Jerusalem in the East is that it is fatally easy for those who would defend Islamic culture to be fearful of the West and to see in any intrusion evidence of a new crusade, and to react in the same way as they did to the old.

FOR FURTHER READING:

J.A. Brundage, *The Crusades, a documentary survey* (Milwaukee, 1962); S.B. Edgington, *The First Crusade*, Historical Association 'New Appreciations in History' No. 37 (London, 1996); J. France, *Victory in the East: a Military History of the First Crusade* (Cambridge, 1994), A. Maalouf, *The Crusades through Arab eyes* (London, 1984); J. Riley-Smith, *The Crusades: a short history* (London, 1987).

John France is Senior Lecturer in Medieval History at the University of Wales and author of Victory in the East: a Military History of the First Crusade *listed above.*

The Emergence of the Christian Witch

P.G. Maxwell-Stuart *examines the impact of early Christianity on notions of magic and definitions of witchcraft.*

As CHRISTIANITY BEGAN to make an impact on the Roman world, the new religion faced two major struggles. On the one hand, it faced a series of deviations from orthodox theology, in the form of heresies principally concerned with the exact nature of Jesus and his relation to God the Father. Second came the challenge of magic. Magical practitioners were ubiquitous in the pagan world, and their stock in trade consisted of claims to exercise powers beyond the merely natural or human.

Prospective converts looked to Christian priests and monks to work magic more effectively than their pagan equivalents, and this remained a requirement as long as there were sizeable areas of Europe to be converted, that is, until at least the twelfth century. Saints played a major role in this preternatural activity. They worked wonders, cured the sick, expelled evil spirits and, when death took them, their relics continued the good work. Hence, amulets of all kinds, re-cast in Christian guise, pursued the miraculous or magical ends once sought purely by pagan magic.

Yet when non-Christians realised that Jesus himself was credited with miraculous cures and exorcisms, and that the new Church was offering rituals, such as baptism and the Eucharist, which purported to protect its converts by driving away evil spirits, and to change bread and wine into the body and blood of the new god, they maintained that Jesus himself had been a magician, a wonder-worker of a familiar type, and that what his Church called 'sacraments' were no different from rites of magic.

This posed a problem for the Church. Christian missionaries could draw on pagan willingness to accept the possibility of the miraculous more or less without reservation, and hence belief in Christ's resurrection and the efficacy of the sacraments; but they also had to explain why the miracles of Christ himself, or those of the Apostles or later saints were genuine, whereas those of pagan magicians such as the first-century AD Simon Magus or his contemporary, Apollonius of Tyre, were fraudulent.

As well as being accommodated by the Christians, magic was also reinterpreted in the light of the new religion's developing theology. Crucial to this re-interpretation were the figures of Satan and the *daimones*, spirits, conceived as intermediaries between the spiritual and material worlds of paganism. Dai-

mones became evil spirits and in that guise were associated with every branch of magic because of the supposed pact between them and human beings. The Christian perception of creation itself underwent a change as everything took on a Manichaean aspect: God was mirrored by Satan, (even though Satan was always acknowledged, at least in theory, to be weaker and not divine); creation became a battle-ground between good and evil, with humans allowed, by free will, to choose which side they would fight upon; and angels were divided into ranks and had their counterparts in Hell.

Sources of malicious preternatural power, such as the evil eye, continued to exercise potent sway over people's belief and imagination, although now they could be countered by rites and symbols made Christian, while those who inflicted the effects of the evil eye and malicious magical intention upon their neighbours were likely to be seen as adherents of Satan, and therefore idolaters and apostates from the Christian faith.

As a result, the early Christian state came to treat magicians of any kind and their clients as potential trouble-makers or even enemies. The collection of edicts known as the Theodosian Code (AD 428), which contained legal *pronunciamenti* from more or less the whole of the fourth century, forbade consultation of magicians or diviners, regarded necromancy as highly dangerous, since it sought to foretell the future by raising and communicating with the dead, and imposed the death penalty on practitioners of magic. Those who confessed to working harmful or poisonous magic (*maleficium* and *veneficium*), or had been found guilty thereof by due process of law, were not allowed to appeal against their sentences and their families were liable to lose any possible inheritance; nor were convicted defendants able to benefit from any Imperial pardons issued in honour of Easter or to celebrate a birth in the Imperial family. Indeed, being a worker of harmful magic was considered sufficient cause for a woman to sue her husband for divorce, as though he were a murderer or a violator of graves, and some of the edicts went as far as to describe magic in medical terms, as a pollution which contaminates those who come into contact with it.

The state, being the state, consistently attached the death penalty to such practices as these. The Church, however, did not. Its condemnations were just as consistent and just as vehement, but it felt unable, whatever the provocation, to inflict the ultimate penalty. Eager to cure rather than punish what was perceived as spiritual illness, the Church tended to administer, in a spirit of stern rebuke tempered by maternal concern, spiritual remedies in the form of prescribed fasting and prayer. From a plethora of church councils between the fourth and eighth centuries, we can derive a picture of the range of magical activities [that] attracted the wrath of the Christian Church. Women were forbidden to keep watch in cemeteries, presumably for fear that they might rifle the graves or invoke the ghosts of the dead; people were not to call angels by names not to be found in Scripture, a prohibition clearly aimed at the long-standing habit of including Hebrew and Egyptian names in magical invocations; while excessive devotion to certain legitimate angels, such as Michael, was also forbidden, presumably on the grounds that this might be mistaken for something akin to pagan worship.

In late antiquity, anyone,
cleric or layman, might practise
magic in some form and at some time.

'Witches', magicians, diviners and the other practitioners of the occult sciences did not exist on the margins of society in late antiquity; nor were they confined to a particular group by virtue of their age, sex, or education. Anyone at all, cleric or layman, might practise magic in some form at one time or another. We should also avoid drawing strict boundaries between magic, religion and the natural sciences. Parents with a sick child, for example, might offer prayers for its recovery, turning to the priest for exorcism if the illness were of a kind which warranted that assistance, and seeking the help of an apothecary or amateur herbalist for infusions or poultices whose ingredients might or might not be gathered in accordance with astrological calculations, and put together and administered to the accompaniment of prayers or magical formulae or both. Magic was not an exotic recourse to which people turned when religion or 'science' in the form of medicine had failed or seemed to fail them. It was a valid alternative way of seeking to exercise power, or tap into the hidden forces of creation, for personal benefit, even if the official line of both church and state declared that magic was a dubious activity best left alone. In practice, even those very officials might ignore their own prohibitions and behave as everyone else. No one questioned the possible reality of at least some of the effects of magic. Yet it was the danger to the soul and body inherent in that reality that caused the church and state to fear the effects of magic; hence their condemnations, decrees and punishments against it.

In the world of late antiquity or the early Middle Ages, it is impossible to define someone as a witch (as opposed, for example, to an amateur herbalist, a heretic or a scold), and none of the legislation of the time attempted to do so. Offenders were designated offenders by virtue of their performing various actions or wearing certain objects declared by the legislation to be condemned or forbidden. For all practical purposes, the 'witch' had not yet been invented. There were only practitioners of various kinds of magic, both male and female, who might belong to any rank of ecclesiastical or lay society, and whose actions might, or might not, bring them within the compass of canon or secular law, depending on external factors which were usually local but could, from time to time, be more general.

Perhaps the most important factor to influence ecclesiastical and state authority in relation to magic was the ever-present problem of heresy. Deviation from doctrinal orthodoxy had been fought by the Church ever since the earliest years of its establishment, and it was therefore inevitable that it would take a dim view of any manifestations of magic which it did not itself approve or control. Thus, for example, Christian prayers offered with a view to affecting the weather were approved; pagan prayers and rituals offered to achieve the same were not. As a result magic and heresy were almost bound to be perceived as two sides of the same coin.

The consequences of this were significant. The more closely the two were associated, the more likely it was that official perceptions of magic would resemble official perceptions of heresy. Paganism and magic would come to be seen, not as hitherto a loose diversity of questionable activities which depraved or foolish individuals persisted in doing for their own selfish ends, but more an organised movement with its own quasi-theology and liturgy, a distorted mirror of the true faith and the true Church, one with its own god, its own angels, its own 'miracles', and its own worshippers. Once perceived in this way, the impulse to uproot heresy, as it was later to come to be uprooted with the help of the secular authorities doing their pious duty, became potentially very strong. Thus, in 1437, Pope Eugenius IV issued a bull addressed to all inquisitors, deploring the fact that so many people were practising various forms of magic, worshipping evil spirits, and making pacts with them. In consequence of this, he said, these people were to be arrested, brought before inquisitorial tribunals and, with the assistance of the local bishops, tried in accordance with canon law, after which they were to be punished. If necessary, the Pope added, the secular authorities should be called on to render their assistance.

By the later Middle Ages Christian teaching on *daimones* had become a key element in explaining how witches were able to operate and why God allowed them to do so. Alfonso de Spina (died 1469), writing in Latin but recording some Spanish terms for spirits and witches, noted some of their names and types.

> Just as good angels and blessed souls are divided into nine ranks, so evil spirits fell from these nine into another nine categories, and damned souls along with them. Those evil spirits who belonged to the higher grades of the [heavenly] hierarchy became correspondingly worse and more inferior in that part of the meridian whose ruler the Psalmist has called 'the destruction that wastes at noonday'. But there are popular names for many of these spirits and their various grades. Some are called fates, others (in Spanish)

The first known depiction of a witch flying on a broomstick is from Martin le Franc's *Champion des Dames*, 1440. In the manuscript she is described as a *Vaudoise* (Waldensian heretic).

duende, others *incubi* and *succubi*. Some of them cause wars; others eat and drink with human beings and appear in their dreams. Some are said to be generated from the smell given off by a man and a woman during sexual intercourse, or from planetary rays. Some are hermaphrodites; some are clean and others filthy. Some deceive men and women who are called *jorguinas* or *brujas* in Spanish. Many people claim to have seen spirits of this type and stick to the truth of their assertion.

The significance of this for witches is plain. The daimones, in pre-Christian times neutral or even benign figures, had gradually been re-interpreted as evil spirits who mirrored in their organisation and graded powers the angelic hierarchy. By their fall from Heaven through the increasingly inferior stages into which the material world was divided, they arrived in the sublunary, elemental region, where they degenerated and suffered the same imperfections as humankind, though to a lesser degree and without the same limitations. They became associated with the practice of magic in any form, and the conception of magic was so tainted by this association that it became virtually impossible for Christian theologians to dissociate the practice of magic from traffic with evil spirits; when de Spina discussed *jorguinas* and *brujas* (different words for 'witch'), he used a verb *illudere* capable of more than one meaning. The spirits, he said, 'deceive' them in the sense of 'playing with' them or 'making fools of' them, as well as 'using them for sexual pleasure'. His is thus a complex description of a sinister relationship.

The notion of a pact between human beings and daimones became deep-seated, and in consequence any act of magic was liable to be interpreted as the effect of a diabolical alliance between an evil spirit and the human operator. Moreover, as the Middle Ages proceeded, the habit of blaming evil spirits for any kind of misfortune grew. God might be all-powerful and all-merciful, but he was prepared to permit Satan and his evil spirits

to punish people's sins or to test their faith, as the biblical case of Job demonstrated. The serried ranks of angels and evil spirits became opposing armies in a continual war between good and evil; it could therefore be argued that any human being who practised magic was liable to be doing so with the help of Satan and thus to be an enemy of God.

The situation was summed up by the fifteenth-century theologian, Pedro Ciruelo:

> Anyone who maintains a pact or treaty of friendship with the Devil commits a very grave sin because he is breaking the first commandment and is sinning against God, committing the crime of treason or *lèse majesté*. His action is also contrary to the religious vow he made when he was baptised. He becomes an apostate from Christ, and an idolater who renders service to the enemy of God, the Devil.

Matters had now begun to reach the stage where the image of what is now seen as the typical early modern witch of the Sabbat could begin to emerge, although the grounds for the details of her behaviour had been laid a long time before the fifteenth century. In *c*.1115, for example, Guibert de Nogent recorded in his autobiography *Monodiae* (Solitary Songs) details of the behaviour of certain heretics from Soissons. They would meet, he said, in underground chambers where they would light candles and then, coming up behind a woman who was lying on her stomach with her naked buttocks on view for everyone to see, they would 'present the candles to her' (by which Guibert probably meant they inserted them briefly into her anus). After these ritual acts, the candles were extinguished, everyone shouted 'Chaos!' and indiscriminate sexual intercourse took place. Any baby which might result from this copulation was then brought to another meeting and thrown from one person to another through the flames of a large fire until the child was dead, after which its body was reduced to ashes, made into bread, and eaten as a kind of blasphemous sacrament.

These details were by no means unique, and similar tales had long been told of all kinds of heretics and, in the early days, of Christians themselves. Yet they were adapted with only certain changes to give the picture of witches' Sabbats, which rapidly became the norm. By the beginning of the fifteenth century, for example, the heretical sect known as 'Waldensians' or 'Vaudois' had become identified with sorcerers and witches, and Vauderie and Vaudoiserie were used as synonyms of 'sorcery' or 'witchcraft'; the amalgamation of the notion of heresy with the notion of magic was now complete and with magic, it seems, as a whole, although the emphasis did tend to be upon its maleficent operations.

But if the Sabbat itself could be related to anti-heretic propaganda, the witches' flight thither had other, folkloric roots. A description of something similar is to be found in the *Canon Episcopi*, a piece of canon law dating from *c*.906.

> Certain wicked women turn themselves round to face the other way behind Satan and, led astray by hallucinations and figments of their imaginations created by

Serried ranks of angels surround the celestial spheres in this pre-Copernican cosmology.

evil spirits, believe and maintain that during the hours of night they ride upon certain beasts along with Diana (a goddess of the pagans), or with Herodias and an innumerable host of women, traversing many areas of the earth in the silent dead of night; that they obey her commands as though she were their mistress, and that on specific nights they are called to her service.

Perhaps the most notable aspect of records concerning the flight is the degree of scepticism which attended them. The *Canon Episcopi* itself calls such stories hallucinations and figments of the imagination. Burchard of Worms, in the early eleventh century, condemned these and other claims to magical ability, and prescribed a penance of forty days on bread and water for seven consecutive years for anyone admitting to believe in them; while in the twelfth century John of Salisbury, in a passage devoted to dreams and visions, declared that there were some people, driven by their sins and the free rein they gave to their wickedness, who were allowed by God to come to such a pitch of madness that they believed (in the most wretched and lying manner) that something they were experiencing in spirit was actually happening to them bodily. He gives as an ex-

ample attendance at a Sabbat in the train of the pagan goddess Herodias. The Dominican Jordanes of Bergamo introduced medical explanations into the discussion and in *c*.1460 gave it as his opinion that evil spirits worked upon the witch's humours, stirring them up so that they ascended to the brain and there created all kinds of imaginings, which caused the witch to believe that he or she had the power to work magic, be transported from place to place, and attend the Sabbat to worship the Devil.

Despite these doubts, however, the story of witches' flights had a certain allure. Thus in the mid-thirteenth century Thomas of Cantimpré recounted the anecdote of a nobly-born girl who, at the same hour each night, was carried away bodily by evil spirits, and although her brother, a monk, did his best to prevent this from happening by grasping her firmly in his arms, as soon as the hour arrived she disappeared. In the early fifteenth century, Johannes Nider, whose *Formicarius* is an important repository of key ideas in the development of the theory of witches' behaviour, was told about the experience of a fellow-Dominican who arrived at a village to be confronted by a woman who claimed that at night she flew with Diana; and although neither Nider nor his informant believed her story, the fact of its being

Courtesy of the author

A witch is carried off by the devil on horseback in this 16th-century woodcut.

told is enough to indicate that belief in such flight was common. Then in *c.*1440 Martin le Franc, secretary to the anti-Pope Felix V, wrote a long poem, *Champion des Dames*, in which two speakers exchanged views on witches and their wicked practices. One of them described women going to the Sabbat on foot or on sticks, 'flying through the air like birds', and the manuscript illustrated the point with two marginal miniatures showing one woman astride a besom and the other riding a long, stout staff. Significantly, they flew under the heading 'Vaudoises'.

By the second half of the fifteenth century, then, there had come into existence a notion of the witch which was not com-pletely at variance with earlier conceptions and models of the magical operator, but which tended to concentrate on certain newly developed 'theatrical' (as opposed to everyday magical) aspects of her behaviour. In much of the literature which was beginning to specialise in these aspects, the witch now seems to have been visualised more or less as distinctively female. What is more, her activities were described as those of a person who was less a depraved individual and more a willing member or adherent of an organised anti-Christian sect of Devil-worshippers whose aim was to help Satan corrupt the society of the faithful and thereby swell the ranks of the damned in Hell.

FOR FURTHER READING

B. Ankarloo & S. Clark (eds.), *The Athlone History of Witchcraft and Magic in Europe, Vol. 2* (Athlone Press, 1999); V. Flint, *The Rise of Magic in Early Mediaeval Europe* (Clarendon 1991); S. Houdard, *Les sciences du diable: quatre discours sur la sorcellerie* (Cerf, Paris 1992); N. Jacques-Chaquin & M. Préaud (eds.), *Le sabbat des sorciers en Europe, xve-xviiie siècles* (Grenoble, 1993); H. Maguire (ed.), *Byzantine Magic* (Dumbarton Oaks, 1995); P.G. Maxwell-Stuart, *Witchcraft in Western Europe and the New World, 1400–1800,* (Macmillan, 2000) and *Witchcraft: A History* (Tempus, 2000).

P.G. Maxwell-Stuart is honorary lecturer at St Andrews University. His new book *Witchcraft: A History* is published by Tempus in November 2000 at £19.99/$32.50. Call 01453-883300 (UK) or 1-888-313-2665 (USA).

Women Pilgrims of the Middle Ages

'There's no discouragement
Shall make him once relent
His first avowed intent
To be a pilgrim.'

Women, however, endured vexations of their own as Diana Webb outlines.

Do you not realise you are a woman and cannot go just anywhere?' With these words, the holy man Abba Arsenius, somewhere around the beginning of the fifth century, rebuked 'a very rich and God-fearing virgin of senatorial rank' from Rome who had sought him out in his Egyptian solitude. His anxiety was on his own account, not on hers: 'it is through women that the enemy wars against the Saints'. He conjured up a nightmare vision that she would encourage her Roman sisters to 'turn the sea into a thoroughfare with women coming to see me'. Pious women were in this period indeed eagerly engaged in pilgrimages, which often combined visiting the Holy Places with seeking out prominent holy men. Arsenius was not alone in feeling that God-fearing virgins should be discouraged from this inappropriate mobility and encouraged to gratify their ascetic impulses in seclusion. It was a sentiment with a big future.

However popular pilgrimage became in the medieval centuries, and however meritorious it was generally believed to be, it was never officially regarded as indispensable to salvation. This of course made it easier to forbid it to certain Christians, and from its earliest days it was the object of criticism. This tended to focus on two issues which frequently became inextricably intertwined. On the one hand, the idea that the holy could be found concentrated in particular places was thought to contradict the essentially spiritual nature of Christianity; on the other, gadding about to shrines could easily degenerate into mere tourism or worse, a spiritually aimless wandering affording opportunity for all sorts of immorality away from the eyes of neighbours and superiors.

In principle these criticisms applied to pilgrimage undertaken by men and women alike. What came to be the standard version of the religious life in the West, Benedictine monasticism, enjoined stability on both monks and nuns. St Benedict's well-known denunciation of wandering monks amounted to a rejection of a conception of pilgrimage which had taken root especially among Celtic Christians: the perpetual uprooting of the self from familiar surroundings into penitential wandering, possibly lifelong and not always directed to particular shrines. To judge from the words of an Irish female recluse to St Columbanus, some time around 560, women who sought perfection within this tradition were aware of some limitations:

> I, too, as far as I have been able have gone out to war.
> It is fifteen years since I left my home and sought out
> this place of pilgrimage... and if my fragile sex had not
> stood in the way, I would have crossed the sea and
> sought out a place of more fitting pilgrimage.

Did the words 'fragile sex' denote moral or physical weakness, or both?

It certainly became the orthodox view that stability and seclusion were particularly vital to female religious, and it followed that they should be debarred from pilgrimage as from other excuses to leave the cloister. Not all women were nuns, however. Did the belief that women could not 'go about as they pleased' influence later attitudes to the practice of pilgrimage by laywomen?

It might justly be contended that neither men nor women were often totally free to go as they pleased in the Middle Ages. Few were exempt from the supervisory power of social or ecclesiastical superiors. Monks, like nuns, were bound to seek permission to leave the cloister. The male serf was no less securely tied to the soil than his womenfolk; Richard II's government tried to prevent both male and female serfs from leaving their appointed places 'by colour of pilgrimage'. Noble men and ladies were well-advised to seek licence and safe-conduct from their rulers if they wished to travel abroad. It is against this background that any greater degree of reserve about female freedom of movement has to be assessed, and we need also to ask exactly from what roots it grew. Did wandering women pose a moral and spiritual threat principally to men or to themselves? Was there, perhaps, concern that because they were more vulnerable to physical danger while travelling, they inevitably imposed a burden of responsibility and protection on men? It may of course be difficult to disentangle these lines of thought; and one man's views might be ambivalent.

In 747, St Boniface wrote to Cuthbert, Archbishop of Canterbury, advising him to take steps to prevent 'matrons and veiled women' from making frequent pilgrimages to Rome. 'There are very few towns in Lombardy or Frankland or Gaul' he wrote, 'where there is not a courtesan or a harlot of English stock. It is a scandal and a disgrace to your whole church.' It has been suggested that this letter shows Boniface changing his mind about the desirability of female pilgrimage. Some years earlier he had written to the Abbess Eadburga, refusing to take it upon himself to advise her for or against a pilgrimage to Rome, but quoting with approval the words of 'our sister Wiethburga', who had found peace of mind at the shrine of St Peter. We know from a letter of King Aethelberht II of Kent that Eadburga in fact made her pilgrimage and met Boniface himself at Rome, perhaps in 745 when he attended a council there. Does the letter to Archbishop Cuthbert, only a few years later, indicate sudden misgivings Boniface had not felt earlier? Or was he neither the first nor the last man in recorded history to express generalised doubts about women which he did not feel about individuals who were well known to him?

Boniface identifies two classes of women, *matronae* (married women or, more likely, widows) and nuns, who were by the middle of the eighth century flocking from England to Rome. We can follow the imaginary trails left by these two classes of female pilgrim down through the centuries to a fictional Canterbury in 1370: one trail ends with Chaucer's Prioress, who perhaps really should not have been out of her cloister, and the other with the Wife of Bath, a *matrona* several times over. Her activities may have raised eyebrows, but was her right to go on pilgrimage open to question?

In 791, less than half a century after Boniface's letter to Cuthbert, the Synod of Friuli legislated to safeguard and enforce the enclosure of 'monasteries of maidens living under a rule'. The relevant canon includes a specific prohibition of pilgrimage, and the terms it employs are suggestive:

> At no time whatsoever shall it be permitted to an abbess or any nun to go to Rome and tour other holy places, if Satan should transform himself into an angel of light and suggest it to them as if for the sake of prayer. For no one can be so obtuse or stupid as not to realise how irreligious and blameworthy it is [for them] to have dealings with men because of the necessities of travel....

That women, lay or religious, could not travel without men in their company was a truth universally acknowledged. For female religious this was (or should have been) an insuperable difficulty; for female pilgrims in general it was a problem, as we shall see more fully later.

In theory strict enclosure was required of monks and nuns alike. Four hundred years after the Synod of Friuli, efforts were being made in England to limit the mobility of religious in general. A legatine council held at York in June 1195 by Archbishop Hubert Walter, for example, ruled that monks, regular canons and nuns should not be permitted to leave their houses without just cause and without appropriate escort. Pilgrimage was mentioned among the causes of 'wandering' which were to be forbidden. However, the saving clause 'without specific and reasonable cause' potentially furnished a very elastic loophole, and the additional note that nuns in particular were not to leave the cloister unless accompanied by the abbess or prioress indicated that enclosure was not in fact expected to be total.

Later legislation repeated these prohibitions, tending to focus more narrowly on nuns. Cardinal Ottobuon Fieschi's legatine council of 1268 in London decreed that the abbess and other superiors were only to leave the convent in case of evident necessity, the other nuns never, but again there was the inevitable saving clause, 'unless for just and reasonable cause'. Here, no specific mention was made of pilgrimage and when in 1298 Pope Boniface VIII pronounced on the subject in the ominously entitled Bull *Periculoso* he focused on secular and legal business as the causes most likely to drag nuns out of the cloister. The English bishops dutifully disseminated this Bull. Archbishop Thomas Corbridge of York, interpreting it as enjoining 'perpetual enclosure', made a spirited attempt to enforce it on the nuns of his diocese, which evidently met with an equally spirited response. In 1344 Bishop Hamo de Hethe of Rochester complained that the nuns of Malling had been infringing on their enclosure in all sorts of ways, including wandering around the country 'by colour of pilgrimage and visiting your friends', and he exacted an oath of amendment from the abbess and convent.

Some restrictions were clearly widely accepted. Philip VI of France failed to persuade Pope Clement VI to grant the benefits of the 1350 Roman Jubilee Indulgence to 'enclosed nuns' who, among other classes of people, were not able to make the journey. The name of only one nun, the Abbess of Barking, appears among the permissions granted by the English royal government to go to Rome for the Jubilee. It was not just in 1350 that this was exceptional. No other nun appears among the fairly abundant records of royal permissions to go abroad on pilgrimage which survive in the Patent and Close Rolls in the thirteenth and fourteenth centuries. Abbots occur occasionally, while monks sometimes went with or without the permission of their superiors. Domestic pilgrimage, which leaves less mark on the record, was probably less contentious, and it is a fair inference that it was on modest little pilgrimages within the kingdom that nuns like Chaucer's Prioress betook themselves from time to time. Occasionally the popes gave permission for a female recluse—a different category of religious woman—to go on pilgrimage.

What of the Prioress's fellow-pilgrim, the Wife of Bath, and other *matronae?* There was no legislation to stop married women going on pilgrimage, even without their husbands, as long as they had obtained a public statement of their spouse's permission, a requirement laid down by the Council of Westminster in 1195 which in theory applied to married people of both sexes. Two hundred years later, Margery Kempe of Lynn was well aware of the need for her husband's consent to her pilgrimages, but she resisted the demand of the hostile 'doctor' who arraigned her in the chapter-house at York, while she was visiting the shrine of St William, that she should be able to produce a written permission:

> Sir, my husband gave me permission with his own mouth. Why do you proceed in that way with me more than you do with other pilgrims who are here, and who have no letter any more than I have?'

Occasionally feminine disobedience to husbands in the matter of pilgrimage appears as a motif in a miracle-collection of saint's *Life*. There is an example among the tenth-century miracles of Ste Foy at Conques: a woman in an advanced state of pregnancy had come to the shrine against her husband's will and was suddenly seized by the pains of impending labour. The saint intervened and on consideration of the gift of a ring from the woman's finger arrested the course of nature, so that she could return safely to her husband and give birth in due time. This and other miracle-collections provide abundant evidence that women were constant customers of the saints, petitioning or giving thanks on their own account, sometimes on that of their husbands, above all on that of their children.

Women expected to have access to popular relics. Early in the ninth century mixed crowds flocked to the abbey of Fleury when new relics were brought there. As women could not enter the monastery church, the relics were exhibited at fixed times in a marquee outside. A similar well-publicised instance occurred in the thirteenth century at the Cistercian abbey of Pontigny. Edmund of Abingdon, late Archbishop of Canterbury, was buried there in 1240 and on his canonisation in 1246 flocks of pilgrims had recourse to his tomb, including many Englishwomen of rank. Popes Innocent IV and Alexander IV successively issued special permissions for women to enter the abbey to do reverence to the saint. The chronicler of another Cisterican house, Meaux in Yorkshire, many years later gave a sardonic version of these events. The monks of Pontigny, he said, had favoured the women's devotion and, still more to the point, had been reluctant to forego their offerings. So they had detached the saint's arm and exhibited it separately at the gates of the monastery, 'so that the women were not totally disappointed of their devotion, and they themselves obtained no small profit from their offerings'. God and the saint himself, however, were not best pleased by these proceedings, and refused to work any more miracles.

Another monastic establishment, the cathedral priory of Durham, prevented women from approaching the shrines of St Cuthbert. This exclusion had a different result. Two-thirds of the miracles recorded in the late twelfth century as performed by Godric (d. 1170), the saint of neighbouring Finchale, benefited women, and in at least one instance St Cuthbert himself directed the sufferer to Finchale for her cure. Other saints and

shrines catered for a distinctively feminine clientele. In the earlier sixteenth century Sir Thomas More poked gentle fun at housewives who spent more on a pilgrimage to the housekeeper-saint Zita in order to find lost keys than the keys were worth in the first place.

Women, it may be suggested, were essential contributors to the shrine economy; and it seems that their right to participate in pilgrimage, as it became more and more integral to lay religious practice, was taken largely for granted. Restrictions on that participation, particularly on long-distance pilgrimage, may well have been imposed as much by practical as by moralistic considerations. A head-count of pilgrims would undoubtedly show men in a large majority, and there were good reasons why this should be so. Such head-counts of course are not easy to achieve, for lack of sufficiently detailed evidence, but one example can be quoted. The *Opera*, or office of works, of St James in the cathedral of the Tuscan city of Pistoia from about 1360 kept a record of its almsgiving to pilgrims, mostly *en route* to Compostela. Between 1360 and 1460 some 3,000 pilgrims were recorded, most though not all of them by name. (There must have been many more, because there is a gap in the record from 1407–17.) The interesting fact is that only two hundred or so of the named pilgrims were women and the vast majority of them, for some reason, performed their pilgrimages before 1400 rather than after.

Among these few women, however, were some of lowly social rank (a laundress and a cook) and one or two who went both to Compostela and the Holy Land. The popularisation of pilgrimage down the social scale, which potentially opened it up to such women, must also, however, have created many situations in which the man went on pilgrimage and the woman stayed behind to mind the shop. Wives with their husbands, mothers with their sons, and perhaps above all widows, in groups or suitably accompanied according to their rank, nonetheless, figure prominently among recorded pilgrims of the central and later Middle Ages.

The young Dominican friar, Felix Fabbri of Ulm, gives a vivid picture of the six rich old women who took ship with him at Venice on his first pilgrimage to Jerusalem in 1480. They were 'through old age scarcely able to support their own weight'. Some of the noblemen in the party objected to their presence, but they proved their worth when sickness broke out on the ship between Cyprus and the Holy Land and they, completely unscathed, nursed the rest of the company. Felix compared them favourably with the one woman, the wife of a Flemish pilgrim, who was on the ship he took on his second pilgrimage in 1483: 'restless and inquisitive', she realised all men's worst fears, he complained, 'as she ran hither and thither incessantly about the ship... wanting to hear and see everything.'

The spiritual value of pilgrimage, for men or women, might be debatable, though it was widely believed in; its physical hazardousness was beyond dispute. It would have been a rash man who set off to Compostela or the Holy Land, or indeed on any considerable journey, totally unaccompanied. Many all-male parties of pilgrims got together for the sake of safety and company, whether or not they knew one another previously, and women sometimes attached themselves to such groups of men

The abbey church of Vezelay, central France, built from the late 12th century, attracted pilgrims in their thousands to its relics of St. Mary Magdalene.

or to family parties. There is an illustrative anecdote in the life of Bona (d. 1207), who lived as a semi-recluse under the supervision of the Augustinian canons of San Martino in Pisa. At an early age she acquired the habit of seeing Christ, his mother, her sisters and St James in visions, and they subsequently accompanied her on her various pilgrimages. She was especially devoted to St James and on her frequent journeys to and from Compostela, she was sometimes escorted by an old man whom she, if no one else, knew to be the saint himself. More normally she travelled in groups of the usual kind, 'with other pilgrims'. On one of these journeys, a male pilgrim got separated from the rest of his party and was promptly set upon by a robber. We are given this illustration of the dangers of solitude only because Bona took it upon herself to intervene, knowing that being wounded and left for dead was the least of the pilgrim's worries; he had two unconfessed mortal sins on his conscience which would damn him unless she cured him. (She got him his money back as well, and converted the robber to the religious life: a good day's work.)

On another occasion, Bona went to the superiors who had charge of her and asked for permission to go on pilgrimage to Rome. This was granted, but she was asked with whom she proposed to travel. Merrily she replied, 'Guido, Guida and Pietro', meaning by Guido and Guida Christ himself and the Virgin, her 'guides'. Perhaps aware that there was a lingering reservation in the minds of her superiors, she asked that a servant called Jacopo, 'who had often accompanied her', should go with her to a riverside meadow where she expected to meet her three escorts. Jacopo's evidently burning desire to be allowed to accompany her to Rome himself is let down gently; he is deeply suspicious of the youth and beauty of Guido-Christ, and needs a great deal of reassurance, to the amusement of all the party, that Bona is not going to be the object of this particular guide's improper attentions.

It is hard to imagine the life of a male pilgrim-saint including such elaborate reference to the provision for his safety *en route*. In the case of women such as Bona, vowed to the religious life, there was, of course, additional reason for anxiety, since their chastity was their indispensable stock in trade. Two centuries later, Margery Kempe of Lynn, who despite the numerous children she had borne in her early sinful life, had to her own satisfaction mastered the difficult art of how to become a virgin, felt a keen anxiety on the same account. Although Christ himself had assured her that he would keep her 'from all wicked men's power', Margery shows recurrent concern about how, and by whom, she was to be escorted on her various pilgrimages. Abandoned at Venice by the party with which she had gone to the Holy Land, she met Richard the 'broken-backed man' who, it had been foretold, would accompany her. He was nervous of the responsibility, not unreasonably thinking that one man, unarmed, was no great defence for a woman against the hazards of the road. At Assisi, he was only too glad to hand her over to the care of Margaret Florentyne, who had come from Rome for the indulgence of the Portiuncula fittingly accompanied by 'many knights of Rhodes, many gentlewomen and a fine equipage'.

Later in life, having escorted her widowed German daughter-in-law back home, Margery undertook the pilgrimage to Wilsnack on the assurance of the company of a man who promised to see her home to England; but he turned out to be in a perpetual state of nerves and, she thought, made every effort to be rid of her. Finding herself again abandoned, she made her way to Aachen with a group of rather verminous poor people and saw the relics. Meeting here 'a worthy woman' from London, who was travelling more conventionally as 'a widow with a large retinue', she thought herself assured of company home, but was disappointed. She then joined forces with a solitary poor friar, but that she should travel alone with him seemed improper to an innkeeper's wife, who got her accepted into a passing party of pilgrims. In the next town she tried once again to attach herself to the widow from London and was harshly rebuffed. Back in company with the poor friar, who by all accounts was having almost as bad a time as she was, she suffered horribly from fears of rape, especially at night: 'She dared trust no man; whether she had reason or not, she was always afraid.'

It was a stressful experience, especially given Margery's anxious personality, but by no means an unintelligible one, nor one that would seem altogether unfamiliar to many modern female travellers. The poor friar, who represents millions of nameless innocuous men throughout the ages, had, she acknowledged, 'been most kindly and decently behaved to her during the time that they travelled together'. It would be interesting to have his journal: did it add to the stress of *his* journey—like that of the broken-backed Richard years before, or the querulous man on the road to Wilsnack—that he felt responsible for this woman?

It was not primarily the extra hazards that female travellers faced that Abba Arsenius had in mind when he suggested that the pious Roman virgin could not go just anywhere. His view of the restrictions that women should observe were in later centuries enforced (insofar as they were successfully enforced) only on some women, those who entered the institutionalised religious life. Laywomen who wanted to go on pilgrimage obviously encountered certain problems which flowed from their gender and its perceived frailties. (The pilgrim who in 1370 gave birth to a male child in the hospital of San Jacopo at Pistoia was an extreme case.) The monk-custodians of popular relics might, with some grumbling, have to take steps to safeguard their purity against invading female pilgrims; but the devotion and the offerings of these women were worth having. It is hard to imagine the shrines of the Middle Ages without their female clientele.

FOR FURTHER READING:

Jonathan Sumption, *Pilgrimage: An Image of Medieval Religion* (Faber, 1975); Ronald Finucane, *Miracles and Pilgrims* (Macmillan, 1995); Benedicta Ward, *Miracles and the Medieval Mind* (Wildwood House, 1987); Michael Goodich, *Violence and Miracle in the Fourteenth Century: Private Grief and Public Salvation;* Chicago University Press, 1994); On Margery, *The Book of Margery Kempe,* translated into modern English by B.A. Windeatt (Penguin Classics, 1985); Clarissa Atkinson, *Mystic and Pilgrim: The Book and the World of Margery Kempe* (Cornell University Press, 1983).

Diana Webb is Lecturer in Medieval History at King's College, The University of London, and the author of Patrons and Defenders: The Saints in the Italian City States *(I.B. Tauris, 1996).*

Britain 1300

Bruce Campbell *argues that a unique conjunction of human and environmental factors went into creating the crisis of the mid-14th century*

In 1258 a parliament held at Oxford—the first to include two representatives per county—imposed the so-called provisions of Oxford on Henry III (r.1216–72) to curb his royal power. The same year, in Wales, Llywelyn ap Gruffyd (r.1246–82) assumed the title of Prince of Wales and began to consolidate his power base in Gwynedd. Across the Irish Sea Brian Ó Neill of Tyrone was engaged in a similar enterprise: at Cáeluisce near Belleek he was given the 'kingship of the Gaels of Ireland' by Fedlimid Ó Conchobair and Tadg Ó Briain. Their confederation was the first co-ordinated Gaelic resistance to Anglo-Norman expansion. In Scotland, however, the young Alexander III (r.1249–86) would have to wait another three years before he assumed personal rule in 1262, whereupon one of his first and greatest achievements would be to negotiate the treaty of Perth with Magnus VI, king of Norway, thereby securing the Western Isles to Scotland.

Meanwhile, early in 1258, somewhere in the tropics, a major volcanic eruption occurred. Particles from the eruption were ejected high into the stratosphere, shrouding earth in a 'dry fog'. In Britain the ensuing cool, wet summer followed a year of 'excessive and long rains' and produced one of the worst harvests of the thirteenth century. Record wheat prices were accompanied by dearth and famine. Atmospheric circulation remained disturbed for several years, resulting in 1262 in a summer that was exceptionally dry and hot. In Ireland drought-induced famine fanned the spread of disease. It could have been even worse. In 1258 and 1259 bubonic plague had spread west from central Asia, where it was endemic, into southern Turkey. On that occasion the deadly pandemic got no further, and in Britain and Ireland the environmental disturbance of 1258–62 caused only a momentary faltering in the established demographic and economic expansion. It was, however, a harbinger of things to come.

From the late thirteenth century the climate became cooler and more prone to extremes, heightened storm surges in the North Sea threatened reclaimed coastal marshlands, and pestilences of animals and humans became rife. In 1300 Britain stood on the threshold of what environmentally was to be its most apocalyptic half-century.

A range of archaeological indicators identify the years between 1315 and 1353 as a time of pronounced environmental hiatus on a global scale. The historical record confirms this period as exceptionally hazardous and unhealthy for both humans and domesticated animals. All of northern Europe suffered famine during the terrible years 1315–17 and in Britain there were further serious harvest failures in 1331, 1346 and 1351. As if this were not enough, in 1319–20 cattle herds were ravaged by disease—probably rinderpest—and over the next thirty years recurrent outbreaks of infectious murrain and scab ensured high levels of mortality in sheep. These biological catastrophes can hardly have been unconnected with the disturbed environmental conditions that prevailed. The same is probably true of plague, a disease of rodents transferred by fleas to humans, which—as in 1258—began its terrible spread across Europe at precisely the point of greatest environmental stress.

It now seems likely that the extreme weather conditions that caused harvest failure and famine and the various pestilences of animals and humans were all part of a single prolonged episode of environmental disturbance. Viewed in this light, these events assume far greater magnitude than historians have been inclined to ascribe to them. No socio-economic system exposed for so long to such variety of severe shocks could have withstood them unscathed, let alone one at Europe's stage of development in the early fourteenth century. Agricultural producers, in particular, had to contend with a series of environmental hazards outside their control and far beyond their comprehension. In England, historians have represented the fourteenth-century crisis as 'population outstripping resources', 'feudal over-exploitation of the production system', and 'the price paid for burgeoning warfare'. Yet when nemesis in the form of plague eventually came, it was essentially non-economic in origin.

The resources upon which the population depended for food, drink, fuel, raw materials and export earnings were essentially organic: the product of plants and animals. Lead, tin and iron were the only significant exceptions. Likewise, technology was mainly reliant upon human and animal muscle power augmented by the renewable power sources of wind and water applied to mills, boats, and ships. In this sense, Britain was still a green and pleasant land. Yet, as Alfred Crosby has pointed out, the mills present in practically every settlement bestowed upon Britain, in common with much of the rest of northern Europe, 'a greater proportion of individuals who understood wheels, levers, and gears than any other region on earth'. Machines needed to be maintained, soil fertility renewed, and flocks and herds restocked. Sustaining output was an enduring challenge. In areas of common-field agriculture local communities enacted by-laws and appointed officials—reeves, messors and haywards—to ensure that resources were managed effectively in the collective interest. In coastal areas there was also intra- and inter-community co-operation in the maintenance of sea defences and drainage dykes. Everywhere the effort to prevent the degradation of resources was a struggle, even when the climate was clement.

Organic waste was recycled everywhere: Norwich sold 'night-soil' to farmers within a 5-mile radius.

By 1300 tillage had been extended almost to its physical limits: only common pastures and the private parks and royal forests set aside as hunting grounds for the nobility proved immune to the advance of the plough. Royal forest was subject to forest law and this was deeply resented, hence the popularity of tales that told of outlaws who poached the king's deer. These forests, too, were at their medieval maximum. In areas of woodland, upland and marsh there had also been much reclamation to accommodate an expanding livestock population. Around 1300, 8 to 10 million sheep supplied wool for the export trade alone. There were also more horses than ever before, both for riding and for draught. Hay was a vital commodity, and carefully managed, artificial hay meadows were the most highly valued of all possible land uses. The key to producing more from the land now lay in fuller participation in international markets, greater specialisation, more intensive use of labour and capital, and the development of more sophisticated agrosystems, in which arable and pastoral husbandry were closely integrated. Already farmers in eastern Norfolk and eastern Kent—agriculturally the two most advanced regions—were employing methods akin to those whose wider adoption was to constitute the agricultural revolution of the eighteenth century. Elsewhere farming methods were far less advanced and husbandmen worked hard often for disappointing returns.

Farmers worked both with and against nature. Organic waste was recycled almost everywhere, either by feeding it to pigs or spreading it on the land—cities like Norwich sold 'night-soil' and other biodegradable refuse to farmers within a five-mile radius. Natural predators were dealt with by hawking, hunting and hiring boys to scare off birds. The rabbit, which had been intro-

duced for its meat and fur in the twelfth century, was beginning to become sufficiently acclimatised and numerous to pose a serious nuisance to cereal farmers. Everywhere fields were infested with weeds which threatened a throttle the grain and competed with it for scarce soil nitrogen. At best farmers could contain the weed problem: against recurrent outbreaks of rust and other parasitic infestations of grain crops they were effectively defenceless. Bread incorporating seeds from weeds could have hallucinatory effects. Cases of ergotism—poisoning produced by a fungus affecting rye and other cereals—were frequent.

Surviving examples of medieval smoke-blackened thatch have preserved samples of crops harvested six or seven centuries ago. All the grains were significantly taller than the dwarf varieties grown today. In contrast, preserved animal bones show that livestock were of debased stature relative both to Romano-British livestock and those of the eighteenth century. Probably breeds had become genetically debased. Pastures, too, had become degraded through repeated heavy stocking. Consequently, carcass weights, milk yields and fleece weights were relatively modest and ripe for systematic improvement in later centuries. Keeping flocks and herds up to strength required constant care and attention. Disease and the asset-stripping activities of executors and crown officials could undo years of effort at a stroke. Wales, the north of England, and Scotland served as reservoirs of replacement animals for pastoral producers in the English lowlands, most of whom had long since abandoned any attempt at complete self-sufficiency.

Wood for fuel and timber for construction and a host of other purposes were among the most essential of renewal resources. The more closely settled and intensively exploited parts of the countryside were almost devoid of woodland and such as existed was jealously guarded and closely managed. Communal ovens were one way of conserving fuel; in large conventual and aristocratic households, communal kitchens and hearths were another. Strictly, monasteries should have had only one heated room, apart from the kitchen; but this rule, made in southerly climes, proved hard to enforce in cool and rainy Britain. Scarcity of fuel was a greater constraint upon London's growth than scarcity of food. Smiths and other industrial workers in the capital were already turning to coal shipped from the north-east, which was also finding a market in port towns on both sides of the North Sea. Irrespective of social status, most houses at this time must have been smoky, draughty and cold; all social classes placed a premium upon heavy fur-lined clothing. Communities mostly in the north and west with free access to an abundance of peat therefore enjoyed a significant advantage.

Britain in 1300 was almost certainly more crowded than ever before. There has been much debate among historians over the size of the population. For England a figure of 4.25 million to 4.5 million is consistent with the agricultural resources of the country, and Wales and Scotland between them are unlikely to have contained more than a further million. However, some have argued for a population of 6 million for England alone. If this is correct, it would not have been exceeded until well into the eighteenth century. What ever the population size, it was relatively unevenly distributed in England at least. In the most

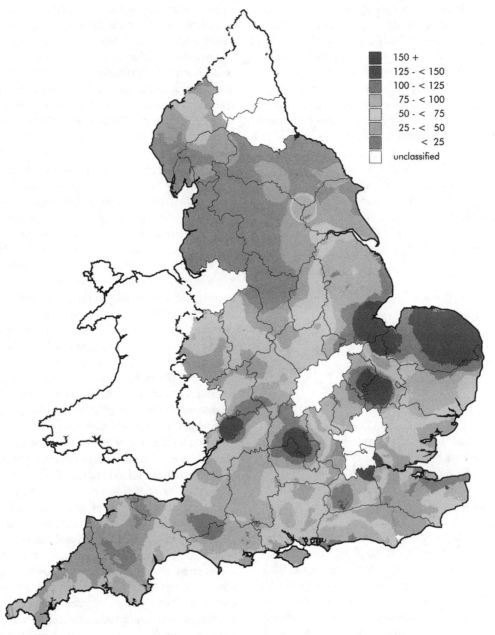

150 +
125 - < 150
100 - < 125
75 - < 100
50 - < 75
25 - < 50
< 25
unclassified

Map showing taxpayers per ten square miles, 1327 and 1332, with the intensively farmed region around the Wash, England's demographic centre of gravity.

congested districts there may have been in excess of 400 people per square mile, but much lower population densities were generally the rule. Norfolk was the most populous county, closely followed by Cambridgeshire, Huntingdonshire, and Lincolnshire. Significantly lower densities prevailed north and west of a line from the Humber to the Severn and the Exe, and in the highlands of Wales and Scotland densities must have been lower still. Nor, at this point, were the Home Counties around London as relatively populous as they were to become. England's demographic centre of gravity lay very much around the Wash. This reflected institutional and historical factors which often ante-dated the Normal Conquest. Later centuries would see the population map of England redrawn, with many settle-

ments that had been thriving in 1300 shrinking or abandoned entirely.

In England the population varied as much in status as it did in distribution. This was a male-dominated age and there were many grades and conditions of men: laymen and churchmen, townsmen and countrymen, lords and peasants, great magnates and minor country gentlemen, merchants and hucksters, franklins and petty freeholders, substantial customary tenants and poor cottars, and a growing class of landless who laboured, begged and stole. Serfdom, in which three-quarters of the rural population had been entrapped at the time of Domesday, had long been on the wane. By 1300 serfs were outnumbered by freemen, and about 60 per cent of all tenanted land was held by some form of free tenure. Freemen had reproduced themselves more rapidly than customary tenants and the extensive land reclamation and colonisation of the twelfth and thirteenth centuries had tended to create free, rather than unfree, tenancies. Moreover, customary rents and obligations, once fixed, were hard to raise. Custom now protected serfs from some of the more arbitrary actions of lords—including, in most cases, the raising of rental obligations. Customary tenants holding 15–30 acres for a fixed rent were often comparatively well off at this time of scarce land, high rents, and low real wages.

The more enlightened landlords employed cooperation, not coercion, in dealing with their tenants.

On most manors substantial customary tenants filled the most important offices and helped operate the manorial courts. Notwithstanding some celebrated struggles of serfs against their lords, the more enlightened landlords, such as Ramsey Abbey, employed co-operation rather than coercion in dealing with their tenants. Social control was difficult to maintain without good landlord-tenant relations. Only a minority of customary tenants were expected to perform regular work on the lord's demesne; hired labour was better motivated and cheaper to supervise. Within the economy at large, wage labour may have accounted for about a fifth to a quarter of the total labour expended in producing goods and services, with family labour accounting for the lion's share of the remainder: Lords also increasingly preferred money rents to labour rents, lay lords receiving seven-eighths of their income in that form by the early fourteenth century. This was possible because the economy was more based on money than ever before, with three times more coinage *per capita* in real terms than in 1086. The population had grown in response to the absence of serious mortality crises coupled with expanding employment opportunities, as the European economy became more commercialised and integrated. The great cities of Italy and Flanders were the nerve centres of that economy. Their growth owed much to the absence until the end of the thirteenth century of major European wars. In England it was war that in 1275 first led kings to tax and manipulate trade. Until then, except for the tolls charged by towns through which goods passed, conditions of free trade had effectively prevailed. Latin provided merchants with a common language for international trade and silver and gold, a common currency. As a result trading volumes had risen everywhere, with the value of English overseas trade trebling over the course of the thirteenth century. An increasing share of that trade was channelled through London, where native merchants vied for its control with foreign merchants. London alone among British cities regularly attracted merchants from all of the countries with which Britain conducted trade. Lombard Street in the City of London takes its name from the great Italian companies who based themselves in the heart of the metropolis.

Since 1000, lowland Britain had become covered by a close network of towns. In Wales and Scotland the bulk of these were deliberate foundations and their streets and property boundaries still display evidence of formal planning. Many English towns were of similar origin, including several that had risen to commercial prominence—Newcastle-upon-Tyne, Kingston-upon-Hull, Boston, King's Lynn, Liverpool and Salisbury. Together, developing administration and trade had reshaped the league-table of town. London—second only to Paris among northern European cities—headed that table, the undisputed national focus of commercial, cultural, legal, administrative and political life. The capital's population of perhaps 75,000 was supported by a sophisticated system of provisioning which guaranteed the city's food supply in even the worst harvest years.

Monks, nuns, friars, clerics, and clerks accounted collectively for about one in ninety of the total population. This was institutionalised celibacy on an impressive scale. Fast advancing fashions and techniques of art, architecture and musical composition helped make religion the great consumer product of the age, offering something to suit almost every purse. Cathedrals, convents, churches, chapels, chantries, altars, retables, statues, monuments, windows, books, vestments and choral masses were all available to be endowed, adorned or purchased by those with the wherewithal to do so. Pilgrimages and crusades provided both the pretext and the means for those inclined to travel.

Monarchs and magnates with their retinues and households, merchants, mongers and hawkers with their wares, armies with their cavalries, infantries and baggage trains, prelates, priests and pilgrims, carters and drovers on land and boatmen and sailors on river and sea were all on the move. Even bonded villeins regularly took to the road to transport demesne produce to market or estate headquarters. The roads, many of them inherited from the Romans, were in better shape than in centuries to come when traffic would be heavier, while unit transport costs compared favourably with those of the eighteenth century. Except in the remoter and less developed parts of the country, the horse had largely replaced the slower ox for haulage. Under private initiative, most major rivers had been bridged while ferries operated at crossings too wide to be bridged. Tolls helped repay the investment. Travellers could purchase lodging, food and drink in most settlements. Writs issued by Exchequer officials at Westminster would be acted upon in the furthest corners of the realm, usually within a matter of weeks. Information and instructions travelled fast.

Bulk goods travelled more slowly and more cheaply by water. England's major navigable rivers, especially those that flowed east, carried a busy traffic. Boats of varying capacities were readily available for hire, as were warehouses and granaries in the principal towns. From 1296 Edward I (r. 1272–1307) would exploit this infrastructure to assemble the mountain of grain, beans, and bacon required to provision his armies and garrisons in Scotland. This lively riverine activity interconnected with an equally busy seaborne trade. The superior prosperity of Britain's east-cost ports demonstrates that maritime commerce was far more strongly orientated towards the North

Sea than the Atlantic. Flanders, the northern terminus of the great overland trade route to Italy and the Mediterranean, was the focus of most northern European seaborne trade, and its great cloth-working towns the destinations for the bulk of the wool that dominated both English and Scottish exports. From the closing years of the thirteenth century, however, trade was increasingly disrupted by warfare. In particular, the trans-Alpine trade route became more risky. Piracy and the conscription of merchant vessels to serve naval needs also became blights upon North Sea shipping.

The invention of spectacles lengthened the working life of all who made a living from the written word.

The thirteenth century had witnessed a process of state building in England and Scotland. In England the common law had developed and royal justice rose to eclipse seigniorial justice. At the same time, the crown's constant need for revenue from taxation and other sources fed the growth of an increasingly depersonalised administration, reliant upon the written word. Central government was aided by a host of clerks and facilitated by royal officials in the shires—sheriffs, escheators, and, from the early fourteenth century, justices of the peace. Public record-keeping fostered private record-keeping, as manifest in England's unique wealth in extant manorial records. Without widespread literacy the transition could not have been made from memory to written record.

The recent invention of spectacles lengthened the working life of clerks, scribes and all who made their living from or relied upon the written word. The mechanical clock likewise introduced the possibility of better time-keeping and payment by the hour. Britons, like their fellow Europeans, were becoming more preoccupied with measurement and quantification, heralding the scientific achievements of later centuries. Attitudes towards money and concepts of profit also began to change. By the second quarter of the fourteenth century Italian merchants had invented double-entry bookkeeping but already from the late thirteenth century the monks of Norwich Cathedral Priory were beginning to experiment with profit-and-loss accountancy. Under the pressure of commercial change canon lawyers began to reformulate the position of the Church on the lending of money for interest.

In England it was now firmly believed that English ways were best and there was a growing desire in some quarters to extend those ways to Wales and Scotland. Emigration had already carried English settlers and some others deep into south Wales, Ireland and Scotland. In Scotland these immigrants mostly settled in the newly founded boroughs but in south Wales and Ireland they occupied both town and country. The cultural, demographic, and economic impacts of settlement were tremendous. Politically, alien communities were created which long remained defiantly separate from those around them and

which helped further English economic, political, and military domination of the greater part of the British Isles.

Edward I harboured an ambition to create a single empire on Britain and by 1306 it looked as though he was on the brink of fulfilling that aim. By 1272 Llywelyn ap Gruffyd felt sufficiently secure in his base of Gwynedd to refuse homage to Edward. He misjudged Edward, who in 1277 wheeled the English military machine into north Wales and forced Llywelyn to acknowledge his overlordship. Renewed Welsh rebellion in 1282 was crushed more ruthlessly and in 1284 the principality was annexed to the English crown. To consolidate and defend his conquest Edward encircled Llywelyn's former mountain stronghold of Snowdonia with a ring of stone castles of the most up-to-date military design. He intended Caenarfon Castle as a royal residence and modelled its walls on those of the imperial city of Constantinople.

The opportunity to intervene in Scotland came in 1290 when, disastrously, there was a failure in the Scottish direct line of succession. Edward was invited to arbitrate and chose John Balliol, whom he required to swear fealty to him and accede to his claimed right to hear appeals from Scots courts. When in 1296 John renounced his fealty, Edward forced him to abdicate and invaded Scotland with the intention of annexing it. Notwithstanding England's superior resources, this eventually proved ruinous to England. At their peak in the Falkirk campaign of 1298, the armies fielded by the English against the Scots numbered over 25,000 men. Keeping such large forces in the field at such a distance was a huge undertaking and a great strain upon the administration and the economy. Nevertheless, all was ultimately in vain.

Scottish independence was forged in its war of independence against England, as were anti-English Scottish sentiments. Following the crushing defeat of Edward II (r.1307–27) by Robert the Bruce (r.1306–29) at Bannockburn in 1314, the Scots took their war to the enemy, raiding deep into northern England, burning, destroying, and driving off cattle to great economic harm. The once peacefully settled border counties would not know security again until the union of the Scottish and English crowns in 1603. In 1315 a Scottish army was also despatched to Ireland—since 1171 a Lordship of the English crown—to cut off this important source of supplies to English armies in Scotland, open up a pan-Celtic front against the English, and create a kingdom for Roberts's brother, Edward Bruce. This dealt a blow to the English colony in Ireland from which it never recovered, converting it from a source of profit to a drain upon the English purse as crown control shrank to the lands of the Pale.

Until the last quarter of the thirteenth century, war in Europe had been relatively localised and short-lived. Kings and magnates had mostly done their fighting against the 'infidel' in Spain or the Holy Land. In the closing years of the century, large-scale warfare returned to Europe. England spent much of the new century fighting a war on three fronts: against the French, the Scots and the Irish. War was destructive—of property, goods, and confidence. It was also costly. Kings took out loans to finance their wars and bribe their allies, often bankrupting those from whom they borrowed. Edward I expelled the Jews in 1290 after they were of no further financial use to him.

Europe's bankers, the Italian super-companies, now served him better. His grandson, Edward III, would borrow even more heavily in order to finance the opening stages of the Hundred Years' War. Edward III (r.1327–77) was one of several militaristic monarchs who by reneging upon huge loans contributed to the collapse of a succession of Italian merchant banks. The shock waves were felt throughout the European monetary system. Meanwhile, English kings had begun to tax trade and use the once-lucrative wool export trade to coerce the Flemings into providing support against the French. As the burden of taxation mounted and law and order broke down, brigands and pirates preyed with increasing effect upon the all important long-distance trade. The long boom was over and as markets contracted so commercial recession deepened and poverty increased.

This, and the adverse environmental changes, was the background to the worst subsistence crisis and greatest crisis of public health in recorded British history. There were at least half a million excess deaths during the Great European Famine of 1315–22. A generation later a further 1.25 to 2 million would perish in the Black Death of 1348–49. Governments had no way of dealing with catastrophes on this scale—indeed, during the Black Death England's found it difficult to keep functioning at all—nor was it yet accepted that it was the responsibility of government to take action. Instead, family support, private charity, and the Church were relied upon for welfare, relief, and spiritual consolation, irrespective of whether their means were adequate to the need. Hence the devastating toll exacted by these disasters. As populations collapsed in England, Wales, Scotland, and Ireland so the tide of English power receded. An era had culminated.

For Further Reading

R. H. Britnell, *the Commercialisation of English Society 1000–1500* (Manchester University Press, 1996); B. M. S. Campbell (ed.), *Before the Black Death: Studies in the 'Crisis' of the Early Fourteenth Century* (Manchester University Press, 1991), R. R. Davies, *Domination and Conquest: the Experience of Ireland, Scotland and Wales 1100–1300* (Cambridge University Press, 1990); C. McNamee, *The Wars of the Bruces: Scotland, England and Ireland, 1306–1328* (Tuckwell Press, 1997); E. Miller and J. Hatcher, *Medieval England: Towns, Commerce and Crafts 1086–1348* (Longmans, 1995); M. Prestwich, *Edward I* (Guild Publishing, 1988); Alfred Crosby, *The Measure of Reality: Quantification and Western Society 1250–1600* (CUP, 1997).

Bruce M. S. Campbell is Professor of Medieval Economic History at The Queen's University of Belfast.

This article first appeared in *History Today,* June 2000, pp. 10-17. © 2000 by History Today, Ltd. Reprinted by permission.

Ready Aim Fire!

A Risky Experiment Reveals How Medieval Engines Of War Brought Down Castle Walls

By Evan Hadingham

Iɴ ᴛʜᴇ ɴᴏᴠᴇᴍʙᴇʀ ᴛᴡɪʟɪɢʜᴛ, ᴀ ᴅᴀɴᴋ ᴡɪɴᴅ sᴛɪʀs ᴀᴄʀᴏss loch ness, sweeping a curtain of penetrating drizzle toward the shore. I take my place in line and grasp a rope thickly caked with Scottish mud. Four dozen of us begin a rhythmic chant, swaying together as we haul on the twin ropes fastened to the giant wooden war machine. This is a trebuchet, a fearsome, poorly understood superweapon of the Middle Ages, which we've been constructing in a swampy field beside the loch for the past two weeks, and are about to fire for the first time.

Although the trebuchet is said to have revolutionized siege warfare eight centuries ago and to have been a potent instrument of both the Islamic and Mongol conquests, few details of its actual capabilities and performance have survived. Medieval drawings of these gravity-powered catapults are seldom realistic; for example, the soldiers who operate them are frequently depicted as taller than the castle walls they are assaulting. And when chronicles refer to machines that fling huge stone balls and crack castle walls to their foundations, it is natural to suspect more than a hint of exaggeration. Was the trebuchet really the ultimate 13th-century deterrent many historians have supposed it to be?

At this moment such questions are academic. We're intent on hoisting one end of a 29-foot beam of Douglas fir, pivoted like an outsize teeter-totter, high into the air over our heads. It takes every muscle we've got, since the end we're raising has 6½ tons of specially cast lead ingots bolted to it. At the moment of firing, a trigger will release the beam, and the massive weight will swing toward earth, flipping the other end of the beam skyward. As that other end flies up, it will pull on a rope sling cradling a stone ball, and fling the ball in a lofty, soaring trajectory down the field.

Or so we hope. But the sight of so many tons poised above us stirs apprehension. Will our machine really hurl a 250-pound stone ball 200 yards, as it's supposed to do? Or could the ball come crashing down on our skulls instead?

The answer from the history books is not wholly encouraging. For instance, when William the Lion, king of the Scots, set up a machine to assault the English defenders of Wark Castle in 1174, the first rock tumbled feebly out of the sling and hit one of his own knights whose armor fortunately protected him from serious harm. Others were not so lucky: a 13th-century account of the siege of Seville speaks of a rock that spun backward out of a trebuchet, killing a man.

The word "trebuchet" has uncertain orgins. In its most primitive form, the trebuchet consists of a pivoted beam with a sling at one end and ropes at the other.

To help forestall such mishaps we have modern engineering on our side. Our trebuchet is mostly the brainchild of Col. W.

Wayne Neel, who teaches mechanical engineering at the Virginia Military Institute in Lexington, Virginia. With his pipe and tartan cap, Wayne cuts a Holmesian figure as he hovers around the machine, constantly absorbed in steely calculation and reflection.

"The way I first approached the design was not the way a 20th-century engineer would do it," Wayne explains. "Instead, I tried to take the medieval approach." Medieval craftsmen, he knew, were illiterate and had no elaborate math to guide them. Instead, they used simple whole-number ratios and geometric arcs that allowed them to plan a design and transfer it to timber using the most elementary of aids: a set of dividers, a square and a plumb bob.

After figuring out the basics, Wayne was relieved to come across an Arabic work from 1463 entitled *The Elegant Book of Trebuchets;* this work quotes ratios and proportions very similar to those he had deduced from the old drawings and his own intuition. All that was left was to ensure the safety of the design. Stepping outside the medieval world, Wayne applied standard engineering formulas to calculate the machine's bending and breaking stresses. He also crafted meticulous working scale-model trebuchets, which propel small foil-wrapped packages of butter across restaurant rooms with startling violence.

Wayne's ideas were translated into a full-sized machine as part of a *NOVA* public television miniseries on experimental archaeology. (The episode on trebuchets aired on PBS February 1, 2000.) *NOVA* flew in a team of more than 50 craftsmen, nearly all from an organization of traditional carpenters, the Timber Framers Guild of North America. *NOVA* wanted a machine that not only would replicate original trebuchet performance but as far as possible reflect the techniques of the Middle Ages.

Accordingly, a medieval craft village sprang up beside the loch. The air rang with the clanging of the blacksmith's anvil on which iron fittings for the machine were bashed out. In one corner, the "leadheads" (with modern safety masks) melted down 14,000 pounds of scrap lead for the trebuchet weights. Elsewhere, a mason patiently chiseled out ammunition, each sandstone ball identically sized so that the trebuchet would perform consistently from one shot to the next. Most curious of all, a wooden lathe was in operation; an improbable device, it was powered by a five-foot-diameter, hand-cranked wheel. The lathe operator used a sharp "lathe hog" to shave rapidly spinning pieces of wood into a desired shape. The result was an array of miraculously well-finished axles, capstans and other cylindrical wooden components.

The demands of television selected this soggy field for picturesqueness not practicality, and this complicated the timber framers' task. The track leading into the site was too steep for the delivery of timber, which had to come by barge from the loch instead. In October, it starts getting dark here by 4 P.M., and then there's the drizzle. Yet all the obstacles forged an exceptional bond between the timber framers. To a casual visitor, it looked like there was no one in charge. Communication on the site flowed quietly, almost telepathically, from one craft expert to the next: a rope adjusted here, a beam trimmed there. Under the pressures of a real siege with lives at stake,

medieval carpenters must have worked with similar speed and coordination.

Casting an acerbic eye on the proceedings is Hew Kennedy, whose green Wellington boots and tweeds proclaim him a member of the landed gentry. Kennedy owns a Shropshire manor filled with armor and more than a decade ago, was one of the first to dabble in trebuchet building. Assembling tree trunks and a 60-foot-long wooden beam, he installed his machine at the top of a sloping farm field, then began startling his neighbors by hurling drums of flaming gasoline, upright and grand pianos, dead farm animals, even a one-ton car. Although not a true replica of a medieval design, Kennedy's machine convinced him of the trebuchet's effectiveness: "If you chuck a thing that heavy at a stone wall, it will shatter it. Stone missiles are a lot more effective than upright pianos."

The word "trebuchet" has uncertain origins. The roots of the machine go back to at least the fifth century B.C. in China. In its most primitive form, it consisted of a pivoted beam with a sling at one end and ropes at the other. A stone would be placed in the sling and a team of men would haul on the ropes, swinging the beam up into the air.

Throughout the Crusades, dozens of these human-powered machines would be ranged against a castle wall, and it was said that some engines were pulled by teams of several hundred men. In retaliation, the defenders remodeled the towers with platforms broad enough to accommodate their own trebuchets. During the siege of Jerusalem in A.D. 1099, a Saracen defender was caught spying on the Crusaders' siege machinery; the unfortunate infiltrator was bound hand and foot, loaded into a catapult and hurled fatally back toward the city walls.

He began startling his neighbors by hurling drums of flaming gasoline, grand pianos, dead farm animals.

Finally, in the late 12th century (still well before the advent of gunpowder in the West), an unknown Islamic or Crusader engineer hit upon the idea of adding heavy weights to one end of the pivoted beam, thereby vastly multiplying the machine's potential size and destructiveness. In fact, the counterweight trebuchet was the first step in the development of large-scale mechanized warfare. When Britain's King Henry III assaulted Kenilworth Castle in 1266, he kept nine trebuchets working day and night, letting loose such a rain of destruction that stones collided in midair. The added power of the counterweight trebuchet meant that missiles could be lobbed in a high, curving arc right over the castle walls, bursting with devastating shrapnel-like effect amidst the beleaguered defenders. The trebuchet even introduced the practice of biological warfare. At Carolstein in 1422, Lithuanian attackers shot the bodies of dead soldiers into the castle along with 2,000 cart-

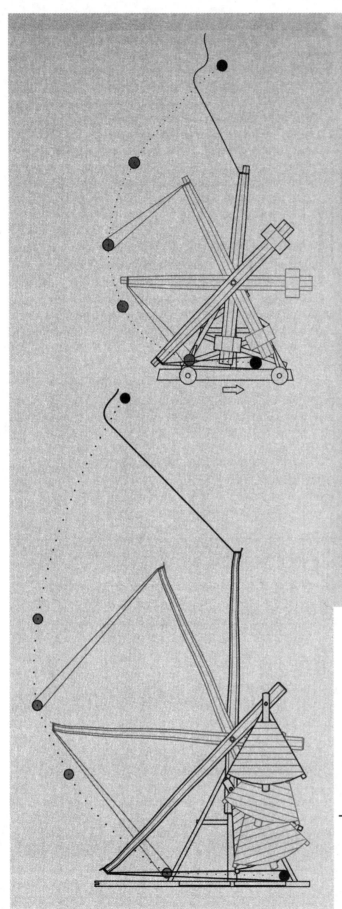

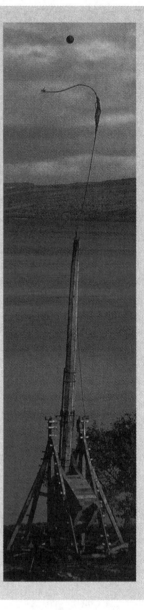

Photographs by Patrick Ward

A trebuchet consists of a giant, pivoting beam with weights on one end and a sling to deliver a missile attached to the other. The weighted end is raised and, when the machine is fired, it falls to earth. The sling pulls the ammunition, flinging it upward with great force and releasing it at the crucial moment. Neel's siege machine (top diagram) has fixed weights and is on wheels; the weights in Beffeyte's trebuchet (bottom) are in a hinged basket.

As the end flies up, it will pull on a rope sling cradling a stone ball, and fling the ball in a lofty, soaring trajectory down the field.

loads of manure in a reportedly successful attempt to spread infection.

No one was more adept and ruthless at the game of siege warfare than Edward I of England (familiar to fans of the movie *Braveheart* as "Longshanks"). For three months in 1304, a mere 50 Scots held seemingly impregnable Stirling Castle under relentless attacks from Edward. The defenders had only one trebuchet, which soon broke. Ranged against them were no less than 13 machines, each sizable enough to have a pet name such as the "Vicar" or the "Parson." The royal accounts note that church roofs for miles around were stripped of lead for counterweights. Edward built a timber viewing stand for Queen Margaret and the ladies of the court from which they could watch the spectacular firing at a safe distance.

As the siege wore on, 50 of Edward's laborers toiled over the ultimate war machine, which they named the Loup de Guerre, or the "War Wolf." We have few details of this formidable weapon, but evidently the defenders, now reduced to about 30, had had enough. Their offer of surrender, however, was turned down. So eager was Edward to see the War Wolf in action that he would not discuss terms until it was completed and had lobbed a few missiles at the castle wall.

What did it take to make a machine like the War Wolf? Did the need for high-power, precision artillery give birth to a genuine science of trebuchet design? Our team beside the loch is about to find out.

One overlooked idea that we'll test is adding wheels to the base of a trebuchet, as shown in several 13th-century manuscripts. Common sense suggests that wheels would be useful merely for aiming the machine or moving it closer to castle walls. Wayne has discovered, however, that scale models without wheels often topple over after firing. Wheeled models, on the other hand, not only stay upright but actually roll forward as the weighted end of the beam swings down. This is a simple consequence of gravity, since the rolling action allows the weight to fall a straighter vertical path. It means that more energy is squeezed out of the counterweight's fall, so the missile will be flung farther. The rolling motion also has the effect of dampening forces that tend to topple the machine or shake it apart.

So this elementary design feature may well turn out to be a brilliant stroke of medieval engineering—that's if our 30-ton replica behaves identically to Wayne's models, and rolls forward on its wheels as it fires. Based on years of hurling pianos, Hew Kennedy is skeptical. "It's very difficult to hit a target wall, and wheel's won't help," he asserts. "In a model it's OK if it lurches all over the place, but in a full-sized model we should tie it down."

A more fundamental argument in trebuchet design centers on the counterweight. Medieval drawings frequently show machines with a large hinged basket that rotates around the end of the beam, rather than a fixed weight. The operators filled up the basket with sand, rocks or any heavy material at hand. A comparison of the drawings suggests that hinged trebuchets mostly replaced the fixed type, so they may have possessed a hidden mechanical advantage. Wayne suspects that the swinging of the basket would give an extra "kick" to the machine and fling the

projectile farther, similar to the action of wheels. An account by a 13th-century chronicler, Aegidio Colonna, seems to support Wayne's hunch. Colonna observed that hinged machines shot farther than those with fixed weights (but added a disparaging note that they also shot less accurately).

Such distinctions might be academic trifles if *NOVA*'s producer hadn't decided to spice up the program by commissioning a second trebuchet, now rising in the same swampy field alongside the first. When finished, this second contraption will feature a hinged basket and an immobile base, in contrast to the fixed lead weights and wheels of Wayne's device. And it will be the work of a designer with a very different background to Wayne's.

Renaud Beffeyte, a shrewd, good-humored Frenchman, is a master carpenter rather than an engineer. He is also perhaps the world's only full-time trebuchet maker, the creator of more than 30 machines for castles and museums around the world since 1984. A giant oak log has been landed by barge, and by the time the timber framers have finished trimming it, Renaud is confronted with a slender throwing arm no less than 42 feet long. This will require a trebuchet far bigger than Renaud—or anyone else since the Middle Ages—has attempted to build.

To meet the challenge, Renaud turns to the sole existing medieval "blueprint" for a trebuchet. (Unfortunately, only one fragment of the plan—the layout of the base—survives.) It fills one of 33 pages of a notebook compiled by a man named Villard de Honnecourt, who lived in northern France in the early 13th century. The notebook offers a unique glimpse of the mind of a master architect or engineer, a medieval Leonardo, although Villard's precise professional status and career are unknown. He crammed the pages of his notebook with meticulous plans of abbeys and cathedrals, designs for labor-saving gadgets and perpetual motion machines, and sketches of nudes and insects.

Renaud had long dreamed of building a trebuchet based on Villard's plan but was always intimidated by its enormous scale, since the sketch implies a machine more than five stories tall. Now, faced with the 42-foot-long throwing arm, Renaud decides that the opportunity has finally come to realize Villard's ambitious design. What began as a competition to build two rival machines quickly turns into an intense cooperative effort, as the timber framers struggle to assemble intricately fitted wooden structures.

At last, after two week's heroic effort, the moment of truth arrives. I find myself in line with four dozen others on the ropes, hoisting the heavy end of Wayne's throwing arm as high as it will go. Hastily the timber framers scramble to insert a long metal trigger pin into the tackle that holds the ropes fast. Now they must load the machine. The ammunition consists of a 250-pound sandstone ball, which they roll into position on a long plank set directly underneath the throwing arm. A rope sling is then carefully fastened so that it cradles the ball at one end while the other loops over a wooden prong protruding from the arm. When the trigger is pulled and the arm flies up, the sling will pull the ball off the plank and fling it upward in a high arc. At the crucial moment, one end of the sling will slip off the prong, releasing the ball.

By now I have retired to a safe distance, since standing next to our untried machine feels like sitting on a keg of gunpowder with a sizzling fuse. A dozen men get ready to pull on the rope attached to the trigger pin. Someone yells "fire in the hole!" The men yank… and nothing happens. The pin is stuck fast, imprisoned by friction and the three-ton load on the trigger chain. The men fumble and struggle, then suddenly the pin flies free of the tackle. There is an eerie moment as the apparatus seems to hang in suspension. Then, with a low rumble the ball slides forward, and in a surprisingly graceful motion it soars up and arcs over the machine, finally flying free of the rope at a heart-stopping 60 feet above the ground. Off it sails through the gray skies until, with a mighty thump and spatter, it finds a mark in the distant mud. A police radar gun clocks the ball's speed at 127 miles per hour.

Although the display of brute mechanical power is exhilarating, the ball has fallen short. Our machine is aiming at a specially built target wall 200 yards away; it is five feet thick at the base and modeled after the upper battlements of a medieval castle, with narrow slots for archers to shoot through. If our trebuchets are to be any good as siege engines, they must pound away reliably at a specific patch of wall, at a safe distance from defenders' arrows.

Wayne judges that the sling released the ball late, so that it flew in too flat a trajectory. Now he shortens the sling by one foot, so the ball will be released sooner and curve higher into the air, thus traveling farther up the field. For good measure, Wayne rubs a little lard on the wooden prong so that the sling will slip off the end more readily.

Feeling bolder for the second shot, I stick close to the machine and Wayne, who is thinking aloud about his engineering predictions. "The frame should roll forward around six feet," he remarks. This time, the ball is released smoothly, in a higher arc, and whizzes by the right-hand edge of the wall, missing it by inches. The timber framers yell in exultation and tear up the field in pursuit. Wayne, however, puffs on his pipe and steps coolly up to the machine with his tape measure. The entire frame has been rolling back and forth in sympathy with the swinging of the great arm, the timber groaning in protest. Now, as the machine comes to rest, Wayne bends over and measures. "A little over five feet," he mutters in satisfaction. The wheeled frame has worked much as he anticipated, adding additional force to the ball while dampening the stresses of firing.

It takes four more shots until, finally, there's a direct hit: a ball careens into the arrow slot in the middle of the wall, pulverizing the masonry and ejecting a fountain of dirt and rubble out the wall's back side. Could it be due to the kilts that the timber framers have just put on for good luck? More likely, it is thanks to Wayne's tiny adjustments to the length of the sling and the position of the frame. After a mere half-dozen shots, the machine has proved that it can fire with surprising precision and consistency.

With this satisfying result, work now redoubles on Renaud's machine. How will the absence of wheels and the different counterweight design affect its performance? When finally complete, the machine stands 54 feet tall, and its long, slender throwing arm now looks decidedly fragile. For its first shot, Renaud cautiously orders the counterweight basket to be loaded with a mere two tons of sand.

"A heavy silence descended on the work site, normally so animated," Renaud wrote afterward. "Everyone was waiting, and I was feeling the pressure. I stepped back to calm myself by taking time to contemplate 'the beast.' She was truly magnificent—powerful, balanced of noble breed. Then I sensed a real harmony and a mounting confidence. I silently thanked my operative ancestor, Willard de Honnecourt, and his little secrets of geometry."

With too little ballast in the basket, the first ball hops feebly into the air and thumps to earth just over 100 feet away. So more sand is added while Renaud watches nervously to see if the arm will break. Now the machine shoots in a high, lobbing arc, much higher than the trajectory of Wayne's machine—so high, in fact, that it cannot reach the wall. Although there is only one day to go before the end of the project, Renaud's prospects look good if he can figure out a way to flatten the path of the ball.

The next day dawns despondently with snow that turns into driving rain. The ropes become mired in mud, and fingers are numb with the effort of wringing them dry. When the weather clears, Renaud tries a new strategy. The throwing arm of his machine has an iron finger on the end, in place of the wooden prong of Wayne's. With the help of a welding torch, Renaud bends the prong forward, so that the sling will slip off the end just a fraction of a second later. This does the trick, for now the shots become near misses indeed, whizzing barely inches above the top of the battlements. Renaud will score a bull's-eye if the path of the ball can be lowered by a whisker. But is such a fine adjustment possible? With a hammer, one of the timber framers taps gingerly at the base of the iron finger. He's bending it forward barely perceptibly—a couple of millimeters—when Renaud motions him to stop.

The sky grows black again with an impending storm. The ropes are stretched and frayed, the stone ball almost too greasy to roll into position. This is clearly Renaud's final chance. For the last time, the trigger flies out of the tackle and the ball rumbles down the plank. Up it goes, arching against the storm clouds over the loch, then bearing down on the battered wall. Thanks to the tiny shift in the prong, the ball's path is now two feet lower, and the missile lands with a resounding crash squarely on the top of the battlements. Masonry explodes in all directions, and the entire wall bows out under the impact. Renaud tosses his cap into the air. "Yeah!" he shouts. "Just a little—just two millimeters apart—and we get the best shoot!" Despite many differences in design and construction, both Wayne's and Renaud's machines have performed with startling precision and predictability.

Medieval historian Michael Prestwich, who witnessed the NOVA experiment, was left in no doubt of the trebuchet's impact. "For the first time I had a real sense of how formidable these siege engines could be," he notes. "With a few shots, it's obvious you could do tremendous damage. In the struggle between attackers and defenders that marked every siege, it's very clear to me now that the appearance of a trebuchet on the scene must have shifted the balance radically in favor of attack."

Drying out from our victory beside a log fire, we reflect on lessons no history book could have taught us. Our trebuchets had called for subtle geometry, expert rigging and fastidious timberwork. Centuries before Newton, trebuchet engineers had developed a seat-of-the-pants expertise that involved repeated observation, testing, and a skillful gasp of mechanics. While medieval chroniclers hint at the terrifying impact of machines like the War Wolf, they are mostly silent on the ingenuity invested in their design and construction.

Only modern experiment could reveal that these unwieldy contraptions were in practice reliable, high-precisian instruments of war, foreshadowing the weapons of far worse conflicts to come.

Evan Hadingham, Science Editor of NOVA *on PBS, has written books on prehistory and archaeology. Patrick Ward photographed Letter Boxers for the April 1998* SMITHSONIAN. *He works in the United Kingdom.*

From *Smithsonian* magazine, June 2000, pp. 78-87. © 2000 by Evan Hadingham.

War-Games of Central Italy

Modern Italian cities hold annual intramural games dating back to the Middle Ages. **Raymond E. Role** *explores their evolution and the cultural, political and social landscape where these paramilitary sports originated.*

ITALY'S ENERVATING SUMMERS are invigorated by the pageantry of annual sporting events, with Siena's bare-back horse race, *La Corsa del Palio*, being the most famous. Unforgettable as visual experiences, full of the bold patterns and colours of period costumes, these events have roots that reach deep into a less languid medieval past.

Almost a century before the First Crusade (1095–99), Christendom's first counter-assaults against Islam had been launched from Pisa and Genoa, re-opening western Mediterranean sea routes and stimulating a revival of commerce and industry in the Italian peninsula on the foundations of the urban network of ancient Rome. Over the following centuries, their growing economic power enabled Italian cities to develop the most advanced culture in Europe; yet they remained volatile and violent places.

Beginning around the year 1080 in a few cities like Pisa and Lucca, the commune, a republican form of political system, emerged, and by 1143 communes had been established in all major cities from Rome to the Alps. City-dwellers were elevated to citizenship by taking an oath of obedience to the commune, which in effect governed a city-state whose inhabitants spanned all circumstances and means. Italian nobility increasingly participated in the commercial life of the cities, while the urban merchant class steadily increased its

wealth, so that many of the distinctions between these two classes diminished. They began to share a common style of life, and became the cities' political class.

As the rural nobility began living in cities during the early twelfth century, they brought their aristocratic mentality with them. Soon city folk of middling rank were emulating the nobles' ostentatious, arrogant and violent behaviours, including the vendetta. With lawlessness endemic among the urban elite, the custom of the vendetta seems to have spread quickly to all levels of society, so no medieval citizen was ever far from a potential street fight.

> *The very fabric of the medieval Italian city was a constant invitation to future violence.*

Men instinctively turned first to their relatives and then to their friends for protection. Kinship ultimately determined status, power and security. By the mid-twelfth century, large kinship groups, or clans, had incorporated themselves into defensive alliances or *consorterie*, while groups of smaller, unrelated families had bound themselves together by solemn

oaths into mutual defence associations called 'tower societies'. Consequently, communal governments had constantly to struggle to assert their nascent right to govern and to establish their authority over an unruly populace, while simultaneously striving to unify their citizenry into something more than a quarrelsome tangle of rival factions.

Within the walls of the cities, inhabitants' mutual fear can be seen reflected in their arrangement of housing—a patchwork of neighbourhoods, each the stronghold either of a *consorteria* or of a 'tower society'. The architectural nucleus of such a neighbourhood was its stout stone or brick tower, like those surviving at San Gimignano or Lucca's Torre Guinigi, designed for throwing, shooting or catapulting projectiles at rival fellow-citizens and/or their property nearby. Built tightly around this fortification were the houses of the members of its *consorteria* or its 'tower society', along with their parish church. This whole complex formed a compact urban refuge, whose narrow alleyways could be easily barricaded off and defended when vendettas flared up. The very fabric of the medieval Italian city was a constant invitation to future violence.

Even beyond the city walls, this parochial mentality can be seen in the medieval map of northern and central Italy—a patchwork of city-states, each trying to expand at the expense of the other. The survival of a city as an independent state ultimately rested on its armed forces, which comprised combat units levied from each of its semi-autonomous neighbourhoods. If the internal divisions from within the city were allowed to reach the battlefield, they could destroy military cohesion and possibly endanger the city itself.

Legislative attempts to curb bloodfeuds occurred as early as 1100 when Pisa limited the height of towers and forbade private possession of catapults, mangonels, crossbows and ammunition. City governments, often in concert with the local bishops, demanded oaths of peace *en masse* from their citizens and extracted sums of money from past offenders as surety bonds. Punishments usually took the form of fines, confiscation of property, razing of family palazzi or towers, permanent exile or death—but the clannish nature of the vendetta was so engrained that some legislation, such as the Florentine Ordinances of Justice enacted in 1293, went so far as to punish not only those guilty of violence, but their innocent relatives as well. Some punishments even included a grant of immunity from prosecution to victims' families, in order to allow its members to take revenge with impunity upon the peace-breakers, their close relatives, even their children as yet unborn.

Communal governments also developed a safety-valve to release built-up rancour at a diminished level of violence, and in doing so demonstrated their authority over their disorderly constituents. They coupled major annual religious festivals with a government-sponsored intramural game, or *giocca*, a mock combat pitting contestants from rival neighbourhoods against one another. This offered a non-lethal outlet with, hopefully, a cathartic outcome as a substitute for the vendetta. Such events were preceded by impressive religious-civic processions, formally manifesting the government's jurisdiction. Today, the direct descendants of these paramilitary games come alive each summer.

Almost as old as the communes themselves was the most widespread of all the intramural games, the *Giocca di Mazzascuda;* or the Game of Club and Shield, where fully armoured foot soldiers

sought to drive their opponents from the field with blows from wooden maces. Known to have been played at various times in almost every city throughout Tuscany and Umbria, and at Pavia and Gubbio too, this 'sport' was probably played widely elsewhere in Italy as well.

From at least the early thirteenth century, the communal government of Pisa encouraged its citizens to play the *Giocca di Mazzascuda* annually between Christmas and Shrove Tuesday. To underscore governmental control and sponsorship, a field was set up directly in front of Palagio Maggiore, Pisa's seat of government, in the city's main piazza, the Piazza dei Anziani (now Piazza dei Cavalieri di San Stefano). This large circular enclosure, surrounded by a cordon of chains with entrances at two opposing points, was guarded from dawn to dusk by Pisa's police forces to maintain order among combatants and spectators alike. This field of honour was available daily, except Sundays, for privately arranged contests, either single or group combat, a handy place to settle a grudge, even a score, or repay an insult. On January 17th, the feast day of St Anthony Abbot, the government also sponsored a large group combat, similar to a popular knightly tournament called a *melée*, or *battagliaccia*. This civic 'sport' allowed even humble citizens to publicly display their martial skills on foot in the same vainglorious way as the noble citizens displayed their derring-do on horseback. For centuries this annual martial exercise kept its citizen-soldiers in fighting trim, but in 1406 Pisa lost its independence to the Florentines, who swiftly confiscated the Pisans' arms, including their wooden maces for playing the *Giocca di Mazzascuda.*

Undiminished by Florentine rule, however, internecine violence continued at Pisa throughout the fifteenth century, taking on the form of rock-throwing incidents between the then unarmed neighbourhood factions, often staged impromptu on the narrow bridges spanning the Arno. Since little was needed to convert this spontaneous mayhem into a new government-sponsored martial arts tournament, Lorenzo de' Medici, towards the end of the century, encouraged the establishment of the *Giocca del Ponte* to be held

on June 17th, the feast day of San Ranieri, patron saint of Pisa. The earliest form of the *Giocca del Ponte* probably consisted of two numerically equal squads of combatants, armed with blunt weapons and protected by shields and armour, contesting the crossing of a bridge. There were no rules, but the first squad to bludgeon its way across to the opponent's side won.

The rules of the *Giocca del Ponte* were made slightly more genteel in the early sixteenth century, by limiting contestants to just six per side, defining the martial techniques permitted and eliminating some of the game's more entertaining 'plays' such as tossing a heavily armoured opponent into the Arno. Gone too were the traditional wooden club and shield, replaced by the *targone*, a long narrow type of wooden shield, a meter long with a semi-circular top 25cm wide, tapering to a blunt point 5cm wide. Fitted with horizontal wooden hand grips top and bottom, the *targone* could be used both defensively, to parry opponents' blows, and offensively, to push and to 'butt end' by gripping its handles or to club by holding its small end. The *Battagliaccia del Giorno di San Antonio* was also reinstated on January 17th, preserving the no-holds-barred style of 'play'—a kind of minor league event where aspiring combatants could hone their skills.

In the late sixteenth century the game was reorganised into just two large opposing teams, called Tramontana and Mezzogiorno, representing the northern and southern sides of the city divided by the Arno, each incorporating the neighbourhood squads. This arrangement forced those in adjacent neighbourhoods—normally the most mutually antagonistic and vendetta-prone groups—to work together as teammates and future comrades-in-arms. Organized in military fashion into six companies of sixty each, with a captain and commanded by a general, these small armies battled against each other for two hours (later reduced to one hour and then to forty-five minutes). These rule changes ushered in a period of increased popularity for the *Giocca del Ponte*, that lasted from 1600 to 1785, when Pietro Leopoldo I, Grand Duke of Tuscany, an enlightened Austrian, banned it, considering it a barbarous anachronism.

After a suspension of over a century and a half, Pisa's city government reinstated the annual *Giocca del Ponte*, in 1947. Its combatants then became contestants in a modernised game, a tense 'push-of-war' with neighbourhood squads pushing in opposite directions against a seven-ton carriage, or *carrello*, mounted on a fifty-metre metal track running the length of Ponte di Mezzo. Reborn as Tramontana and Mezzogiorno, each team now composed of six squads of twenty, still representing the same neighbourhoods on opposite sides of the Arno, compete in six consecutive contests. As riotous as the conclusion of any single contest may be, the end of the deciding contest that awards the annual victory to either Tramontana or Mezzogiorno is pandemonium—with unofficial fireworks and the unfurling of homemade banners, while the winners' side of the Arno is brilliantly lit up, leaving the losing side to brood in twilight.

Florence's **Calcio** *derives from a conditioning exercise for Roman legionaries akin to rugby.*

Medieval Florence had its own version of the *Giocca di Mazzascuda*, but also had long played an indigenous ball game called *Calcio*, a descendant of *Arapasto*, a conditioning exercise for Roman legionaries akin to rugby but more violent. It was not until the early fourteenth century, when Florence's communal government was first able to divide the city into four sub-divisions or *quartieri*, that it also began to sponsor a *Calcio* tournament at Carnevale. Its purpose was to force adjacent neighbourhoods in each *quartiere*, from which Florence also mustered its militia, to work together as teammates, just as at Pisa.

Each quartiere fielded a team of twenty seven players for a three-game, 'sudden death' tournament played on a rectangular field (one hundred metres by

forty six), set-up in one of the city's larger piazzas, usually Piazza Santa Croce or Piazza Signoria. The object was to throw a 25cm diameter ball into the opponent's goal, a net 1.2 metres high stretching the full width of the field—one point if successful, but a half-point to the opponent if unsuccessful. The rules were almost nonexistent. Played annually until the late 1700s, this cross between wrestling, boxing, rugby, basketball and soccer was reinstated with its original rules and staged in its traditional venues in 1930. Known today as *Calcio Storico Fiorentino*, it continues as an annual outlet for (still quite lively) intramural animosities. In 1997, the final match had to be cancelled when disgruntled fans from one *quartiere* violently assaulted a player from a rival *quartiere* as he left his home, in retaliation for his particularly foul play in the semifinal match; and the 1998 final was marred when fans purposely injured an opposing player by throwing fireworks into the field during the pre-game festivities.

If old habits refuse to die at Florence, they are as healthy as ever at Siena, whose very urban structure on its three hills has caused dissension for so long that the city was already referred to in the plural by the ancient Romans—the Sienas. During the Dark Ages, residents descended from the hills into the valley between them to trade with each other in a large, open field, a market site that was to become the heart of the medieval city, Piazza del Campo. Commercial disputes regularly led from quarrels to blows and bloodshed, particularly during the weeks before Lent when scarcity caused high prices. After 1125, a communal government was established in a tripartite manner with each hill becoming a political unit of the city, or *terziere*, with equal representation in the government. Each had its own internal governmental structure.

These initial building blocks of Sienese political life must have been the clan and the 'tower society', which provided Siena's armed forces. A series of devastating wars, along with the Black Death outbreaks in 1348 and thereafter, combined to decrease drastically the numerical strength of *consorteria* and 'tower society' alike, so that by the late 1400s,

the survivors had to seek protection from each other by banding together in a new type of association called a *contrada*. A *contrada* was begun by unrelated families living in a neighbourhood as a corporation with a written constitution, laws, membership requirements, dues, officers, a court, a headquarters, a parish church, a patron saint, geographical boundaries, an army, a heraldic symbol, colours, a banner, allies, enemies and vendettas. Originally numbering as many as sixty, depopulation caused some *contrade* to merge until the last geographic revision, in 1729, reduced them to their present number, seventeen. Today, the Sienese *contrada*, demilitarised yet militant, retains all of its other original elements. It is still a mutual aid society and social club. Needy members are aided by funds raised from its dues, philanthropic contributions, rental properties, bar and social events such as dances. Each *contrada* sponsors a club for women and another for children, while its headquarters are bar [and] are a focus for male social activity. With both its original structure and social mission preserved, the *contrada* is more modernised than evolved, generating an intense sense of identity and loyalty among those born within its boundaries.

The **Giocca della Pugna** *seemed to satisfy the bloodlust of the Sienese, with 1,200 participating in a citywide contest in 1324.*

Faced with an already centuries-old culture of intramural violence, Siena's earliest communal governments sought to condone and control what they could not eliminate by also initiating an annual Sienese version of the *Giocca di Mazzascuda* 'played' at the end of Carnevale. Called the *Giocca dell' Elmora*, the Game of the Helmet, it was a citywide group combat, pitting Siena's most populous *terziere* against the other two. For generations, thousands of Sienese, paricipating under their military banners, wielding wooden weapons (maces, swords and spears) and throwing stones, ought to drive their fellow citizens from Piazza del Campo under the watchful eyes of their elected officials looking on from the windows of Palazzo Pubblico, the seat of government. Sheer numbers, however, made effective control nearly impossible. When even the intervention of the city's police forces still failed to prevent ten fatalities in 1291, sufficient political will was finally generated to ban the 'game' permanently.

Besides the *Giocca dell' Elmora*, its less life-threatening and much older, possibly Etruscan relative, the *Giocca della Pugna*, or the Fist Fight, was a favourite pastime in medieval Siena. Wearing cloth caps with protective cheek-pieces tied together under the chin similar to the sparring headgear of modern boxers, and with their fists wrapped in cloth bindings to protect their knuckles, participants sought to drive their fellow citizens from one of the city's piazzas. Whether arranged in advance or held impromptu between just two neighbourhoods in a nearby piazza, or organized by the communal government between the full *terzieri* in Piazza del Campo, the Giocca della Pugna seemed to satisfy the bloodlust of the Sienese, judging from the participation of 1,200 in a citywide *pugna*, in 1324. During the Renaissance, bans did little to dull the appetite for the 'game' among the Sienese, who staged a *pugna* just as heartily in 1536 to celebrate the visit of newly crowned Holy Roman Emperor, Charles V, as they did nearly twenty years later to raise their own morale during the siege of the city by his Imperial troops. *La pugna* survived even Napoleon, with the students of Siena University's class of

1816 being the last to enjoy the exhilaration of this 'sport'.

Siena's communal government, like those of other cities in Italy, originally linked their paramilitary games to celebrations of some annual religious festivals, but by the mid-twelfth century it had also coupled as many as six horse races with other religious events. Beginning at some point outside the city walls, these horse races ran a course, point-to-point or *al lungo*, through Siena's streets to a finishing line at the cathedral, where the winner received as a prize, a bolt of expensive cloth, or *palio*. Later, a single *contrada*, in celebration of the feast day of its patron saint, would periodically stage a *palio*, inviting others to participate. It is uncertain when the *contrade* began to send entrants to the annual citywide races, but by the last half of the fifteenth century they sponsored all the contestants.

After Siena lost its independence to Florence in 1555, Duke Cosimo I de' Medici, fearing massive public gatherings, reduced the number of races to just one, honouring St Mary, patron saint of Siena, on August 15th, in commemoration of her Assumption. In 1656, a second race was permitted on July 2nd to commemorate the Visitation and the purely local feast day of St Mary of Provenzano—a race run *alla tonda*, three times around Piazza del Campo, allowing viewing of the race start-to-finish for the first time. So exciting was this new form that a third race, also *alla tonda*, was soon added on August 16th. Although the older race, *al lungo*, on August 15th failed to survive the nineteenth century, the other two races, both now called *La Corsa del Palio*, have been run continuously ever since, under the sponsorship of the competing *contrade*. Such longevity is due in part to the incorpora-

tion within them of many aspects of Siena's former paramilitary games and races so that, with the partisan enthusiasm for all of them distilled into these two events, *La Corsa del Palio* releases the seemingly eternal fanaticism of the *contrade*.

Lucca's *Tiro dei Balestrieri*, where cross-bow men test their archery skill, Arezzo's *Giostra del Saracino* and Pistoia's *Giostra del Orso*, where teams of modern-day knights tilt at the quintain, and Gubbio's *La Corsa dei Ceri*, where teams race up-hill carrying thousand-pound weights, are some of the other sporting events whose origins are entwined in their cities' history. Each is unique yet quintessentially Italian, not so much folkloristic re-enactments as modern expressions of the passions that generated their institution.

FOR FURTHER READING

Violence and Civil Disorder in Italian Cities, 1200–1500, ed. Lauro Martines (University of California Press, 1972); D. and F. W. Kent *Neighbors and Neighborhood in Renaissance Florence: the District of the Red Lion in the Fifteenth Century* (J.J. Augustin Publisher, New York, 1982); Nicholas A. Eckstein *The District of the Green Dragon: Life and Social Change in Renaissance Florence* (Leo S. Olschki Editore, Florence, 1990); E. Cristiani, *Nobilità e Popolo nel commune di Pisa* (Instituto Italiano Per Gli Studi Storici, Naples 1962); L. Artusi, *Il Palagio Parte Guelfa e il Calcio in Costume a Firenze* (Edizioni Scramasax, Florence 1997); W. Heywood *Palio e Ponte* (Hacker Art Books, New York, 1969); A. Dundes & A. Falussi *La Terra in Piazza* (University of California Press, 1975); V. Grassi *Le Contrade di Siena e le loro feste: il Palio attuale* (2 Vol., Periccioli Editore, Siena, 1972).

Raymond E. Role is a practising architect and freelance writer based in Lucca, Italy.

How a Mysterious Disease Laid Low Europe's Masses

In the 1300s, a third of the population died of plague brought by fleas, shocking the medieval world to its foundations.

Charles L. Mee Jr.

In all likelihood, a flea riding on the hide of a black rat entered the Italian port of Messina in 1347, perhaps down a hawser tying a ship up at the dock. The flea had a gut full of the bacillus *Yersinia pestis*. The flea itself was hardly bigger than the letter "o" on this page, but it could carry several hundred thousand bacilli in its intestine.

Scholars today cannot identify with certainty which species of flea (or rat) carried the plague. One candidate among the fleas is *Xenopsylla cheopis*, which looks like a deeply bent, bearded old man with six legs. It is slender and bristly, with almost no neck and no waist, so that it can slip easily through the forest of hair in which it lives. It is outfitted with a daggerlike proboscis for piercing the skin and sucking the blood of its host. And it is cunningly equipped to secrete a substance that prevents coagulation of the host's blood. Although *X. cheopis* can go for weeks without feeding, it will eat every day if it can, taking its blood warm.

One rat on which fleas feed, the black rat *(Rattus rattus)*, also known as the house rat, roof rat or ship rat, is active mainly at night. A rat can fall 50 feet and land on its feet with no injury. It can scale a brick wall or climb up the inside of a pipe only an inch and a half in diameter. It can jump a distance of two feet straight up and four horizontally, and squeeze through a hole the size of a quarter. Black rats have been found still swimming days after their ship has sunk at sea.

A rat can gnaw its way through almost anything—paper, wood, bone, mortar, half-inch sheet metal. It gnaws constantly. Indeed, it *must* gnaw constantly. Its incisors grow four to five inches a year: if it were to stop gnawing, its lower incisors would eventually grow—as sometimes happens when a rat loses an opposing tooth—until the incisors push up into the rat's brain, killing it. It prefers grain, if possible, but also eats fish, eggs, fowl and meat—lambs, piglets and the flesh of helpless infants or adults. If nothing else is available, a rat will eat manure and drink urine.

Rats prefer to move no more than a hundred feet from their nests. But in severe drought or famine, rats can begin to move en masse for great distances, bringing with them any infections they happen to have picked up, infections that may be killing them but not killing them more rapidly than they breed.

Rats and mice harbor a number of infections that may cause diseases in human beings. A black rat can even tolerate a moderate amount of the ferocious *Yersinia pestis* bacillus in its system without noticeable ill effects. But bacilli breed even more extravagantly than fleas or rats, often in the millions. When a bacillus finally invades the rat's pulmonary or nervous system, it causes a horrible, often convulsive, death, passing on a lethal dose to the bloodsucking fleas that ride on the rat's hide.

THE ULTIMATE BACILLUS BREEDER

When an afflicted rat dies, its body cools, so that the flea, highly sensitive to changes in temperature, will find another host. The flea can, if need be, survive for weeks at a time without a rat host. It can take refuge anywhere, even in an abandoned rat's nest or a bale of cloth. A dying rat may liberate scores of rat fleas. More than that, a flea's intestine happens to provide ideal breeding conditions for the bacillus, which will eventually multiply so prodigiously as finally to block the gut of the flea entirely. Unable to feed or digest blood, the flea desperately seeks another host. But now, as it sucks blood, it spits some out at the same time. Each time the flea stops sucking for a moment, it is capable of pumping thousands of virulent bacilli back into its host. Thus bacilli are passed from rat to flea to rat, contained, ordinarily, within a closed community.

For millions of years, there has been a reservoir of *Yersinia pestis* living as a permanently settled parasite—passed back and forth among fleas and rodents in warm, moist nests—in the wild rodent colonies of China, India, the southern part of the Soviet Union and the western United States. Probably there will always be such reservoirs—ready to be stirred up by sudden climatic change or ecological disaster. Even last year, four authentic cases of bubonic plague were confirmed in New Mexico and Arizona. Limited outbreaks and some fatalities have occurred in the United States for years, in fact, but the disease doesn't spread, partly for reasons we don't understand, partly because patients can now be treated with antibiotics.

And at least from biblical times on, there have been sporadic allusions to plagues, as well as carefully recorded outbreaks. The emperor Justinian's Constantinople, for instance, capital of the Roman empire in the East, was ravaged by plague in 541 and 542, felling perhaps 40 percent of the city's population. But none of the biblical or Roman plagues seemed so emblematic of horror and devastation as the Black Death that struck Europe in 1347. Rumors of fearful pestilence in China and throughout the East had reached Europe by 1346. "India was depopulated," reported one chronicler, "Tartary, Mesopotamia, Syria, Armenia, were covered with dead bodies; the Kurds fled in vain to the mountains. In Caramania and Caesarea none were left alive."

Untold millions would die in China and the rest of the East before the plague subsided again. By September of 1345, the *Yersinia pestis* bacillus, probably carried by rats, reached the Crimea, on the northern coast of the Black Sea, where Italian merchants had a good number of trading colonies.

From the shores of the Black Sea, the bacillus seems to have entered a number of Italian ports. The most famous account has to do with a ship that docked in the Sicilian port of Messina in 1347. According to an Italian chronicler named Gabriele de Mussis, Christian merchants from Genoa and local Muslim residents in the town of Caffa on the Black Sea got into an argument; a serious fight ensued between the merchants and a local army led by a Tartar lord. In the course of an attack on the Christians, the Tartars were stricken by plague. From sheer spitefulness, their leader loaded his catapults with dead bodies and hurled them at the Christian enemy, in hopes of spreading disease among them. Infected with the plague, the Genoese sailed back to Italy, docking first at Messina.

Although de Mussis, who never traveled to the Crimea, may be a less-than-reliable source, his underlying assumption seems sound. The plague did spread along established trade routes. (Most likely, though, the pestilence in Caffa resulted from an infected population of local rats, not from the corpses lobbed over the besieged city's walls.)

In any case, given enough dying rats and enough engorged and frantic fleas, it will not be long before the fleas, in their search for new hosts, leap to a human being. When a rat flea senses the presence of an alternate host, it can jump very quickly and as much as 150 times its length. The average for such jumps is about six inches horizontally and four inches straight up in the air. Once on human skin, the flea will not travel far before it begins to feed.

The first symptoms of bubonic plague often appear within several days: headache and a general feeling of weakness, followed by aches and chills in the upper leg and groin, a white coating on the tongue, rapid pulse, slurred speech, confusion, fatigue, apathy and a staggering gait. A blackish pustule usually will form at the point of the fleabite. By the third day, the lymph nodes begin to swell. Because the bite is commonly in the leg, it is the lymph nodes of the groin that swell, which is how the disease got its name. The Greek word for "groin" is *boubon*—thus, bubonic plague. The swelling will be tender, perhaps as large as an egg. The heart begins to flutter rapidly as it tries to pump blood through swollen, suffocating tissues. Subcutaneous hemorrhaging occurs, causing purplish blotches on the skin. The victim's nervous system begins to collapse, causing dreadful pain and bizarre neurological disorders, from which the "Dance of Death" rituals that accompanied the plague may have taken their inspiration. By the fourth or fifth day, wild anxiety and terror overtake the sufferer—and then a sense of resignation, as the skin blackens and the rictus of death settles on the body.

In 1347, when the plague struck in Messina, townspeople realized that it must have come from the sick and dying crews of the ships at their dock. They turned on the sailors and drove them back out to sea—eventually to spread the plague in other ports. Messina panicked. People ran out into the fields and vineyards and neighboring villages, taking the rat fleas with them.

When the citizens of Messina, already ill or just becoming ill, reached the city of Catania, 55 miles to the south, they were at first taken in and given beds in the hospital. But as the plague began to infect Catania, the townspeople there cordoned off their town and refused—too late—to admit any outsiders. The sick, turning black, stumbling and delirious, were objects more of disgust than pity; everything about them gave off a terrible stench, it was said, their "sweat, excrement, spittle, breath, so foetid as to be overpowering; urine turbid, thick, black or red...."

Wherever the plague appeared, the suddenness of death was terrifying. Today, even with hand-me-down memories of the great influenza epidemic of 1918 (SMITHSONIAN, January 1989) and the advent of AIDS, it is hard to grasp the strain that the plague put on the physical and spiritual fabric of society. People went to bed perfectly healthy and were found dead in the morning. Priests and doctors who came to minister to the sick, so the wild stories ran, would contract the plague with a single touch and die sooner than the person they had come to help. In his preface to *The Decameron*, a collection of stories told while the plague was raging, Boccaccio reports that he saw two pigs rooting around in the clothes of a man who had just died, and after a few minutes of snuffling, the pigs began to run wildly around and around, then fell dead.

"Tedious were it to recount," Boccaccio thereafter laments, "brother was forsaken by brother, nephew by uncle, brother by sister and, oftentimes, husband by wife; nay what is more and scarcely to be believed, fathers and mothers were found to abandon their own children, untended, unvisited, to their fate, as if they had been strangers…."

In Florence, everyone grew so frightened of the bodies stacked up in the streets that some men, called *becchini*, put themselves out for hire to fetch and carry the dead to mass graves. Having in this way stepped over the boundary into the land of the dead, and no doubt feeling doomed themselves, the *becchini* became an abandoned, brutal lot. Many roamed the streets, forcing their way into private homes and threatening to carry people away if they were not paid off in money or sexual favors.

VISITING MEN WITH PESTILENCE

Some people, shut up in their houses with the doors barred, would scratch a sign of the cross on the front door, sometimes with the inscription "Lord have mercy on us." In one place, two lovers were supposed to have bathed in urine every morning for protection. People hovered over latrines, breathing in the stench. Others swallowed pus from the boils of plague victims. In Avignon, Pope Clement was said to have sat for weeks between two roaring fires.

The plague spread from Sicily all up and down the Atlantic coast, and from the port cities of Venice, Genoa and Pisa as well as Marseilles, London and Bristol. A multitude of men and women, as Boccaccio writes, "negligent of all but themselves… migrated to the country, as if God, in visiting men with this pestilence in requital of their iniquities, would not pursue them with His wrath wherever they might be…."

Some who were not yet ill but felt doomed indulged in debauchery. Others, seeking protection in lives of moderation, banded together in communities to live a separate and secluded life, walking abroad with flowers to their noses "to ward off the stench and, perhaps, the evil airs that afflicted them."

It was from a time of plague, some scholars speculate, that the nursery rhyme "Ring Around the Rosy" derives: the rose-colored "ring" being an early sign that a blotch was about to appear on the skin; "a pocket full of posies" being a device to ward off stench and (it was hoped) the attendant infection; "ashes, ashes" being a reference to "ashes to ashes, dust to dust" or perhaps to the sneezing "a-choo, a-choo" that afflicted those in whom the infection had invaded the lungs—ending, inevitably, in "all fall down."

In Pistoia, the city council enacted nine pages of regulations to keep the plague out—no Pistoian was allowed to leave town to visit any place where the plague was raging; if a citizen did visit a plague-infested area he was not allowed back in the city; no linen or woolen goods were allowed to be imported; no corpses could be brought home from outside the city; attendance at funerals was strictly limited to immediate family. None of these regulations helped.

In Siena, dogs dragged bodies from the shallow graves and left them half-devoured in the streets. Merchants closed their shops. The wool industry was shut down. Clergymen ceased administering last rites. On June 2, 1348, all the civil courts were recessed by the city council. Because so many of the laborers had died, construction of the nave for a great cathedral came to a halt. Work was never resumed: only the smaller cathedral we know today was completed.

In Venice, it was said that 600 were dying every day. In Florence, perhaps half the population died. By the time the plague swept through, as much as one-third of Italy's population had succumbed.

In Milan, when the plague struck, all the occupants of any victim's house, whether sick or well, were walled up inside together and left to die. Such draconian measures seemed to have been partially successful—mortality rates were lower in Milan than in other cities.

Medieval medicine was at a loss to explain all this, or to do anything about it. Although clinical observation did play some role in medical education, an extensive reliance on ancient and inadequate texts prevailed. Surgeons usually had a good deal of clinical experience but were considered mainly to be skilled craftsmen, not men of real learning, and their experience was not much incorporated into the body of medical knowledge. In 1300, Pope Boniface VIII had published a bull specifically inveighing against the mutilation of corpses. It was designed to cut down on the sale of miscellaneous bones as holy relics, but one of the effects was to discourage dissection.

Physicians, priests and others had theories about the cause of the plague. Earthquakes that released poisonous fumes, for instance. Severe changes in the Earth's temperature creating southerly winds that brought the plague. The notion that the plague was somehow the result of a corruption of the air was widely believed. It was this idea that led people to avoid foul odors by holding flowers to their noses or to try to drive out the infectious foul odors by inhaling the alternate foul odors of a latrine. Some thought that the plague came from the raining down of frogs, toads and reptiles. Some physicians believed one could catch the plague from "lust with old women."

> *Most Christians believed the cause of the plague was God's wrath at sinful Man.*

Both the pope and the king of France sent urgent requests for help to the medical faculty at the University of Paris, then one of the most distinguished medical groups in the Western world. The faculty responded that the plague was the result of a conjunction of the planets Saturn, Mars and Jupiter at 1 P.M. on March 20, 1345, an event that caused the corruption of the surrounding atmosphere.

Ultimately, of course, most Christians believed the cause of the plague was God's wrath at sinful Man. And in those terms, to be sure, the best preventives were prayer, the wearing of crosses and participation in other religious activities. In Orvieto, the town fathers added 50 new religious observances to the municipal calendar. Even so, within five months of the appearance of the plague, Orvieto lost every second person in the town.

There was also some agreement about preventive measures one might take to avoid the wrath of God. Flight was best: away from lowlands, marshy areas, stagnant waters, southern exposures and coastal areas, toward high, dry, cool, mountainous places. It was thought wise to stay indoors all day, to stay cool and to cover any windows that admitted bright sunlight. In addition to keeping flowers nearby, one might burn such aromatic woods as juniper and ash.

The retreat to the mountains, where the density of the rat population was not as great as in urban areas, and where the weather was inimical to rats and fleas, was probably a good idea—as well as perhaps proof, of a kind, of the value of empirical observation. But any useful notion was always mixed in with such wild ideas that it got lost in a flurry of desperate (and often contrary) stratagems. One should avoid bathing because that opened the pores to attack from the corrupt atmosphere, but one should wash face and feet, and sprinkle them with rose water and vinegar. In the morning, one might eat a couple of figs with rue and filberts. One expert advised eating ten-year-old treacle mixed with several dozen items, including chopped-up snake. Rhubarb was recommended, too, along with onions, leeks and garlic. The best spices were myrrh, saffron and pepper, to be taken late in the day. Meat should be roasted, not boiled. Eggs should not be eaten hard-boiled. A certain Gentile di Foligno commended lettuce; the faculty of medicine at the University of Paris advised against it. Desserts were forbidden. One should not sleep during the day. One should sleep first on the right side, then on the left. Exercise was to be avoided because it introduced more air into the body; if one needed to move, one ought to move slowly.

By the fall of 1348, the plague began to abate. But then, just as hopes were rising that it had passed, the plague broke out again in the spring and summer of 1349 in different parts of Europe. This recurrence seemed to prove that the warm weather, and people bathing in warm weather, caused the pores of the skin to open and admit the corrupted air. In other respects, however, the plague remained inexplicable. Why did some people get it and recover, while other seemed not to have got it at all—or at least showed none of its symptoms—yet died suddenly anyway? Some people died in four or five days, others died at once. Some seemed to have contracted the plague from a friend or relative who had it, others had never been near a sick person. The sheer unpredictability of it was terrifying.

In fact, though no one would know for several centuries, there were three different forms of the plague, which ran three different courses. The first was simple bubonic plague, transmitted from rat to person by the bite of the rat flea. The second and likely most common form was pneumonic, which occurred when the bacillus invaded the lungs. After a two- or three-day incubation period, anyone with pneumonic plague would have a severe, bloody cough; the sputum cast into the air would contain *Yersinia pestis*. Transmitted through the air from person to person, pneumonic plague was fatal in 95 to 100 percent of all cases.

The third form of the plague was septocemic, and its precise etiology is not entirely understood even yet. In essence, however, it appears that in cases of septocemic plague the bacillus entered the bloodstream, perhaps at the moment of the fleabite. A rash formed and death occurred within a day, or even within hours, before any swellings appeared. Septocemic plague always turned out to be fatal.

Some people did imagine that the disease might be coming from some animal, and they killed dogs and cats—though never rats. But fleas were so much a part of everyday life that no one seems to have given them a second thought. Upright citizens also killed gravediggers, strangers from other countries, gypsies, drunks, beggars, cripples, lepers and

Jews. The first persecution of the Jews seems to have taken place in the South of France in the spring of 1348. That September, at Chillon on Lake Geneva, a group of Jews were accused of poisoning the wells. They were tortured and they confessed, and their confessions were sent to neighboring towns. In Basel all the Jews were locked inside wooden buildings and burned alive. In November, Jews were burned in Solothurn, Zofingen and Stuttgart. Through the winter and into early spring they were burned in Landsberg, Burren, Memmingen, Lindau, Freiburg, Ulm, Speyer, Gotha, Eisenach, Dresden, Worms, Baden and Erfurt. Sixteen thousand were murdered in Strasbourg. In other cities Jews were walled up inside their houses to starve to death. That the Jews were also dying of the plague was not taken as proof that they were not causing it.

Very rarely does a single event change history itself. Yet an event of the magnitude of the Black Death could not fail to have an enormous impact.

On the highways and byways, meanwhile, congregations of flagellants wandered about, whipping themselves twice a day and once during the night for weeks at a time. As they went on their way they attracted hordes of followers and helped spread the plague even farther abroad.

The recurrence of the plague after people thought the worst was over may have been the most devastating development of all. In short, Europe was swept not only by a bacillus but also by a widespread psychic breakdown—by abject terror, panic, rage, vengefulness, cringing remorse, selfishness, hysteria, and above all, by an overwhelming sense of utter powerlessness in the face of an inescapable horror.

After a decade's respite, just as Europeans began to recover their feeling of well-being, the plague struck again in 1361, and again in 1369, and at least once in each decade down to the end of the century. Why the plague faded away is still a mystery that, in the short run, apparently had little to do with improvements in medicine or cleanliness and more to do with some adjustment of equilibrium among the population of rats and fleas. In any case, as agents for Pope Clement estimated in 1351, perhaps 24 million people had died in the first onslaught of the plague; perhaps as many as another 20 million died by the end of the century—in all, it is estimated, one-third of the total population of Europe.

Very rarely does a single event change history by itself. Yet an event of the magnitude of the Black Death could not fail to have had an enormous impact. Ironically, some of the changes brought by the plague were for the good. Not surprisingly, medicine changed—since medicine had so signally failed to be of any help in the hour of greatest need for it. First of all, a great many doctors died—and some simply ran away. "It has pleased God," wrote one Venetian-born physician, "by this terrible mortality to leave our native place so destitute of upright and capable doctors that it may be said not one has been left." By 1349, at the University of Padua there were vacancies in every single chair of medicine and surgery. All this, of course, created room for new people with new ideas. Ordinary people began wanting to get their hands on medical guides and to take command of their own health. And gradually more medical texts began to appear in the vernacular instead of in Latin.

AN OLD ORDER
WAS BESIEGED

Because of the death of so many people, the relationship between agricultural supply and demand changed radically, too. Agricultural prices dropped precipitously, endangering the fortunes and power of the aristocracy, whose wealth and dominance were based on land. At the same time, because of the deaths of so many people, wages rose dramatically, giving laborers some chance of improving their own conditions of employment. Increasing numbers of people had more money to buy what could be called luxury goods, which affected the nature of business and trade, and even of private well-being. As old relationships, usages and laws broke down, expanding secular concerns and intensifying the struggle between faith and reason, there was a rise in religious, social and political unrest. Religious reformer John Wycliffe, in England, and John Huss, in Bohemia, were among many leaders of sects that challenged church behavior and church doctrine all over Europe. Such complaints eventually led to the Protestant Reformation, and the assertion that Man stood in direct relation to God, without need to benefit from intercession by layers of clergy.

Indeed, the entire structure of feudal society, which had been under stress for many years, was undermined by the plague. The three orders of feudalism—clergy, nobility and peasantry—had been challenged for more than a century by the rise of the urban bourgeoisie, and by the enormous, slow changes in productivity and in the cultivation of arable land. But the plague, ravaging the weakened feudal system from so many diverse and unpredictable quarters, tore it apart.

By far the greatest change in Western civilization that the plague helped hasten was a change of mind. Once the immediate traumas of death, terror and flight had passed through a stricken town, the common lingering emotion was that of fear of God. The subsequent surge of religious fervor in art was in many ways nightmarish. Though medieval religion had dealt with death and dying, and naturally with sin and retribution, it was only after the Black Death that painters so wholeheartedly gave themselves over to pictures brimming with rotting corpses, corpses being consumed by snakes and toads, swooping birds of prey appearing with terrible suddenness, cripples gazing on the figure of death with longing for deliverance, open graves filled with blackened, worm-eaten bodies, devils slashing the faces and bodies of the damned.

Well before the plague struck Europe, the role of the Catholic Church in Western Europe had been changing. The Papacy had grown more secular in its concerns, vying with princes for wealth and power even while attempts at reform were increasing. "God gave us the Papacy," Pope Leo X declared. "Let us enjoy it." The church had suffered a series of damaging losses in the late 1200s—culminating in 1309 when the Papacy moved from Rome to Avignon. But then, the Black Death dealt the church a further blow, for along with renewed fear and the need for new religious zeal came the opposite feeling, that the church itself had failed. Historical changes rarely occur suddenly. The first indications of change from a powerful catalyst usually seem to be mere curiosities, exceptions or aberrations from the prevailing worldview. Only after a time, after the exceptions have accumulated and seem to cohere, do they take on the nature of a historical movement. And only when the exceptions have come to dominate, do they begin to seem typical of the civilization as a whole (and the vestiges of the old civilization to seem like curiosities). This, in any case, is how the great change of mind occurred that defines the modern Western world. While the Black Death alone did not cause these changes, the upheaval it brought about did help set the stage for the new world of Renaissance Europe and the Reformation.

As the Black Death waned in Europe, the power of religion waned with it, leaving behind a population that was gradually but certainly turning its attention to the physical realm in which it lived, to materialism and worldliness, to the terrible power of the world itself, and to the wonder of how it works.

From *Smithsonian* magazine, February 1990, pp. 67–74, 76, 78. © 1990 by Charles L. Mee, Jr. Reprinted by permission of the author.

Saints Or Sinners?
The Knights Templar in
Medieval Europe

During the trials that destroyed one of 14th-century Europe's most celebrated crusading military orders, witnesses claimed all manner of abuses had been going on for years. But how true were these claims? And what did contemporaries think about them and the other military orders—such as the Knights Hospitaller and Teutonic Knights? Helen Nicholson investigates.

In October 1307, by order of Philip IV of France, all the Knights Templar within the French domains were arrested. In November, Pope Clement V sent out orders for the arrest of the Templars throughout Europe. The brothers were accused of a variety of crimes, which were said to be long-established in the order. There were, it was claimed, serious abuses in the admission ceremony, where the brothers denied their faith in Christ. The order encouraged homosexual activity between brothers. The brothers worshipped idols. Chapter meetings were held in secret. The brothers did not believe in the mass or other sacraments of the church and did not carry these out properly, defrauding patrons of the order who had given money for masses to be said for their families' souls.

What was more, it was alleged that the Templars did not make charitable gifts or give hospitality as a religious order should. The order encouraged brothers to acquire property fraudulently, and to win profit for the order by any means possible.

During the trial of the Templars witnesses claimed that the order's abuses had been notorious for many years and

under interrogation, including torture, many brothers confessed to at least some of these crimes. In March 1312, Pope Clement dissolved the Order of the Temple, giving its property to the Order of the Hospital, and assigning the surviving brothers to other religious orders. Despite this, the question of the order's guilt has never been settled. Just what were the accusations made against the Templars before 1300, and were these related to the trial? What did contemporaries think about the other military orders, such as the Knights Hospitaller and the Teutonic Knights?

The Order of the Temple was a military order, a type of religious order. It had been founded in the early twelfth century, in the wake of the Catholic conquest of the Holy Land, to protect pilgrims travelling to the holy places against bandits. This role soon grew to protecting Christian territory in Spain as well as the Holy Land. The order gained its name because the King of Jerusalem had given the brothers his palace in the al-Aqsa mosque, which the Christians called 'the Temple of Solomon', to be their headquarters. In Europe the members' lifestyle was much like that of ordi-

nary monks. The order's rule laid down a strict regime on clothing, diet, charitable giving and other living arrangements. In theory only men could join the order, but in practice some women were also admitted.

The Order of the Temple was the first military order, but others soon followed. The Order of the Hospital of St John of Jerusalem had been founded as a hospice for pilgrims in the eleventh century, but by the 1130s the Hospital was employing mercenaries to protect pilgrims from bandits, and was soon involved in the defence of the frontiers of the Kingdom of Jerusalem alongside the Order of the Temple. These brothers became known as the Hospitallers.

The Hospital of St Mary of the Teutons was set up at the siege of Acre during the Third Crusade (1189–92) to care for German pilgrims and was then relaunched in 1198 as a military order. The brothers were known as the Teutonic Knights. These were the most famous of the international military orders, but the concept was so popular that others were founded wherever Christians confronted non-Christians: in Spain, where the Muslim frontier was slowly retreating, and in the Baltic and Prussia where pagan tribes threatened Christian settlements and converts. From the 1230s onwards the Teutonic order became prominent in the Baltic area.

The concept of the military order was a natural development from the concept of the crusade. Rather than taking up weapons for a short period to defend Christ's people, the members of a military order did so for life. In return, they expected to receive pardon for their sins and immediate entry into heaven if they died in action against the enemies of their faith.

In western Europe, far from the battlefield, some of the clergy were doubtful whether a military order could be a valid religious order. Around 1150, the Abbot of Cluny wrote to Pope Eugenius III that he and many of his monks regarded the brothers of the Temple as only knights, not monks, and believed that fighting the Muslims overseas was less important than suppressing bandits at home. Letters written to encourage the early Templars also hint at this sort of opposition. But the bulk of the surviving evidence is warmly in praise of the Templars, and clergy and knightly classes alike welcomed the new order with generous donations. In fact the Hospital of St John seems to have attracted more donations as it became more of a military order. By 1200 the military orders had become part of the religious establishment and criticism of the concept ceased.

However, other criticism arose which tended to fluctuate with events. During a crusade, while crusaders wrote home with accounts of the military orders' courage and self-sacrifice, criticism was overlooked. Between crusades, as Europeans received news of territorial losses to the Muslims, they forgot the military orders' heroism and concluded that these defeats were God's punishment for sin. For surely God would not allow godly men to suffer such setbacks.

Political views also shaped criticism, especially during the period 1229–50, while pope and emperor were at loggerheads. The Temple, and to a lesser degree the Hospital, supported the pope, while the Teutonic order supported the emperor. So observers sympathetic to the emperor's policies in the Holy Land,

such as Matthew Paris, chronicler of St Albans abbey, criticised the Templars and Hospitallers. Yet there was praise from those who opposed the emperor in the Holy Land, such as Philip of Novara and the Powerful Ibelin family of Cyprus who were Philip's lords.

Chroniclers tended to be critical, for they wished to draw a moral from contemporary events for the edification of future generations. In other forms of literature, romance, epic or farce, the Templars, Hospitallers and Teutonic Knights appeared as brave knights of Christ combating the Muslim menace, or as helpers of lovers, or as good monks. It is interesting that although monks and parish priests came under heavy criticism for their immorality in the 'fables' or farces, the military orders were not criticised. Obviously they were not regarded as womanisers.

Between the Second and Third Crusades of 1148–49 and 1189, the generous donations of money and privileges to the Templars and Hospitallers became a major cause of resentment. This was hardly surprising. All religious orders aroused complaints about their privileges, and the Templars and Hospitallers never attracted such severe criticism as the Cistercians and friars.

But the Templars and the Hospitallers caused particular annoyance because their houses were so widely scattered. Their legal privileges were especially resented. In 1236 Pope Gregory IX wrote to the Templars and hospitallers in western France ordering them not to abuse the privileges granted to them by the papal see. The brothers had been summoning their legal opponents to courts in far-off places which they had no hope of reaching by the specified day, so that they were then fined for failing to appear. The brothers had also been taking annual payments for clergy and laity in return for allowing them to share their legal privileges.

Forty years later, when Edward I's commissioners were conducting the Hundred Roll inquiries to establish where royal rights had been usurped in each locality, there were similar protests. Some people who had no proper connection with the Templars and Hospitallers were claiming their privileges, in Warwick-

shire and Derbyshire there were complaints that the orders' privileges 'impede and subvert all common justice and excessively oppress the people', while the burghers of Totnes and Grimsby had been summoned to courts in the four corners of England by the Hospitallers and Templars respectively.

Despite their extensive possessions, the Templars and Hospitallers were always claiming to be poverty-stricken. They sent out alms-collectors on a regular basis, to collect money from lay-people and clergy for their work in the Holy Land. Matthew Paris was probably expressing a widely-felt discontent when he wrote around 1245:

The Templars and Hospitallers… receive so much income from the whole of Christendom, and, only for defending the Holy Land, swallow down such great revenues as if they sink them into the gulf of the abyss…

Whatever did they do with all their wealth? Some Europeans concluded that they must be using their resources very inefficiently.

The orders were not only wealthy and privileged, they were proud and treacherous. Pride, the first of the seven deadly sins, was already the military orders' most infamous vice by the 1160s. As the years passed it became a stock complaint against the Templars and Hospitallers, as if it was 'their' sin. Pride made the orders jealous of each other and of other Christians, so that they fought each other instead of fighting the Saracens. The Templars and Hospitallers' quarrels became notorious, although in fact the orders went to great lengths to ensure peaceful relations. The troubadour, Daspol, writing in around 1270, neatly summed up the problem: because the Templars and Hospitallers had become proud and greedy and did evil instead of good, they were unable or unwilling to defend the Holy Land against the Saracens.

In 1289 a Flemish satirist, Jacquemart Giélée, depicted the Templars' and Hospitallers' bitter quarrels in his satire, *Renart le Nouvel*, the new Renart, based on the old theme of the unscrupulous fox. A

Hospitaller is shown denigrating the Templars in order to win Renart for his order. After the final loss of Acre in 1291, Pope Nicholas IV suggested that the military order's quarrels had been a contributory factor in the defeat, and many chroniclers and churchmen agreed.

The charge that the Order of the Temple encouraged the brothers to acquire property fraudulently and to win profit by all possible means clearly reflects these complaints against the Templars and Hospitallers. For at least 150 years contemporaries had accused the military orders of lying and cheating because of their greed for wealth. In 1312 the same old criticisms against the Hospitallers arose again at the Council of Vienne, as the pope planned to bestow on them the former property of the Templars.

Interestingly, no critic before 1300 accused the Templars of immorality. In the mid-thirteenth century an English poet, writing in Anglo-Norman French, surveyed the whole of society and accused most of the clergy of womanising, even dropping hints about the Hospitallers. But he exempted the Templars, who were too busy making money to have time for sex:

The Templars are most doughty men and they certainly know how to look after themselves, but they love pennies too much; when prices are high they sell their wheat instead of giving it to their dependants. Nor do the lords of the Hospital, have any desire for buying women's services, if they have their palfreys and horses, I don't say it for any evil…

A more explicit charge of immorality against the Hospitallers appeared in March 1238, when a French crusade was preparing to depart for the Holy Land. Pope Gregory IX wrote a letter of rebuke to the Hospitallers in Acre. He had heard that the brothers kept harlots in their villages, had been cheating the dying into bequeathing their property to them and (among other crimes) that several of the brothers were guilty of heresy. As for the Templars, he only complained that they

were not keeping the roads safe for pilgrims!

Although the Templars were not accused of immorality, they were linked with traditional romantic love. A late thirteenth-century French verse romance, *Sone de Nausay*, depicts the Master of the Temple in Ireland as the go-between in a love affair, while a French Arthurian romance of the same period, *Claris et Laris*, depicts the Templars as friends to lovers. But this was a wholly sympathetic view, and saw the Templars as servants of lovers rather than as lovers themselves. None of the military orders were accused of sodomy, although such accusations were occasionally made against ordinary monks.

There were many other complaints against the military orders before 1300. Perhaps the most significant were the divided opinions over their record of fighting the Muslims (and other non-Christians). Many complained that they were not sufficiently enthusiastic about defending Christendom and winning back lost territory, while others complained that they were too eager to fight those who could be won to Christ by peaceful means.

Some contemporaries alleged that the military orders were unwilling to fight the Muslims because they were secretly in alliance with them. The military orders certainly did make alliances with Muslim rulers on various occasions, but these alliances were intended to promote the Christian cause, not to hinder it.

The chroniclers also alleged that the Muslims exploited the brothers' greed. There was a legend in circulation which recounted how the Christians had failed to capture a Muslim fortress because some of the Christian leaders had been bribed by Muslim gold to raise the siege. This gold subsequently turned out to be copper. This story appeared in various forms and with various parties in the role of dupe from the mid-twelfth century onwards. By the early thirteenth century the Templars had become the dupes, and by the mid-thirteenth century the Hospitallers had joined them. The fortress also changed identity several times! In fact this is a very old story, and versions of it appear in Gregory of Tours' *History of the Franks*, written in the sixth century,

and in the collection of ancient Welsh legends known as the *Mabinogion*.

Many accusations that the military orders were unwilling to attack the Muslims arose from a misunderstanding of the true situation in the Holy Land. The Templars were criticised for refusing to help the Third Crusade besiege Jerusalem in 1191–92, but the brothers believed that the city could not be held after the crusaders had returned home, and that the security of the holy places were better served by attacking Egypt. In 1250, during the crusade of Louis IX of France, Count Robert of Artois decided to lead the vanguard of the crusading army to attack the Muslims in Mansourah. The Templars and Hospitallers advised against this, whereupon the count accused them of laziness and trying to impede the Christian cause and advanced. Anxious not to be accused of cowardice, the military orders accompanied him and, as they had predicted, the Christian army was cut to pieces. This was a terrible defeat, but something of a propaganda coup for the military orders, who had fearlessly died for Christ against hopeless odds.

Other critics felt that the military orders were *too* eager to fight. Thirteenth-century literature depicted the ideal knight as one who only fought when necessary. The military orders' self-sacrifice for Christ seemed rash and irrational. Some of the clergy believed that the orders' love of violence and domination impeded or prevented conversions. This accusation was made against the Templars in the 1180s by Walter Map, Archdeacon of Oxford, and against the Teutonic order by some unknown critics and around 1266–68 by Roger Bacon, an English Franciscan friar imprisoned in Paris for his unorthodox views.

The unknown critics may have been the Polish princes who opposed the expansion of the Teutonic order's power in Prussia. In 1258, letters were sent to Pope Alexander IV from the order's friends in Poland and Prussia, defending them against various accusations. Apparently the brothers had been accused of forbidding the preaching of Christianity to the pagan Prussians, preventing the establishment of churches, destroying old churches, impeding the sacraments and enslaving new converts. Roger Bacon's criticisms echoed these: the Teutonic order wanted to subjugate the Prussians and reduce them to slavery, and refused to stop attacking them in order to allow peaceful preaching. He added that the order had deceived the Roman Church for many years as to its true motives in Prussia.

The peak of criticism of the military orders came around 1250. After this they faded from the chronicles and critical writings. Many critics of the church omitted them. Others showed little actual knowledge of them. Although there was a vast number of newsletters coming from the Holy Land, so the chroniclers could hardly have been short of information on events, they seem to have chosen to ignore this. News was almost invariably bad, and chroniclers probably believed that the loss of the Holy Land was only a matter of time. There were many crises closer to home to occupy their pens.

As a result, after 1250, the image of the military orders expressed in the chronicles and other writing shows a relative improvement. Day-to-day relations between the military orders and their neighbours and the authorities were usually peaceful. Bishops' registers, royal administrative records and the records of the nobility where these survive, show that although there were disputes generally the military orders were obedient subjects and reliable servants. As Walter Map had remarked, whatever the Templars did in the Holy Land, in England they lived peacefully enough.

Despite the sorry state of the Latin Christian settlement in the Holy Land, after 1250 the military orders were still well regarded in Europe. Donations to the orders had fallen in most areas, but all religious orders were suffering in this respect. Some commentators, while agreeing that even the Templars had declined in spirituality along with all other religious orders, depicted them as having previously been among the most spiritual of the religious orders. This was a far cry from their original foundation, when some had doubted that the order could have a spiritual dimension at all!

So, how far were the Templars' accusers of 1307 justified in their case against the order? Contemporaries would certainly have agreed with the charge that they lied and cheated in order to satisfy their greed. Yet there is no hint before 1300 that the Templars did not carry out the sacraments; although the Teutonic order were accused of impeding the sacraments in Prussia. It was true that the proceedings of the order's chapter meetings were kept secret, but this was the custom among military orders.

The accusation that the order did not practice charity and hospitality may have sprung from the rivalry between the Temple and the Hospital. The Hospitallers were always at pains to emphasise their dual hospitable-military role, in contrast to the solely military role of the Templars. A few contemporaries were struck by the difference: a German pilgrim, John of Würzburg, remarked dismissively in around 1170 that the Temple's charitable giving was not a tenth of the Hospital's. Of course, the Order of the Temple did practise charity, as it was obliged to do under its religious rule, but most contemporaries seemed to have regarded the defence of pilgrims as charity in itself.

There is no indication before 1300 of public scandal over the order abusing admission procedures, or of heresy, idolatry or homosexuality within the order. Only the Hospital was accused of heresy. Interestingly, the Teutonic Knights' rivals in Livonia were accusing them of pagan practices and witchcraft by 1306. This suggests that such charges were politically motivated, rather than based on fact.

The accusations of denial of Christ, sodomy and idolatry had been standard accusations against heretics for centuries, most recently against the Waldensians and the Cathars. Therefore, to accuse a rival of such crimes was to accuse them of heresy. Orthodox Christian belief was believed to be essential for the health of society and to ensure God's favour. Heresy was seen as a disease which must be eradicated before it overcame the whole Christian body. Powerful political rivals could use the charge of heresy with devastating effect against their opponents: it had been deployed by

Pope Innocent IV against the emperor Frederick II during the 1240s, and from 1303 by Philip IV's government against Pope Boniface VIII, who had infuriated Philip by asserting the supremacy of the church over secular rulers. Boniface was accused of heresy, sodomy, witchcraft and magic. Later Guichard, Bishop of Troyes, and Louis of Nevers, son of the Count of Flanders, were accused of similar crimes after incurring Philip's enmity.

Certainly any wealthy, privileged religious order with close ties to the papacy, such as the Cistercians, Friars, Hospitallers or Templars, was likely to incur a monarch's enmity. Yet the Templars were no more disliked than other military orders, and less criticised than some other religious orders. They had a long history of faithful service to the French crown. So why were they singled out for attack?

The Templars had a special position in the defence of the Holy Land. According to Jacquemart Giélée, the brothers claimed to be sole 'Defenders of the Holy Church'. They were depicted as principal defenders of the Holy Land by the Parisian poet Rutebuef in 1277. Templars were mentioned in chronicles and literature in general more than other military orders. They were invariably listed first whenever anyone thought about military orders. They had been the first military order, and were one of the richest and most far-flung. Yet this particular prominence also left them particularly vulnerable when they failed in their duty.

When the city of Acre finally fell to the Muslims in May 1291, several reports of the disaster depicted the Templars as chiefly responsible for the defence of the city. The chronicler of Erfut, writing in the summer of 1291, depicted the Templars dying like true knights of Christ, fighting to the last. Thaddeo of Naples, a priest, praised the courage of the brothers of the military orders who died, and portrayed the death of the master of the Temple, William of Beaujeu, as the decisive blow which led to the loss of the Holy Land. For after Acre fell, the remaining Latin Christian possessions in the East surrendered to the Muslims.

But the order's prominence could also be its undoing. The most popular account of the defeat, which was reproduced in many chronicles, dismissed the Templars as totally ineffective and only concerned to save their treasure. The true hero of the tragedy was now Brother Matthew of Claremont, marshal of the Hospital, who was 'a faithful warrior, knight of Christ', and died a martyr's death. Ricoldo of Monte Cruce, a Dominican Friar who was on a preaching mission in the Middle East when he heard of the disaster, compared William of Beaujeu to the notorious King Ahab, husband of Queen Jezebel and the worst king of Israel in the Old Testament. Certainly he was an excellent soldier, but God rejected him because of his sins.

The loss of Acre was not mentioned among the charges brought against the Templars in 1307, but it was understood that the brothers' alleged abuses were responsible for the disaster.

From the evidence, the famous, shocking charges brought against the Templars in 1307 were unknown before 1300. The order was certainly guilty of fraud and unscrupulous greed, but so too were other religious orders. The brothers' real crime was their failure to protect the Holy Land after claiming to be solely responsible for its defence.

FOR FURTHER READING:

M. Barber, 'Propaganda in the Middle Ages: the charges against the Templars', *Nottingham Medieval Studies*, 17 (1973); M. Barber, *The Trial of the Templars* (Cambridge University Press, 1978); M. Barber, *The New Knighthood: a History of the Order of the Temple* (Cambridge University Press, 1993); H. Nicholson, *Templars, Hospitallers and Teutonic Knights: Images of the military orders, 1128–1291* (Leicester University Press, 1993); J. Upton-Ward, (trans.) *The Rule of the Templars: the French text of the Rule of the Order of Knights Templar* (Boydell Press, 1992).

Helen Nicholson lectures in history at the University of Wales College of Cardiff. She is currently working on a translation of the Itinerarium Peregrinorum et Gesta Regis Ricardi, *a chronicle of the Third Crusade.*

UNIT 6

Renaissance and Reformation

Unit Selections

Key Points to Consider

- What does the career of Jacques Coeur tell us about the basic elements of early capitalism?

- Why was the career of Masilio Ficino important in the Renaissance era?

- How did politics change at the beginning of the modern era?

- Did Renaissance humanism influence the place of women in European life? Explain.

- How is Martin Luther viewed?

 **Links: www.dushkin.com/online/**
These sites are annotated in the World Wide Web pages.

Burckhardt: Civilization of the Renaissance in Italy
http://www.idbsu.edu/courses/hy309/docs/burckhardt/burckhardt.html

Centre for Reformation and Renaissance Studies
http://citd.scar.utoronto.ca/crrs/databases/www/bookmarks.html

Elizabethan England
http://www.springfield.k12.il.us/schools/springfield/eliz/ elizabethanengland.html

1492: An Ongoing Voyage/Library of Congress
http://lcweb.loc.gov/exhibits/1492/

History Net
http://www.thehistorynet.com/THNarchives/AmericanHistory/

The Mayflower Web Pages
http://members.aol.com/calebj/mayflower.html

Reformation Guide
http://www.educ.msu.edu/homepages/laurence/reformation/index.htm

Sir Francis Drake
http://www.mcn.org/2/oseeler/drake.htm

Society for Economic Anthropology Homepage
http://nautarch.tamu.edu/anth/sea/

Women and Philosophy Web Site
http://www.nd.edu/~colldev/subjects/wss.html

The departure from medieval patterns of life was first evident in Renaissance Italy. There the growth of capital and the development of distinctly urban economic and social organizations promoted a new culture. This culture, which spread to other parts of Europe, was dominated by townsmen whose tastes, abilities, and interests differed markedly from those of the medieval clergy and feudal nobility. The essay "How Jacques Coeur Made His Fortune" shows how early capitalism functioned in France.

The emerging culture was limited to a minority—generally those who were wealthy. But even in an increasingly materialistic culture it was not enough just to be wealthy. It was necessary to patronize the arts, literature, and learning, and to demonstrate skill in some profession. The ideal Renaissance man, as Robert Lopez observes (in *The Three Ages of the Italian Renaissance*, University of Virginia Press, 1970) "came from a good old family, improved upon his status through his own efforts, and justified his status by his own intellectual accomplishments."

The new ideal owed much to the classical tradition. Renaissance man, wishing to break out of the other-worldly spirituality of the Middle Ages, turned back to the secular naturalism of the ancient world. Indeed, the Renaissance was, among other things, a heroic age of scholarship that restored classical learning to a place of honor. It was classical humanism in particular that became the vogue. The article "Marsilio Ficino, Renaissance Man" exemplifies these ideas. And in the new spirit of individualism, however, humanism was transformed. The classical, "Man is the measure of all things," became, in poet and scholar Leon Alberti's version, "A man can do all things, if he will." No one better illustrates Alberti's maxim than Leonardo da Vinci.

Civic humanism was another Renaissance modification of the classical heritage. It involved a new philosophy of political engagement, a reinterpretation of political history from the vantage point of contemporary politics, and a recognition that men would not simply imitate the ancients but rival them. Of course, humans being what they are, Renaissance humanism had its darker side. And the Renaissance ideal did not fully extend to women, as J. H. Plumb's essay, "Women of the Renaissance," explains.

Renaissance art and architecture reflected the new society and its attitudes. Successful businessmen were as likely as saints to be the subjects of the portraits. Equestrian statues of warriors and statesmen glorified current heros while evoking memories of ancient Rome. Renaissance painters rediscovered nature, which generally had been ignored by medieval artists, often depicting it as an earthly paradise—the appropriate setting for humanity in its new image. And in contrast to the great medieval cathedrals, which glorified God, Renaissance structures focused on humanity.

Some of these developments in art and architecture indicate changes in the role of Christianity and the influence of the Church, which no longer determined the goals of Western civilization as they had during the medieval period. Increasingly, civil authorities and their symbols competed with churchmen and their icons, while Machiavelli (treated in the article by Vincent Cronin) and other writers provided a secular rationale for a new

LUTHER SCHLÄGT DIE 90 SÄTZE AN.

politlical order. Nonetheless, most Europeans, including many humanists, retained a deep and abiding religious faith.

The Reformation, with its theological disputes and wars of religion, is a powerful reminder that secular concerns had not entirely replaced religious ones, especially in northern Europe. The great issues that divided Protestants and Catholics—the balance between individual piety and the Church's authority, the true means of salvation—were essentially medieval in character. Indeed, in their perceptions of humanity, their preoccupation with salvation and damnation, and their attacks upon the Church's conduct of its affairs, Martin Luther, John Calvin, Ulrich Zwingli, and other Protestant leaders echoed the views of medieval reformers. Luther's lasting influence is examined in "Luther: Giant of His Time and Ours." As for Calvinism, see William J. Bouwsma's essay, "Explaining John Calvin," in which the author attempts to correct modern misperceptions of the Swiss reformer.

Taken together, then, the Renaissance and Reformation constituted a new compound of traditional elements—classical and medieval, secular and religious—along with elements of modernity. The era was a time of transition, or as Lynn D. White describes it, "This was a time of torrential flux, of fearful doubt, making the transition from the relative certainties of the Middle Ages to the new certainties of the eighteenth and nineteenth centuries."

How Jacques Coeur Made His Fortune

He made it none too scrupulously, and lost it at the whim of a much wilier scoundrel than himself

Marshall B. Davidson

One should visit Bourges to see the curious house that Jacques Coeur built, wrote Jules Michelet a century or so ago in his gigantic history of France. It was, he added, "a house full of mysteries, as was Coeur's life." Then, in one of the picturesque asides that make his history such a treasury of unexpected discoveries, he went on to describe that house and the man who built it—the self-made man who played banker to King Charles VII of France, and who bailed out that monarch when his kingdom was at stake; the intrepid man of the world who traded privileges with Moslem sultans, Christian popes, and European princes; the implausibly rich parvenu who, within less than twenty years, parlayed a few counterfeit coins into the largest private fortune in France.

By 1443, when construction of his house started, Coeur was quite possibly the wealthiest man in the world. His new dwelling was to be a monument to his worldly success, and according to one contemporary it was "so richly ornamented, so spacious, and yet, withal, so magnificent, that neither princes of the blood, nor the king himself, had any residence comparable to it." That last point was not lost on Charles VII, as, in the end, Coeur had bitter cause to know.

The house still stands in the cathedral town of Bourges, a short drive south of Paris. It is a unique survival, a memorial as much to a time in history as to the man who built it, for Coeur's life spanned a critical period in the destiny of France. In the last decade of his life the agonizing internecine strife and the bloody slaughter that accompanied the Hundred Years' War were, with his substantial aid, finally brought to an end. The English were thrown back across the Channel, and the land was united as it had not been in living memory.

In the course of those protracted disorders the scrambled authority of feudalism gave way to the more orderly rule of the national monarchy, the spirit of chivalry faded before the practical aims of an aspiring bourgeoisie, and the stultifying controls of medieval economy were turning into the growing pains of modern capitalism. To most contemporary eyes such vital changes appeared as a blurred image, like a dissolve in a movie. But Coeur's role in those transitions was so decisive, and he was so perfectly cast for the part he played, that he might well have written the script himself.

It could be said that in Coeur's time double-entry bookkeeping was proving mightier than the sword, for without that instrument of precision and convenience (apparently a fourteenth-century invention), he could hardly have managed his complex affairs. To him, and other businessmen, time—and timekeeping—took on new importance. For time was money made or lost. The easy rhythm of the canonical hours was being replaced by the stern measure of mechanical clocks that counted out the cost of fleeting opportunities, pointed the way to quicker profits, and ticked off interest on loans. And Coeur pressed every advantage. He even used carrier pigeons to bring him advance notice of approaching cargoes so that he could improve his position in the local markets.

From the very beginning Coeur's enterprise was, for better and for worse, closely associated with the interests of his sovereign. Ironically, he first came to public notice in 1429, when, as an associate of the master of the Bourges mint, he was accused of striking coins of inferior alloy. Like so many other functions now considered the exclusive prerogative of government, minting money was then a private concession, albeit by privilege from the king, who took a substantial share of the milling toll as seigniorage, at rates fixed by law. Since no practical system of taxation was yet in force, this was one of the few ways the king could raise money. To meet the demands of the moment, debasing the coinage was approved practice, and the royal "take" could be enhanced by secretly altering the rate of seigniorage—that is, by still further debasing the coinage without advising the public. If the counterfeit was detected, the royal accomplice could disavow the scheme and leave his concessionaires to face the music. And this is what happened to Coeur and his associates in 1429.

Desperate necessities drove Charles VII to practice such duplicity. When he inherited the throne in 1422, the Hundred Years' War was in its eighth grim decade and the fortunes of France were at their lowest ebb. This ill-omened, youthful heir, the tenth child of a madman who disinherited him and of a mother of loose morals who disowned him (it was widely reported that he was a bastard, no matter of shame at the time, but a shadow on his claim to the throne), was holed up in Bourges. An English king reigned in Paris, and English forces occupied all the land from the Channel to the Loire. Philip the Good, the powerful and autonomous duke of Burgundy, tolerated the foreign invader and was allied with him. And Brittany, ever mindful of its own independent traditions, wavered between allegiances.

The years that followed Charles's succession revolved in a murderous cycle of war and brigandage, pestilence and famine. The king could not afford a standing army, and his military leaders were independent contractors who, between battles with the enemy, roamed the land with their mercenaries, raping, stealing, burning, and killing. Under the circumstances, trade and commerce came to a standstill. Merchants took to the road only if they were armed to the teeth. The great international fairs of Champagne, once vital points of exchange for Europe's traffic, were abandoned as the north-south trade shifted to the sea routes between Flanders and the Mediterranean. France came close to ruin.

The winter of 1428–1429 brought a turning point, or at least a promise of deliverance. The English had laid seige to Orléans, the principal city remaining in Charles's rump of a kingdom. Had Orléans fallen there would have been pitifully little left of that kingdom. The city became a symbol of resistance, while the timid young monarch vacillated in his provincial retreat barely sixty miles away. His mocking enemies dubbed him the "king of Bourges" and anticipated the fall of his petty realm. His treasury was empty; it is said he even borrowed money from his laundress. Only by a miracle could he keep his tottering crown.

The miracle materialized when, as if in direct response to the widely whispered prophecy that an armed virgin would appear and drive the English from the land, Joan of Arc was brought before the king at the château of Chinon where he was then holding court. After grilling the maid for three weeks, the king's counselors decided that she was, as she claimed, divinely appointed by "voices" she had heard to save her king and her country. Somehow, Charles found money to provide her with troops, and the siege of Orléans was lifted. Joan then persuaded her wavering monarch to be crowned at Reims, where Clovis had been baptized. By that ritual the stain of bastardy was auto-matically removed, and Charles was indisputably the true king of France. It took him eight more years to win Paris from the English, but when he did ride triumphantly into that city, after its sixteen years of foreign occupation, he came as the rightful Christian king.

It was hardly a coincidence that Coeur and his associates were charged with counterfeiting almost immediately after the "miracle" at Orléans, or that Coeur was pardoned of the crime. Charles had most likely met the payroll for Joan's troops with funds provided by the mint's illegal operations, and as party to the crime he saw that Coeur got off easily. At least there is no better explanation.

In any case, soon after his pardon Coeur set out to make his fortune. He formed a new partnership with his old associates at the mint, this time to deal in "every class of merchandise, including that required by the King, Monseigneur the Dauphin, and other nobles, as well as other lines in which they [the partners] can make their profit."

For precedents in this new venture he looked abroad. The basis of Renaissance prosperity, already so conspicuous in Italy, was the carrying trade between East and West. For centuries Venice had fattened on this commerce, to the point where its successful and friendly business relations with Mongols and Moslems alike had encouraged those infidels to close in on the Christian world. Then, as European knighthood took the Cross to the Holy Land, Venetians supplied and equipped their fellow Christians and ferried them to the battle sites at exorbitant rates.

Venice also continued its flourishing trade in arms, armor, and diverse other goods with the Saracens of Egypt and Palestine. When Pope Benedict XII forbade unauthorized trade with the infidel, the merchants of Venice bought up papal authorizations wherever they could and used them as ordinary bills of exchange. With the Fourth Crusade, the "businessman's crusade," the merchants of Venice made a double killing. They dissuaded the debt-burdened knights from their proclaimed purpose of attacking Alexandria, one of Venice's richest markets, and persuaded them to sack the flourishing Christian capital of Constantinople.

Meanwhile, across the Apennines in Tuscany, enterprising merchants were swarming out of Florence into western Europe, collecting contributions to the Crusades as bankers to the Holy See, advancing money to land-poor feudal lords at fantastic interest rates, and with their ready cash buying up the privileges of the towns. During the Hundred Years' War the powerful Bardi and Peruzzi families equipped both French and English armies for the battlefields, prolonging the conflict and taking over the functions of state when it was necessary to secure their accounts. In return for helping Henry III of England with his running expenses, the Florentines asked for 120 per cent interest on advances and, when repayment was not prompt, added 60 per cent more. In such a company of greedy Christians, Shylock would have seemed hopelessly ingenuous.

During the most agonizing period of the Hundred Years' War, however, the Florentines had gradually abandoned their commercial colonies in France. Now that his time had come, Coeur moved to fill that vacuum with his own business and, with equal speed, to stake a claim among the markets of the

BOTH: ARCHIVES PHOTOGRAPHIQUES

Coeur's mansion is adorned both inside and out with whimsical vignettes of daily life.

The *trompe l'oeil* couple may represent servants watching for their master's return.

East, so profitably exploited by Venice. His first try at emulating the Venetian merchants was a disaster. In 1432 he journeyed to Damascus, an awkward if not perilous place for Christians to be at the time, buying up spices and other exotic commodities for resale in the home markets of France. When his ship foundered off Corsica he lost literally everything but his shirt. He and his shipmates were stripped clean by the islanders.

He seems to have recovered promptly. He had centered his operations at Montpellier on the Mediterranean coast, the only French port authorized by the pope to deal with the infidel East. He threw himself with bounding determination into the development of the city's facilities, pressing the local authorities to improve its docks, dredge essential canals, construct adequate warehouses, and generally improve the advantages for commerce and navigation, even spending his own money when he had to. As he later wrote the king, he had plans for developing a vast maritime empire under the lily banner of France.

Almost from the moment Charles returned to Paris, Coeur's affairs started to move in a steady counterpoint to the affairs of state. Within a year or two he was installed as *argentier*, receiver of the revenues used to maintain the royal establishment. Since in his capacity as merchant he was also the principal purveyor to that establishment, his position was doubly advantageous and ambiguous. And since for the most part the court could be accommodated only by long-term credit, both the advantage and the ambiguity were compounded. It must have been quite easy for Coeur to convince himself that what was good for Jacques Coeur was good for France.

A reciprocal rhythm of commissions and benefits, responsibilities and opportunities, honors and profits, increased in tempo for more than a decade. The king may already have been in debt to Coeur even before the royal entry into Paris, and this relationship became more or less chronic thereafter. The Paris campaign had again exhausted the royal treasury. In an effort to tighten the leaking economy of the state, Charles, possibly advised by his *argentier*, forbade the export of money from his realm except by a special license, which he then granted, apparently exclusively, to Coeur.

In 1440 Charles further recognized Coeur's services by according to him patents of nobility. The following year he appointed him *conseilleur du roi*, in effect minister of finance and, as such, adviser in the revision of the nation's tax structure. Charged with assessing and collecting regional taxes, Coeur sometimes received not only his due commissions but gratuities from local representatives who both respected his influence at court and feared his power as a merchant banker. The "states" of Languedoc, for example, of which Montpellier was the principal port, paid him handsomely for his good offices in the interest of their maritime prosperity—canceling his share of their taxes as a matter of course.

The king, meanwhile, with an unprecedented income from the revenues he received, reorganized his military forces into a paid standing army. He was no longer a mere feudal lord but a monarch able to make policy and enforce it, if need be, with cannon—cannon, cast at the foundries of bourgeois manufacturers, that could reduce the proudest knight's castle to rubble. In 1444 Charles arranged a temporary peace with the English, who still held Normandy and Guyenne. It was at the gay spring *pourparlers* on the banks of the Loire by which the peace was negotiated that Charles first spied the indescribably beautiful Agnes Sorel, "the fairest of the fair," whom he shortly afterward made his mistress. As the king's bedmate, Agnes began to use her influence in matters of state, inaugurating a tradition in French history. As it later turned out, this was a fateful development in the life of Jacques Coeur. The immediate consequence of the truce arrangements, however, was that he could now move into the English-held markets in Rouen and Bordeaux as well as across the Channel.

Coeur's influence was already recognized far beyond the shores of France. In 1446 he served as negotiator between the Knights of Rhodes and the sultan of Egypt. Two years later, through the intercession of Coeur's agents, the sultan was persuaded to restore trading privileges to the Venetians, who had for a time been banned from the Arab world. At the same time,

Coeur consolidated his own position in the Mediterranean and put a cap on his immense commercial structure. Pope Eugenius IV issued a bull authorizing Coeur to trade for five years in his own right, beyond the privileges enjoyed by the port of Montpellier, with the non-Christian world. With this special authority in his pocket, Coeur shifted the base of his maritime enterprise to Marseilles.

One important matter still needed mending. For all Coeur's good offices and his wide reputation, official relations between France and the Arab world were less cordial than suited his interests. In 1447 he persuaded Charles to agree to a formal pact with Abu-Said-Djacmac-el Daher, sultan of Egypt. The French ambassadors, traveling in Coeur's ships and at his expense, arrived in Egypt "in great state" bearing lavish gifts provided by Coeur in the name of the king. The sultan, in turn, arranged an extravagant reception. Coeur's diplomacy triumphed. Peace between the two lands was agreed upon, and French traders received "most favored nation" privileges in Arab ports.

Aided by the gratitude of the Venetians and the Knights of Rhodes, the friendship of the sultan, the favor of the pope, and the indulgence of his king, Coeur secured unassailable advantages at every important point in the world of his day. "All the Levant he visited with his ships," wrote the duke of Burgundy's chronicler some years later, "and there was not in the waters of the Orient a mast which was not decorated with the *fleur-de-lis*." The maritime empire he created remained for several centuries one of the principal bulwarks of French commerce. To carry on his far-flung, highly diversified operations—they had developed into a virtual monopoly of France's exclusive markets—Coeur employed some three hundred agents and maintained branch offices in Barcelona, Damascus, Beirut, Alexandria, and other strategic centers.

The inventories of his warehouses read like an exaggerated description of Ali Baba's caves. "All the perfumes of Arabia" were carried in stock, and spices and confections from the farthest shores; dyes and colors, cochineal and cinnabar, indigo and saffron—and henna to illuminate the king's manuscripts; materials of fabulous richness and variety, and gems supposedly from the navels of sacred Persian and Indian monkeys, which were mounted in precious metals and considered a universal antidote to human ills. He could provide for the court's most extraordinary or exquisite whim: a coat of mail covered with azure velvet for a Scottish archer of the king's bodyguard; a silver shoulder piece and Turkish buckler for Charles of Orléans; silks and sables for Margaret of Scotland; diamonds to set off the incomparable beauty of Agnes Sorel—they were all to be had, including cold cash for the queen of France herself, who offered up her "great pearl" for security.

In order to put his surplus money to work and to spread his risk, Coeur joined associations that profited form the licensing of fairs (reborn since the temporary truce with England), from speculation in salt, and from the exploitation of copper and silver mines of the Lyonnais and Beaujolais. He had interests in paper and silk factories in Florence. He even invested in three-quarters of two English prisoners of war, each worth a handsome ransom.

The list of his varied enterprises is almost endless. Cash was still in short supply among the nobility, the long war had brought ruin to many lordly tenants, and Charles's fiscal reforms were reducing their income from traditional feudal dues. So Coeur accommodated some of the greatest families of the realm by buying up their manor houses and properties until he held more than thirty estates, some including whole villages and parishes within their grounds. All told, the complex structure of his myriad affairs, his control of the production, transport, and distribution of goods, his private banking resources, and his secure grasp on essential markets all suggest something like the first vertical trust in history.

So far, nothing belied the motto Coeur was then having chiseled into the stones of his great town house at Bourges—*A vaillants coeurs rien impossible*, nothing is impossible to the valiant. Coeur's star rose even higher in 1448 when he was sent to Rome by Charles with a select group of ambassadors to help end the "pestilential and horrible" papal schism that for long years had been a great trial to the Church. The French ambassadors entered Rome in a procession of splendor—their cortege included three hundred richly caparisoned and harnessed Arabian horses—and Pope Nicholas V wrote Charles that not even the oldest inhabitants could remember anything so magnificent.

Coeur promptly took center stage. Through his efforts, the rival pope, Amadeo VIII, duke of Savoy, was finally persuaded to renounce his claim to the papal throne and accept a position in the church hierarchy second only to that of Pope Nicholas V. As a reward, Coeur's privilege of dealing with the non-Christian world was extended indefinitely. He was also given a franchise to carry Christian pilgrims to the Holy Land.

There were some who complained of the outrageous cost of that papal mission from which Coeur gained such honor and profit. Coeur had no doubt paid the bills, but whether from his own purse or from the king's treasury would have been difficult to determine. Coeur's wealth was by now beyond imagining. It was reported that his horses were shod with silver. His table service was of gold and silver. Each year, it was said, his income was greater than that of all the other merchants of France combined. "The king does what he can; Jacques Coeur does what he pleases" was a repeated observation. He might even be in league with the devil, they began to say.

Jacques Coeur had indeed reached a singular, and perilous, eminence.

How rich Coeur really was and what resources he could command came out in the years immediately following. The time had come, Charles decided, to break the truce with the English and to push them out of France altogether. To launch and maintain the campaign, however, Charles needed more money than he could find in the royal coffers, and he turned to Coeur for help. Coeur responded by dredging every sou he could manage from the resources available to him and by stretching his almost inexhaustible credit to the limit. By one means or another, he turned over to the king, at the very minimum, two hundred thousand ecus, a sum equal to more than one-fifth of the kingdom's annual tax revenues.

He also took to the field at the king's side. In the victorious procession that entered Rouen on November 10, 1449, Coeur rode in the company of Charles; mounted on a white charger, he was clothed in velvet and ermine and wore a sword embellished with gold and precious stones.

Coeur was now about fifty-five years old. For some twenty years he had enjoyed increasing wealth and prestige. Then, suddenly, the wheel of fortune changed direction. Three months after the ceremonies at Rouen, Agnes Sorel died in childbirth, after having been delivered of the king's fourth child. Rumors spread that she had been poisoned. Almost automatically, a cabal of debtors formed to point a finger at the king's *argentier*, "the money man" of almost magical faculties, who was known to be one of the executors of Agnes's will. To convict Coeur of murder would serve to disembarrass the king and every important member of the court from the claims of their common creditor.

Charles was quick to play his part. One week in July, 1451, he expressed his gratitude to Coeur for his many services; the next week he issued an order for his arrest. Supported by his most recent favorites, the king confronted Coeur with a long list of indictments, starting with the poisoning charge and going back over the years to the counterfeiting charge of 1429, set aside so long ago by the pleasure and the convenience of Charles VII.

No sooner were the dungeon doors closed behind Coeur than "the vultures of the court" started picking away at the estate he could no longer protect. The nobility of France swarmed about the tottering house of Jacques Coeur to redeem their own fortunes from his disgrace. The trial that followed was a mockery. With his enemies as both prosecutors and judges he never had a chance. Even though his accusers confessed that the charge of poisoning Agnes Sorel was false, and the pope pleaded for clemency and justice in the case, Coeur was shunted for several years from prison to prison.

Finally, in May, 1453, at Poitiers, when he was threatened with torture, he issued a statement that led his judges to condemn him, banish him, and confiscate his properties. By a remarkable coincidence, on the day of Coeur's sentence the sorely tried city of Constantinople fell, this time once and for all, to the Turks. It was the end of an era. Less than a week later, the convicted man made an *amende honorable:* kneeling, bareheaded, before a large crowd and holding a ten-pound wax torch in his hands, he begged mercy of God, king, and the courts.

One more adventure remained. For almost a year and a half after his trial, Coeur was kept imprisoned in France, in spite of his banishment, while most of his holdings were seized and sold off. Then, in the autumn of 1454, he managed to escape. Aided by several of his faithful agents, he crossed the Rhone out of France and fled to Rome, where the pope received him with honor. He never returned to France, nor to the house that was his pride.

But he did take to the sea one last time. He arrived in Rome at a crucial moment in the history of the Church and of Western civilization. All Christendom had been shaken by the fall of Constantinople less than two years earlier and felt threatened by further advances of the Ottoman hordes. In the summer of 1456, Coeur, sixty years old and "toiled with works of war," set forth in command of a fleet dispatched by Pope Calixtus III to help retake Constantinople. On the twenty-fifth of November, on the island of Chios, his *vaillant coeur* was stopped, possibly by wounds he suffered in battle.

As he lay dying, Coeur sent one last appeal to Charles, begging the king to show consideration for his children. At this point Charles could afford to be indulgent. In an act of royal compassion he conceded that since "the said Coeur was in great authority with us and rich and abounding in this world's goods and ennobled in his posterity and line... it pleases us to have pity on [his children]," and ordained that what might be salvaged from their father's estate, including the house at Bourges, be returned to them.

It was, after all, little enough for him to do, and in the end Coeur had an ironic revenge. The thought of poisoning continued to haunt the king. Four years later, fearing he might be poisoned by his own son, he refused to eat, and died of starvation.

From *Horizon*, Winter 1976. © 1976 by Forbes, Inc. Reprinted by permission of *American Heritage* magazine, a division of Forbes, Inc.

Marsilio Ficino, Renaissance Man

***Valery Rees looks at the Florentine scholar Marsilio Ficino and finds
a man whose work still speaks to us today.***

IN OCTOBER [1999] it will be 500 years since Marsilio Ficino died in Florence. Although we risk becoming sated with centenaries, some events and individuals stand out as deserving of celebration: Marsilio Ficino is one of these.

If his name is not as well known as those of his illustrious followers, it is not surprising, as we shall see from his career. Nor would this state of affairs have entirely displeased him, for he was a modest man.

Marsilio Ficino was the son of Cosimo de' Medici's physician. Born in 1433, he received his early training in medicine, on the reasonable assumption that he would follow his father's career. However an early interest in philosophy (especially in Lucretius and Plato) soon brought him to Cosimo's attention. Around 1456 Cosimo redirected him to learning more Greek so that he could pursue these studies with greater effect. Cosimo was actively looking for a suitable candidate to translate the texts that were being brought to Florence by his own trading agents as well as by Greek scholars fleeing the fall of Constantinople. Ficino's progress in Greek clearly pleased Cosimo. Early fruits of it were translations of Orphic and Homeric hymns. Then Cosimo gave him two extraordinary gifts: the first, in 1462, was a manuscript of the works of Plato, the only known complete codex of Plato's works. This was almost certainly the very copy which the Greek emperor had

brought to the Council of Florence in 1438 and which had been so much admired by the Italian participants there. The second gift, the following year, was of a villa and land in Careggi, close to Cosimo's own favourite country seat. This facilitated the work of translation, and participation in those meetings of like-minded scholars, poets and statesmen that formed the Platonic Academy of Florence. In fact, Ficino became the leader of that circle, and from his correspondence, which he himself collected and published in twelve volumes in his lifetime, we can see that the circle of his influence was wide indeed.

Ficino started work on the Platonic dialogues at once, but soon Cosimo asked him to lay that aside and concentrate on a text called the *Poimandres* ('Shepherd of Men'), which one of his agents had just acquired in Macedonia. Its contents, written in Greek, were curious: it consisted of writings attributed to Hermes Trismegistus (thrice greatest Hermes) who was thought to be a contemporary of Moses, and was related to or even identified with the divine being Thoth (Tehuti). Tehuti figures in Egyptian representations of the weighing of the heart, ie. the judgement of the soul at death. He had human form but the head of an ibis, recognisable by its long beak. He shared the qualities of the Greek Hermes, as a messenger between divine and human realms, and was the embodiment of eloquence, reason and the discursive

mind. To the Egyptians he was the inventor of language and writing, master of knowledge, with power to guide souls at the time of death.

The importance of finding this Hermetic work cannot be overestimated. One Hermetic text, the *Asclepius*, had been known since Classical times, though often attributed to its reputed Latin translator Apuleius rather than Hermes. Whereas the *Asclepius* clearly deals in mysteries and magic, the *Poimandres* (now generally known as the *Corpus Hermeticum*) is full of powerful poetry highly reminiscent of the biblical books of Genesis and Job and other Hebrew/Aramaic sources. Thus the *Poimandres*, then thought to date from the time of Moses, appeared to provide the much desired missing link between the philosophy of Graeco-Roman antiquity and the revealed wisdom of holy scripture. Moses had been brought up as an Egyptian, and, according to the tradition endorsed by St Augustine, both Plato and Pythagoras had studied in Egypt. Hence the divergent strands of Greek philosophy and Christian apologetics now seemed to share a common source.

In the seventeenth century the Hermetic writings were subjected to intensive critical scrutiny, and their Egyptian origins rejected, in favour of a late Hellenistic date, reflecting a syncretic philosophy that contained elements of the Greek and Hebrew traditions. Yet more recent scholarship tends once more to emphasise the indigenous Egyptian elements within the Hermetic Corpus. But none of this later critical scholarship detracts from the fact that Ficino's generation genuinely believed the Hermetic texts to represent an early link in the chain of transmission of a very ancient and unified tradition of wisdom, which he called the *prisca theologia*, a theology that underlay but predated the coming of Christ. Indeed the subtitle of the *Poimandres* is 'On the Power and Wisdom of God.'

If theology was so old, and included pre-Christian sources within it, no longer need Classical philosophy be regarded as the enemy of religion, as had often been the case. Plato and Pythagoras became respectable, and a *pia philosophia* could be traced back beyond them all the way to Zoroaster, the Sixth century B.C. founder of the Parsee religion, and to the Chaldaean civilisation who were believed to be the most ancient sources. The early Church Fathers, especially Origen and Clement of Alexandria, could be seen as the direct heirs of this tradition.

> *According to Plato, the practice of philosophy is the ascent of the mind from darkness to light.*

The *Poimandres* translation was finished in 1463, and printed in 1471. It immediately became a very popular and influential work. The Platonic dialogues took longer to appear, coming into print only in 1484, though versions of them were being circulated and discussed in manuscript form much earlier. Indeed, the intervening years were extremely fruitful.

When Cosimo died in 1464, Ficino was able to continue his work under the patronage of Cosimo's son, Piero de' Medici, who also appointed him as tutor to his own sons Lorenzo and Giuliano. This period saw the publication of his translations of two Platonic works, Alcinous on *Plato's Doctrine* and the Pla-

tonic *Definitions* of Speusippus. Ten of the dialogues were also ready before Cosimo died as well as Ficino's major commentaries on Plato's *Philebus* (published 1464), on ethics and the highest Good, and on the *Symposium* (published 1469). This period also marks the beginnings of Ficino's public career, with lectures on the Philebus commentary in the Church of Santa Maria degli Angeli in Florence. 'Since philosophy' he said on this occasion, 'is defined by all men as love of wisdom… and wisdom is the contemplation of the divine, then certainly the purpose of philosophy is knowledge of the divine.' This quest was to remain the constant imperative throughout his life and work, a rule to live by as well as a system of thought. According to Plato, 'the minds of those practising philosophy, having recovered their wings through wisdom and justice… fly back to the heavenly kingdom.' The study and practice of philosophy is thus the ascent of the mind from the lower regions to the highest, and from darkness to light. Its origin is an impulse of the divine mind; its middle steps are the faculties and the disciplines which we have described; and its end is the possession of the highest good. Finally, its fruit is the right government of men.

The *Symposium* commentary, known as *De Amore*, is arguably an original work rather than a commentary, so far does it carry Plato's themes into new territory. It became one of the best known and best loved works of interpretation, serving as inspiration for generations of writers on the theme of love, sometimes filtered through its early emulators, Pietro Bembo, Leone Ebreo and Castiglione, then translated into Italian in 1544, and French in 1545 and 1578, and thus making its mark directly or indirectly on English and French literature, in the verses of Sidney, Chapman, Spenser and Shakespeare, of Ronsard and Scève.

Between 1469 and 1473 the work of translation proceeded apace. Yet it appears that these were difficult times for Ficino personally. He speaks of 'a certain bitterness of spirit' and often refers to the influence of Saturn, dominant at his birth, as favouring discipline and contemplation but incurring melancholy also. It was perhaps a time of deep anxi-

ety: working so closely with Plato and the later Platonists brought up many questions of a metaphysical and philosophical nature that Ficino needed to resolve to his own satisfaction, quite apart from the requirement to avoid heresy. By 1473, it seems his concerns were reasonably resolved, and he took ordination as a priest. By 1474, he was sufficiently sure of his ground to complete his own major work, the *Platonic Theology*, though he continued to revise it up to its publication in 1482. It is a master work of exposition of the arguments for the immortality of the soul, aiming at a proper synthesis of Platonic philosophy and Christian theology. His title was not new: Proclus had written on a similar theme in the fifth century. Ficino studied in detail his extant works, as well as those of all the other major writers in the Platonic tradition, both Latin and Greek, Christian and anti-Christian.

> *The concept of an immortal soul did not become an article of Christian dogma until 1512.*

Also in 1474, prompted by his recovery from a serious illness, Ficino published a smaller work on similar themes, known as the *Christian Religion*, and in 1476, a treatise dealing with Paul's rapture into the third heaven, pursuing the idea of a positive interaction between divine inspiration and providence and human imagination and will. His primary concern in all these works was to clarify the underlying concordance between the Christian/Aristotelian outlook of his own education and the apparently contradictory ideas that he found in Plato and the later Platonists. Chief among these was the concept of the immortality of the individual human soul. Aristotle had denied this, and traditional scholastic theology was inconsistent with it. Strange though it may seem to us, the concept of an immortal individual soul did not become an article of Christian dogma until 1512. Other crucial questions included the nature of the will, whether it is free or not; the role of love and beauty in drawing mankind naturally towards the divine; whether only Christians could be so drawn, through Christ's redemption, or whether all peoples share in divine Grace. Similarly, is human love the first step along that path of attraction to the divine, or is it a falling away from spiritual development? These were questions whose changing answers mark a real turning point in European culture. They reverberated through the art and literature of the period, and they became burning issues that rent communities apart during the Reformation. Yet with one slight exception, Ficino managed to present and represent these issues, expanding, expounding and elaborating on their themes without incurring the wrath or censure of the Church.

That wrath could be expressed in many ways: following the failure of the Pazzi conspiracy against the Medici family, Florence was put under interdict by the Pope, and was then attacked in a bitter war. By 1478, largely as a result of the war, there was an outbreak of plague in the city. Ficino's response was to publish a very different work, a practical guide to the treatment of plague. This was written in Tuscan to be immediately accessible and of use to his fellow citizens at a time of great need. It was subsequently translated into Latin by Hieronymus Ricci in 1516 and published alongside Galen's work on fevers, as a standard medical work. It is easy to forget that all Ficino's works of profound contemplation and leisurely presentation were written against a backdrop of intense social and political disturbances.

During the following years, Ficino continued to revise his Plato translations, and to write summaries and commentaries. The complete Plato dialogues were published in 1484, making a reliable version of Plato available to a much wider reading public. They were enormously influential, and a second edition was printed in 1496. Meanwhile a series of later works in the Platonic-Pythagorean tradition followed in 1488, including *Synesius on Dreams; Iamblichus on the Egyptian Mysteries; Psellus on Daemons; Priscan on the Soul; Porphyry and Proclus on Sacrifice and Magic;* the *Mystical Theology and Divine Names of*

Dionysius; and in 1492, the long awaited *Enneads of Plotinus*. Finally, in 1495 he allowed the printing and publication of his *Letters* that he had been collecting and circulating in manuscript form for many years. So successful was this publication that three further editions, or reprintings, followed within two years. At the time of his death in 1499, Ficino was still working on a commentary to St Paul's *Epistles to the Romans*.

Ficino returned again and again to favourite themes, presenting them in order to convince and persuade others. He wrote on light and the sun, on dreams, on resurrection and rebirth; he became interested in astronomy and mathematics, together with their sister arts of astrological influences and natural magic. This was where he narrowly avoided censure, for in the third of his three books *On Life*, magic and astrology play a prominent part, and he had to defend himself from criticism. Interestingly enough, this third book had started out as an attempt to understand and explain a mystifying passage in Plotinus. Ficino was never one to shirk from following the full implications of what he was studying, however unfashionable or disturbing. Nor did he neglect to put what he learned into practice, living a Platonic life and putting all his wisdom and experience at the disposal of others, through teaching, through letters, through sermons but perhaps above all through his own personal example.

He described his life's work to Giovanni Niccolini, Archbishop of Amalfi, at Rome in a letter written shortly before the publication of his Plato translations:

Being initially guided by the authority of Saint Augustine and then being strengthened in resolve by the testimony of many holy Christians, I therefore considered that, since I needed to apply myself to philosophy, it would be well worth doing so mainly in an academy. But wishing the Platonic teaching to shine out further still, since it is related to the divine law of both Moses and Christ as the moon is to the sun, I translated all the books of Plato from Greek into Latin. In addition, so that no one's eyes

would be blinded by seeing [a] new light, I wrote a book by way [of] exposition, divided into eightee[n] parts [The Platonic Theology]. Here the Platonic mysteries are set forth as clearly as possible, so that we may follow Plato's mind rather than his words and so that, removing the poetic veils, we may reveal the Platonic teaching, which is in complete accord with divine law. I believe, and with good reason, that this has been decreed by divine providence, so that all those subtle minds who find it difficult to yield to the sole authority of divine law may at least yield in the end to the reasoning of Plato, which gives its full support to religion.

Through Ficino the writings of the ancients not only became available, but became a powerful enlivening force. He is known to posterity principally for these translations. But he was not the first to explore this literature, nor the first to translate, emulate and adapt what was found to meet the needs of the day. Among the most brilliant of his predecessors, Leonardo Bruni had translated some of Plato's dialogues and had thereby reshaped Florentine political thinking along Republican lines; Valla had developed critical linguistics; Leon Battista Alberti had translated Vitruvius, the key to new ideas of harmony and proportion in art and architecture. Ficino's task was more comprehensive, for he sought not just to borrow, imitate or adapt but to effect a real synthesis between classical philosophy and Christianity. This is what made it ultimately more influential. He would not himself have claimed to be providing anything new, yet his interpretations gave strength and impetus to new ways of looking at the world.

This comes through clearly in his *Letters*. Their hallmarks are clarity, eloquence, honesty and integrity. They show a man engaged in a life-long quest for real and substantial happiness, not just for himself but for all who care to partake of it. He is deeply pious but his piety has been forged in the fires of profound, persistent questioning. As a friend, he is a source of wise counsel,

...ps it up in playful ...g example of this is ...ith Callimachus in ...eries of witty ex- ...neath the banter is a ...Callimachus had had to ...Rome when the Roman ...my was disbanded for trying to ...t against the Pope. The Florentine Academy was also subject to suspicion by association, yet Ficino's correspondence with Callimachus during his lengthy exile is warm and friendly. In his first letter, a response to Callimachus's challenge over the existence of daemons, Ficino shows how Callimachus is nonetheless beneficiary of the gifts of such daemons. When Callimachus complained of fiery spirits, that had caused his house to burn down, Ficino turns serious: picking up his cue from an Orphic poem Callimachus had sent him earlier, he reminds him that fire will bring the ultimate destruction of the whole creation. 'Besides,' he says, 'you were looking for light in your books and your books were turned into light for you.' Then on a more serious note, 'What can we divine from this for you, my friend? You will in the end shine more in death than in life,' for it is the soul that shines, and its light is eternal.

Always of prime concern to Ficino was the life of the soul. Its twin needs, love and reason, form a recurrent motif in his work.

The themes covered in Ficino's letters are of universal, not just historical interest. They include love, pain, coping with adversity; how to study, how to balance the various demands on one's life; they discuss unity and individuality, beauty, medicine and astrology. They expound

Plato, they refer to Hermes and the Neoplatonists, to Augustine and the Church Fathers, they contain passing Biblical commentary, always related to the particular problem that concerns his correspondent at the time. The forms of expression are varied to suit the circumstance, ranging from simple exposition to the imaginative creativity of fables or the famous letter of 1479 to Ferrante, king of Naples, where the spirit of Ferrante's father Alfonso is invoked to deliver a strong moral and spiritual message to his son directly from the realm of the angels. Always of prime concern to Ficino is the life of the soul. Its twin needs, for love and reason (or wisdom and justice, as quoted above, or faith and judgement, devotion and discrimination) form a recurrent motif in his work. When these twin needs are met, the soul recovers its two wings to fly back to its true home.

There are letters to political leaders and princes, to churchmen and scholars, both in Italy and elsewhere: his contacts stretched to England (Colet), the French court (de Gannay), humanists in Germany (Prenninger) and the Low Countries (Paul of Middleburgh) and with Hungary he enjoyed a very fruitful period of collaboration with Matthias Corvinus via Francesco Bandini and Nicholas Bathory. In Italy his correspondents include Lorenzo de' Medici; Ferrante, King of Naples; Federico da Montefeltro, Duke of Urbino; Pope Sixtus IV; Giovanni Cavalcanti the poet; Ermolao Barbaro; Bernardo Bembo; Pier Leone of Spoleto, Marco Barbo, and other scholars and churchmen too numerous to be listed.

The latest volume of these *Letters* in English translation, published in June 1999, deals principally with concerns in Italy in the years 1481–83. It contains the letter to Niccolini quoted above, as well as letters on the war, on daemons, on medicine, the Graces, astrology, and a fascinating series of Apologi or Fables. It also adds to our picture of Ficino as a person.

Ficino's writings were studied closely for many years as a principal means of

access to the great philosophers of ancient Greece and Egypt. Through his translations and commentaries, his teaching and his letters, the wisdom of these texts came vividly to life and helped to shape the thinking of his time. Naturally, his own concerns coloured his interpretation of the past, and this Ficinian Christian Platonism began to have a far-reaching influence.

Through the Medicis, Ficini's ideas blossomed in Florentine art and literature and travelled, via Venice, to Hungary, Germany and France. By the end of the sixteenth century we can find in Shakespeare's plays perfect resonances of Ficini's ideas, though no outward evidence of direct transmission can easily be demonstrated.

As long as Classical influence reigned, Ficini's work continued to inform and inspire. Artists as diverse as Michelangelo and the metaphysical poets bear the stamp of his approach. Although Plato scholarship has now moved on, and for most purposes we have no need to rely on Ficino to decipher the Greeks today, the questions that he tried to answer are still relevant today, and will always remain so. He speaks of the soul, nature, and human behaviour with intelligence, wisdom and compassion. There is still much for us to learn from the writings of this remarkable man.

FOR FURTHER READING

The Letters of Marsilio Ficino (Shepheard-Walwyn, six vols. 1975-1999); A. Goodman & A. MacKay, *The Impact of Humanism on Western Europe* (Longman,1990); M.J.B. Allen, *Plato's Third Eye* (Variorium, 1995); and *Synoptic Art* (Olschki, 1998); C.V. Kaske and J.R. Clarke, *Three Books on Life*, (Binghampton, N.Y. 1998); D. Van Oyen, C. Salaman & William Wharton, *The Way of Hermes*, (Duckworth, 1999.)

Valery Rees has been translating Ficino's letters for many years. She organised the conference 'Marsilio Ficino: His Sources, His Circle, His Legacy' in London in June.

This article first appeared in *History Today*, July 1999, pp. 45-51. © 1999 by History Today, Ltd. Reprinted by permission.

Machiavelli

Would you buy a used car from this man?

Vincent Cronin

Machiavelli—the most hated man who ever lived: charged, down the centuries, with being the sole poisonous source of political monkey business, of the mocking manipulation of men, of malfeasance, misanthropy, mendacity, murder, and massacre; the evil genius of tyrants and dictators, worse than Judas, for no salvation resulted from *his* betrayal; guilty of the sin against the Holy Ghost, knowing Christianity to be true, but resisting the truth; not a man at all, but Antichrist in apish flesh, the Devil incarnate, Old Nick, with the whiff of sulphur on his breath and a tail hidden under his scarlet Florentine gown.

Machiavelli is the one Italian of the Renaissance we all think we know, partly because his name has passed into our language as a synonym for unscrupulous schemer. But Niccolò Machiavelli of Florence was a more complex and fascinating figure than his namesake of the English dictionary, and unless we ourselves wish to earn the epithet Machiavellian, it is only fair to look at the historical Machiavelli in the context of his age.

He was born in 1469 of an impoverished noble family whose coat of arms featured four keys. Niccolò's father was a retired lawyer who owned two small farms and an inn, his mother a churchgoer who wrote hymns to the Blessed Virgin. Niccolò was one of four children; the younger son, Totto, became a priest,

and the idea of a confessional occupied by a Father Machiavelli is one that has caused Niccolò's enemies some wry laughter.

Niccolò attended the Studio, Florence's university, where he studied the prestigious newly-discovered authors of Greece and Rome. Like all his generation, he idolized the Athenians and the Romans of the Republic, and was to make them his models in life. This was one important influence. The other was the fact that Florence was then enjoying, under the Medici, a period of peace. For centuries the city had been torn by war and faction; but now all was serene, and the Florentines were producing their greatest achievements in philosophy, poetry, history, and the fine arts.

This point is important, for too often we imagine the Italian Renaissance as a period of thug-like *condottieri* and cruel despots forever locked in war. We must not be deceived by the artists. Uccello and Michelangelo painted bloody battles, but they were battles that had taken place many years before. If we are to understand Machiavelli, we must picture his youth as a happy period of civilization and peace: for the first time in centuries swords rusted, muscles grew flabby, fortress walls became overgrown with ivy.

In 1494, when Machiavelli was twenty-five, this happiness was shattered. King Charles VIII of France invaded Italy to seize the kingdom of Naples; Florence lay on his route. In the Middle Ages the Florentines had fought bravely against aggressors, but now, grown slack and effete, they were afraid of Charles's veterans and his forty cannon. Instead of manning their walls, they and their leading citizen, Pietro de' Medici, meekly allowed the French king to march in; they even paid him gold not to harm their country.

This debacle led to internal wars, to economic decline, in which Niccolò's father went bankrupt, to much heartsearching, and to a puritanical revolution. Savonarola the Dominican came to rule from the pulpit. Thundering that the French invasion was punishment for a pagan way of life, he burned classical books and nude pictures and urged a regeneration of Florence through fasting and prayer. The French just laughed at Savonarola; he lost the confidence of his fellow citizens and was burned at the stake in 1498.

In that same year, Machiavelli became an employee of the Florentine Republic, which he was to serve ably as diplomat and administrator. Machiavelli scorned Savonarola's idea of political regeneration through Christianity; instead, he persuaded the Florentines to form a citizen militia, as was done in Republican Rome. In 1512 Florence's big test came. Spain had succeeded France as Italy's oppressor, and now, at the instigation of the Medici, who had been exiled from Florence in 1494 and wished to return, a Spanish army of five thousand marched against Tuscany. Four thousand of Machiavelli's militia were defending the strong Florentine town of Prato. The Spaniards, ill-fed and unpaid, launched a halfhearted attack. The Florentines, instead of resisting, took to their heels. Prato was sacked, and a few days later Florence surrendered without a fight. The Medici returned, the Republic came to an end, Machiavelli lost his job and was tortured and exiled to his farm. For the second time in eighteen years he had witnessed a defeat that was both traumatic and humiliating.

In the following year an out-of-work Machiavelli began to write his great book *The Prince*. It is an attempt to answer the question implicit in Florence's two terrible defeats: what had gone wrong? Machiavelli's answer is this: for all their classical buildings and pictures, for all the Ciceronian Latin and readings from Plato, the Florentines had never really revived the essence of classical life—that military vigor and patriotism unto death that distinguished the Greeks and Romans. What then is the remedy? Italy must be regenerated—not by Savonarola's brand of puritanism, but by a soldier-prince. This prince must subordinate every aim to military efficiency. He must personally command a citizen army and keep it disciplined by a reputation for cruelty.

But even this, Machiavelli fears, will not be enough to keep at bay the strong new nation-states, France and Spain. So, in a crescendo of patriotism, Machiavelli urges his prince to disregard the accepted rules of politics, to hit below the belt. Let him lie, if need be, let him violate treaties: "Men must be either pampered or crushed, because they can get revenge for small injuries but not for fatal ones"; "A prudent ruler cannot, and should not, honor his word when it places him at a disadvantage and when the reasons for which he made his promise no longer exist"; "If a prince wants to maintain his rule he must learn how not to be virtuous."

Machiavelli develops his concept of a soldier-prince with a couple of portraits. The first, that of the emperor Alexander

Severus, is an example of how a prince should not behave. Alexander Severus, who reigned in the third century, was a man of such goodness it is said that during his fourteen years of power he never put anyone to death without a trial. Nevertheless, as he was thought effeminate, and a man who let himself be ruled by his mother, he came to be scorned, and the army conspired against him and killed him. Machiavelli scorns him also: "Whenever that class of men on which you believe your continued rule depends is corrupt, whether it be the populace, or soldiers, or nobles, you have to satisfy it by adopting the same disposition; and then *good deeds are your enemies.*"

Machiavelli's second portrait is of Cesare Borgia, son of Pope Alexander VI, who carved out a dukedom for himself and then brought it to heel by appointing a tough governor, Ramiro. Later, says Machiavelli, Cesare discovered that "the recent harshness had aroused some hatred against him, and wishing to purge the minds of the people and win them over… he had this official (Ramiro) cut in two pieces one morning and exposed on the public square… This ferocious spectacle left the people at once *content and horrified.*"

The words I have italicized show Machiavelli's peculiar cast of mind. He grows excited when goodness comes to a sticky end and when a dastardly deed is perpetrated under a cloak of justice. He seems to enjoy shocking traditional morality, and there can be little doubt that he is subconsciously revenging himself on the Establishment responsible for those two profound military defeats.

Machiavelli wrote *The Prince* for Giuliano de' Medici. He hoped that by applying the lessons in his book, Giuliano would become tough enough to unite Italy and drive out the foreigner. But Giuliano, the youngest son of Lorenzo the Magnificent, was a tubercular young man with gentle blue eyes and long sensitive fingers, the friend of poets and himself a sonneteer. He was so soft that his brother Pope Leo had to relieve him of his post as ruler of Florence after less than a year. Preparations for war against France taxed his feeble constitu-

tion; at the age of thirty-seven he fell ill and died. Machiavelli's notion of turning Giuliano into a second Cesare Borgia was about as fantastic as trying to turn John Keats into a James Bond.

This fantastic element has been overlooked in most accounts of Machiavelli, but it seems to me important. Consider the *Life of Castruccio Castracani*, which Machiavelli wrote seven years after *The Prince*. It purports to be a straight biography of a famous fourteenth-century ruler of Lucca, but in fact only the outline of the book is historically true. Finding the real Castruccio insufficiently tough to embody his ideals, Machiavelli introduces wholly fictitious episodes borrowed from Diodorus Siculus's life of a tyrant who really was unscrupulous: Agathocles. As captain of the Syracusans, Agathocles had collected a great army, then summoned the heads of the Council of Six Hundred under the pretext of asking their advice, and put them all to death.

Machiavelli in his book has Castruccio perform a similar stratagem. Just as in *The Prince* the second-rate Cesare Borgia passes through the crucible of Machiavelli's imagination to emerge as a modern Julius Caesar, so here a mildly villainous lord is dressed up as the perfect amoral autocrat. In both books Machiavelli is so concerned to preach his doctrine of salvation through a strong soldier-prince that he leaves Italy as it really was for a world of fantasy.

Machiavelli had a second purpose in dedicating *The Prince* to Giuliano de' Medici (and when Giuliano died, to his almost equally effete nephew Lorenzo). He wished to regain favor with the Medici, notably with Pope Leo. This also was a fantastic plan. Machiavelli had plotted hand over fist against the Medici for no less that fourteen years and was known to be a staunch republican, opposed to one-family rule in Florence. Pope Leo, moreover, was a gentle man who loved Raphael's smooth paintings and singing to the lute; he would not be interested in a book counseling cruelty and terror.

How could a man like Machiavelli, who spent his early life in the down-to-earth world of Italian politics, have yielded to such unrealistic, such fantastic hopes? The answer, I think, lies in the fact that he was also an imaginative artist—a playwright obsessed with extreme dramatic situations. Indeed, Machiavelli was best known in Florence as the author of *Mandragola*. In that brilliant comedy, a bold and tricky adventurer, aided by the profligacy of a parasite, and the avarice of a friar, achieves the triumph of making a gulled husband bring his own unwitting but too yielding wife to shame. It is an error to regard Machiavelli as primarily a political theorist, taking a cool look at facts. *The Prince* is, in one sense, the plot of a fantastic play for turning the tables on the French and Spaniards.

What, too, of Machiavelli's doctrine that it is sometimes wise for a prince to break his word and to violate treaties? It is usually said that this teaching originated with Machiavelli. If so, it would be very surprising, for the vast majority of so-called original inventions during the Italian Renaissance are now known to have been borrowed from classical texts. The Florentines valued wisdom as Edwardian English gentlemen valued sport—the older the better.

In 1504 Machiavelli wrote a play, which has been lost, called *Masks*. It was in imitation of Aristophanes' [The] *Clouds*, the subject of which is the Sophists, those men who claimed to teach "virtue" in a special sense, namely, efficiency in the conduct of life. The Sophists emphasized material success and the ability to argue from any point of view, irrespective of its truth. At worst, they encouraged a cynical disbelief in all moral restraints on the pursuit of selfish, personal ambition. Florentines during their golden age had paid little attention to the Sophists, preferring Plato, who accorded so well with Christianity and an esthetic approach to life; but after the collapse in 1494 it would have been natural for a man like Machiavelli to dig out other, harder-headed philosophers.

The source for his doctrine of political unscrupulousness may well have been the Sophists as presented in Aristophanes' play. The following sentence from one of Machiavelli's letters in 1521 close to many lines in *The Clouds*: "For that small matter of lies," writes Machiavelli, "I am a doctor and hold my degrees. Life has taught me to confound false and true, till no man knows either."

In *The Prince* this personal confession becomes a general rule: "One must know how to color one's actions and to be a great liar and deceiver."

How was it that an undisputably civilized man like Machiavelli could advise a ruler to be cruel and deceitful and to strike terror? The answer lies in the last chapter of *The Prince*, entitled "Exhortation to liberate Italy from the barbarians." Often neglected, it is, in fact, the most deeply felt chapter of all and gives meaning to the rest. "See how Italy," Machiavelli writes, "beseeches God to send someone to save her from those barbarous cruelties and outrages"—he means the outrages perpetrated by foreign troops in Italy, a land, he goes on, that is "leaderless, lawless, crushed, despoiled, torn, overrun; she has had to endure every kind of desolation."

Machiavelli is a patriot writing in mental torment. He seldom mentions the deity, but in this chapter the name God occurs six times on one page, as an endorsement for this new kind of ruler. Machiavelli really believes that his deceitful prince will be as much an instrument of God as Moses was, and this for two reasons. First, Italy is an occupied country, and her survival is at stake; and just as moral theologians argued that theft becomes legitimate when committed by a starving man, so Machiavelli implies that deceit, cruelty, and so on become legitimate when they are the only means to national survival.

Secondly, Machiavelli had seen honest means tried and fail. Savonarola had hoped to silence cannon by singing hymns; Machiavelli himself had sent conscripts against the Spaniards. But the Italians had been then—and still were—bantams pitted against heavyweights. They could not win according to the rules, only with kidney punches. And since they had to win or cease to be themselves—that is, a civilized people as compared with foreign "barbarians"—Machiavelli argues that it is not only right but the will of God that they should use immoral means.

We must remember that *The Prince* is an extreme book that grew out of an extreme situation and that its maxims must

be seen against the charred, smoking ruins of devastated Italy. The nearest modern parallel is occupied France. In the early 1940's cultivated men like Camus joined the Resistance, committing themselves to blowing up German posts by night and to other sinister techniques of *maquis* warfare. Like Machiavelli, they saw these as the only way to free their beloved country.

But the most original and neglected aspect of Machiavelli is his method. Before Machiavelli's time, historians had been the slaves of chronology. They started with the Creation, or the founding of their city, and worked forward, year by year, decade by decade, chronicling plague, war, and civil strife. Sometimes they detected a pattern, but even when they succeeded in doing so, the pattern was *sui generis*, not applicable elsewhere. Machiavelli was the first modern historian to pool historical facts from a variety of authors, not necessarily of the same period, and to use these facts to draw general conclusions or to answer pertinent questions.

He applies this method notably in his *Discourses on Livy*, and among the questions he answers are these: "What causes commonly give rise to wars between different powers?" "What kind of reputation or gossip or opinion causes the populace to begin to favor a particular citizen?" "Whether the safeguarding of liberty can be more safely entrusted to the populace or to the upper class; and which has the stronger reason for creating disturbances, the 'have-nots' or the 'haves'?"

Machiavelli does not wholly break free from a cyclical reading of history—the term Renaissance is itself a statement of the conviction that the golden age of Greece and Rome had returned. Nor did he break free from a belief in Fortune—what we would now call force of circumstance—and he calculated that men were at the mercy of Fortune five times out of ten. Nevertheless, he does mark an enormous advance over previous historical thinkers, since he discovered the method whereby man can learn from his past.

Having invented this method, Machiavelli proceeded to apply it imperfectly.

He virtually ignored the Middle Ages, probably because medieval chronicles were deficient in those dramatic human twists, reversals, and paradoxes that were what really interested him. This neglect of the Middle Ages marred his study of how to deal with foreign invaders. Over a period of a thousand years Italy had constantly suffered invasion from the north; the lessons implicit in these instances would have helped Machiavelli to resolve his main problem much better than the more remote happenings he chose to draw from Livy. For example, at the Battle of Legnano, near Milan, in 1176, a league of north Italian cities won a crushing victory over Frederick Barbarossa's crack German knights. The Italians didn't employ duplicity or dramatic acts of terrorism, just courage and a united command.

So much for Machiavelli's teaching and discoveries. It remains to consider his influence. In his own lifetime he was considered a failure. Certainly, no soldier-prince arose to liberate Italy. After his death, however, it was otherwise. In 1552 the Vatican placed Machiavelli's works on the Index of Prohibited Books, because they teach men "to appear good for their own advantage in this world—a doctrine worse than heresy." Despite this ban, Machiavelli's books were widely read and his political teaching became influential. It would probably have confirmed him in his pessimistic view of human nature had he known that most statesmen and thinkers would seize on the elements of repression and guile in his teachings to the exclusion of the civic sense and patriotism he equally taught.

In France several kings studied Machiavelli as a means of increasing their absolutism, though it cannot be said that he did them much good. Henry III and Henry IV were murdered, and in each case on their blood-soaked person was found a well-thumbed copy of *The Prince*. Louis XIII was following Machiavelli when he caused his most powerful subject, the Italian-born adventurer Concini, to be treacherously killed. Richelieu affirmed that France could not be governed without the right of arbitrary arrest and exile, and that in case of danger to the state it may be well that a hundred innocent men should perish. This was *raison d'état*, an exaggerated version of certain elements in *The Prince*, to which Machiavelli might well not have subscribed.

In England Machiavelli had little direct influence. England had never been defeated as Florence had been, and Englishmen could not understand the kind of desperate situation that demanded unscrupulous political methods. The political diseases Machiavelli had first studied scientifically were in England called after his name, rather as a physical disease—say Parkinson's—is called not after the man who is suffering from it but after the doctor who discovers it. Machiavelli thus became saddled with a lot of things he had never advocated, including atheism and any treacherous way of killing, generally by poison. Hence Flamineo in Webster's *White Devil*:

O the rare trickes of a Machivillian!
Hee doth not come like a grosse plodding slave
And buffet you to death: no, my quaint knave—
Hee tickles you to death; makes you die laughing,
As if you had swallow'd a pound of saffron.

The eighteenth century, with its strong belief in man's good nature and reason, tended to scoff at Machiavelli. Hume wrote: "There is scarcely any maxim in *The Prince* which subsequent experience has not entirely refuted. The errors of this politician proceed, in a great measure, from his having lived in too early an age of the world to be a good judge of political truth." With Hume's judgment Frederick the Great of Prussia would, in early life, have agreed. As a young man Frederick wrote an *Anti-Machiavel*, in which he stated that a ruler is the first servant of his people. He rejected the idea of breaking treaties, "for one has only to make one deception of this kind, and one loses the confidence of every ruler." But Frederick did follow Machiavelli's advice to rule personally, to act as his own commander in the field, and to despise flatterers.

Later, Frederick began to wonder whether honesty really was the best policy. "One sees oneself continually in danger of being betrayed by one's allies, forsaken by one's friends, brought low by envy and jealousy; and ultimately one finds oneself obliged to choose between the terrible alternative of sacrificing one's people or one's word of honor." In old age, Frederick became a confirmed Machiavellian, writing in 1775: "Rulers must always be guided by the interests of the state. They are slaves of their resources, the interest of the state is their law, and this law may not be infringed."

During the nineteenth century Germany and Italy both sought to achieve national unity, with the result that writers now began to play up Machiavelli's other side, his call for regeneration. Young Hegel hails the author of *The Prince* for having "grasped with a cool circumspection the necessary idea that Italy should be saved by being combined into one state." He and Fichte go a stage further than Machiavelli: they assert that the conflict between the individual and the state no longer exists, since they consider liberty and law identical. The necessity of evil in political action becomes a superior ethics that has no connection with the morals of an individual. The state swallows up evil.

In Italy Machiavelli's ideal of a regenerated national state was not perverted in this way and proved an important influence on the *risorgimento*. In 1859 the provisional government of Tuscany, on the eve of national independence, published a decree stating that a complete edition of Machiavelli's works would be printed at government expense. It had taken more than three hundred years for "a man to arise to redeem Italy," and in the event the man turned out to be two men, Cavour and Garibaldi. Both, incidentally, were quite unlike the Prince: Cavour, peering through steel-rimmed spectacles, was a moderate statesman of the center, and Garibaldi a blunt, humane, rather quixotic soldier.

Bismarck was a close student of Machiavelli, but Marx and Engels did not pay much attention to him, and the Florentine's books have never exerted great influence in Russia. In contemporary history Machiavelli's main impact ha been on Benito Mussolini. In 1924 Mussolini wrote a thesis on *The Prince*, which he described as the statesman's essential vade mecum. The Fascist leader deliberately set himself to implement Petrarch's call quoted on the last page of *The Prince:*

Che l'antico valore
Nell' italici cor non è ancor morto.
Let Italians, as they did of old,
Prove that their courage has not
    grown cold.

After a course of muscle building, Mussolini sent the Italian army into Ethiopia to found a new Roman Empire. He joined Hitler's war in 1940, only to find that he had failed to impart to modern Italians the martial qualities of Caesar's legions. The final irony occurred in 1944, when the Nazis were obliged to occupy northern Italy as the only means of stopping an Allied walkover, and Italy again experienced the trauma of 1494 and 1512. Mussolini's failures discredit, at least for our generation, Machiavelli's theory that it is possible for one man to effect a heart transplant on a whole people.

What is Machiavelli's significance today? His policy of political duplicity has been found wanting in the past and is probably no longer practicable in an age of democracy and television. His policy of nationalism is also beginning to date as we move into an era of ideological blocs. His insistence on the need for military preparedness has proved of more durable value and is likely to remain one of the West's key beliefs. His technique for solving political problems through a study of the past is practiced to some extent by every self-respecting foreign minister of our time.

Was Machiavelli, finally, an evil man? He made an ethic of patriotism. In normal times that is a poisonous equation, but defensible, I believe, in the context of sixteenth-century Italy. Machiavelli wrote on the edge of an abyss: he could hear the thud of enemy boots, had seen pillage, profanation, and rape by foreign troops. Imaginative as he was, he could sense horrors ahead: the ending of political liberty and of freedom of the press, which put the lights out in Italy for 250 years. He taught that it is civilized man's first duty to save civilization—at all costs. Doubtless he was mistaken. But it is not, I think, the mistake of an evil man.

From *Horizon*, Autumn 1972. © 1972 by Forbes, Inc. Reprinted by permission of *Horizon* magazine, a division of Forbes, Inc.

Women of the Renaissance

J. H. Plumb

François Villon, the vagabond poet of France, wondered, as he drifted through the gutters and attics of fifteenth-century Paris, where were the famous women of the days long past? Where Hélöise, for whom Abelard had endured such degradation? Where Thaïs, Alis, Haremburgis, where the Queen Blanche with her siren's voice, where were these fabled, love-haunted, noblewomen, of more than human beauty? Gone, he thought, gone forever. Even the rough Viking bards sang of their heroic women, of Aud the Deep-minded, who "hurt most whom she loved best." The lives of these fateful, tragic women, medieval heroines of love and sorrow became themes of epic and romance that were told in the courts of princes; yet even as Villon bewailed their loss, men were growing tired of them.

The age of heroes was dying. The unrequited love of Dante for Beatrice, the lyrical attachment of Petrarch for Laura, and, in a different mood, the agreeable pleasantries of Boccaccio, had domesticated love, making it more intimate. The dawn of a carefree, less fate-ridden attitude to woman was gentle, undramatic, and slow beginning way back with the wandering troubadours and the scholars who moved from castle to farm, from monastery to university, singing their lighthearted lyrics to earn their keep:

Down the broad way do I go,
Young and unregretting,
Wrap me in my vices up,
Virtue all forgetting,

Greedier for all delight
Than heaven to enter in:
Since the soul in me is dead,
Better save the skin.
Sit you down amid the fire,
Will the fire not burn you?
Come to Pavia, will you
Just as chaste return you?
Pavia, where Beauty draws
Youth with finger-tips,
Youth entangled in her eyes,
Ravished with her lips.

So sang the nameless Archpoet, young, consumptive, in love, as he wandered down to Salerno to read medicine. The time was the twelfth century—three hundred years before the haunting love poems of Lorenzo de' Medici were written. Yet the sentiments of both men were a part of the same process, part of the lifting tide of Southern Europe's prosperity, of its growing population, of the sophistication that wealth and leisure brought, for in leisure lies dalliance. The wandering scholars were few; their mistresses, chatelaines or girls of the town. Yet they were the naive harbingers of a world that was to reach its fullness in Italy in the fifteenth century.

It was the new prosperity that influenced the lives of women most profoundly. It brought them fresh opportunities for adornment; it increased their dowries and their value. It emancipated many from the drudgery of the household and from the relentless, time-consuming demands of children. Women entered more fully into the daily lives and pursuits of men. And, of course, the new delights of the Renaissance world—painting, music, literature—had their feminine expression. Much of the artistic world was concerned with the pursuit of love in all its guises. Women were a part of art.

Except for the very lowest ranks of society, women were inextricably entangled in the concept of prosperity, and their virtue was a marketable commodity. They were secluded from birth to marriage, taught by women and priests, kept constantly under the closest supervision in the home or in the convent. Marriage came early: twelve was not an uncommon age, thirteen usual, fifteen was getting late, and an unmarried girl of sixteen or seventeen was a catastrophe. Women conveyed property and could often secure a lift in the social scale for their families. Even more important was the use of women to seal alliances between families, whether princely, noble, or mercantile. The great Venetian merchants interlocked their adventures overseas with judicious marriages at home. The redoubtable Vittoria Colonna was betrothed at the age of four to the Marquis of Pescara to satisfy her family's political ambition. Lucrezia Borgia's early life was a grim enough reminder of the dynastic value of women. Her fiancés were sent packing, her husbands murdered or declared impotent, so that Alexandere VI could use her again and again in the furtherance of his policies.

In less exalted ranks of society women were still traded. It took Michelangelo years of horse trading to buy a young Ridolfi wife for his nephew and so push his family up a rank in Florentine society. Marriages so arranged were symbolic of power and social status as well as wealth, and their celebration, in consequence, demanded the utmost pomp and splendor that the contracting parties could afford. Important Venetian marriages were famed for an extravagance that not even the Council of Ten could curb.

The festivities began with an official proclamation in the Doge's Palace. The contracting parties and their supporters paraded the canals *en fete*. Gondoliers and servants were dressed in sumptuous livery; the facades of the palaces were adorned with rare Oriental carpets and tapestries; there were bonfires, fireworks, balls, masques, banquets, and everywhere and at all times—even the most intimate serenades by gorgeously dressed musicians. Of course, such profusion acted like a magnet for poets, dramatists, rhetoricians, painters, and artists of every variety. For a few ducats a wandering humanist would pour out a few thousand words, full of recondite references to gods and heroes; poets churned out epithalamiums before they could be asked; and painters immortalized the bride, her groom, or even, as Botticelli did, the wedding breakfast. And they were eager for more mundane tasks, not for one moment despising an offer to decorate the elaborate *cassoni* in which the bride took her clothes and linen to her new household. Indeed, the competitive spirit of both brides and painters in *cassoni* became so fierce that they ceased to be objects of utility and were transformed into extravagant works of art, becoming the heirlooms of future generations.

The artistic accompaniment of marriage became the height of fashion. When the Duke and Duchess of Urbino returned to their capital after their wedding, they were met on a hilltop outside their city by all the women and children of rank, exquisitely and expensively dressed, bearing olive branches in their hands. As the Duke and Duchess reached them, mounted choristers accompanied by nymphs à *la Grecque* burst into song—a special cantata that had been composed for the newlyweds. The Goddess of Mirth appeared in person with her court, and to make everyone realize that jollity and horseplay were never out of place at a wedding, hares were loosed in the crowd. This drove the dogs insane with excitement, to everyone's delight. No matter how solemn the occasion, marriage always involved coarse farce, usually at the climax of the wedding festivities, when the bride and the groom were publicly bedded. Although there was no romantic nonsense about Italian weddings—certainly few marriages for love—everyone knew that the right, true end of the contract was the bed. The dowager Duchess of Urbino, something of a blue-stocking and a Platonist and a woman of acknowledged refinement, burst into her niece's bedroom on the morning after her marriage and shouted, "Isn't it a fine thing to sleep with the men?"

Marriage for the women of the Renaissance gave many their first taste of opulence, leisure, and freedom. They were very young; the atmosphere of their world was as reckless as it was ostentatious; and furthermore, they had not chosen their husbands, who frequently were a generation older than they. Their men, who often were soldiers or courtiers living close to the razor-edge of life, fully enjoyed intrigue, so the young wife became a quarry to be hunted. As she was often neglected, the chase could be brief. Even Castiglione, who was very fond of his wife, treated her somewhat casually. He saw her rarely and made up for his absence with affectionate, bantering letters. Of course, she was a generation younger than he and therefore hardly a companion. Such a situation was not unusual: a girl of thirteen might excite her mature husband, but she was unlikely to entertain him for long. She fulfilled her tasks by bearing a few children and running a trouble-free household, and neither matter was too onerous for the rich. Nurses took over the children as soon as they were born; a regiment of servants relieved wives of their traditionally housewifely duties. So the leisure that had previously been the lot of only a few women of very high birth became a commonplace of existence for a multitude of women.

The presence of these leisured women in society helped to transform it. It created the opportunity for personality to flourish, for women to indulge the whims of their temperaments—free from the constraining circumstances of childbirth, nursery, and kitchen. There were men enough to adorn their vacant hours. Italy was alive with priests, many of them urbane, cultured, and idle, whose habit acted as a passport, hinting a security for husbands that their actions all too frequently belied. Nevertheless, they were the natural courtiers of lonely wives, and they swarmed in the literary salons of such distinguished women as Elisabetta Gonzaga at Urbino, the Queen of Cyprus at Asolo, or Vittoria Colonna at Rome.

Soldiers as well as priests needed the sweetness of feminine compassion to soften their tough and dangerous lives. Fortunately, military campaigns in Renaissance Italy were short and usually confined to the summer months, and so the horseplay, the practical jokes, and the feats of arms that were as essential to the courtly life as literary conversations or dramatic performances were provided by the knights.

In addition to soldiers and priests, there were the husbands' pages, all in need of the finer points of amorous education. For a princess, further adornment of the salon was provided by an ambassador—often, true enough, a mere Italian, but at times French or Spanish, which gave an exotic touch that a woman of fashion could exploit to her rivals' disadvantage. Naturally, these courts became highly competitive: to have Pietro Bembo sitting at one's feet, reading his mellifluous but tedious essays on the beauties of Platonic love, was sure to enrage the hearts of other women. In fact, the popularity of Bembo illustrates admirably the style of sophisticated love that the extravagant and princely women of Italy demanded.

Pietro Bembo was a Venetian nobleman, the cultivated son of a rich and sophisticated father who had educated him in the height of humanist fashion at the University of Ferrara, where he acquired extreme agility in bandying about the high-flown concepts of that strange mixture of Platonism and Christianity that was the hallmark of the exquisite. Petrarch, of course, was Bembo's mentor, and like Petrarch he lived his life, as far as the pressures of nature would allow him, in literary terms. He fell verbosely and unhappily in love with a Venetian girl; his ardent longings and intolerable frustrations were committed elegantly to paper and circulated to his admiring friends.

This experience provided him with enough material for a long epistolary exchange with Ercole Strozzi, who was as addicted as Bembo to girls in literary dress. Enraptured by the elegance of his sentiments, Strozzi invited Bembo to his villa near Ferrara, doubtless to flaunt his latest capture, Lucrezia Borgia, as well as to indulge his insatiable literary appetite. However, the biter was quickly bitten, for Bembo was just Lucrezia's cup of tea. A mature woman of twenty-two, thoroughly versed in the language as well as the experience of love, she was already bored with her husband, Alfonso d'Este, and tired of Strozzi. Soon she and Bembo were exchanging charming Spanish love lyrics and far larger homilies on aesthetics. After a visit by Lucrezia to Bembo, sick with fever, the pace quickened. Enormous letters followed thick and fast. Bembo ransacked literature to do homage to Lucrezia; they were Aeneas and Dido, Tristan and Iseult, Lancelot and Guinevere—not, however, lover and mistress.

For a time they lived near each other in the country while Ferrara was plague-ridden. Proximity and the furor of literary passion began to kindle fires in Bembo that were not entirely Platonic, and, after all, Lucrezia was a Borgia. Her tolerant but watchful husband, however, had no intention of being cuckolded by an aesthete, and he rattled his sword. Bembo did not relish reliving the tragedy of Abelard; he might love Lucrezia to distraction, but he cherished himself as only an artist can, so he thought it discreet to return to Venice (he had excuse enough, as his brother was desperately sick). There he consoled himself by polishing his dialogue, *Gli Asolani*, which already enjoyed a high reputation among those to whom it had been circulated in manuscript. Resolving to give his love for Lucrezia its final, immortal form, he decided to publish it with a long dedication to her. To present her with his divine

thoughts on love was a greater gift by far, of course, than his person. Doubtless both Lucrezia and her husband agreed; whether they read further than the dedication is more doubtful.

Bembo had written these highfalutin letters—informal, mannered, obscure, and so loaded with spiritual effusions on love, beauty, God, and women that they are almost unreadable—during a visit to that tragic and noblewoman Caterina Cornaro, Queen of Cyprus. The daughter of a Venetian aristocrat, she had been married as a girl to Giacomo II of Cyprus for reasons of state and declared with infinite pomp "daughter of the republic." Bereaved of both husband and son within three years, she had defied revolution and civil war and maintained her government for fourteen years until, to ease its political necessities, Venice had forced her abdication and set her up in a musical-comedy court at Asolo. There she consoled herself with the world of the spirit, about which Bembo was better informed than most, and he was drawn to her like a moth to a flame. Her court was elegant, fashionable, and intensely literary. *Gli Asolani*, published by Aldus in 1505, made Bembo the archpriest of love as the *Courtier* was to make Castiglione the archpriest of manners. Indeed, Bembo figures in the *Courtier*, and Castiglione adopted his literary techniques. These two subtle and scented bores were destined to turn up together, and nowhere was more likely than the court of Elisabetta Gonzaga at Urbino, for her insatiable appetite for discussion was equal to their eloquence; her stamina matched their verbosity; and night after night the dawn overtook their relentless arguments about the spiritual nature of love. Neither, of course, was so stupid as to think that even the high-minded Caterina or Elisabetta could live by words alone, and Bembo, at least, always interlarded the more ethereal descriptions of Platonic love with a warm eulogy of passion in its more prosaic and energetic aspects. Indeed, he was not above appearing (not entirely modestly disguised) as an ambassador of Venus, in order to declaim in favor of natural love. After six years of this excessively cultured refinement at

Urbino, Bembo became papal secretary to Leo X in Rome. Appropriately, at Rome the word became flesh, and Bembo settled into the comfortable arms of a girl called Morosina, who promptly provided him with three children. It is not surprising, therefore, that Bembo's interests became more mundane, turning from Platonic philosophy to the history of Venice. After the death of his mistress, the life of the spirit once more claimed him, and he entered the College of Cardinals in 1538. More than any other man of his time, he set the pattern of elegant courtship, so that the flattery of the mind, combined with poetic effusions on the supremacy of the spirit, became a well-trodden path for the courtier. It possessed the supreme advantage of passionate courtship without the necessity of proof—a happy situation, indeed, when the object was both a blue stocking and a queen.

Yet it would be wrong to think that the gilded lives of Renaissance princesses were merely elegant, sophisticated, and luxurious or that flirtation took place only in the most refined language. Few could concentrate their thoughts year in, year out, on the nobility of love like Vittoria Colonna. She, who inspired some of Michelangelo's most passionate poetry, even into old age, could and did live in an intense world of spiritual passion, in which the lusts of the flesh were exorcised by an ecstatic contemplation of the beauties of religion. She managed to retain her charm, avoid the pitfalls of hypocrisy, and secure without effort the devotion of Castiglione and Bembo as well as Michelangelo. Even the old rogue Aretino attempted to secure her patronage, but naturally she remained aloof. In her the Platonic ideals of love and beauty mingled with the Christian virtues to the exclusion of all else. Amazingly, no one found her a bore. However, few women could live like Vittoria: they sighed as they read Bembo, became enrapt as they listened to Castiglione, but from time to time they enjoyed a quiet reading of Boccaccio and, better still, Bandello.

Matteo Bandello had been received as a Dominican and spent many years of his live at the Convento delle Grazie, at Milan, which seems to have been a more exciting place for a short-story teller than might be imagined. He acted for a time as ambassador for the Bentivoglio and so came in contact with that remarkable woman Isabello d'Este Gonzaga, whose court at Mantua was as outstanding for its wit, elegance, and genius as any in Italy. There Bandello picked up a mistress, which put him in no mind to hurry back to his brother monks. At Mantua, too, he laid the foundations of his reputation for being one of the best raconteurs of scandal in all Italy, Aretino not excepted. How true Bandello's stories are is still a matter of fierce warfare among scholars, but this they agree on: they did not seem incredible to those who read them. That being so, they give a hair-raising picture of what was going on at courts, in monasteries, in nunneries, in merchant houses, in the palaces and the parsonages of Italy. The prime pursuit, in the vast majority of Bandello's stories, is the conquest of women, and to achieve success, any trick, any falsehood, any force, is justifiable. His heroes' attitude toward success in sex was like Machiavelli's toward politics—the end justified any means. The aim of all men was to ravish other men's wives and daughters and preserve their own women or revenge them if they failed to do so. Vendettas involving the most bloodcurdling punishments were a corollary to his major theme. In consequence, Bandello's stories, cast in a moral guise, nevertheless read like the chronicles of a pornographer. Here are the themes of a few that were thought to be proper entertainment for the lighter moments of court life or for quiet reading by a bored wife: the marriage of a man to a woman who was already his sister and to his daughter; the adultery of two ladies at court and the death of their paramours, which is a vivid record of sexual pleasure and horrifying punishment; the servant who was decapitated for sleeping with his mistress; the death through excessive sexual indulgence of Charles of Navarre; Gian Maria Visconti's burial of a live priest; the autocastration of Fra Filippo—and so one might go on and on, for Bandello wrote hundreds of short stories, and they were largely variations of a single theme. The women of the Renaissance loved them, and few storytellers were as popular as Bandello (such abilities did not go unmarked, and he finished his career as Bishop of Agen). Nor was Bandello exceptional: there were scores of writers like him. Malicious, distorted, exaggerated as these tales were, they were based on the realities of Italian life. Undoubtedly the increased leisure of men and women released their energies for a more riotous indulgence of their sexual appetites.

However daring the Italian males of the Renaissance were, the prudence of wives and the vigilance of husbands prevailed more often than not. The Emilia Pias, Elisabetta Gonzagas, Isabello d'Estes, Lucrezia Borgias, Costanza Amarettas, and Vittoria Colonnas were rare—particularly for cardinals and bishops ravenous for Platonic love. So in Rome, in Florence, in Venice, and in Milan there developed a class of grand courtesans, more akin to geisha girls than to prostitutes, to the extent that the *cortesane famose* of Venice despised the *cortesane de la minor sorte* and complained of their number, habits, and prices to the Senate (they felt they brought disrepute on an honorable profession). Grand as these Venetian girls were, they could not compete with the great courtesans of Rome, who not only lived in small palaces with retinues of maids and liveried servants but also practiced the literary graces and argued as learnedly as a Duchess of Urbino about the ideals of Platonic love.

Italy during the Renaissance was a country at war, plagued for decades with armies. A well-versed condottiere might battle with skill even in the wordy encounters of Platonic passion, but the majority wanted a quicker and cheaper victory. For months on end the captains of war had nothing to do and money to spend; they needed a metropolis of pleasure and vice. Venice, with its quick eye for a profit, provided it and plucked them clean. There, women were to be had for as little as one *scudo*, well within the means even of a musketeer. And it was natural that after Leo X's purge, the majority of the fallen from Rome should flow to Venice. That city, with its regattas, *feste*, and carnivals, with its gondolas built for seclusion and sin, became a harlot's paradise. The trade in women became more profitable and extensive than it had been since the days of Imperial Rome. The Renaissance recaptured the past in more exotic fields than literature or the arts.

Life, however, for the noblewomen of the Renaissance was not always cakes and ale; it could be harsh and furious: the male world of war, assassination, and the pursuit of power frequently broke in upon their gentle world of love and dalliance. Indeed, Caterina Sforza, the woman whom all Italy saluted as its *prima donna*, won her fame through her dour courage and savage temper. Castiglione tells the story of the time she invited a boorish condottiere to dinner and asked him first to dance and then to hear some music—both of which he declined on the grounds that they were not his business. "What is your business, then?" his hostess asked. "Fighting," the warrior replied. "Then," said the virago of Forlì, "since you are not at war and not needed to fight, it would be wise for you to have yourself well greased and put away in a cupboard with all your arms until you are wanted, so that you will not get more rusty than you are." Caterina was more a figure of a saga than a woman of the Renaissance. Three of her husbands were assassinated. At one time she defied the French, at another Ceasare Borgia, who caught her and sent her like a captive lioness to the dungeons of Sant' Angelo. She told her frantic sons that she was habituated to grief and had no fear of it, and as they ought to have expected, she escaped. Yet tough and resourceful as she was, Caterina could be a fool in love—much more than the Duchess of Urbino or Vittoria Colonna. Time and time again her political troubles were due to her inability to check her strong appetite, which fixed itself too readily on the more monstrous of the Renaissance adventurers. So eventful a life induced credulity, and like the rest of her family, Caterina believed in the magical side of nature, dabbled in alchemy and mysteries, and was constantly experimenting with magnets that would produce family harmony or universal salves or celestial water or any other improbable elixir that the wandering hucksters wished on her. At any age, at any time, Catarina would have been a remarkable woman, but the

Renaissance allowed her wild temperament to riot.

Certainly the women of the Renaissance were portents. Elisabetta Gonzaga and Isabello d'Este are the founding sisters of the great literary salons that were to dominate the fashionable society of Western Europe for centuries. But the courts of Italy were few, the families that were rich enough to indulge the tastes and pleasures of sophisticated women never numerous. The lot of most women was harsh; they toiled in the home at their looms or in the fields alongside their men. They bred early and died young, untouched by the growing civility about them, save in their piety. In the churches where they sought ease for their sorrows, the Mother of God shone with a new radiance, a deeper compassion, and seemed in her person to immortalize their lost beauty. Even the majority of middle-class women knew little of luxury or literary elegance. Their lives were dedicated to their husbands and their children; their ambitions were limited to the provision of a proper social and domestic background for their husbands; and they were encouraged to exercise prudence, to indulge in piety, and to eschew vanities. Yet their lives possessed a civility, a modest elegance, that was in strong contrast to the harsher experiences and more laborious days of medieval women. Their new wealth permitted a greater, even if still modest, personal luxury. They could dress themselves more finely, acquire more jewels, provide a richer variety of food for their guests, entertain more lavishly, give more generously to charity. Although circumscribed, their lives were freer, their opportunities greater. It might still be unusual for a woman to be learned or to practice the arts, but it was neither rare nor exotic. And because they had more time, they were able to create a more active social life and to spread civility. After the Renaissance, the drawing room became an integral part of civilized living; indeed, the Renaissance education of a gentleman assumed that much of his life would be spent amusing women and moving them with words. As in so many aspects of life in Renaissance Italy, aristocratic attitudes of the High Middle Ages were adopted by the middle classes. Courtesy and civility spread downward, and the arts of chivalry became genteel.

Child's Play in Medieval England

Nicholas Orme investigates toys, games & childhood in the Middle Ages.

'Play up! play up! and play the game' The ringing chorus of Sir Henry Newbolt's famous cricket poem *Vitai Lampada* (1908) sums up some characteristic Victorian and Edwardian views about play. How children played was important, and adults should regulate and direct it. Cricket and suchlike games promoted endurance, self-discipline and team spirit. These qualities were needed for the health of society and government at home, and of the British Empire beyond.

Newbolt, of course, was only one in a long line of people who thought in this way. The notion that children's play could be used for educational and social purposes goes back to the ancient Greeks, if not beyond. Medieval England was no exception. Studying its toys and games tells us much about adult views of children and play. But it also reveals a good deal about children themselves, and casts light on what has become, in recent times, a controversial issue.

Forty years ago, the French historian Phillipe Ariès argued, in a famous book called *Centuries of Childhood*, that childhood in the Middle Ages did not exist in its modern sense. Children were regarded by adults with relatively little affection, and followed a way of life not greatly different from that of their elders. More recent historians have disputed this notion, pointing to plentiful signs of parental affection and arguing that childhood, by its very nature, must always have been much the same.

In this debate play is a crucial topic. Did adults encourage it? If so, did they see it as recreational (providing toys, for example) or as educational (making children play in particular ways)? Did children play as their elders told them, or did they invent their own games, away from adults and even against their wishes?

These questions can be answered, because we know a good deal about play in medieval England. Toys have been found in archaeological digs, though they are limited to objects of metal and sometimes wood which have survived in the ground. Pictures in medieval manuscripts show a wide range of children's activities, from board games to physical sports such as running and wrestling. Literary sources help as well. Religious works, romances, dictionaries and financial records all have something to say about play, and the result is a rich body of evidence, not only about how children played but what they and their elders thought on the subject.

Our first toys, after we start life as babies, are ones we are given by adults. And adults certainly gave children toys in medieval England, from infancy onwards. The Cornish writer John Trevisa talks in 1398 of nobel babies, playing with 'a child's brooch', an object similar in function to the bright plastic toys that are given to babies today to bite and handle. Rattles existed by the sixteenth century, when William Horman, who wrote a handbook for teaching Latin, talked of buying one to stop a baby crying. Buying a rattle implies mass production, and manufactured rattles occur as archaeological finds in London by the sixteenth century. They are made of a lead-tin alloy and consist of a ball containing a bead and attached to a handle. This reduced the number of dangerous edges, and kept the rattling agent out of reach.

As children grew older, their toys became more complicated. The top is mentioned as early as the story of Apollonius of Tyre, written in about 1060, and a specimen from the period, made of maple wood, has been excavated at Winchester. It is 6.9 centimetres high, with pointed ends at top and bottom, and a groove for whipping. Windmills appear in fifteenth-century pictures: both the modern kind that blow against the wind and ones to be wound up with a string that revolves when you pull it.

All these toys were 'unisex', but medieval children, like modern ones, soon grew aware of their gender and modelled their activities on those of their gender parents. Coroners' records show that accidents to boys tended to arise as they followed their father about his work, and to girls as they followed their mother. Boy's toys, then as now, often took military forms, and two metal soldiers have been found in London, dating from around the reign of Edward I. Each is a knight in armour on horseback, holding a sword. They are about five centimetres high, made in a mould and must have been mass produced; very likely they were painted.

Girls, of course, had dolls—objects that are probably as old as *Homo sapiens*, though the word goes back only to the seventeenth century. The earlier term was 'popper' or 'puppet'. They came in several varieties and more than one kind of material. Cloth dolls are mentioned in a religious text of 1413 which likens idle knights and squires to 'legs of clouts [cloths], as children make poppets for to play with while they are young'. Simple wooden dolls, truncheon-shaped with a head and simple body, are well attested in Tudor and Stuart England, and some survive. They were painted and suitable for dressing with costumes.

By Tudor times, if not before, dolls were manufactured and sold commercially. Many were imported, particularly the wooden ones which were easily transported. William Turner's *Herbal* (1562) talks of 'little puppets and mammets which come to be sold in England in boxes'. In 1582 the crown set a duty of 6s 8d on each gross of imported 'puppets or babies for children'. The duty, amounting to just over a halfpenny per doll, implies that they were sold for sixpence each.

Modern dolls often have tea-sets, and these too have their medieval equivalents. The London excavations have turned up model utensils moulded from lead-tin alloy, evidently mass-produced, probably in England. Jugs, ewers, plates and cups have all been found, as well as little tripod cauldrons and skillets, robust enough to be filled with water and warmed on a hearth. A related toy, also from the tudor period, consists of an ornate cupboard, stamped out of a flat sheet of alloy. The stamped-out profile could be bent to re-create the cupboard in three dimensions, the ancestor of a modern assembly kit.

There was, in short, a toy industry in medieval England by at least 1300. Wealthy parents could buy made toys for their children at fairs or in towns. Lesser people were less able to afford them, but that did not preclude a father using his carpentry skills instead (as mine did in the Second World War toy famine) or a mother hers of sewing. Children too were not passive in this respect, nor solely dependent on their elders for things to play with. Rich and poor alike made toys of their own from anything lying about.

Gerald of Wales, describing his childhood at Manorbier Castle in Pembrokeshire in the 1150s, recalls how he and his brothers played with sand and dust (perhaps on the nearby beach). They built towns and palaces, and he made

churches and monasteries. But the best account of children's own toy-making comes from a fifteenth-century Scottish gentleman named Rait, who wrote about the seven ages of life. Talking of childhood, he observes how children, once they are three, begin to make things to play with. They build small houses with sticks, used bread to form ships, and make a horse from a stick, a spear from a plant-stem or a doll from some rags.

This little knight on horseback, c.1300, is made from moulded metal and would probably have been painted.

The same was true of games. We encounter games organised by adults, but medieval children spent a lot of time playing on their own with one another, as modern children do. Some games, like running, needed no equipment. Others used little objects of no value but easily found. Cherry-stones were rolled, thrown or flicked into a hole in a game called 'cherry-pit'. Cob-nuts, large cultivated hazel-nuts, were employed in the same way: you threw a nut at a heap of other nuts and took the number you hit or scattered.

In 1532 Sir Thomas More imagined a bad schoolboy playing games instead of going to school: 'cherry-stone, marrow bone, buckle-pit, spurn point, cobnut, or quoiting'. It is not clear what all these games consisted of, but at least four of them centred on waste items of food or

clothing, easily found. A later, Elizabethan, source talks of children playing with lace-tags, pins, cherry-stones and counters. Like cob-nuts, these could be used both as the tools of a game and as currency for measuring gains and losses.

The value placed by the young on such trifles is revealed by the most detailed archaeological study yet made of a site used by children. The Carmelite friary at Coventry, dissolved in 1538, became for a time the grammar school of the town. The friary church was turned into the classroom and the choir stall into the pupils' desks. During this period, numerous small objects fell into the foundations beneath the stalls and were recovered by excavation in the 1970s. Many were of iron or copper, such as arrowheads, buckles, buttons, pins, fragments of knives, and small trinkets including a cross, bells and a Jew's harp.

Prominent in the collection were large numbers of little copper tags from the ends of laces, about 400 of them, probably 'money' for games like the one above. There were also beads of glass paste, and bone, two children's teeth, discs and counters made from tile and shale, and small balls similar to marbles made of green and red sandstone, brick and clay.

Nobody has recorded how these objects were played with, but one person passed by as children were playing with them and noted down some of the words they used. This estimable man was a mysterious recluse known only as Geoffrey, who lived in the Dominican friary of King's Lynn in the mid fifteenth century. In 1440 Geoffrey compiled a dictionary for schools entitled *Promptorium Parvulorum* ('a prompter for little ones'). It is a work of great distinction, the first significant English-to-Latin dictionary, the first English dictionary too since it arranges large numbers of English words in alphabetical order, and the first dictionary to take an interest in children.

Not only did Geoffrey include words common throughout society, but names of toys and games which he defined as 'children's play'. They were evidently playground words because they are seldom recorded in other sources, making him the forerunner of those like Pe and Iona Opie who have researched 'the lore and language of schoolchildren'. He gives four words for spinning tops: 'top' itself, ''prill', 'spilcock' and 'whirligig'; three words for running and chasing games: 'running', 'buck hide' and 'base play'. He mentions children playing 'shuttle' (meaning shuttlecock) and 'tennis', and swinging on a swing or see-saw which he calls a 'totter' or 'merrytotter'. It took an unusual person to notice these things.

Active games were universal too. Children ran and chased each other, competed at throwing stones or wrestling, swam and fished (in the case of boys), and played various kinds of ball games against walls, in the streets or over fields. Some of this energy took military forms. Small boys in the twelfth century played a game called 'knights' with plantains, similar to conkers. Boys in the later Middle Ages shot arrows with bows. Adults encouraged this, wanting boys to grow up to play their part in what was, for most men, a military society. The Statute of Winchester of 1285 required every male over the age of fifteen to posses weapons in accordance with his rank. The population needed to be armed to deal with robbers and rebels, and to provide men for the wars with the Welsh, the Scots and the French.

Noble boys had military toys. In 1279, for example, Edward I's son Alonso, aged five, owned a little castle and siege engine to use against it. His younger brother, later Edward II, had a castle made for him when he was six, by his cook, John Brodeye. This was painted and so spectacular that it was shown to the Queen in Westminster Hall the marriage feast of Edward's sister Margaret.

Real weapons made their appearance almost as early. Henry, another child of Edward I, had two arrows bought of his age in 1274 when he was five, and Henry was provided with eight at about the same age, 'some greater and some smaller, for to learn the king to play in tender age'. By the time he was seven, he had a little 'harness" or suit of armour. Children's bows were a distinct commodity by 1475 when the wood for them was imported from Spain. One was bought for the five-year-old Prince

Arthur, son of Henry VII in 1492, and his sister Margaret shot a buck at Alnwick, with another in 1503 when she was fourteen.

The crown tried to affect the play of young people in general. Although the Statute of Winchester required all men to own at least bows and arrows, the national skill at archery seemed inadequate in the very heyday of the Hundred Years War. In 1365 Edward III complained that people followed 'dishonest and useless' games like stone-casting, ball games and cock-fighting, and ordered the male population to practise on feast days with bows and arrows or bolts. The Stature of Cambridge (1388) ordered all 'servants' (a term implying young men) to give up quoits, dice, stone-casting and skittles, and to do archery practice on Sundays and festivals. In 1512 the law was extended to younger children. All men with boys in their houses, aged between seven and seventeen, were ordered to provide them with a bow and two arrows, and to bring them up to shoot. Justices of the Peace were told to enforce the statue, and every town had to set up 'butts' or targets for use.

These policies anticipated nineteenth-century ones. The battle of Agincourt was won on the playing fields of Kenilworth, like that of Waterloo on the fields of Exon. But by no means all children's military activity was regulated and directed by adults. Children have always been liable to war by themselves, sometimes disrupting their elders' peace and quiet. In 1400, six months after Richard II had been overthrown by Henry IV, the children of London gathered together and chose themselves kings. The chronicle-writer Adam of Usk, who tells us this, believed that they congregated 'in thousands . . . made war upon each other and fought to their utmost strength, whereby many died'. In the end, the new king had to order their parents and masters to stop them.

Nor were these wars unique. Richard Carew, the Cornish historian, records how a year before the Prayer Book Rebellion of 1549, at a time of religious unrest, the boys of Bodmin School divided into two factions: the old religion against the new. There were battles, and one boy even made a gun that fired from a can-

dlestick, causing the schoolmaster to intervene decisively with his birch! Five years later, after the failure of Wyatt's rebellion in January 1554, boys gathered in Finsbury Fields outside London in March 'to play a new game: some took Wyatt's part and some the queen's and made a combat in the fields'. The Spanish ambassador reckoned the number at 300 and heard that several were wounded; 'most of them', he wrote, 'have been arrested and shut up in the Guildhall'.

This willingness of children to take the initiative in play, not just to wait for adults to direct them, can be seen in the way they observed the calendar. Medieval life was highly seasonal, affected by light, weather, crops and the Church's cycle of fasts and festivals. Adults had their round of Christmas, Lent, Easter and so on, which children shared in, but children had their own observances, semidetached from their elders.

As early a the thirteenth century, a Franciscan friar and preacher, Thomas Docking, remarked that a child 'has his own particular favourite times of the year. In spring, he follows the ploughers and sowers; in summer and autumn, he accompanies those gathering the grapes'. The Tudor poet Alexander Barclay noticed the same in about 1518. Lent is a time for playing tops; in summer, boys busy themselves in looking for fruit; when winter comes, they get bladders, fill them with peas till they rattle, then use them for handball or football. The periods Barclay mentions—Lent, the fruit season, and the time when pigs were killed (usually in November)—all feature in other sources.

Lent, the first of these seasons, was preceded by Shrove Tuesday in February or early March, depending on the date of Easter, to which it was tied. This was a major date in the children's calendar. The last day before the Lenten fast, it was a public holiday, and one when children (or at any rate boys) had their own activity: cock-fighting. William FitzStephen, describing London at the end of the twelfth century, tells us that

Every year, on the day called Shrove Tuesday, boys from the schools bring fighting cocks to their master, and the whole morning is given up to boyish sport; for they have a holiday in the schools that they may watch their cocks do battle.

Children's cockfighting continued throughout the later Middle Ages, and indeed in some places down to the eighteenth century. It is hard for us to empathise with, but it was approved by adults and even set as a subject for Latin composition. A school notebook, probably from St Albans, contains a whole Latin poem about a real cock-fight, telling how a boy named Chelyng brought to school a cock called Kob, and how this put the other birds to flight. 'Kob' or 'Cob' means a male swan; the bird was obviously large and aggressive.

Shrove Tuesday was also a day for football, and Lent which followed was a season of outdoor games as the weather improved yet still remained bracing enough for active pursuits. The battles of 1400 happened in Lent and those of 1554 were in March, nearly all of which fell within Lent that year. Barclay associated tops (another outdoor activity) with this season, a linkage confirmed by other observers. One wonders if this was an echo of the scourging of Jesus on Good Friday, or of the whipping of penitent sinners, which also took place during Lent. A second burst of excitement took place in late summer. June to September was the season of harvest and fruit-picking, in which children were likely to be involved, licitly or illicitly. The English 'Luttrell Psalter' of 1335–40 has a picture of a boy up a tree, apparently picking cherries, with an angry man beneath. When summer ended, nutting was popular, and at Eton by 1560–61 the boys of the college had a holiday for it, probably on September 14th, Holy Cross Day.

A further autumn custom, roasting beans, occurs in a unique reference among the miracles of Henry VI, relating to the late fifteenth century. A house at Berkhamsted was nearly burnt by a bonfire in late September, before being saved by the dead king's intervention.

This fire, says the miracle recorder, was the result of 'a children's game', 'for children are accustomed in the autumn to burn beans or peas in their stalks, so that they may eat them half burnt'.

The third time of activity unfolded as winter approached. Winter started on all Saints' Day, 1 November, and the killing of animals for winter food began on this day. The slaughter of pigs in particular, by providing bladders for ball games, may have inaugurated the football season. Now that households were well-stocked with autumn fruit and ale, and with the stimulation of dark nights, young people (especially boys) began to go about dressed up, singing songs and asking for money or food.

The most famous example of this practice relates to St Nicholas Day (6 December) and Childermas or Holy Innocents' Day (December 28th), when churches encouraged boys to dress up as a boy-bishop and his attendants, and to lead the services in a piece of licensed role-reversal. The boys then went out of church and round the neighbouring parish, collecting food and money, a custom that was also done by children on two days in November: St. Clement and St. Katherine (November 23rd and 25th).

In 1541 the government of Henry VIII—now well into the Reformation of the Church—decided to forbid these customs. A royal proclamation ordered them to cease: another example of adults trying to control what children did. The sequel is instructive. The king's writ ran inside churches, and the boy-bishop services disappeared. Outside churches, however, children could not be stopped from going around and begging for food and money. Boys continued to ask for apples, pears, money or drink on St Clement's Day, and boys (and sometimes girls) on St Katherine's Day. The customs died out only in recent times.

Play, then, tells us a good deal about medieval society—which was, in major respects, a modern one. The relationship between adults and children worked in ways which we still recognise. Many parents were indulgent to their children, pro-

viding them with toys and giving them time to play. Children played in a wide variety of ways—imaginatively, skilfully, athletically and violently—developing their minds, bodies and social skills. Adults tried at times to regulate play: partly to keep children in order, partly to give them skills for adult life (in this case, military ones), and (by the Reformation) to inculcate the right kinds of religion.

Children had to do what their elders wanted, to some extent, but they were never fully under adult control. They gravitated to one another and formed a culture of their own. John Trevisa observed how the young 'love talkings and counsels of such children as they are, and forsake and avoid [the] companies of the old'. They were capable of doing more than their elders liked, when they fought in the streets and fields, and of doing less when they ignored the orders of 1541. To sum up, parents did take an interest in children, and children had their own special culture. We can answer Ariès's thesis with a resounding 'No!'. Childhood has always been much the same. Boys, after all, will be boys—and girls be girls.

FOR FURTHER READING

Joseph Strutt, *The Sports and Pastimes of the People of England*, ed. William Hone (London, 1876); Nicholas Orme, *From Childhood to Chivalry; the education of the English kings and aristocracy 1066–1530* (London and New York, 1984), and *Medieval Children* (London, 2001), Sally Crawford, *Childhood in Anglo-Saxon England* (Stroud, 2000); M. R. James (ed), *The Romance of Alexander* (Oxford, 1933), William Horman, *Vulgaria* (London, 1519, reprinted Amsterdam, 1975); W. Endrei and L. Zolnay, *Fun and Games in Old Europe* (Budapest, 1986); Pierre Riché and Danièle Alexandre-Bidon, *L'Enfance au Moyen Age* (Paris, 1994).

Nicholas Orme is Professor of History at Exeter University. His book *Medieval Children* was published by Yale University Press last month, priced £25.

Luther: Giant of His Time and Ours

Half a millennium after his birth, the first Protestant is still a towering force

It was a back-room deal, little different from many others struck at the time, but it triggered an upheaval that altered irrevocably the history of the Western world. Albrecht of Brandenburg, a German nobleman who had previously acquired a dispensation from the Vatican to become a priest while underage and to head two dioceses at the same time, wanted yet another favor from the Pope: the powerful archbishop's chair in Mainz. Pope Leo X, a profligate spender who needed money to build St. Peter's Basilica, granted the appointment—for 24,000 gold pieces, roughly equal to the annual imperial revenues in Germany. It was worth it. Besides being a rich source of income, the Mainz post brought Albrecht a vote for the next Holy Roman Emperor, which could be sold to the highest bidder.

In return, Albrecht agreed to initiate the sale of indulgences in Mainz. Granted for good works, indulgences were papally controlled dispensations drawn from an eternal "treasury of merits" built up by Christ and the saints; the church taught that they would help pay the debt of "temporal punishment" due in purgatory for sins committed by either the penitent or any deceased person. The Pope received half the proceeds of the Mainz indulgence sale, while the other half went to repay the bankers who had lent the new archbishop gold.

Enter Martin Luther, a 33-year-old priest and professor at Wittenberg University. Disgusted not only with the traffic in indulgences but with its doctrinal underpinnings, he forcefully protested to Albrecht—never expecting that his action would provoke a sweeping uprising against a corrupt church. Luther's challenge culminated in the Protestant Reformation and the rending of Western Christendom, and made him a towering figure in European history. In this 500th anniversary year of his birth (Nov. 10, 1483), the rebel of Wittenberg remains the subject of persistent study. It is said that more books have been written about him than anyone else in history, save his own master, Jesus Christ. The renaissance in Luther scholarship surrounding this year's anniversary serves as a reminder that his impact on modern life is profound, even for those who know little about the doctrinal feuds that brought him unsought fame. From the distance of half a millennium, the man who, as Historian Hans Hillerbrand of Southern Methodist University in Dallas says, brought Christianity from lofty theological dogma to a clearer and more personal belief is still able to stimulate more heated debate than all but a handful of historical figures.

Indeed, as the reformer who fractured Christianity, Luther has latterly become a key to reuniting it. With the approval of the Vatican, and with Americans taking the lead, Roman Catholic theologians are working with Lutherans and other Protestants to sift through the 16th century disputes and see whether the Protestant-Catholic split can some day be overcome. In a remarkable turnabout, Catholic scholars today express growing appreciation of Luther as a "father in the faith" and are willing to play down his excesses. According to a growing consensus, the great division need never have happened at all.

Beyond his importance as a religious leader, Luther had a profound effect on Western culture. He is, paradoxically, the last medieval man and the first modern one, a political conservative and a spiritual revolutionary. His impact is most marked, of course, in Germany, where he laid the cultural foundations for what later became a united German nation.

When Luther attacked the indulgence business in 1517, he was not only the most popular teacher at Wittenberg but also vicar provincial in charge of eleven houses of the Hermits of St. Augustine. He was brilliant, tireless and a judicious administrator, though given to bouts of spiritual depression. To make his point on indulgences, Luther dashed off 95 theses condemning the system ("They preach human folly who pretend that as soon as money in the coffer rings, a soul from purgatory springs") and sent them to Archbishop Albrecht and a number of theologians.*

The response was harsh: the Pope eventually rejected Luther's protest and demanded capitulation. It was then that Luther began asking questions about other aspects of the church, including the papacy itself. In 1520 he charged in an open letter to the Pope, "The Roman Church, once the holiest of all, has become the most licentious den of thieves, the most shameless of brothels, the kingdom of sin, death and hell." Leo called Luther "the wild boar which has invaded the Lord's vineyard."

The following year Luther was summoned to recant his writings before the Diet of Worms, a council of princes convened by the young Holy Roman Emperor Charles V. In his closing defense, Luther proclaimed defiantly: "Unless I am convinced by testimony from Holy Scriptures and clear proofs based on reason—because, since it is notorious that they have erred and contradicted themselves, I cannot believe either the Pope or the council alone—I am bound by conscience and the Word of God. Therefore I can and will recant nothing, because to act against one's conscience is neither safe nor salutary. So help me God." (Experts today think that he did not actually speak the famous words, "Here I stand. I can do no other.")

This was hardly the cry of a skeptic, but it was ample grounds for the Emperor to put Luther under sentence of death as a heretic. Instead of being executed, Luther lived for another 25 years, became a major author and composer of hymns, father of a bustling household and a secular figure who opposed rebellion—in all, a commanding force in European affairs. In the years beyond, the abiding split in Western Christendom developed, including a large component of specifically "Lutheran" churches that today have 69 million adherents in 85 nations.

The enormous presence of the Wittenberg rebel, the sheer force of his personality, still broods over all Christendom, not just Lutheranism. Although Luther declared that the Roman Pontiffs were the "Antichrist," today's Pope, in an anniversary tip of the zuc-

chetto, mildly speaks of Luther as "the reformer." Ecumenical-minded Catholic theologians have come to rank Luther in importance with Augustine and Aquinas. "No one who came after Luther could match him," says Father Peter Manns, a Catholic theologian in Mainz. "On the question of truth, Luther is a lifesaver for Christians." While Western Protestants still express embarrassment over Luther's anti-Jewish rantings or his skepticism about political clergy, Communist East Germany has turned him into a secular saint because of his influence on German culture. Party Boss Erich Honecker, head of the regime's *Lutherjahr* committee, is willing to downplay Luther's antirevolutionary ideas, using the giant figure to bolster national pride.

Said West German President Karl Carstens, as he opened one of the hundreds of events commemorating Luther this year: "Luther has become a symbol of the unity of all Germany. We are all Luther's heirs."

After five centuries, scholars still have difficulty coming to terms with the contradictions of a tempestuous man. He was often inexcusably vicious in his writings (he wrote, for instance, that one princely foe was a "faint-hearted wretch and fearful sissy" who should "do nothing but stand like a eunuch, that is, a harem guard, in a fool's cap with a fly swatter"). Yet he was kindly in person and so generous to the needy that his wife despaired of balancing the household budget. When the plague struck Wittenberg and others fled, he stayed behind to minister to the dying. He was a powerful spiritual author, yet his words on other occasions were so scatological that no Lutheran periodical would print them today. His writing was hardly systematic, and his output runs to more than 100 volumes. On the average, Luther wrote a major tract or treatise every two weeks throughout his life.

The scope of Luther's work has made him the subject of endless reinterpretation. The Enlightenment treated him as the father of free thought, conveniently omitting his belief in a sovereign God who inspired an authoritative Bible. During the era of Otto von Bismarck a century ago, Luther was fashioned into a

nationalistic symbol; 70 years later, Nazi propagandists claimed him as one of their own by citing his anti-Jewish polemics.

All scholars agree on Luther's importance for German culture, surpassing even that of Shakespeare on the English-speaking world. Luther's masterpiece was his translation of the New Testament from Greek into German, largely completed in ten weeks while he was in hiding after the Worms confrontation, and of the Old Testament, published in 1534 with the assistance of Hebrew experts. The Luther Bible sold massively in his lifetime and remains today the authorized German Protestant version. Before Luther's Bible was published, there was no standard German, just a profusion of dialects. "It was Luther," said Johann Gottfried von Herder, one of Goethe's mentors, "who has awakened and let loose the giant: the German language."

Only a generation ago, Catholics were trained to consider Luther the archheretic. Now no less than the Vatican's specialist on Lutheranism, Monsignor Aloys Klein, says that "Martin Luther's action was beneficial to the Catholic Church." Like many other Catholics, Klein thinks that if Luther were living today there would be no split. Klein's colleague in the Vatican's Secretariat for Promoting Christian Unity, Father Pierre Duprey, suggests that with the Second Vatican Council (1962–65) Luther "got the council he asked for, but 450 years too late." Vatican II accepted his contention, that in a sense, all believers are priests; while the council left the Roman church's hierarchy intact, it enhanced the role of the laity. More important, the council moved the Bible to the center of Catholic life, urged continual reform and instituted worship in local languages rather than Latin.

One of the key elements in the Reformation was the question of "justification," the role of faith in relation to good works in justifying a sinner in the eyes of God. Actually, Catholicism had never officially taught that salvation could be attained only through pious works, but the popular perception held otherwise. Luther recognized, as University of Chicago Historian Martin Marty explains, that everything "in the system of Catho-

ic teaching seemed aimed toward ap-
easing God. Luther was led to the idea
f God not as an angry judge but as a for-
iving father. It is a position that gives
he individual a great sense of freedom
nd security." In effect, says U.S. Histo-
ian Roland Bainton, Luther destroyed
he implication that men could "bargain
vith God."

Father George Tavard, a French Cath-
lic expert on Protestantism who teaches
n Ohio and has this month published
ustification: An Ecumenical Study
Paulist; $7.95), notes that "today many
Catholic scholars think Luther was right
nd the 16th century Catholic polemi-
ists did not understand what he meant.
Both Lutherans and Catholics agree that
ood works by Christian believers are
he result of their faith and the working
f divine grace in them, not their per-
onal contributions to their own salva-
ion. Christ is the only Savior. One does
ot save oneself." An international Luth-
ran-Catholic commission, exploring the
asis for possible reunion, made a joint
tatement along these lines in 1980. Last
month a parallel panel in the U.S. issued
 significant 21,000-word paper on justi-
ication that affirms much of Luther's
hinking, though with some careful
edging from the Catholic theologians.

There is doubt, of course, about the
egree to which Protestants and Catho-
ics can, in the end, overcome their dif-
erences. Catholics may now be
ermitted to sing Luther's *A Mighty For-
ress Is Our God* or worship in their naive languages, but a wide gulf clearly
emains on issues like the status of Prot-
stant ministers and, most crucially, pa-
al authority.

During the futile Protestant-Catholic
eunion negotiations in 1530 at the Diet
f Augsburg, the issue of priestly celi-
acy was as big an obstacle as the faith
s. good works controversy. Luther had
arried a nun, to the disgust of his Cath-
lic contemporaries. From the start, the
arriage of clergy was a sharply defined
ifference between Protestantism and
Catholicism, and it remains a key barrier
oday. By discarding the concept of the
oral superiority of celibacy, Luther es-
blished sexuality as a gift from God. In
eneral, he was a lover of the simple
leasures, and would have had little pa-

tience with the later Puritans. He spoke
offhandedly about sex, enjoyed good-
natured joshing, beer drinking and food
("If our Lord is permitted to create nice
large pike and good Rhine wine, presumably I may be allowed to eat and drink").
For his time, he also had an elevated
opinion of women. He cherished his wife
and enjoyed fatherhood, siring six children and rearing eleven orphaned nieces
and nephews as well.

But if Luther's views on the Catholic
Church have come to be accepted even
by many Catholics, his anti-Semitic
views remain a problem for even his
most devoted supporters. Says New
York City Rabbi Marc Tanenbaum:
"The anniversary will be marred by the
haunting specter of Luther's devil theory
of the Jews."

Luther assailed the Jews on doctrinal
grounds, just as he excoriated "papists"
and Turkish "infidels." But his work titled *On the Jews and Their Lies* (1543)
went so far as to advocate that their synagogues, schools and homes should be
destroyed and their prayer books and
Talmudic volumes taken away. Jews
were to be relieved of their savings and
put to work as agricultural laborers or expelled outright.

Fortunately, the Protestant princes ignored such savage recommendations,
and the Lutheran Church quickly forgot
about them. But the words were there to
be gleefully picked up by the Nazis, who
removed them from the fold of religious
polemics and used them to buttress their
20th century racism. For a good Lutheran, of course, the Bible is the sole authority, not Luther's writings, and the
thoroughly Lutheran Scandinavia vigorously opposed Hitler's racist madness. In
the anniversary year, all sectors of Lutheranism have apologized for their
founder's views.

Whatever the impact of Luther's anti-
Jewish tracts, there is no doubt that his
political philosophy, which tended to
make church people submit to state authority, was crucial in weakening opposition by German Lutherans to the Nazis.
Probably no aspect of Luther's teaching
is the subject of more agonizing Protestant scrutiny in West Germany today.

Luther sought to declericalize society
and to free people from economic bur-

dens imposed by the church. But he was
soon forced, if reluctantly, to deliver
considerable control of the new Protestant church into the hands of secular rulers who alone could ensure the survival
of the Reformation. Luther spoke of
"two kingdoms," the spiritual and the
secular, and his writings provided strong
theological support for authoritarian
government and Christian docility.

The Lutheran wing of the Reformation was democratic, but only in terms of
the church itself, teaching that a plow-
man did God's work as much as a priest,
encouraging lay leadership and seeking
to educate one and all. But it was Calvin,
not Luther, who created a theology for
the democratic state. A related aspect of
Luther's politics, controversial then and
now, was his opposition to the bloody
Peasants' War of 1525. The insurgents
thought they were applying Luther's
ideas, but he urged rulers to crush the revolt: "Let whoever can, stab, strike, kill."
Support of the rulers was vital for the
Reformation, but Luther loathed violent
rebellion and anarchy in any case.

Today Luther's law-and-order approach is at odds with the revolutionary
romanticism and liberation theology that
are popular in some theology schools. In
contrast with modern European Protestantism's social gospel, Munich Historian Thomas Nipperdey says, Luther
"would not accept modern attempts to
build a utopia and would argue, on the
contrary, that we as mortal sinners are incapable of developing a paradise on
earth."

Meanwhile, the internal state of the
Lutheran Church raises other questions
about the lasting power of Luther's vision. Lutheranism in the U.S., with 8.5
million adherents, is stable and healthy.
The church is also growing in Third
World strongholds like racially torn
Namibia, where black Lutherans predominate. But in Lutheranism's historic
heartland, the two Germanys and Scandinavia, there are deep problems. In East
Germany, Lutherans are under pressure
from the Communist regime. In West
Germany, the Evangelical Church in
Germany (E.K.D.), a church federation
that includes some non-Lutherans, is
wealthy (annual income: $3 billion), but
membership is shrinking and attendance

at Sunday services is feeble indeed. Only 6% of West Germans—or, for that matter, Scandinavians—worship regularly.

What seems to be lacking in the old European churches is the passion for God and his truth that so characterizes Luther. He retains the potential to shake people out of religious complacency. Given Christianity's need, on all sides, for a good jolt, eminent Historian Heiko Oberman muses, "I wonder if the time of Luther isn't ahead of us."

The boldest assertion about Luther for modern believers is made by Protestants who claim that the reformer did nothing less than enable Christianity to survive.

In the Middle Ages, too many Popes and bishops were little more than corrupt, luxury-loving politicians, neglecting the teaching of the love of God and using the fear of God to enhance their power and wealth. George Lindbeck, the Lutheran co-chairman of the international Lutheran-Catholic commission, believers that without Luther "religion would have been much less important during the next 400 to 500 years. And since medieval religion was falling apart, secularization would have marched on, unimpeded."

A provocative thesis, and a debatable one. But with secularization still marching on, almost unimpeded, Protestants and Catholics have much to reflect upon as they scan the five centuries after Luther and the shared future of their still divided churches.

—By Richard N. Ostling. Reported by Roland Flamini and Wanda Menke-Glückert/Bonn, with other bureaus.

---

*Despite colorful legend, it is not certain he ever nailed them to the door of the Castle Church.

Explaining John Calvin

John Calvin (1509–64) has been credited, or blamed, for much that defines the modern Western world: capitalism and the work ethic, individualism and utilitarianism, modern science, and, at least among some devout Christians, a lingering suspicion of earthly pleasures. During [a] recent American presidential campaign, the two candidates appealed to "values" that recall the teachings of the 16th-century churchman, indicating that what William Pitt once said of England—"We have a Calvinist creed"—still may hold partly true for the United States. But the legend of the joyless tyrant of Geneva obscures both the real man, a humanist as much as a religious reformer, and the subtlety of his thought. Here his biographer discusses both.

Villiam J. Bouwsma

Our image of John Calvin is largely the creation of austere Protestant churchmen who lived during the 17th century, the century following that of the great reformer's life. The image is most accurately evoked by the huge icon of Calvin, familiar to many a tourist, that stands behind the University of Geneva. There looms Calvin, twice as large as life, stylized beyond recognition, stony, rigid, immobile, and—except for his slightly abstracted disapproval of whatever we might imagine him to be contemplating—impassive.

Happily, the historical record provides good evidence for a Calvin very different from the figure invoked by his 17th-century followers. This Calvin is very much a man of the 16th century, a time of religious strife and social upheaval. His life and work reflect the ambiguities, contradictions, and agonies of that troubled time. Sixteenth-century thinkers, especially in Northern Europe, were still grappling with the rich but inherent legacy of the Renaissance, and their characteristic intellectual constructions were less successful in reconciling its contradictory impulses than in balancing among them. This is why it has proved so difficult to pigeon-hole such figures as Erasmus and Machiavelli or Montaigne and Shakespeare, and why they continue to stimulate reflection. Calvin, who can be quoted on both sides of most questions, belongs in this great company.

Born in 1509 in Noyon, Calvin was brought up to be a devout French Catholic. Indeed, his father, a lay administrator in the service of the local bishop, sent him to the University of Paris in 1523 to study for the priesthood. Later he decided that young John should be a lawyer. Accordingly, from 1528 to 1533, Calvin studied law. During these years he was also exposed to the evangelical humanism of Erasmus and Jacques Lefèvre d'Étaples that nourished the radical student movement of the time. The students called for salvation by grace rather than by good works and ceremonies—a position fully compatible with Catholic orthodoxy—as the foundation for a general reform of church and society on the model of antiquity.

To accomplish this end, the radical students advocated a return to the Bible, studied in its original languages. Calvin himself studied Greek and Hebrew as well as Latin, the "three languages" of ancient Christian discourse. His growing interest in the classics led, moreover, to his first publication, a moralizing commentary on Seneca's essay on clemency.

Late in 1533, the French government of Francis I became less tolerant of the Paris student radicals, whom it saw as a threat to the peace. After helping to prepare a statement of the theological implications of the movement in a public address delivered by Nicolas Cop, rector of the University, Calvin found it prudent to leave Paris. Eventually he made his way to Basel, a Protestant town tolerant of religious variety.

Up to this point, there is little evidence of Calvin's "conversion" to Protestantism. Before Basel, of course, he had been fully aware of the challenge Martin Luther posed to the Catholic Church. The 95 Theses that the German reformer posted in Wittenberg in 1517 attacked what Luther believed were cor-

...ons of true Christianity and, by implication, the authors of those errors, the Renaissance popes. Luther, above all, rejected the idea of salvation through indulgences or the sacrament of penance. Excommunicated by Pope Leo X, he encouraged the formation of non-Roman churches.

In Basel, Calvin found himself drawing closer to Luther. Probably in part to clarify his own beliefs, he began to write, first a preface to his cousin Pierre Olivétan's French translation of the Bible, and then what became the first edition of the *Institutes*, his masterwork, which in its successive revisions became the single most important statement of Protestant belief. Although he did not substantially change his views thereafter, he elaborated them in later editions, published in both Latin and French, in which he also replied to his critics; the final versions appeared in 1559 and 1560.

The 1536 *Institutes* had brought him some renown among Protestant leaders, among them Guillaume Farel. A French Reformer struggling to plant Protestantism in Geneva, Farel persuaded Calvin to settle there in late 1536. The Reformation was in trouble in Geneva. Indeed, the limited enthusiasm of Geneva for Protestantism—and for religious and moral reform—continued almost until Calvin's death. The resistance was all the more serious because the town council in Geneva, as in other Protestant towns in Switzerland and southern Germany, exercised ultimate control over the church and the ministers.

The main issue was the right of excommunication, which the ministers regarded as essential to their authority but which the town council refused to concede. The uncompromising attitudes of Calvin and Farel finally resulted in their expulsion from Geneva in May of 1538.

Calvin found refuge for the next three years in Protestant Strasbourg, where he was pastor of a church for French-speaking refugees. Here he married Idelette de Bure, a widow in his congregation. Theirs proved to be an extremely warm relationship, although none of their children survived infancy.

During his Strasbourg years, Calvin learned much about church administration from Martin Bucer, chief pastor there. Attending European religious conferences, he soon became a major figure in the international Protestant movement.

Meanwhile, without strong leadership, the Protestant revolution in Geneva foundered. In September of 1541, Calvin was invited back, and there he remained until his death in 1564. He was now in a stronger position. In November the town council enacted his *Ecclesiastical Ordinances*, which provided for the religious education of the townspeople, especially children, and instituted his conception of church order. It established four groups of church officers and a "consistory" of pastors and elders to bring every aspect of Genevan life under the precepts of God's law.

The activities of the consistory gave substance to the legend of Geneva as a joyless theocracy, intolerant of looseness or pleasure. Under Calvin's leadership, it undertook a range of disciplinary actions covering everything from the abolition of Catholic "superstition" to the enforcement of sexual morality, the regulation of taverns, and measures against dancing, gambling, and swearing. These "Calvinist" measures were resented by many townsfolk, as was the arrival of increasing numbers of French Protestant refugees.

The resulting tensions, as well as the persecution of Calvin's followers in France, help to explain the trial and burning of one of Calvin's leading opponents, Michael Servetus. Calvin felt the need to show that his zeal for orthodoxy was no less than that of his foes. The confrontation between Calvin and his enemies in Geneva was finally resolved in May of 1555, when Calvin's opponents overreached themselves and the tide turned in his favor. His position in Geneva was henceforth reasonably secure.

But Calvin was no less occupied. He had to watch the European scene and keep his Protestant allies united. At the same time, Calvin never stopped promoting his kind of Protestantism. He welcomed the religious refugees who poured into Geneva, especially during the 1550s, from France, but also from

England and Scotland, from Italy, Germany, and the Netherlands, and even from Eastern Europe. He trained many of them as ministers, sent them back to their homelands, and then supported them with letters of encouragement and advice. Geneva thus became the center of an international movement and a model for churches elsewhere. John Knox, the Calvinist leader of Scotland, described Geneva as "the most perfect school of Christ that ever was on the Earth since the days of the Apostles." So while Lutheranism was confined to parts of Germany and Scandinavia, Calvinism spread into Britain, the English-speaking colonies of North America, and many parts of Europe.

Academic efforts to explain the appeal of Calvinism in terms of social class have had only limited success. In France, his theology was attractive mainly to a minority among the nobility and the urban upper classes, but in Germany it found adherents among both townsmen and princes. In England and the Netherlands, it made converts in every social group. Calvinism's appeal lay in its ability to explain disorders of the age afflicting all classes and in the remedies and comfort it provided, as much by its activism as by its doctrine. Both depended on the personality, preoccupations, and talents of Calvin himself.

Unlike Martin Luther, Calvin was a reticent man. He rarely expressed himself in the first person singular. This reticence has contributed to his reputation as cold and unapproachable. Those who knew him, however, noted his talent for friendship as well as his hot temper. The intensity of his grief on the death of his wife in 1549 revealed a large capacity for feeling, as did his empathetic reading of many passages in Scripture.

In fact, the impersonality of Calvin's teachings concealed an anxiety, unusually intense even in an anxious age. He saw anxiety everywhere, in himself, in the narratives of the Bible, and in his contemporaries. This feeling found expression in two of his favorite images for spiritual discomfort: the abyss and the labyrinth. The abyss represented all the nameless terrors of disorientation and the absence of familiar boundaries. The labyrinth expressed the anxiety of entrapment: in religious terms, the inability of human beings alienated from God to escape from the imprisonment of self-concern.

One side of Calvin sought to relieve his terror of the abyss with cultural constructions and patterns of control that might help him recover his sense of direction. This side of Calvin was attracted to classical philosophy, which nevertheless conjured up for him fears of entrapment in a labyrinth. Escape from this, however, exposed him to terrible uncertainties and, once again, to the horrors of the abyss. Calvin's ideas thus tended to oscillate between those of freedom and order. His problem was to strike a balance between the two.

He did so primarily with the resources of Renaissance humanism, applying its philological approach to recover a biblical understanding of Christianity. But humanism was not only, or even fundamentally, a scholarly movement. Its scholarship was instrumental to the recovery of the communicative skills of classical rhetoric. Humanists such as Lorenzo Valla and Erasmus held that an effective rhetoric would appeal to a deeper level of the personality than would a mere rational demonstration. By moving the heart, Christian rhetoric could stimulate human beings to the active reform of both themselves and the world.

Theological system-building, Calvin believed, was futile and inappropriate. He faulted the medieval Scholastic theologians for relying more on human reason than on the Bible, which spoke uniquely to the heart. The teachings of Thomas Aquinas, and like-minded theologians, appealed only to the intellect, and so were lifeless and irrelevant to a world in desperate need.

As a humanist, Calvin was a *biblical* theologian, prepared to follow Scripture even when it surpassed the limits of human understanding. And its message, for him, could not be presented as a set of timeless abstractions; it had to be adapted to the understanding of contemporaries according to the rhetorical principle of decorum—i.e. suitability to time, place, and audience.

Calvin shared with earlier humanists an essentially biblical conception of the human personality, not as a hierarchy of faculties ruled by reason but as a mysterious unity. This concept made the feelings and will even more important aspects of the personality than the intellect, and it also gave the body new dignity.

Indeed, Calvin largely rejected the traditional belief in hierarchy as the general principle of all order. For it he substituted the practical (rather than the metaphysical) principle of *utility*. This position found expression in his preference, among the possible forms of government, for republics. It also undermined, for him, the traditional subordination of women to men. Calvin's Geneva accordingly insisted on a single standard of sexual morality—a radical departure from custom.

Calvin's utilitarianism was also reflected in deep reservations about the capacity of human beings to attain anything but practical knowledge. The notion that they can know anything absolutely, as God knows it, so to speak, seemed to him deeply presumptuous. This helps to explain his reliance on the Bible: Human beings have access to the saving truths of religion only insofar as God has revealed them in Scripture. But revealed truth, for Calvin, was not revealed to satisfy human curiosity; it too was limited to meeting the most urgent and practical needs, above all for individual salvation. This practicality also reflects a basic conviction of Renaissance thinkers: the superiority of an active life to one of contemplation. Calvin's conviction that every occupation in society is a "calling" on the part of God himself sanctified this conception.

But Calvin was not only a Renaissance humanist. The culture of 16th-century Europe was peculiarly eclectic. Like other thinkers of his time, Calvin had inherited a set of quite contrary tendencies that he uneasily combined with his humanism. Thus, even as he emphasized the heart, Calvin continued to conceive of the human personality as a hierarchy of faculties ruled by reason; from time to time he tried uneasily, with little success,

to reconcile the two conceptions. This is why he sometimes emphasized the importance of rational control over the passions—an emphasis that has been reassuring to conservatives.

Calvin's theology has often been seen as little more than a systematization of the more creative insights of Luther. He followed Luther, indeed, on many points: on original sin, on Scripture, on the absolute dependence of human beings on divine grace, and on justification by faith alone. Other differences between Calvin and Luther are largely matters of emphasis. His understanding of predestination, contrary to a general impression, was virtually identical to Luther's; it was not of central importance to his theology. He believed that it meant that the salvation of believers by a loving God was absolutely certain.

In major respects, however, Calvin departed from Luther. In some ways he was more radical, but most of his differences suggest that he was closer to Catholicism than Luther, as in his insistence on the importance of the historical church. He was also more traditional in his belief in the authority of clergy over laity, perhaps as a result of his difficulties with the Geneva town council. Even more significant, especially for Calvinism as a historical force, was Calvin's attitude toward the everyday world. Luther had regarded this world and its institutions as incorrigible, and was prepared to leave them to the devil. But for Calvin this world, created by God, still belonged to Him; it remained potentially His kingdom; and every Christian was obliged to devote his life to make it so in reality by reforming and bringing it under God's law.

Calvin's thought was less a theology to be comprehended by the mind than a set of principles for the Christian life: in short, spirituality. He was more concerned with the experience and application of Christianity than with mere reflection about it. His true successors were Calvinist pastors rather than Calvinist theologians. Significantly, in addition to devoting much of his energy to the training of other pastors, Calvin was himself a pastor. He preached regularly: some 4,000 sermons in the 13 years after his return to Geneva.

alvin's spirituality begins with the conviction that we do not so much "know" God as "experience" him indirectly, through his mighty acts and works in the world, as we experience but can hardly be said to know thunder, one of Calvin's favorite metaphors for religious experience. Calvin also believed that human beings can understand something of what God is like in the love of a father for his children, but also—surprisingly in one often identified with patriarchy—in the love of a mother. He denounced those who represented God as dreadful; God for him is "mild, kind, gentle, and compassionate."

Nevertheless, in spite of this attention to God's love for mankind, Calvin gave particular emphasis to God's power because it was this that finally made his love effective in the work of redemption from sin. God, for Calvin, represented supremely all the ways in which human beings experience power: as energy, as warmth, as vitality, and, so, as life itself.

Sin, by contrast, is manifested precisely in the negation of every kind of power and ultimately of the life force given by God. Sin *deadens* and, above all, deadens the feelings. Saving grace, then, must be conceived as the transfusion of God's power—his warmth, passion, strength, vitality—to human beings. It was also essential to Calvin's spirituality, and a reflection of his realism, that this "transfusion" be not instantaneous but gradual.

Calvin's traditional metaphor for the good Christian life implied activity: "Our life is like a journey," he asserted, but "it is not God's will that we should march along casually as we please, but he sets the goal before us, and also directs us on the right way to it." This way is also a struggle.

Complex as his ideas were, it is easy to see how the later history of Calvinism has often been obscured by scholars' failure to distinguish among (1) Calvinism as the beliefs of Calvin himself, (2) the beliefs of his followers, who, though striving to be faithful to Calvin, modified his teachings to meet their own needs, and (3) more loosely, the beliefs of the Reformed tradition of Protestant Christianity, in which Calvinism proper was only one, albeit the most prominent, strand.

The Reformed churches in the 16th century were referred to in the plural to indicate, along with what they had in common, their individual autonomy and variety. They consisted originally of a group of non-Lutheran Protestant churches based in towns in Switzerland and southern Germany. These churches were jealous of their autonomy; and Geneva was not alone among them in having distinguished theological leadership. Ulrich Zwingli and Heinrich Bullinger in Zurich and Martin Bucer in Strasbourg also had a European influence that combined with that of Calvin, especially in England, to shape what came to be called "Calvinism."

Long after Calvin's death in 1564, the churchmen in Geneva continued to venerate him and aimed at being faithful to his teaching under his successors, first among them Theodore de Bèze. But during what can be appropriately described as a Protestant "Counter Reformation," the later Calvinism of Geneva, abandoning Calvin's more humanistic tendencies and drawing more on other, sterner aspects of his thought, was increasingly intellectualized. Indeed, it grew to resemble the medieval Scholasticism that Calvin had abhorred.

Predestination now began to assume an importance that had not been attributed to it before. Whereas Calvin had been led by personal faith to an awed belief in predestination as a benign manifestation of divine providence, predestination now became a threatening doctrine: God's decree determined in advance an individual's salvation or damnation. What good, one might wonder, were one's own best efforts if God had already ruled? In 1619 these tendencies reached a climax at the Synod of Dort in the Netherlands, which spelled out various corollaries of predestination, as Calvin had never done, and made the doctrine central to Calvinism.

Calvinist theologians, meanwhile, apparently finding Calvin's loose rhetorical style of expression unsatisfactory, began deliberately to write like Scholastic theologians, in Latin, and even appealed to medieval Scholastic authorities. The major Calvinist theological statement of the 17th century was the *Institutio Theologiae Elencticae* (3 vols., Geneva, 1688) of François Turretin, chief pastor of Geneva. Although the title of this work recalled Calvin's masterpiece, it was published in Latin, its dialectical structure followed the model of the great *Summas* of Thomas Aquinas, and it suggested at least as much confidence as Thomas in the value of human reason. The lasting effect of this shift is suggested by the fact that "Turretin," in Latin, was the basic theology textbook at the Princeton Seminary in New Jersey, the most distinguished intellectual center of American Calvinism until the middle of the 19th century.

Historians have continued to debate whether these developments were essentially faithful to Calvin or deviations from him. In some sense they were both. Later Calvinist theologians, as they abandoned Calvin's more humanistic tendencies and emphasized his more austere and dogmatic side, found precedents for these changes in the contrary aspects of his thought. They were untrue to Calvin, of course, in rejecting his typically Renaissance concern with balancing contrary impulses. One must remember, however, that these changes in Calvinism occurred during a period of singular disorder in Europe, caused by, among other things, a century of religious warfare. As a result, there was a widespread longing for certainty, security, and peace.

One or another aspect of Calvin's influence has persisted not only in the Reformed churches of France, Germany, Scotland, the Netherlands, and Hungary, but also in the Church of England, where he was long as highly regarded as he was by Puritans who had separated from the Anglican establishment. The latter organized their own churches, Presbyterian or Congregational, and brought Calvinism to North America 300 years ago.

Even today these churches, along with the originally German Evangelical and Reformed Church, remember Calvin—that is, the strict Calvin of Geneva—as their founding father. Eventually Calvinist theology was also widely accepted by major groups of American Baptists; and even Unitarianism, which broke away from the Calvinist churches of New England during the 18th century, reflected the more rational impulses in Calvin's theology. More recently, Protestant interest in the social implications of the Gospel and Protestant Neo-Orthodoxy, as represented by Karl Barth and Reinhold Niebuhr, reflect the continuing influence of John Calvin.

Calvin's larger influence over the development of modern Western civilization has been variously assessed. The controversial "Weber thesis" attributed the rise of modern capitalism largely to habits encouraged by Puritanism, but Max Weber (1864–1920) avoided implicating Calvin himself. Much the same can be said about efforts to link Calvinism to the rise of early modern science;

Puritans were prominent in the scientific movement of 17th-century England, but Calvin himself was indifferent to the science of his own day.

A somewhat better case can be made for Calvin's influence on political theory. His own political instincts were highly conservative, and he preached the submission of private persons to all legitimate authority. But, like Italian humanists of the 15th and 16th centuries, he personally preferred a republic to a monarchy; and in confronting the problem posed by rulers who actively opposed the spread of the Gospel, he advanced a theory of resistance, kept alive by his followers, according to which lesser magistrates might legitimately rebel against kings. And, unlike most of his contemporaries, Calvin included among the proper responsibilities of states not

only the maintenance of public order but also a positive concern for the general welfare of society. Calvinism has a place, therefore, in the evolution of liberal political thought. His most durable influence, nevertheless, has been religious. From Calvin's time to the present, Calvinism has meant a peculiar seriousness about Christianity and its ethical implications.

William J. Bouwsma, 65, is Sather Professor of History at the University of California, Berkeley. Born in Ann Arbor, Michigan, he received an A.B. (1943), an M.A. (1947), and a Ph.D. (1950) from Harvard. He is the author of, among other books, Venice and the Defense of Republican Liberty *(1968) and* John Calvin: A Sixteenth-Century Portrait *(1988).*

From *The Wilson Quarterly*, New Year's 1989 edition, pp. 68–75. © 1989 by William J. Bouwsma. Reprinted by permission of the author.

Holbein

Court Painter of the Reformation

Andrew Pettegree charts Hans Holbein's path from Germany to England and
points to the ironies of his reputation as a great Protestant painter.

Hans Holbein, who was born 500 years ago this year, was one
of the great painters of the northern Renaissance. Born and
raised in Augsburg, he achieved lasting fame in England, as the
leading artist at the court of Henry VIII. Holbein's paintings of
the king, his wives and courtiers, provide some of the most famous images of the age, and enshrined his place in the trinity of
the great German artists of the Reformation: Dürer, Holbein,
and Cranach. Yet there is a certain irony in celebrating Holbein
as a great Protestant painter. Holbein's career was closely inter-
woven with the events of the Reformation. He was patronised
by some of its leading figures, and produced some fine examples of the new Protestant art. But personally he viewed Protestantism with some distaste, not least for its adverse effect on the
artistic traditions in which he had been raised.

Hans Holbein came from a family of artists. His father, Hans
Holbein the elder, was an accomplished painter of religious
paintings who had made a distinguished career in the German
city of Augsburg. His altarpiece for the city's Moritzkirche was
one of the most important paintings recently commissioned by
the city fathers. Holbein's two sons, Hans and Ambrosius (also
a talented painter, though he would die tragically young), would
have received their early training in their father's workshop, before in 1514 the two boys moved together from Augsburg to
Basle. For young men eager to make their way in the world this
was a shrewd choice. In the early decades of the sixteenth century Basle was one of the greatest cities of Europe, and certainly
one of its most cultivated and cultured. Strategically placed on
the crossroads of Europe's major trade routes, the city and its
university were already famous through their association with
Erasmus and the other leaders of the new intellectual movement
of humanism.

Most importantly, Basle was also one of Europe's leading
centres of book production, and it is quite possibly this which
attracted the young artists to the city. In this period the new science of book publishing offered rich opportunities for the

graphic arts, but it was only the richest and best established publishing houses which had the capital to embark on prestige
projects which required elaborate illustrated title-pages, borders, and text illustrations.

In Basle, Holbein quickly made his name as one of the finest
exponents of the new arts of the design of woodcuts and engravings. Among his work during this period was a superb series of
illustrations for bibles and Old Testaments published in 1522,
1524 and 1526, the years when the awakening interest in the
new evangelical teachings of Martin Luther produced an almost
insatiable demand for vernacular scripture. Holbein's designs
had no particular confessional slant: he also provided the designs for illustrations of conventional devotional literature. But
he used these years to cultivate contacts among Basle's ruling
élite, particularly the humanist milieu which would provide
some of the most outspoken exponents of religious change. His
first portraits were of members of this artistic and civic set, pictures which testify both to his growing skill as a portrait painter,
and to his established position in the city's artistic hierarchy.

In 1526 this prosperous and precociously successful career
was rudely disturbed by contemporary political events. By this
time the shockwaves unleashed by Luther's criticisms of the
church hierarchy were making their effects known all over the
German-speaking world, and even as cultivated a metropolis as
Basle was not immune to their impact. At the heart of Protestantism was a call for a return to the primitive simplicity of the
original Gospel message. The new evangelical preachers vehe-
mently denounced anything in the old church that detracted
from this, and some of the most violent criticism was reserved
for the religious images and artwork, which in the old church,
they believed, had become almost an alternative focus of religious devotion. In towns which adopted the evangelical agenda,
the abolition of the mass was often accompanied by the wholesale destruction of religious art; even magnificent pieces, such
as the Augsburg altarpiece recently created by Holbein's father.

Courtesy of the National Portrait Gallery, London.

Henry VIII shadowed by Henry VII in Holbein's cartoon for the Whitehall Mural—a proclamation of Tudor stability. The painting no longer survives. Holbein's talents were such that once in England he quickly graduated from general painting and decorating jobs in the king's new palaces to producing key images of the reign such as this.

For artists such as Holbein the potential consequences were obvious. It was no just that the demand for religious paintings was greatly diminished: the whole purpose of their vocation seemed to be under question.

As the Reformation gathered pace in Basle, Holbein decided the time had come to try his fortunes elsewhere. His passport to new opportunities was provided by his humanist friends and Holbein left Basle with letters of recommendations to friends in Antwerp and England from no less a figure than Desiderius Er-

asmus. 'The arts are freezing here', wrote Erasmus to Pieter Gilles in Antwerp; so 'he [Holbein] is on his way to England to pick up some angels'. (The angel was an English gold coin; the pun on the Latin for English, *Angli* was typical Erasmus.)

Once again Holbein had chosen well. In England, he was immediately assured of the patronage and friendship of Thomas More, Erasmus' familiar friend, and at this point at the height of his powers and influence. More provided Holbein with two of his more important early commissions: a group portrait of the extended More family, now sadly lost and known only from later copies and a preparatory sketch, and the wonderful, haunting portrait of More himself, now in the Frick Collection of New York. Holbein captured exactly the painful ambiguity of the intellectual in office: the man of letters as statesman, the powerful lines of his heavy chain of office contrasting vividly with the thoughtful, slightly troubled features; even at More's moment of glory Holbein seems to anticipate the painful choices which would bring Thomas to his destruction. It remains the defining, perhaps unduly flattering, image of More; for Holbein it was a triumphant advertisement of his mastery of the techniques of renaissance portraiture, previously almost unknown in England.

More was a grateful and generous patron. It was he who provided Holbein with the crucial introductions to the king, that enabled him to be taken on as one of the Henry's salaried court painters. Initially, Holbein's work as court painter was far from glamorous. The king had employed him largely to work on the new decorative schemes with which Henry was adorning his many newly constructed palaces. But proximity to the great, in however humble a capacity, was what counted in sixteenth-century society, and it took little time for Holbein's exceptional gifts as a portrait painter to be widely known around the court. Soon he was once again in demand.

At this point in the sixteenth century the native English artistic tradition lagged far behind the continent. The artistic lessons of the Renaissance were yet to leave their mark on the few native painters who attempted the new art of portraiture, and the English court eyed the portraits produced at the more sophisticated Continental courts with frank envy. The only alternative was to send to the Continent for more accomplished practitioners. As Sir Thomas Elyot, a leading English scholar and author, put it in 1531: 'We are constrained, if we will have anything well painted, carved, or embroidered, to abandon our own countrymen and resort to strangers.'

It soon became obvious that even among these immigrant artists, Holbein was an exceptional talent. The painter quickly established an extended clientele among the statesmen, courtiers and adventurers who flocked to Henry's court. His uncanny ability to capture the personality of an individual sitter make his portraits some of the most lifelike and believable images of the sixteenth century. At Henry's court he was in a class of his own.

This was, of course, a talent which had to be used with discretion. Henry's court was a brutal place, where the struggle for the king's favour was fought with little mercy. Many of those who sat for Holbein were ruthless adventurers hardened by the cynical politics of the day. The revealing drawings Holbein made in preparation for his portraits often capture something of hardness in his sitters, but the drawings were intended for Holbein's eyes only, and the final portrait created a far more noble and flattering image. The full extent of Holbein's artistry is revealed only if one places the two side by side, as one can for instance with his portrait of the courtier Simon George. The portrait drawing, which survives in a superb collection of almost one hundred similar preparatory sketches in the Royal Collection at Windsor, does not mask the brutal ambition of a young man on the make; the finished oil painting, on the other hand (all the sitter would see) was a masterpiece of studied elegance.

With his most important patron, the king himself, Holbein would risk no liberties. Henry employed Holbein both for conventional portraits and for more ambitious projects, such as the group portrait of the king with his parents and third wife, Jane Seymour, intended to proclaim and celebrate the new stability of the tudor dynasty after the long awaited birth of a male heir, the future Edward VI. For this monumental painting (again sadly lost), Holbein was able to draw on the design he had accomplished for another of his 'political' paintings, the famous full length portrait of the two French ambassadors, recently cleaned and restored by the National Gallery. Modern scholarship reveals this as one of the most subtle and innovative of all Holbein's English paintings, a design full of emblematic symbolism which perfectly evoked the intricate, understated world of European court diplomacy.

The French embassy took place at a critical moment in English politics as Henry VIII, desperate for approval of his divorce and re-marriage to Anne Boleyn, sought to assure the continuing friendship of France's king to counter-balance the assured hostility of the Emperor Charles V, the nephew of the spurned wife, Katherine of Aragon. None of this tension is revealed in the inscrutable features of Holbein's sitters, though the critical importance of the mission is suggested by the decision to portray the ambassadors full length, a privilege otherwise reserved for patrons of royal rank.

The portrait is at once monumental and enigmatic, the impassive dignity of the ambassadors contrasting with the youthfulness of their faces, as the two men pose in rather uncomfortable formality around a table crammed with astronomical instruments and other impediments. At first sight these objects seem quite irrelevant to their mission, but to the educated eye all convey a subtle coded message. The astronomical instruments, the broken string on the lute on the lower table, the Lutheran hymn book, all hint at a world out of joint and the perils of the religious disunity which would surely follow from Henry's new religious and matrimonial policies.

This was a form of emblematic representation with which Holbein was entirely comfortable from his long training in the polite humanist world of Basle, but in the turbulent world of English politics such elegant understatement was already increasingly irrelevant. In his later years in England Holbein was obliged to create images much more overtly partisan in character. His new patron, the Vicegerent in Spirituals, Thomas Cromwell, had now emerged as one of the leading figures in the increasingly confident evangelical party, and Holbein played his part in the new evangelical propaganda. Indeed it was for Cromwell that Holbein produced one of his most remarkable original designs, the title page for Coverdale's new English translation of the Bible.

This design clearly draws inspiration from one of the most original pictorial designs of the new Protestant movement: the New and Old Covenant of Lucas Cranach, a pictorial representation of the core Lutheran doctrine of Justification by Faith. But here in Holbein's rendition the theme is restated and stripped of much of its polemical intent. Panels of scenes of the Old and New Testament are (as with Cranach's design) ranged along the left- and right-hand borders, but the original central panel of Man's redemption is replaced by an imposing representation of Henry VIII handing the vernacular scriptures to his assembled prelates and councillors. Nothing could more perfectly have captured the constraints which governed the reception of Continental evangelism in Henry's kingdom.

Subtle and pragmatic, Holbein seemed to have the perfect temperament to prosper in the maelstrom in Henry's court. On occasions, however, the painter's artistry could bring his patrons into unanticipated difficulties. In 1539 the king was in search of a new wife, and Holbein was sent off to the Continent to take the portrait of the potential brides. Two of his pictures from this expedition survive; the full length painting of Christina of Denmark, now in the National Gallery in London, and his miniature of the successful candidate, Anne of Cleves. It is often asserted that Henry was only persuaded to marry Anne by seeing Holbein's flattering portrait, though there were also pressing diplomatic reasons for such a match. Whatever the reason, when Henry finally laid eyes on his new bride he conceived an instant aversion to her, which spelled the end of both the marriage and its architect, Thomas Cromwell.

Holbein, the painter, again emerged unscathed from this debacle, and it is interesting the whereas authors and printers often fell victim to the confessional politics of the age, painters were seldom held accountable for the ideological content of their work. In this respect, contemporaries seem to have taken a pragmatic view of the artist's role: his task was to do his patron's bidding, without his own personal convictions forming an important part of the equation. This is not to say that artists were not themselves often deeply touched by the religious issues of the day. Albrecht Dürer was a late but apparently sincere convert to the doctrines of the Reformation, and the role of Lucas Cranach as the court artist of Luther's Wittenberg was crucial to the creation of the first memorable visual images of Protestantism. Cranach, at least, was an enthusiastic and committed supporter of Luther's movement, and a close personal friend of the reformer. Hans Holbein, on the other hand, while he cleverly accommodated his output to the changing demands for art in Protestant centres, does not seem to have been deeply touched by its religious messages.

Something of this is evident in Holbein's conduct of his own affairs in his last years. Although after 1528 Holbein spent almost all of the remainder of his life in England, he never became an English citizen, preferring to keep open the option of a return to Basle. At one point he made to the Basle Council an undertaking to return within two years, if the Council would in the meantime pay for the upkeep of his wife and children, who had remained in the city. Sadly, this seems to have been a bargain he never intended to keep. When Holbein died of the plague in London in 1544, he left behind debts and two illegitimate children, fathered during his English years.

This sorry tale is in many ways typical of the inconsistencies of this turbulent and morally ambiguous age. Artists like Holbein brought forth many noble works of art: in his case not only portraits but the splendid book illustrations and title-pages like that of the Coverdale Bible. But they could often do this without a deep level of intellectual commitment. Rather they were reacting as professional artists to a changing market. The restriction of opportunities for religious art and commissions for new church altarpieces made it vitally necessary to explore new avenues and opportunities. Nor should men like Holbein be too lightly condemned. For it is to their ingenuity and initiative that we owe the essentially new secular art forms of the modern era—portrait, landscape, and the Dutch genre paintings of everyday life—that emerged as the pictorial arts became emancipated from their medieval dependence on the church. And this,

despite its initial destructiveness, is one of the central artistic legacies of the Reformation.

FOR FURTHER READING:

The Holbein anniversary has strangely not inspired the expected rush of new studies. Derek Wilson, *Hans Holbein, Portrait of an Unknown Man* (Phoenix, 1996) is the most accessible; Oskar Bätschmann and Pascal Grenier, *Hans Holbein* (Reaktion, 1997) the most scholarly. Helen Langdon, *Holbein* (Phaedon Colour Library, 1973) is still reliable. Susan Foister, Ashok Roy and Martin Wyld, *Holbein's Ambassadors* (National Gallery/Yale, 1997) is the splendidly informative catalogue of the National Gallery exhibition. For the wider context, David Howarth, *Images of Rule, Art and Politics in the English Renaissance, 1485–1649* (Macmillan, 1997); Lorne Campbell, *Renaissance Portraits* (Yale, 1990); Carl Christiansen, *Art and the Reformation in Germany* (Athens, Ohio, 1979).

Andrew Pettegree *is Professor of Modern History in the University of St Andrews, and Director of the St Andrews Reformation Studies Institute.*

WHO WAS SHAKESPEARE?

William Rubinstein *continues his survey of topics*
of enduring popular debate by examining the controversy
surrounding the true identity of England's famous bard.

William shakespeare may well have been the greatest man England has ever produced, but he is also one of the most elusive. Virtually everything known of the facts of his life seem to belie the transcendent genius of his plays and poems. His parents were illiterate; he grew up in a small provincial town in which lived no more than a handful of educated men. His schooling ended at thirteen. There is no evidence that he owned a book. No manuscript definitely known to be by him survives. There are only six copies of his apparent signature, all on legal documents, where the name may have been written by a lawyer or clerk. Of the seventy-five known contemporary documents in which Shakespeare is named, not one concerns his career as an author. Most are legal and financial documents which depict him as a particularly cold, rapacious, and successful local businessman and property developer.

Shakespeare's life between his marriage in 1582 to Anne Hathaway and his emergence as an actor and presumed writer nearly ten years later is a mystery period in which biographers have credited him with all manner of employment, as a law clerk, soldier, schoolmaster, traveller on the Continent, and so on, for which there is no evidence whatsoever. At the age of about forty-seven, after being at the centre of one of the world's greatest cultural renaissances for more than twenty years, he suddenly retired

from London to Stratford, living there quietly until he died five years later.

Seven years after Shakespeare's death, in 1623, a huge memorial volume appeared, produced by several of his former theatrical associates, which contained nearly all of his plays (many printed in full for the first time). This First Folio does not mention or acknowledge his family in Stratford, although it seems inconceivable that they did not retain some effects left by him that would have been useful to the First Folio's editors. There is no evidence that any member of his family (or anyone else in Stratford) owned a copy; indeed, his two surviving daughters were illiterate.

Since Shakespeare's recognition in the late eighteenth century as the pre-eminent English national writer, hundreds of archivists, researchers, and historians have poured over thousands of contemporary manuscripts and published works in an effort to learn something—anything— about Shakespeare the man. Their efforts have been almost entirely in vain. During the twentieth century, only a handful of details emerged. In 1909 two American researchers, Charles and Hilda Wallace, trawling the Public Record Office, discovered the previously unknown Bellot-Mountjoy lawsuit at which Shakespeare testified. In 1931 Leslie Hotson, another American, discovered a curious, almost inexplicable, 1596 writ for the arrest of Shakespeare and two others issued by a

criminal figure in Southwark. Potentially, perhaps the most important document uncovered, first noticed in the 1920s by Sir E.K. Chambers, the greatest modern scholar of Shakespeare's life, was the will of Alexander Hoghton of Lea, Lancashire, made in 1581, which left a small legacy to a 'William Shakeshafte now dwelling with me', apparently as a tutor to his children. Many believe that Shakespeare was 'Shakeshafte' and spent several years as a tutor in two wealthy Lancashire Catholic stately homes, those of the Hoghtons of Hoghton Tower and Sir Thomas Hesketh of Rufford. E.A.J. Honigmann, who has done most to popularise the 'lost years in Lancashire' thesis, has discovered that there is a long-standing tradition in the Hoghton family that Shakespeare was employed in their home for two years in his youth. The Lancashire thesis has been adopted by many recent biographers. And some historians have speculated further that the young Shakespeare may have gone from one of the Lancashire households to London as a member of a players' company. Others believe that during the 'lost years' Shakespeare was already an actor with a troupe of strolling players. The Earl of Worcester's Men for example, are known to have visited Stratford-on-Avon on several occasions between 1568 and 1582, and definitely employed Edward Alleyn (the founder of Dulwich College). Shakespeare may have made his way to London with this acting troupe, eventually settling there as a playwright and theatre-owner. Alleyn could well have hired Shakespeare as an actor in London.

Though plausible, these theories have been heavily disputed, not least because there is nothing other than the Hoghton will to connect Shakespeare with Lancashire. For centuries biographers have been puzzled as to how he acquired such a detailed knowledge of the law of his day, and there has been much speculation that he spent his 'lost years' as a law student or clerk. If Shakespeare was a perambulating actor during the 'lost years' he cannot also have readily been a law clerk, or acquired a working knowledge of court life or European politics.

In 1818 Richard Phillips, writing in *The Monthly Magazine*, interviewed J.M. Smith, a descendant through his mother from Shakespeare's sister Joan. Smith told Phillips that

… he had often heard [her] state that Shakespeare owed his rise in life, and his introduction to the theatre, to his accidentally holding the horse of a gentleman at the door of the theatre, on his first arriving in London. His appearance led to enquiry and subsequent patronage.

Dr Samuel Johnson, writing in 1765, also claimed that Shakespeare began in London as the organiser of a firm that took care of the horses of theatre-goers.) This story perhaps deserves more credibility than most about the life of Shakespeare, since it is the only such anecdote to come from a member of his own family, albeit a very distant one. It appears, however, directly to contradict the most popular current versions of how Shakespeare came to London.

In striking contrast to the obscurity of his background there is the achievement of Shakespeare the writer. This son of an illiterate provincial butcher had the largest vocabulary of any writer in English in history, using about 37,000 different words in his works, twice as many, for instance, as the Cambridge-educated John Milton. Shakespeare coined hundreds of phrases (such as 'into thin air', 'time-honoured', and the 'be-all and

end-all'), which are widely imagined to be proverbial. He apparently also coined at least 1,500 English words, including 'addiction', 'alligator', 'birthplace', 'cold-blooded', 'critic', 'impede', and 'amazement'. Shakespeare was also, apparently, the first writer to use the word 'its' as a third person possessive. He wrote convincingly of court life, foreign intrigues, and the affairs of kings and courtiers, subjects of which he could have had no direct knowledge. As well as law, his works reveal a mastery of science, of classical and European literature, and of other specialised fields, which seem utterly incongruous—indeed, inexplicable—in a poorly-educated country actor. It is this incredible incongruity which has led so many to question whether the Stratford man wrote the plays attributed to him—not, as is often alleged by orthodox scholars, snobbery on the part of proponents of other writers, who allegedly insist that only a nobleman could have been England's national poet, not a commoner of humble background.

Proponents of an alternative 'Shakespeare' do not question that Shakespeare of Stratford existed: he was baptised in April 1564, married in November 1582, and died there in April 1616. They do not dispute that he was an actor and theatre share-holder in London, and died relatively wealthy. But they do question whether he wrote the plays attributed to him, arguing that he acted as a front-man for the real author, that clues exist in his works to this effect, and that the autobiographical material in his works is at variance with the known facts of his life.

Orthodox biographers reject the question of authorship. They have a point: no one suggests that the works of any of Shakespeare's contemporaries were written by someone else. No one in Shakespeare's lifetime or for the next 200 years questioned that he wrote the plays (although this has been disputed by unorthodox biographers), and Several of his contemporaries, most clearly Ben Jonson, appear to have regarded the Stratford man as having written them. This group attribute Shakespeare's achievement to his unique 'genius'. But Shakespeare's skill involved the successful blending of plot, characterisation, language and dra-

matic effect in an original way. It seems almost inconceivable that someone from an illiterate home could be a literary genius, let alone the greatest of them all. Furthermore, the previous century had been one of political, religious and economic turmoil. The fundamental aim of Stratford's local elite was to enforce intellectual, political and religious conformity by every possible means. This appears to be at odds with Shakespeare's unprecedented ability to empathise with his characters, among them foreigners, Catholics, Jews, Moors and women, bringing them to life. Orthodox biographers surely gloss over these incongruities too readily.

The first man explicitly to believe that Shakespeare's works were written by someone else was the Reverend James Wilmot (1726–1808), a Warwickshire clergyman who lived near Stratford. Wilmot's doubts were aroused by his inability to find a single book belonging to Shakespeare despite searching in every old private library within a fifty-mile radius of Stratford. He was also unable to locate any authentic anecdotes about Shakespeare in or around Stratford. Wilmot's father, like him an Oxford graduate, was a 'gentleman' of Warwick. He might well have met persons who knew Shakespeare, and could certainly have known those who had met his surviving daughters, yet he too had evidently heard nothing about him from any local source. From this and other evidence, Wilmot concluded that the real author of Shakespeare's plays was Sir Francis Bacon, whose activities, it seemed, provided much of the knowledge of court life and politics found in the plays.

Wilmot's claims, which encompassed virtually everything said by subsequent anti-Stratfordians, remained unknown until 1932. In the mid-nineteenth century, however, a number of writers independently concluded that Bacon wrote Shakespeare's plays. Chief among them was an American, coincidentally named Delia Bacon, who, in 1857, published the earliest book expounding this theory, *The Philosophy of the Plays of Shakespeare*. By the late nineteenth century, works propounding the Bacon-was-Shakespeare theory had proliferated, though gener-

ney did their cause more harm than good, being chiefly based on alleged secret codes and ciphers in the plays 'proving' that Bacon was the author. The tide of Baconians receded sharply in the twentieth century, as Shakespeare studies became overwhelmingly centred in university English departments. Here, the anti-Stratfordian position is associated with non-academic autodidacts and crackpots; the idea that a serious scholar would take up such a position is viewed as ludicrous. Nevertheless, the anti-Stratfordian cause widened to include other 'Shakespeare claimants' besides Bacon and, in the last twenty years, has made a comeback, especially in the United States, enjoying a certain respectability even in some academic circles.

So, if not Shakespeare of Stratford, then who? Probably the strongest candidate is Edward de Vere, 17th Earl of Oxford (1550–1604), whose biography as the putative author of Shakespeare's plays appears almost too good to be true. Inheritor of the senior earldom in England, and as such hereditary Lord Great Chamberlain, he was educated at Cambridge and studied law at Gray's Inn. Brought up in the household of Lord Burghley (1520–98), his future father-in-law, with its library of nearly 3,000 books, he was tutored by his uncle Arthur Golding, the translator of Ovid's *Metamorphoses*, from which many of Shakespeare's plays are derived. Oxford travelled on the Continent, spending a year in Italy. He was known in his lifetime as a successful playwright and poet, although little of his work survives, and the surviving poems in his own name stop soon after the name 'Shakespeared' (as he was often known) first appeared in print. He held a lease on Blackfriars Theatre and had his own acting company, although much of his life remains a mystery. In 1605 Oxford's daughter was married to the Earl of Montgomery, to whom the First Folio was jointly dedicated (along with William Herbert, 3rd Earl of Pembroke).

The case for Oxford was first made in 1920 by a schoolmaster, John Thomas Looney, in a work entitled 'Shakespeare' Identified. Looney's book was praised by a host of enthusiasts who

gradually made Oxford the most popular of the 'Shakespeare claimants', replacing Bacon.

The most convincing evidence for the Oxford claim emerges from the Sonnets, which seem to many to be related to incidents in the author's life, although precisely what these were is a complete mystery. The Sonnets were first published in 1609, in a limited edition with an inscrutable dedication about which more has been written than anything of its kind in the Shakespeare canon. Many historians believe that they were written in the early 1590s (or even before). Certainly in 1598 a London schoolmaster commented on Shakespeare's 'sugred Sonnets among his private friends'. The 1609 edition of the Sonnets include a series of recommendations from the poet, apparently to an aristocrat, to marry and father children. Most historians believe that the addressee was Henry Wriothesley, 3rd Earl of Southampton (1573–1624), to whom Shakespeare dedicated his poems *Venus and Adonis* in 1593 and *The Rape of Lucrece* in 1594. Sonnet 10 asks the man addressed to 'Make thee another self for love of me'. Many of the Sonnets speak of the poet as 'old' and lame, and as one who has recently suffered shame and ignominy. The homoerotic nature of some of the early Sonnets remains a highly controversial point.

It is simply inconceivable that, in Elizabethan England, the actor son of a butcher would urge a powerful earl to marry and beget children 'for love of me'. Shakespeare of Stratford was plainly not homosexual: he was married at eighteen and had fathered three children by the age of twenty-one. Moreover, the tone of this Sonnet is utterly different from the flattery and abject self-abasement found elsewhere in Shakespeare's dedications to Southampton. The Sonnets repeatedly demonstrate a familiarity with a range of subjects from classical literature to the aristocratic high life. If they were written around 1592–94, as many believe, it is difficult to see why Shakespeare, who was twenty-eight in 1592, would describe himself as 'old'. There is no evidence from any source that he was 'lame', or that he suffered from shame and ignominy (apart from the attack on

him in Robert Greene's posthumous 1592 work *Groatsworth of Wit*); his alleged close association with an earl is evidence that the opposite was true. Although Shakespeare of Stratford dedicated two of his works to Southampton, no direct links between the two men have ever been found, and there is no contemporary evidence (as opposed to anecdotes from much later) that Southampton ever heard of Shakespeare.

Those who believe that the Earl of Oxford was Shakespeare, however, argue that the Sonnets fit his life like a glove. Oxford was born in April 1550, and was thus in his forties when the Sonnets were probably written (Sonnet 2 begins 'When forty winters shall besiege thy brow'). He was, apparently, lame, knew the shame of having been banished from court and of being sent to the Tower (for his involvement with Catholics), and was accused in 1576 by the courtier Charles Arundel of being a 'buggerer of boys'. In 1590 he tried unsuccessfully to arrange a marriage between his daughter Elizabeth (who was also Lord Burghley's granddaughter) and Lord Southampton.

Sceptics have suggested a number of alternative explanations to account for the Sonnets. Some historians—most notably Katharine M. Wilson, in *Shakespeare's Sugared Sonnets* (1974)—have claimed that they were merely a series of imaginative poems on a number of themes, for whatever reason, proposed to him as subjects to write about. Others have claimed that the Sonnets were autobiographical, but were written as if by Southampton's mother (who could ask her son to marry 'for love of me'), or were written in the 1600s rather than in the previous decade, with one of the dedicatees of the First Folio in 1623, William Herbert, third Earl of Pembroke (1580–1630) in mind, not Lord Southampton.

Proponents of Oxford as Shakespeare also claim his identity can be detected in Shakespeare's most famous play, *Hamlet*. They argue that Polonius is a caricature of Lord Burghley, Oxford's father-in-law. As in the case of the Sonnets, it seems improbable that Shakespeare of Stratford would have dared to lampoon

Burghley as occurs in the play (where Polonius is stabbed to death by Hamlet).

Ernest Jones, the pioneer psychiatrist, attempted in 1910 to depict Hamlet as suffering from an Oedipus complex, and saw the date of Shakespeare's father's death (September 1601) as significant in the writing of the play. But the differences between the story of Hamlet and Shakespeare's life are surely immense and his father was certainly not murdered. Furthermore, Thomas Nashe, a contemporary of Shakespeare, referred in 1589 to 'whole Hamlets, I should say handfulls of tragical speeches', indicating that a play by this name was performed in that year and probably at least a few years earlier. Known to scholars today as 'Ur-Hamlet', this lost play is often attributed to Thomas Kyd, a playwright mentioned by Thomas Nashe in the same paragraph, although there is no evidence that he was the author. Shakespeare's *Hamlet* was first registered in 1602. He may have borrowed the theme for his play from this earlier drama, but this is unlike his working methods, and some believe that Shakespeare himself, rather than Kyd, was the author of the earlier play. The problem here is that Shakespeare was only twenty-five in 1589, and younger if the play was written earlier. Proponents of Oxford as Shakespeare argue that many of the plays were actually written much earlier than the normal chronology, beginning in the early 1580s, and point out that there were many 'Ur' plays in circulation, too early for Shakespeare (b.1564) to have written them, but not too early for Oxford (b.1550). By 1596, a play about Hamlet was certainly being performed, because one contemporary refers to

… the Visard of ye ghost which cried so miserably at ye Theator like an oister wife, Hamlet, revenge.

Numerous other links between Shakespeare's plays and Oxford have been postulated. Oxford invested and lost £3,000 with a London merchant named Michael Lok (or Lock), possibly the prototype of 'Shylock', which is unknown in Jewish nomenclature. In *The Merchant of Venice*, Antonio posts bond for 3,000 ducats with Shylock, with 'a pound of flesh' as security.

Yet many obstacles also exist to accepting Oxford as Shakespeare. The most formidable is the fact that Oxford died in June 1604 while Shakespeare continued to write plays probably until 1613–14. According to most mainstream chronologies, as many as ten plays (as well as the Sonnets) first appeared after 1604. Oxford's supporters claim that no new play appeared between 1604 and 1608, and that no contemporary reference in any of Shakespeare's plays can be dated after 1603. They also point to the celebrated, mysterious dedication of the Sonnets by 'T.T.' (Thomas Thorpe, its publisher), which wishes 'all happiness and that eternitie promised by our ever living poet' to the enigmatic dedicatee, 'Mr W.H.'. Oxfordians (and others) point out that 'ever living' was used by Elizabethans only of someone already deceased, which Oxford—unlike Shakespeare—was in 1609, when the Sonnets appeared. They claim that the plays first performed after 1604 were all written earlier and, as it were, 'released' after Oxford's death.

But is there anything that actually ties Oxford to Shakespeare's plays? The Folger Library in Washington DC owns Oxford's 1579 Bible, which contains about 1,000 underlined or marked passages and forty marginal notes, apparently in the Earl's handwriting. In 1992 a detailed examination of these annotations was made by Roger Stritmatter and Mark Anderson, two American Oxfordians, who found that more than a quarter of the marked passages in the Folger Bible turned up as direct references in Shakespeare's plays, among them more than a hundred references that had not previously been noted by Shakespearean scholars, but which are clearly or probably the sources of Shakespeare's phraseology.

According to Oxfordians (and to proponents of other 'Shakespeares'), the William of Stratford was an actor, playbroker, and businessman who was manifestly incapable of writing the plays attributed to him, but whose actual role was to serve as a front man and producer of the plays, lending his name to them because their real author, a nobleman or high official, could not write directly under his own name for the theatre. Hints that Shakespeare of Stratford was not the author were given at the time: for instance, the name of the alleged author appears as 'Shake-speare' in fifteen out of thirty-three plays published before the First Folio appeared, as well as in the first publication of the Sonnets and many other references. Shakespeare's name was never hyphenated in any legal or commercial document clearly relating to the Stratford man, while no other Elizabethan author had his name spelled in this manner.

Had the plays and poems been written anonymously, it seems likely that today Oxford would be the leading candidate for their authorship, and that no one would argue that Shakespeare of Stratford wrote the plays. Many suppose that the authorship question is a relic of nineteenth-century autodidactism and has been superseded by contemporary historical criticism several university courses in America now at least experiment with the proposition that Oxford wrote the plays. Balanced articles on the Shakespeare authorship question have appeared in recent years in mainstream American magazines and on American public television. A similar organised movement has grown up in Britain (headed by the Earl of Burford, a descendant of Oxford), although it has not yet wholly discarded its eccentric label, as its counterpart in America seems to have done.

Oxford's candidacy also suffers from the fact that he is not by any means the only plausible Shakespeare claimant. Bacon has been supposed by some to have been the author of Shakespeare for far longer. He was certainly everything that the Stratford man was not: an aristocrat, Lord Chancellor, and possibly the most learned man of his day. In recent years Bacon's candidacy has been overshadowed by comparison with Oxford's, for he was no poet and his genius appears to differ fundamentally from Shakespeare's. Much of the former 'evidence' 'demonstrating' that Bacon was Shakespeare consists of elaborate, far-fetched anagrams and secret codes found in the plays, which are singularly unconvincing. Yet a number of possible links between Bacon and Shakespeare do exist, some of them remarkable. In 1867 a manuscript came to light in the London home of the Duke of Northumberland. It is a cover-sheet used as a wrapper for twenty-two old manuscripts, that had been extensively scribbled upon some time around 1596. Thought by some to have belonged to Sir Henry Neville, Bacon's nephew, it bears the wording

> ... by Mr. ffrancis Bacon
> Essaies by the same author
> William Shakespeare
> Rychard the Second
> Rychard the Third
> Asmund and Cornelia
> Ile of Dogs frmnt [fragment]
> by Thomas Nashe
> William Shakespeare...

It also carries extracts from the works of Bacon and Shakespeare. Baconians naturally regard it as highly significant, but sceptics believe it is simply a list of works in a library, possibly, therefore, showing that Bacon was not Shakespeare. Baconians also point to one of the few contemporary sources which apparently question whether Shakespeare wrote the works attributed to him, the *Satires* of Joseph Hall (1597–98), which apparently claim that Bacon wrote Shakespeare's *Venus and Adonis*. Additionally, in 1985 a remarkable wall-painting was discovered by workmen renovating an old inn in St Albans, where Bacon lived. Dated to about 1600, it apparently depicts the hunt scene in Shakespeare's *Venus and Adonis*, and

Baconians have also pointed out that St Albans is mentioned fifteen times in Shakespeare's works, whereas Stratford never is. Had this wall-painting been discovered in an old inn in Stratford-upon-Avon, it would, of course, be taken as strong evidence that Shakespeare of Stratford wrote the plays.

> *The thesis that someone else was the author, and the Stratford man a front, is not at all absurd.*

There are further candidates. William Stanley, 6th Earl of Derby (1561–1642), has had his supporters since the publication of a 1918 work by a French scholar arguing the case for him, in part because of his intimate knowledge of the Court of Navarre, the scene of *Love's Labour Lost*. Roger Manners, 5th Earl of Rutland (1576–1612), has his proponents. The candidacy of Christopher Marlowe (1564–93), has been argued for many years. It became well-known in 1955 with the publication of a book by the American Calvin Hoffman, who argued, without a shred of evidence, that Marlowe was not in fact killed in a tavern brawl at the age of twenty-nine, but survived surreptitiously to write Shakespeare's plays. Among other suggestions is one that a group of authors, possibly headed by Bacon, wrote Shakespeare's

works. Against this, however, is the fact that all of Shakespeare's works are similar in style.

Most historians of Shakespeare will, unquestionably, continue to believe the orthodox view, that the poorly-educated man from the obscure market town was the author of the greatest works of English literature. The fact that contemporaries apparently took for granted that Shakespeare was the author is crucial here, as is the fact that Shakespeare's dramatic style can be seen to evolve from the crude *grand guinol* of *Titus Andronicus* to the majestic tragedies of the 1600s—*Hamlet, Macbeth, and King Lear*. Yet the thesis that someone else was the author, and the Stratford man a front or agent of some kind, is not at all absurd. What is certain is that the 'authorship question' is unlikely ever to be settled comprehensively, and may well become more heated in the future than it has been in the past.

FOR FURTHER READING

S. Schoenbaum, *Shakespeare's Lives* (Oxford, 1991); Park Honan, *Shakespeare: A Life* (Oxford, 1999); John Michell, *Who Wrote Shakespeare?* (London, 1996); Diana Price, *Shakespeare's Unorthodox Biography* (Westport, Conn., 2001); Joseph Sobran, *Alias Shakespeare* (New York, 1997).

William D. Rubinstein is Professor of Modern History at the University of Wales, Aberystwyth.

This article first appeared in *History Today*, August 2001, pp. 28-35. © 2001 by History Today, Ltd. Reprinted by permission.

Index

Index

Test Your Knowledge Form

We encourage you to photocopy and use this page as a tool to assess how the articles in *Annual Editions* expand on the information in your textbook. By reflecting on the articles you will gain enhanced text information. You can also access this useful form on a product's book support Web site at *http://www.dushkin.com/online/*.

NAME: _____   DATE: _____

TITLE AND NUMBER OF ARTICLE: _____

BRIEFLY STATE THE MAIN IDEA OF THIS ARTICLE: _____

LIST THREE IMPORTANT FACTS THAT THE AUTHOR USES TO SUPPORT THE MAIN IDEA:

WHAT INFORMATION OR IDEAS DISCUSSED IN THIS ARTICLE ARE ALSO DISCUSSED IN YOUR TEXTBOOK OR OTHER READINGS THAT YOU HAVE DONE? LIST THE TEXTBOOK CHAPTERS AND PAGE NUMBERS:

LIST ANY EXAMPLES OF BIAS OR FAULTY REASONING THAT YOU FOUND IN THE ARTICLE:

LIST ANY NEW TERMS/CONCEPTS THAT WERE DISCUSSED IN THE ARTICLE, AND WRITE A SHORT DEFINITION:

We Want Your Advice

ANNUAL EDITIONS revisions depend on two major opinion sources: one is our Advisory Board, listed in the front of this volume, which works with us in scanning the thousands of articles published in the public press each year; the other is you—the person actually using the book. Please help us and the users of the next edition by completing the prepaid article rating form on this page and returning it to us. Thank you for your help!

ANNUAL EDITIONS: Western Civilization, Volume 1, Twelfth edition

ARTICLE RATING FORM

Here is an opportunity for you to have direct input into the next revision of this volume.
We would like you to rate each of the articles listed below, using the following scale:

1. **Excellent: should definitely be retained**
2. **Above average: should probably be retained**
3. **Below average: should probably be deleted**
4. **Poor: should definitely be deleted**

Your ratings will play a vital part in the next revision.
Please mail this prepaid form to us as soon as possible.
Thanks for your help!

RATING	ARTICLE
	1. Stonehenge: How Did the Stones Get There?
	2. Hatshepsut: The Female Pharaoh
	3. The Cradle of Cash
	4. The Coming of the Sea Peoples
	5. Grisly Assyrian Record of Torture and Death
	6. Scythian Gold
	7. Olympic Self-Sacrifice
	8. Was Socrates a Democrat?
	9. Alexander: The Great Mystery
	10. Love and Death in Ancient Greece
	11. Cleopatra: What Kind of a Woman Was She, Anyway?
	12. Ancient Rome and the Pirates
	13. Sudden Death
	14. Jews and Christians in a Roman World
	15. The Other Jesus
	16. Ecstasy in Late Imperial Rome
	17. Who the Devil Is the Devil?
	18. The Emperor's State of Grace
	19. The Survival of the Eastern Roman Empire
	20. In the Beginning, There Were the Holy Books
	21. Charlemagne's Elephant
	22. The Most Perfect Man in History?
	23. The Amazing Vikings
	24. An Iberian Chemistry
	25. The Capture of Jerusalem
	26. The Emergence of the Christian Witch
	27. Women Pilgrims of the Middle Ages
	28. Britain 1300
	29. Ready, Aim, Fire!
	30. War-Games of Central Italy
	31. How a Mysterious Disease Laid Low Europe's Masses
	32. Saints or Sinners? The Knights Templar in Medieval Europe
	33. How Jacques Coeur Made His Fortune
	34. Marsilio Ficino, Renaissance Man
	35. Machiavelli
	36. Women of the Renaissance

RATING	ARTICLE
	37. Child's Play in Medieval England
	38. Luther: Giant of His Time and Ours
	39. Explaining John Calvin
	40. Holbein: Court Painter of the Reformation
	41. Who Was Shakespeare?

(Continued on next page)

BUSINESS REPLY MAIL
FIRST-CLASS MAIL PERMIT NO. 84 GUILFORD CT

POSTAGE WILL BE PAID BY ADDRESSEE

McGraw-Hill/Dushkin
530 Old Whitfield Street
Guilford, Ct 06437-9989

NO POSTAGE
NECESSARY
IF MAILED
IN THE
UNITED STATES

ABOUT YOU

Name   Date

Are you a teacher? ☐   A student? ☐
Your school's name

Department

Address   City   State   Zip

School telephone #

YOUR COMMENTS ARE IMPORTANT TO US!

Please fill in the following information:
For which course did you use this book?

Did you use a text with this ANNUAL EDITION?   ☐ yes ☐ no
What was the title of the text?

What are your general reactions to the *Annual Editions* concept?

Have you read any pertinent articles recently that you think should be included in the next edition? Explain.

Are there any articles that you feel should be replaced in the next edition? Why?

Are there any World Wide Web sites that you feel should be included in the next edition? Please annotate.

May we contact you for editorial input?   ☐ yes ☐ no
May we quote your comments?   ☐ yes ☐ no